Negotiating the Secular and the Religious in the German Empire

New German Historical Perspectives

Series Editor: Paul Betts (Executive Editor)

Established in 1987, this special St Antony's Series on New German Historical Perspectives showcases pioneering new work by leading German historians on a range of topics concerning the history of modern Germany and Europe. Publications address pressing problems of political, economic, social and intellectual history informed by contemporary debates about German and European identity, providing fresh conceptual, international and transnational interpretations of the recent past.

Volume 10
Negotiating the Secular and the Religious in the German Empire: Transnational Approaches
Edited by Rebekka Habermas

Volume 9
Humanitarianism and Media, 1900 to the Present
Edited by Johannes Paulmann

Volume 8
Space and Spatiality in Modern German-Jewish History
Edited by Simone Lässig and Miriam Rürup

Volume 7
Poverty and Welfare in Modern German History
Edited by Lutz Raphael

Volume 6
Anti-Liberal Europe: A Neglected Story of Europeanization
Edited by Dieter Gosewinkel

Volume 5
A Revolution of Perception? Consequences and Echoes of 1968
Edited by Ingrid Gilcher-Holtey

Volume 4
Popular Historiographies in the 19th and 20th Centuries: Cultural Meanings, Social Practices
Edited by Sylvia Paletschek

Volume 3
Work in a Modern Society: The German Historical Experience in Comparative Perspective
Edited by Jürgen Kocka

Volume 2
Crises in European Integration: Challenges and Responses
Edited by Ludger Kühnhardt

Volume 1
Historical Concepts between Eastern and Western Europe
Edited by Manfred Hildermeier

Negotiating the Secular and the Religious in the German Empire

Transnational Approaches

Edited by Rebekka Habermas

berghahn
NEW YORK·OXFORD
www.berghahnbooks.com

First published in 2019 by
Berghahn Books
www.berghahnbooks.com

© 2019, 2025 Rebekka Habermas
First paperback edition published in 2025

All rights reserved. Except for the quotation of short passages
for the purposes of criticism and review, no part of this book
may be reproduced in any form or by any means, electronic or
mechanical, including photocopying, recording, or any information
storage and retrieval system now known or to be invented,
without written permission of the publisher.

Library of Congress Cataloging-in-Publication Data

Names: Habermas, Rebekka, 1959- editor.
Title: Negotiating the secular and the religious in the German Empire :
transnational approaches / edited by Rebekka Habermas.
Description: New York : Berghahn Books, 2019. | Series: New German historical
perspectives ; Volume 10 | Includes bibliographical references and index.
Identifiers: LCCN 2018056522 (print) | LCCN 2019002379 (ebook) | ISBN
9781789201529 (ebook) | ISBN 9781789201512 (hardback : alk. paper)
Subjects: LCSH: Germany--Religion--19th century. | Germany--Religion--20th
century. | Transnationalism. | Secularism--Germany--History--19th century.
| Secularism--Germany--History--20th century. | Germany--Social
conditions--1871-1918.
Classification: LCC BL980.G3 (ebook) | LCC BL980.G3 N44 2019 (print) | DDC
200.943/09034--dc23
LC record available at https://lccn.loc.gov/2018056522

British Library Cataloguing in Publication Data

A catalogue record for this book is available from the British Library

EU GPSR Authorized Representative

LOGOS EUROPE, 9 rue Nicolas Poussin, 17000, LA ROCHELLE, France
Email: Contact@logoseurope.eu

ISBN 978-1-78920-151-2 hardback
ISBN 978-1-83695-064-6 paperback
ISBN 978-1-83695-202-2 epub
ISBN 978-1-78920-152-9 web pdf

https://doi.org/10.3167/9781789201512

Contents

Introduction
    Negotiating the Religious and the Secular in Modern
    German History   1
    Rebekka Habermas

I. RELIGIOUS AND SECULAR: Scientific Debates

1. A Secular Age? The 'Modern World' and the Beginnings of the
   Sociology of Religion   33
   Wolfgang Knöbl

2. The Silence on the Land: Ancient Israel versus Modern Palestine
   in Scientific Theology   56
   Paul Michael Kurtz

II. RELIGIOUS AND SECULAR: Public Debates

3. What Does It Mean To Be 'Secular' in the German Kaiserreich?
   An Intervention   101
   Lucian Hölscher

4. Secularism in the Long Nineteenth Century between the
   Global and the Local   115
   Rebekka Habermas

III. RELIGIOUS AND SECULAR: Negotiating Boundaries

5. Retrieving Tradition? The Secular–Religious Ambiguity in
   Nineteenth-Century German-Jewish Anarchism   147
   Carolin Kosuch

6. Catholic Women as Global Actors of the Religious and
   the Secular   171
   Relinde Meiwes

7. Negotiating the Fundamentals? German Missions and the
   Experience of the Contact Zone, 1850–1918   196
   Richard Hölzl and Karolin Wetjen

Index   235

Introduction
Negotiating the Religious and the Secular in Modern German History

Rebekka Habermas

In August 2016, the *New York Times* published an article under the headline, 'From Burkinis to Bikinis: Regulating What Women Wear'. The article is illustrated with two photographs. The first one shows a very formally dressed policeman on the beach of Rimini, on the Adriatic Coast of Italy, in 1957, writing a ticket for a woman wearing a bikini. Wearing a bikini (a swimsuit named after the Bikini Atoll Islands in the Pacific, which had become famous after the American nuclear bomb tests of 1946 in that region) was prohibited. At that time, the Italian government as well as most Italians argued in favour of the bikini ban on religious grounds. Following this line of argument, the bikini offended the Christian, in this case Catholic, religion. The second photograph shows three French policemen, dressed just as neatly as their Italian colleague decades before, forcing a woman sitting on the beach of a French town to remove her long-sleeved shirt. This photo was taken in August 2016, and the policemen are enforcing a ban on 'inappropriate clothing on beaches', colloquially referred to as the 'burkini ban', which had been issued some days earlier. Those who are supporting this ban argue that they are defending the secular, which is violated by religious, particularly Muslim, clothing habits.

There were neither bikinis nor burkinis in the German Empire, even though the most common bathing suits at that time were very similar to what is understood nowadays as a burkini – nor had there been major conflicts about Muslim or Catholic clothing habits. However, the recent burkini debate and the steadily growing research field that deals with these and similar contemporary conflicts are perfectly suited as a starting point for an exploration of the religious landscape of nineteenth-century Germany. Until recently this landscape has been described with analytical notions such as secularization or the revitalization of religion.

Since the 1990s, many historians have argued that those common explanations are misleading and that a new set of analytical tools and perspectives is needed to comprehend the significance of religion in the period. However, the question of which methodologies are most appropriate is still open to debate. I argue that contemporary debates concerning the place of the 'burkini' in the public sphere can provide us with helpful points of departure for future research concerning nineteenth-century Germany.

What we can learn from these debates, as I want to show in this Introduction, is that we firstly should connect religious and secular studies. As illustrated with these recent examples from European beaches, and as scholars like Talal Asad have convincingly argued, our understanding of the secular is closely linked to our understanding of the religious, and vice versa. The religious and the secular are anything but stable categories, let alone unproblematic articulations of universal meaning. They are instead relational categories, mutually shaping and reshaping each other as much as different confessions shape each other's identities.[1] Following this perspective, debates on religious phenomena are also always discussions about the frontiers of the secular and thereby about the making and unmaking of the religious and the secular.[2] However, connecting secular with religious studies is easier said than done – this is, first of all, due to research deficits regarding secular studies within historical disciplines. While religious histories have been increasing in popularity for several decades, historians – in contrast to sociologists and anthropologists – have only very recently detected the secular, secularity or secularities as topics of historical research. Historians, therefore, rely on the help of disciplines such as anthropology and sociology, where secular studies have been in steady growth for some years, and where a whole range of ideas on how to think about the secular have emerged.

Secondly, transnational perspectives are crucial here, because, during the long nineteenth century, and above all at the turn of the twentieth century, debates concerning the religious and the secular almost always referred to spaces beyond a given state's borders. In our own times, the Burkini debate, while reflecting French national legislation, has expressed and reinforced cultural concerns beyond the republic's borders. However, the transnational or even global perspectives that are needed for such an opening up of national frameworks are not without pitfalls, which is something particularly emphasized by postcolonial studies, pointing to some crucial shortcomings concerning topics such as religion and secularity. On the one hand, therefore, we need to account for processes of global entanglement, but simultaneously need to acknowledge the limitations of transnational approaches themselves.

How to Put the Religious and the Secular in One Analytical Frame?

The common sense among many historians of the modern period, 'that "religion" is a specific sphere which can be left to a few specialists', to quote John Seed,[3] has lasted for a very long time, particularly among historians working on imperial Germany. This long-lasting ignorance was particularly widespread among German historians, who all shared the same Weberian vision of nineteenth-century Germany as a country experiencing an increasing disenchantment and decline of religious worldviews. The underlying assumption – not always openly declared – was that modernity is secular per se.[4] And as the foundation of the German nation state, in 1871, was defined as a crucial hallmark of modernity, it seemed to be a logical consequence that the German Empire would be framed as a period that lacked strong religious forces and that, therefore, studies in religion would be superfluous. With only some rare exceptions, such as Wolfgang Schieder's article on Catholic pilgrimage, published in 1974,[5] German historians tended to ignore religious phenomena or to understand religion from a quite narrow, functional, point of view, either highlighting Catholicism as a form of clerical social control, or Protestantism's role as a legitimizing ideology for state and dynasty.[6]

It was mainly due to the works of British and American historians such as Richard Evans, David Blackbourn, Jonathan Sperber and Lavina Anderson, all four pioneers in the field of modern German religious history, that the topic was liberated from this shadowy and peripheral existence.[7] They not only claimed that religion was worthy of study in its own right, but also broadened the perspective beyond questions of its alleged backwardness and repressive dimensions. Step by step, the assumptions that nineteenth-century Germany was characterized by a process of secularization became less and less convincing. E.P. Thompson's seminal book, *The Making of the English Working Class*, doubtless also had some impact in this context, underlining as it did the religious origins of social protest movements in Britain. And certainly, the debate, initiated by Barbara Welter, dealing with the question if there had been something like a specific feminine religiosity in the nineteenth century, opened up new perspectives on the relationships between religiosity and gender.[8] Last but not least, nineteenth- and twentieth-century historians learnt much from early modernist and medieval historians' works, such as Lucien Febvre's *Luther* and the studies of Natalie Zemon Davis, pointing out the symbolic, political as well as economic powers that religion was able to develop.[9] These new studies also benefited from a broader understanding of religion, which had emerged in cultural and social anthropology from scholars like Clifford Geertz, defining religion as a system of meanings.[10]

Little by little, an ever-growing number of studies made it obvious that religion could neither be reduced to a Marxist perspective of religion as the 'opiate of the people', nor to a Foucauldian understanding of religion as a form of social discipline and control. Above all, it became clear that modernity and religion are anything but mutually exclusive. A couple of historians began to draw attention to Jewish history,[11] others to Protestantism, the dominant confession in Germany during the long nineteenth century, which had long been neglected, or simply treated as part of the ideological furniture of the imperial state after

1871.¹² As a consequence, the religious nature of charitable associations, particularly those of female origin, were explored and an entire new world of female middle-class life – be it in these associations or as deaconess or in Catholic congregations – was discovered.¹³ Finally, the prominent roles of inter-confessional rivalry within the emergence of German nationalism in the nineteenth century came clearly into focus, as well as the salience and importance of the culture wars waged during the 1870s between Catholics and liberals.¹⁴ At the same time, these and many other studies opened up new perspectives as they led to a rereading of Max Weber's secularization thesis and, therewith, initiated a debate on how to understand German religious sociologists, as well as other scholars such as Emile Durkheim, who are still highly influential among historians today.¹⁵ It became more and more obvious that these theories also need to be understood in the light of confessional debates, and that they are, therefore, rather contributions to the then ongoing culture wars than narratives offering a timeless theory.¹⁶

Along with this growing field of research, an until then overlooked highly vibrant religious landscape was discovered, consisting of dozens of different religious, spiritualistic and sectarian groups, including mission associations at home and abroad.¹⁷ Instead of a decrease in religion's significance over the nineteenth century, an increase in religious associations and religious engagement, far beyond the narrow range of churches, was brought to light. Some even spoke of a 'devotional revolution', a term first used by Emmet Larkin to describe Irish religious life in the nineteenth century.¹⁸ However, this revisionist interpretation has also been subject to criticism, because it was only some parts of society that could be described as becoming increasingly religious, whereas others were turning their backs on the churches and piety. On top of that, the relationship between the state and the church was undergoing fundamental changes.

Against the backdrop of this still growing, rich research field, it is all the more surprising how little we know about the secular. Almost all historians seem to take the secular for granted and, therefore, consider it to be a worthless subject. With the exception of Michael Gross's and Ari Joskowicz's studies on liberal anti-Catholicism, as well as studies of the 1870s culture wars arguing for a more nuanced portrayal of liberal views, the secular side remains undiscovered.¹⁹ The secular is an almost blank space on the historical research map. However, even though almost nobody seems to make the effort necessary to analyse what exactly was understood by the secular, secularities or secularization, almost all studies share the rarely spoken about but extremely widespread assumption that the secular is somehow the opposite side of religion or the mere absence of religion, and that it is needless to come to a precise definition, let alone to study this absence. However, there are some exceptions, like the study of Hermann Lübbe, analysing the concept of secularism in Germany's intellectual world from a 'history of ideas' perspective, and a rare handful of studies on freethinker societies or the atheistic school programmes pioneered by social democrats.²⁰ It has only been very recently that a new, however quite narrow, interest in the secular has emerged among historians. Studies like Todd Weir's book on *Secularism and Religion in Nineteenth-Century Germany*, published in 2014, focuses e.g. on free-thinking associations which explicitly defined themselves as secular.[21] The works of Lübbe as well as Weir are rare studies of this subject, exceptions proving the general rule.

Having pointed out this surprising lack of studies of the secular (which is not a German exception but very typical for almost all aspects of European history),[22] it is all the more remarkable that the number of studies of non-European secularities – in India, Japan and Egypt, to name just a few[23] – is steadily growing. One can even say that the new interest in historical secularisms in recent years has been sparked off outside and not inside Europe. This remarkable disinterest in the history of secularities, as well as the open ignorance of what was understood by whom under the term 'secular' in European history, is, I would argue, no mere coincidence. It is rather due to the very history of the historical discipline – one only has to think of Prussian state historians such as Treitschke and many others. Their self-understanding relied heavily on the notion that they had liberated themselves from the shackles of theology.[24] This almost total lack of historical research on the secular self-fashioning and self-understanding in the long nineteenth century must be understood as a clear and eloquent sign of a particular professional blindness due to epistemological constraints within the academic discipline of history. Among these constraints, what stands out as most pervasive is the rather narrow definition of the secular as a universal category referring to a mere lack of religion. By perpetuating this essentialist and ahistorical definition, historians until today, metaphorically speaking, are still working in the shadow of Max Weber.

Against the backdrop of this particular professional blindness, it comes as no surprise that other disciplines such as anthropology, sociology, and religious studies have been less reluctant to study the secular and secularities.[25] Even more, some argue that secular studies within these disciplines are already declining.[26] And again, the debate among anthropologists, apart from a few exceptions, such as studies on East Germany,[27] was fuelled by scholars focusing on non-European spaces or entangled spaces, like the French beach where Muslim women and French state representatives meet. Whereas public debates had already launched in the 1990s, the discussions within these academic disciplines gained momentum in 2003 with the publication of Talal Asad's book on *Formations of the Secular*.[28] Under his influence the alleged self-evident character of the secular as a blank space or as something that exclusively refers to the separation of church and state, opening up the possibility for modernity and the making of nation states, which bans religion to the private sphere, came under criticism. Instead of following this line of argumentation, Asad and others argue that the secular and the religious are rather more relational and, therefore, more fluid than essentially fixed categories. Following Asad, there is no such thing as one universal meaning of the secular – instead, the secular as much as the religious depends on time and place.

Further, he replaces the classic modernization theory narrative in so far as he rejects the assumption that the secular emerged as a religion-free space out of a sphere dominated by backward-looking religious authorities. Instead, he tells another story, asserting that the category religion first came into use in the early modern period, precisely at the moment of closer contact between Europeans and non-Europeans when the one group became defined as 'Nature Folk', believing in fetishes, and the other as 'Culture Folk', who had religion.[29] Finally, in the eighteenth century, a secular concept of superstition was developed: no longer defined as 'heresy', using canonical terminology, superstition was now regarded as a state of being that deserved to be pitied, a state of 'illusion and oppression before people could be liberated from them'.[30] Lastly, another important definition, developed by Talal Asad, is the term 'secularism'. Secularism is defined as a political doctrine, emerging in Europe, something made and remade by the modern state, and needing a clearly demarcated space that it classifies and regulates and that is closely connected to modernity, while excluding the non-European space from that very modernity.

To be short, Asad's deconstructionist view opens up new possibilities of understanding and interpretation. Particularly challenging for historical studies are three aspects of his understanding of secular and secularism. First of all, he needs to be credited for having drawn our attention to the long overlooked and only at first glance self-evident fact that the secular is more than a lack of religion, and that secularism is more than the idea of separating church and state, and cannot therefore be reduced to a narrow legal perspective, let alone ignored as a whole topic. Against the backdrop of his ideas, nineteenth-century debates, such as those initiated by Max Weber and Emile Durkheim, as well as by representatives of the Catholic Church and members of parliament, such as the centre party deputy, Ludwig Windhorst, should be understood less as a fight between a new group of liberal secularists and backward-looking representatives of a passing religious order, than as the very moment where an essentialist understanding of the secular was developed and theorized by exactly these scholars and politicians. Secondly, Asad shows that the religious and secular landscapes are constantly being made and remade, and thereby lack a fixed, essential identity.[31] Thirdly, his suggestions are stimulating in so far as he shows how these categories are part of power relations, and, thereby anything but neutral.[32] Instead, they are very often connected to other value-laden notions such as 'modernity' and 'civilization'.[33]

However, even though we owe stimulating new insights to the work of Talal Asad, we should not underestimate the objections brought forward by a range of critiques. Nor do I want to argue for a wholesale adaptation of Asad's suggestions. On the contrary, from a historical point of view, further criticism can be added. First and foremost, I cannot share his definition of secularism as a particular liberal ideology equipped with almost overwhelming power. This concept of secularism is far too static, leaving out all dynamics between Europe and other parts of the world.[34] It is also far too state centred, assuming an extremely powerful and, at the same time, abstract state, ignoring the forces of civil society as well as daily life routines, without mentioning emotional aspects. What is more, the dominant role of the state in the making of secularism, and with that the dominance of a political secularism, is anything but convincing.[35] Narrowly linked to this critique is the objection that Asad neglects the roles that competing religious groups have had in the formation of secularism.[36] Todd Weir criticizes Asad for assuming far too narrow a linkage between secularism and Western liberalism, which ignores a large group of radical socialist activists who were engaged in a straightforward secular agenda, at least in nineteenth century Europe.[37]

Another critic addresses the way the making and unmaking of the secular is often described as a process taking place in splendid isolation from other processes. Many sociological secular studies, and most of all Asad's genealogical narrative that starts in an early modern history of conquest in the New World, and leads to the liberal modern state, ignore the broader picture of these negotiations of the secular and religious, and therefore tend to simplify and lead to misunderstandings. For instance, in the nineteenth and twentieth centuries, the new boundaries between the secular and the religious were narrowly connected to questions of class and gender, mutually shaping and reshaping each other – one only has to think of the obvious link between female bodies and French secular policies concerning the Burkini.

However, by taking up these critical arguments, I do not want to throw the baby out with the bathwater. Instead, I think a fresh look on these debates among anthropologists could challenge historical studies, irrespective of whether they follow Asad's perspectives or not. Some suggestions made among secular studies scholars of anthropology and sociology might well turn out to be helpful for empirical historical analysis. However, regardless of which perspective seems more valuable, Asad's understanding of the secular as something constantly undergoing definition and redefinition in dialogue with the religious, opens up new perspectives beyond classical, diametrically opposed theories of secularization on the one hand, and religious revival on the other.

How to Entangle the Secular and the Religious?

If one aim of this volume is to come to a better understanding of the long nineteenth century beyond classical theories of secularization by connecting the study of phenomena, groups, topics and conflicts, named by contemporaries or today's experts, either religious or secular, into one analytical frame, another leading idea is to widen the perspective in geographical terms. Thanks to the ongoing Burkini discussion and to related debates, this idea is not new. In recent years, historical and other disciplines have begun to look beyond their national framework and detected that a denser net of transnational connections is a much less recent development than many sociological globalization theories had assumed.[38] Economic, political, as well as many other kinds of contacts are of considerable longevity, even though the intensity and the character may have indeed changed over the last centuries. However, historians, as well as others, used to link processes of globalization, understood in a rather broad sense as a time–space compression and as a denser net of contacts, to modernity and, therewith, as aforementioned, almost automatically to secularity, understood as a mere lack of religion. It took some time until historians found out that not only the economy and politics but also religion may have been of global character.

It was moreover around 2000 that a growing number of studies, analysing the religious history beyond national boundaries, gathered momentum. Many new insights were gained. One of the important ones, brought to light by these studies, is the fact that a much larger and much more important net of religious contacts already existed in the nineteenth century all around the globe, connecting Europe with Africa, Asia with America, and Australia with India, just to name a few surprising contacts. Missionaries, for instance, established worldwide networks, connecting not only people but initiating an almost global trade in books and religious symbols, but also in travelling concepts, clothing regimes and normative orders.[39] Related to these studies, a whole group of scholars began to explore philanthropic associations and early NGOs, and their construction of a web of global humanitarianism.[40] Other studies, focusing on transnational entanglements, concentrated on the European dimension of culture wars, and compared the entangled modes of working-class religion in Europe and North America,[41] or analysed transnational flows of religious personnel, such as the export of French nuns to England.[42]

Another crucial insight gained by these studies is concerned with the dynamics emerging from these contacts. Knowledge studies, like the seminal investigation of Tomoko Masuzawa on *The Invention of World Religion*, show that categories such as religion, magic and fetishism, as well as, the notion of 'world religion' itself, emerged at the end of nineteenth century as a result of colonial encounters, and that they became increasingly important via academic writings and events, such as the World Parliament of Religions in Chicago.[43] Further effects of religious encounters can be observed in the fostering of already existing belief systems and even in the emergence of political movements, which were engendered by religious contacts. Peter van der Veer, for instance, outlines how British missionaries in India contributed to the formation of a national muscular Hinduism in this period.[44]

Other studies, openly labelled as world histories, such as Bayly's *The Birth of the Modern World*,[45] published early in the new millennium, were less interested in the emergence of new notions of difference due to religious encounters, emphasizing instead the similarities of religious phenomena that could be observed all around the world. He, for instance, detected 'a growing uniformity of styles and social functions' in Christian as well as Muslim and other religious communities.[46] Bayly also emphasizes a new worldwide religious trend of highlighting the rational, and 'condemning superstitious … and magical beliefs'.[47] A similar argument underlines the unifying force of worldwide contacts, which concerned the global role that religion played in processes of nation building in the nineteenth century.⁴⁸

To summarize, transnational, global and world histories have enlarged our understanding of the nineteenth century's religious landscape. Furthermore, these studies can claim an even more important merit: while revising the earlier assumption that globalization and religion are mutually exclusive, these studies showed that religion is linked to processes of globalization and that the most influential global players, at least in the nineteenth century, were religious men and women, like missionaries, connecting entire continents, sometimes even before a worldwide net of trade had been established. Religion, therefore, turned out to be a driver of globalization, one of the most crucial modernizing processes, instead of constituting a 'backward' or 'irrational' phenomenon.

Having emphasized the broad and innovative field of global and transnational historical studies in religious history brings me to the question of how secular studies beyond national boundaries emerged in history. Is there a field of global historical studies of the secular that is understood, on the one hand, less as a religion-free space (in the Weberian perspective) but as something constantly made and remade, and, on the other hand, as a specific ideology? Is there a global or transnational history of the making and unmaking of the secular and of different secularities? Or are global history approaches as uninterested in the secular as national history approaches have turned out to be? To be up front with the answer, the degree to which secularisms are understudied in transnational let alone global histories does not differ in any respect from what we have seen in the field of national history writing.

This lack of interest becomes most obvious when taking a closer look at the world or global history of the long nineteenth century, the subdiscipline aiming at a total coverage and therefore most likely to pay attention to a phenomenon, such as the making and unmaking of the secular. Although most recently published world histories criticize the Weberian secularization thesis, and even though some replace it with more precise descriptions, and others like Bayly emphasize that 'the nineteenth century saw the triumphal re-emergence and expansion of "religion"', there is no global or world history that investigates what the secular actually looked like.⁴⁹ Even those studies that emphasize that a Weberian style of secularization as the only possible way of contemporary self-understanding,⁵⁰ do not take into account, or even investigate, other concepts of the secular and the plurality of possible secularisms. Some pages on laïcité and atheism, as a peculiar and culturally specific development in France, or on philosophical objections to superstition and the foundation of the theosophical society as a product of globalization, is all that is expounded in these works.⁵¹ Global and transnational history thereby suffer from a similar imbalance as the aforementioned studies' focus on national histories: in both cases a growing field of religious history studies is counterbalanced by an almost total lack of historical research on secularism or the secular.⁵² On top of that, the rare global histories that do address the secular share the same essentialist conception of the phenomenon as those historians focusing on a narrow national level: the secular as a set of ideas put forward by associations such as the Freethinker Society in Europe and North America. Set against the backdrop of this surprising continuity in research gaps between national and global histories, it goes without saying that there is no world history putting the secular and the religious into one analytical frame.

Despite global history's enormous merits, (particularly when it comes to a re-evaluation of religion's roles within global processes), the approach not only shares some of the blind spots observed in national histories, but also adds new problems to the research field. First of all, and very generally speaking, global histories, at least those focusing on the nineteenth century, tend to ignore all parts of the world beyond Europe, North America, and those parts of Asia that belonged to the British Empire.[53] Examples, or even in-depth analysis, of African and Australian regions, or places in New Zealand or New Guinea, are rare. To be very clear about that, it can be conclusively justified to leave out a region for more or less pragmatic reasons, even though that contradicts the claim raised by the term 'global history'. And indeed, concentrating on particular regions, such as Europe, Asia and North America, while other regions only 'appear scantily in world historical interpretations' – as Manning has recently pointed out[54] – has for a long time been also due to pragmatic reasons, as world history is mostly based not on first-hand research but on the studies of others, most of which is written in English.[55] But, given the tremendous increase in research resources concerning these global regions in recent years, such excuses are no longer valid. Some scholars have even argued that this ignoring of Africa and Oceania is not due to mere coincidence but rather to a particular blindness that has a history as long and powerful as the history of the blind spots concerning the secular, for which academic historiography has to be held accountable. The left out regions follow a long and powerful tradition – partly established by Hegel – of mapping Europe and Asia as the alleged realm of progress, modernity and, therefore, history, juxtaposed in opposition to regions such as Oceania and Africa, described as lacking civilization, history and the ability to progress.[56] To put it in a nutshell, these histories tend to offer double perspectives, which we know to be extremely problematic, at least since we learned from postcolonial studies to be more aware of the age-old politics of ignorance. Or to quote Patrick Manning, the logic of world histories and their practice of modelling the past contribute to a 'prioritization of elite and civilizational perspectives – stemming from one-sided understanding of human innovation'.[57] These exclusive perspectives of world histories, therefore, whether deliberate or not, are in danger of creating the impression that all other regions are less, if at all, important places in terms of innovation.

Ignoring Africa and Oceania, furthermore, has serious effects on which kinds of belief systems are left out and which are paid attention to. This narrow scope results in ignoring all belief systems beyond what became known in the nineteenth century as 'world religions',[58] such as so-called fetishism, magical customs, voodoo, natural religions or simply superstition. They thus tended to overlook everything that did not fit the definition of a scripture-based or monotheistic belief system. By losing sight of all belief systems beyond world religions, the concept of world religion[59] is doubled instead of deconstructed. What that means can be seen best when taking a short look into the two most prominent world histories of the nineteenth century. The global histories written by Bayly and Osterhammel mention belief systems beyond world religions only in so far as they refer to European missionaries and their often futile attempts to spread the gospel among non-Christians, who often had little to say about the variety of religions, faith and belief systems that existed in the so-called mission field in the first place.[60] The effects of this form of silencing are as powerful as the silencing of entire continents – they often go hand in hand. This leads to an impression of the nineteenth century as an era dominated by world religions whereas other belief systems somehow vanished, or at least lacked the power to, for example, fuel politics, count as an identity marker, or serve as ingredients of new hybrid belief systems. Against the backdrop of what we know about the mechanics of empowerment by religion, particularly within subaltern communities in general, and for many independence movements in particular, this implicit assumption is anything but convincing. Moreover, this exclusion and silencing, above all, helped to foster elite and western-oriented approaches, reinforcing categories such as the notion of 'world religion', which is neither innocent, nor an analytically useful term.[61]

To sum up, even though global histories have enriched the field of religious and secular studies by emphasizing the role religion played within globalization processes, as a means of hybridization and homogenization as well as beyond, they are prone to serious shortcomings.[62] As postcolonial studies have argued, one might even presume that world history contributes as much to a specific perspective on globality, which is not beyond postcolonial legacies, as national histories used to reinforce a particular nineteenth-century version of power, modernity and progress, which was allegedly located exclusively in European nation states.[63]

These critical remarks should not be misunderstood as a plea for a renationalization of historical approaches. The contrary can be learned from these debates.[64] Historians interested in studying the making and unmaking of the religious and the secular in long-nineteenth-century German history can benefit from the questions raised in these debates about the limits and challenges of entangled perspectives, as much as they can benefit from the discussions about secular studies within anthropology.

The Secular and the Religious Entangled in Modern German History

Even though the Burkini debate, as well as others, made it very clear that questions concerning the secular and the religious are closely bound together, shaping and reshaping each other in a way that urges us to engage more in the study of the secular, as well as to broaden its scope beyond national boundaries, the concrete new insights we might gain for a study of modern German history are still hard to grasp. Moreover, the perspectives and tools, I have tried to outline in this Introduction, seem to be full of pitfalls and shortcomings, further hampering, or at least complicating, historical explorations.

A number of this volume's contributors met at the European Studies Centre of St Anthony's, Oxford, in spring 2014, to try to rethink the secular and the religious in the German Empire from a broader perspective.[65] Some of the contributions in this volume were discussed there, while others have been added separately, in order to paint to a fuller picture of the religious as well as the secular landscape in the long nineteenth century, and especially the decades around the turn of the century. The aim was to cover a broad range of different historiographical approaches, such as intellectual history, conceptual history, history of science, social history, and approaches that trace discursive traditions or follow a biographical perspective. Another aim was to combine studies that focus more on the religious with studies that address more the secular side of a given phenomenon. And finally, the global dimensions and conditions of the making and unmaking of the religious and the secular was paid special attention.

The volume is divided into three parts. Part I discusses the production of knowledge around 1900 in two academic disciplines, the sociology of religion and Protestant theology, that were of major importance for the formation of new understandings of the secular and the religious. The second part sheds light on the contemporary debates in the field of secular and religious matters, that go beyond academia. The central questions at stake here are: what was understood by religion, and what was meant by secular; and how were these meanings related to each other and how (far) did the given definitions contradict each other? The third part brings together contributions that deal with phenomena as diverse as political anarchism and missions. The aim here is to explore how and where exactly negotiations of the religious and secular took place, and to better understand the exact meaning these debates had in the German states and empire.

However manifold and varied the emerging field of religious studies was around 1900 – among them titles on missionary activities, religion psychology and anthropology – it can be said that the sociology of religion and Protestant theology were probably the two most influential, academic disciplines, at least in the German academic landscape. The volume, therefore, starts with the headline 'Religious and Secular: Scientific Debates', with two chapters that illuminate how and which new borders between religion, and secularity and secularism emerged within sociology of religion and Protestant theology. Although these two starting chapters focus on different groups of scholars, there is no doubt that they are negotiating similar and entangled questions of how to define religion as well as secularity/secularism.

Wolfgang Knöbl's chapter on 'A Secular Age? The "Modern World" and the Beginnings of the Sociology of Religion' focuses on the beginning of the sociology of religion in Germany and France, and traces the very making of the terms 'religion' and 'secularity/secularism' within academia around 1900. He argues that even though the evolvement of religious studies was the result of transnational entanglements, the particular outlook of this new academic field in France and Germany was due to particular and very different national traditions. Max Weber's concepts of religion, which emphasize religion as a safe haven for the autonomous individual, as well as his understanding of secularity and secularism, varied in many respects from the French model of Emile Durkheim. The latter understood religion as a crucial and even indispensable part of any given society, and is, therefore, less concerned with questions of secularism. This comparative perspective enables us to see the particular traditions that Weber's concept of the secular is based on, and hence sheds new light on how particular intellectual as well as political challenges that German intellectuals had to deal with at the turn of the century shaped Weber's secularization thesis. But Knöbl's analysis does not stop here. He also reminds us of the heavy Eurocentric baggage that we have inherited from the sociology of religion, whether in its Weberian or Durkheimian versions, and their different concepts of religion and secularity/secularism.

Paul Michael Kurtz's chapter on 'The Silence on the Land: Ancient Israel versus Modern Palestine in Scientific Theology' illustrates how the growing interest of Protestant theology in Palestine around 1900 contributed to a new idea of Christian religion as well as to a religionizing of the scientific and, thus, negotiated new borders between the religious and the secular. He studies the emergence of a new interest in Palestine, that can be observed among German Protestant scholars from 1880 onwards. He describes an ever-growing number of inquiries into biblical texts, and an almost endless number of philological works on ancient Israel, which went hand in hand with countless contemporary efforts to decipher a whole range of ancient languages, all leading to a rewriting of the Old Testament. This rewriting led to a new rift between Israel and Judaism, on the one hand, and the emergence of a narrative about a clear historical continuity between Christian religion and ancient Israel, on the other hand. It resulted in a new mapping of what was understood as Christian religion. At the same time, this new interest in the Bible pushed scholars to Palestine, looking for a past that could allegedly still be found in the present day, and, thus, establishing new academic associations and research institutes. But Kurtz not only describes how modern German Protestantism and Christian religion were made and remade around 1900 by digging in places that remained part of the Ottoman Empire, but also shows how these studies and archaeological sites helped to colonize a present place, and how scientific enterprises and disciplines, such as archaeology, were endowed with a spiritual quality.

The second part of the volume is headlined 'Religious and Secular: Public Debates'. Even though the various debates dealing with issues of religion and secularity that reached out to a broader public were all related to the academic sphere, and clear distinctions cannot be made, the two chapters in this part broaden out perspectives, and focus on how notions of the secular and, thereby, of the religious, were negotiated within different layers of the society. Lucian Hölscher takes a closer look at the debates that mostly took place within Protestantism, and underlines the varieties of secularisms negotiated within these circles, while Rebekka Habermas tries to come to a better understanding of the essential core of what, at that time, was understood by 'the secular'.

Lucian Hölscher's chapter, 'What Does It Mean To Be "Secular" in the German Kaiserreich? An Intervention', is mainly focusing on Protestant Germany against the backdrop of Britain and France. In contrast to the approaches of Knöbl and Kurtz, which can be described as intellectual history, Hölscher, as a conceptional historian, is mainly focusing on the debates that took place in intellectual circles. The methodological tools of conceptional history bring the inseparable interconnectedness of secular and religious perspectives within German Protestantism to light. Instead of an antagonistic concept of the secular and religious, Hölscher underlines the broad variety of notions of the secular within Protestantism, and stresses how the interconfessional situation within Protestantism, and not only the culture wars of the 1870s, played a crucial role for the religious, and thereby secular, landscape of the German Empire. This led to the development of several peculiar German secularisms, and one of these, as he argues, was a new kind of religion, civic in character, combining aspects of what was considered secular combined with elements of liberal Protestantism.

Rebekka Habermas's chapter on 'Secularism in the Long Nineteenth Century between the Global and the Local' also tries to come to a more precise definition of the secular. She chooses a broader frame, although the German Empire is the starting point and main focus. The turn of the century is privileged to address the entanglements between the German metropole and its recently acquired colonies. It is within this entangled nation that notions of the secular, as put forward not only in the freethinker associations and among social democrats, but by men from various backgrounds, in most cases not very prominent at the time and completely forgotten nowadays, are analysed. Tracing this production of the secular in weekly magazines and other journals, the chapter shows that the secular was something more than just a lack or absence of religion, it was at the core of a highly emotional debate. Many groups such as confessional charitable associations as well as liberal party leaders were involved in these debates, and even though they disagreed on almost every point, they shared two basic convictions. They defined the secular as something more common among men than women and as an almost exclusively European phenomenon. Everything else was open to an increasingly spirited and vibrant debate, which, as the chapter argues, gives us new insights into the high degree of emotionality at stake in the making of the secular and the religious.

At first sight, the three chapters in Part III have little in common, since they are contributions that deal with leading Jewish anarchists, Catholic women's congregations, and missionaries in German colonies around the turn of the century. And yet, all three contributions of this third part, entitled 'Religious and Secular: Negotiating Boundaries', deal with the same phenomenon: the constant making and unmaking of the religious and secular. This happens in places as diverse as anarchist circles, the everyday life of religious women and African contact zones. The contributions explore how fluid the boundaries between the religious and the secular were, and argue that these constantly renewed borders can be seen in connection with global entanglements – some more, some less.

Carolin Kosuch's chapter 'Retrieving Tradition? The Secular–Religious Ambiguity in Nineteenth-Century German-Jewish Anarchism' on the two leading Jewish anarchists, Gustav Landauer and Erich Mühsam, opens up the arena, leaving the almost exclusively Christian frame, while simultaneously combining questions concerning the secular and the religious with political issues. She chooses a comparative biographical approach combined with a history of ideas, asking how the political concepts of Gustav Landauer and Erich Mühsam, and their ideas of a transnational anarchism were related to the secular, as well as their Jewishness. As Kosuch argues, much of the anarchist programme was also due to a specific legacy of acculturation, which Landauer and Mühsam were less able to cope with compared to their fathers. Studying anarchism from a biographical perspective and in relation to secular ideas, as well as Judaism, enriches the history of political ideas in that it is able to show that even seemingly atheistic theoretical constructs and political programmes owed a great deal to religion. At the same time, she shows how difficult it is to come to a clear-cut definition of what might be called secular, atheistic or worldly.

Relinde Meiwes's chapter 'Catholic Women as Global Actors of the Religious and the Secular' traces the global networks of female congregations, and explores how their daily work always transcended the border to the secular, even though these were women bound by oath to genuine religious work. Meiwes places religious women at the forefront and shows that the very success of the congregations in the German Empire was due to the possibility of crossing the border between the secular and the religious, even though religious orders, particularly those for women, had a long tradition of mainly emphasizing the positive effects of a cloistered life removed from all worldly affairs. At the same time, this transcending of borders seemingly opened up new opportunities, which was particularly attractive for women. Instead of fostering the boundaries between the religious and the secular worlds, the nuns were steadily blurring the lines and, thus, changing notions of religious and secular work. No less surprising is the extent to which these religious orders, which depended on transnational networks, built up new connections. It is needless to underline that the transnational experience also shaped the work in Europe.

Richard Hölzl and Karolin Wetjen's chapter, 'Negotiating the Fundamentals? German Missions and the Experience of the Contact Zone, 1850–1918', follows the work of Catholic as well as Protestant missionaries in the colonies and at home, studying how they shaped and reshaped the boundaries between the secular and the religious and, at the same time, occupied a central role in

European colonialism. Wetjen and Hölzl centre their perspective on the making of the boundaries between the secular and the religious by missionaries in colonial discourse, in theology, and in their practical work. Focusing on the practical as well as on the performative aspect of missionary work, and comparing Protestant to Catholic missionaries in German East Africa, they are able to shed new light on how concepts of the superstitious, the magic and the religious, as well as the secular, emerged in the mission field and how this affected the perspectives that were brought forward in Germany. Here, the interconnectedness includes not only Europeans but also Africans, as well as Protestants and Catholics, and those believing in so called fetish religions. At the same time, it becomes obvious that German colonialism was considerably less secular than is currently acknowledged in many studies.

If we try to summarize the main insights these three parts have to offer, focusing on scholarly debates as well as on discussions beyond academia, and on some few episodes of the political and social life around 1900, it quickly becomes clear that the German Empire can neither be described as a place where religion either decreased or increased, nor is there convincing evidence for a rise or a fall in secular ideas, let alone practices. Instead, some examples, such as the female congregations, show a growing influence of religious work, while other chapters bring to light an increasing importance of so-called civil religion, which was very similar to the secular and atheistic ideas of Jewish anarchists like Mühsam and Landauer.

Instead of unambiguous evidence of either a rise or a fall in religious belief and practice, the chapters show that men and women were steadily working and reworking the boundaries between what they considered to be secular and religious. In their daily work, missionaries never really made clear distinctions between a religious and a secular colonial sphere, even though they wrote entire books on the nature of religion. Sisters from congregations had no difficulties blurring the lines between religious and worldly work; anarchists, like Erich Mühsam, called themselves atheists even though their programme was deeply rooted within Jewish traditions. Max Weber fought for a seemingly academic definition of the secular, which contained nakedly anti-Catholic elements. Neither do we find clear evidence regarding global dimensions, be it among Anarchists, missionaries, sociologists or secularists. Instead, some, like the missionaries, developed increasingly intense ties to Germany, while others, like the French sociologists, stayed within rather national intellectual traditions.

It must therefore be conceded that these chapters do not contribute to the debate concerning the levels of religious practice in the German Empire, nor do they reveal a totally new Kaiserreich. However, they may change some questions and, little by little, rearrange some of the assumptions still to be found at the heart of many historical studies. Against the backdrop of these chapters and many other aforementioned titles, a more nuanced and ambivalent but also more vivid picture of the last decades of the nineteenth century and of the beginning of the twentieth century emerges. This seems to have been a time when many theoretical concepts and legal reforms, but also everyday practices and intellectual mindsets, concerning such terms such as religion, atheism, secularity, fetishism and superstition, were negotiated with a newfound intensity. To put it in a nutshell, this period of German history should be described as a time of negotiations about the secular and the religious rather than as a moment of secularization or religious revival. It was a time when notions such as 'world religion' came into being,[66] when other terms like 'secularization' gained new significance, and when debates emerged between those who feared and those who welcomed falling levels of church attendance and challenges to established religious practices.

Rather than delineate an increase or decrease in religion or secularism in nineteenth-century Germany, the contributions of this volume bring to light a multitude of secular worldviews, belief systems and rituals. They thus uncover a large number of differences in how the borders between the secular and the religious are made and remade. The ideas about what was considered secular or religious varied between civil religion and atheism; some understood certain missionary practices as belonging to a secular sphere, while they themselves believed in their deeply religious nature. Even though some of these practices and worldviews were surely more powerful than others, able to influence legislation processes or determine what would be written down in school books and what would be left out, these many differences are of crucial importance if one wants to understand the signature of the era, which can best be described as one of multiple secularisms.[67] These differences are as well particularly relevant as they bring to light what Talal Asad defined as a secularism, a particular state policy, as well as a specific liberal ideology, which needs to be understood as part of a dynamic field with many different agencies rather than as the singular dominant discourse.

Finally, the chapters bring to light that many, though not all, of these negotiations were connected to different but always very particular parts of the world. This entanglement created new networks, as well as forms of hybridization or homogenization, and fostered new ideas and interests, as underlined by Knöbl for the new discipline of sociology of religion. The missionaries, for example, as Hölzl and Wetjen argue, brought back home strange and, until then rarely heard of, religious, magical and superstitious belief systems,[68] while in the meantime more and more religious women gained global working experiences because congregations were founded and maintained all over the world. However, these networks did not prevent the emergence of particular national concepts of the religious, as Hölscher shows. On the contrary, many national peculiarities were born out of precisely these global entanglements.

Against the backdrop of these peculiarities, it is perhaps surprising that Germany's beaches have not yet served as stages for a new round in the negotiation of the religious and the secular. However, evidence is growing that changes lie ahead in the Federal Republic, and, as in the long nineteenth century, the key question will not represent a straightforward choice between secularization or a revitalization of the religious, but rather how and where we should draw the boundaries between these fluid and contested categories.

Rebekka Habermas is professor of modern German history at the University of Göttingen, and has been Richard von Weizsäcker Professor at Oxford and Theodor Heuss Professor at the New School in New York. She has authored several books on German nineteenth-century history, among others *Frauen und Männer des Bürgertums: Eine Familiengeschichte* (Vandenhoeck & Ruprecht, 2000); *Thieves in Court: The Making of the German Legal System in the Nineteenth Century* (Cambridge University Press, 2016); and *Skandal in Togo: Ein Kapitel deutscher Kolonialherrschaft* (Fischer, 2016).

Notes

I am indebted to Antonie Habermas (Munich) and to Victoria Morick and Lena Glöckler (Göttingen) for their generous and very helpful readings. I am also indebted to Karolin Wetjen (Göttingen) for the several readings she undertook; her advice has been of enormous help. I am also grateful for the many pieces of advice received from the anonymous reviewers.

1. H. Walser-Smith and C. Clark. 'The Fate of Nathan', in H. Walser-Smith (ed.), *Protestants, Catholics and Jews in Germany, 1800–1914* (Oxford: Berg, 2001), 5–7.
2. By the term 'religion-making', the agency of the many can be brought to light, instead of exclusively focusing on the power of the state. Even if it has to be admitted that the terms 'religion-making from above' and 'religion-making from below', as proposed by Dressler and Mandair, are not without shortcomings, as they silence the interconnectedness of both, they open up new possibilities for understanding questions of change and for escaping from the state-centredness of Asad's concept of secularism. M. Dressler and A.S. Mandair, 'Introduction: Modernity, Religion-Making, and the Postsecular', in idem (eds), *Secularism and Religion-Making* (Oxford: Oxford University Press, 2011), 3–37. For the related notion 'Christianity-making', see the excellent analysis of K. Wetjen. 'Religionspädagogische Resonanzen und die Mission: "Christianity Making" im missionarischen Bildungsraum am Ende des 19. Jahrhunderts', in D. Kaebisch and M. Wermke (eds), *Transnationale Grenzgänge und Kulturkontakte: Historische Fallbeispiele in religionspädagogischer Perspektive* (Leipzig: Evangelische Verlagsanstalt, 2016), 23–38.
3. J. Seed, '"Secular" and "Religious": Historical Perspectives', *Social History* 39 (2014), 3. M.L. Anderson, 'Die Grenzen der Säkularisierung', in H. Lehmann (ed.), *Säkularisierung, Dechristianisierung, Rechristianisierung im neuzeitlichen Europa* (Göttingen: Vandenhoeck & Ruprecht, 1997), 194–222, argues that German historians only discovered religion very late because German academia is dominated by protestants, which mainly means members of the so-called *Kulturprotestantismus*. Another reason might be the long-lasting dominance of the *Sonderweg* thesis.
4. Prominent is e.g. M. Weber, 'Wissenschaft als Beruf (1919)', in D. Kaesler (ed.), *Schriften 1884–1922* (Stuttgart: Kröner, 2002), 488.
5. W. Schieder, 'Kirche und Revolution: Sozialgeschichtliche Aspekte der Trierer Wallfahrt von 1844', *Archiv für Sozialgeschichte* 14 (1974), 419–54.

6. R. Evans, 'Religion and Society in Modern Germany', *European Studies Review* 12 (1982), 249–88. The most important exception is F. Schnabel, *Deutsche Geschichte im neunzehnten Jahrhundert*, 4 vols (Freiburg: Herder, 1929; repr. Munich: Deutscher Taschenbuch, 1987). He dedicated one entire volume of his comprehensive multi-volume study on German history to 'religious forces'. The second important exception is T. Nipperdey, *Religion im Umbruch Deutschland 1870–1918* (Munich: Beck, 1988).
7. Evans, 'Religion and Society in Modern Germany'; J. Sperber, *Popular Catholicism in Nineteenth-Century Germany* (Princeton, NJ: Princeton University Press, 1984); D. Blackbourn, *Marpingen: Apparitions of the Virgin Mary in Bismarckian Germany* (Oxford: Clarendon Press, 1993);. M.L. Anderson, *Windhorst: A Political Biography* (Oxford and New York: Clarendon Press, 1981).
8. B. Welter, 'The Feminization of American Religion: 1800–1860', in M.S. Hartmann and L. Banner (eds), *Clio's Consciousness Raised: New Perspectives on the History of Women* (New York: Octagon Books, 1976), 137–57.
9. L. Febvre, *Un destin. Martin Luther* (Paris: Rieder, 1928).
10. C. Geertz, 'Religion als kulturelles System', in idem (ed.), *Dichte Beschreibung: Beiträge zum Verstehen kultureller Systeme* (Frankfurt/Main: Suhrkamp, 1983), 44–95.
11. For other as well historically grounded reasons, a third strand of German research of the 1990s began to focus on Jewish history, also beyond anti-Semitism. Cf. M. Kaplan, *The Making of the Jewish Middle Class:. Women, Family and Identity in Imperial Germany* (New York: Oxford University Press, 1991); T. van Rahden, *Juden und andere Breslauer: Die Beziehungen zwischen Juden, Protestanten und Katholiken in einer deutschen Großstadt von 1860 bis 1925* (Göttingen: Vandenhoeck & Ruprecht, 2000); U. Jensen, *Gebildete Doppelgänger: Bürgerliche Juden und Protestanten im 19. Jahrhundert* (Göttingen: Vandenhoeck & Ruprecht, 2005).
12. L. Hölscher, 'Die Religion des Bürgers: Bürgerliche Frömmigkeit und protestantische Kirche', *Historische Zeitschrift* 250 (1990), 595–630; R. Habermas, 'Weibliche Religiosität oder: Von der Fragilität bürgerlicher Identitäten', in K. Tenfelde and H.U. Wehler (eds), *Wege zur Geschichte des Bürgertums* (Göttingen: Vandenhoeck & Ruprecht, 1994), 125–48.
13. C.M. Prelinger, *Charity, Challenge, and Change: Religious Dimensions of the Mid-Nineteenth-Century Women* (New York: Greenwood Press, 1987); R. Meiwes, *'Arbeiterinnen des Herrn': Katholische Frauenkongregationen im 19. Jahrhundert* (Frankfurt/Main: Campus, 2000).
14. H.G. Haupt and D. Langewiesche (eds), *Nation und Religion in Europa* (Frankfurt/Main and New York: Campus, 2004); M.B. Gross, *The War against Catholicism: Liberalism and the Anti-Catholic Imagination in Nineteenth-Century Germany* (Ann Arbor: The University of Michigan Press, 2005); C. Clark and W. Kaiser (eds), *Culture Wars: Secular–Catholic Conflict in Nineteenth-Century Europe* (Cambridge: Cambridge University Press, 2003); M. Borutta, *Antikatholizismus: Deutschland und Italien im Zeitalter der europäischen Kulturkämpfe* (Göttingen: Vandenhoeck & Ruprecht, 2010).
15. Particularly important, for the broad field of studies of religious emotions, see the pioneering work of Monique Scheer: M. Scheer, P. Eitler and B. Hitzer, 'Feeling and Faith: Religious Emotions in German History', *German History* 32(3) (2014), 343–52.
16. M. Borutta, 'Genealogie der Säkularisierungstheorie: Zur Historisierung einer großen Erzählung der Moderne', *Geschichte und Gesellschaft* 36(3) (2010), 347–76.
17. D. Sawicki, *Leben mit den Toten: Geisterglauben und die Entstehung des Spiritismus in Deutschland 1770–1900* (Paderborn: Schöningh, 2002); C. Ribbat, *Religiöse Erregung:*

Protestantische Schwärmer im Kaiserreich (Frankfurt/Main: Campus, 1996); U. Linse, *Geisterseher und Wunderwirker: Heilssuche im Industriezeitalter* (Frankfurt/Main: Fischer Taschenbuch, 1996). H.W. Smith, *Protestants, Catholics and Jews in Germany, 1800–1914* (Oxford: Berg, 2001). For the role of missionaries, see R. Habermas and R. Hölzl (eds), *Mission Global: Eine Verflechtungsgeschichte seit dem 19. Jahrhundert* (Cologne: Böhlau, 2014).

18. E. Larkin, 'The Devotional Revolution in Ireland', *American Historical Review* 77(3) (1972), 625–52.
19. Gross, *The War against Catholicism*; A. Joskowicz, *The Modernity of the Others: Jewish Anti-Catholicism in Germany and France* (Stanford, CA: Stanford University Press, 2014); Clark and Kaiser, *Culture Wars*; Borutta, *Antikatholizismus*; H. Walser-Smith, *German Nationalism and Religious Conflict: Culture, Ideology, Politics, 1870–1914* (Princeton, NJ: Princeton University Press, 1995).
20. H. Lübbe, *Säkularisierung: Geschichte eines ideenpolitischen Begriffs* (Freiburg: Herder, 1965). S. Enders, *Moralunterricht und Lebenskunde* (Bad Heilbonn: Julius Klinkhardt, 2002). And even from a broader historical perspective the secular only begins to obtain attention as French laïcité; see J.W. Scott, *The Politics of the Veil* (Princeton, NJ and Oxford: Princeton University Press, 2007); and in respect to Jewish history, for instance: L.M. Leff, 'The Jewish Oath and the Making of Secularism in Modern France', *The Baeck Institute Year Book* 58 (2013), 23–34.
21. T.H. Weir, *Secularism and Religion in Nineteenth-Century Germany: The Rise of the Fourth Confession* (Cambridge: Cambridge University Press, 2014). Indeed the merit of his study was to raise the question of what it was exactly that contemporaries understood under the umbrella term 'secular'. Weir studies the members of the rather small but in many respects influential group of secularists organized in associations like the *Deutsche Gesellschaft für ethische Kultur* or as part of the Social Democrat Party, ranging from worldview secularists emphasizing the insights of natural science to more overtly political advocates of state secularization, and it underlines the variety among these groups. However, this study cannot (and does not intend to) reach to the emotional or everyday life of the secular, let alone to the interplay between the religious and the secular beyond these quite small and elitist groups in the city. Nor does it include institutional questions of the secular and the religious. See also T. Matysik, 'Secularism, Subjectivity, and Reform: Shifting Variables', in G. Eley, J. Jenkins and T. Matysik (eds), *German Modernities from Wilhelm to Weimar: A Contest of Futures* (London, Oxford and New York: Bloomsbury, 2016), 215–34.
22. There are a number of studies of French laïcité, the most recent and prominent study focusing on the latest regulations concerning 'the veil' of the French government, is Scott, *The Politics of the Veil*, particularly 90–123; studies concerning the United States can also be found, see S. Jacoby, *Freethinkers: A History of American Secularism* (New York: Metropolitan Books, 2004). It is worth noting that Judaism as well has been studied for some years under the perspective of secularism: see A. Joskowicz and E.B. Katz (eds), *Secularism in Question: Jews and Judaism in Modern Times* (Philadelphia: University of Pennsylvania Press, 2015). Also the making of modern Turkey has been studied under a perspective of secularism: see C.V. Findleyn, *Turkey, Islam, Nationalism, and Modernity: A History, 1787–2007* (New Haven, CT: Yale University Press, 2010); M. Dressler, *Writing Religion: The Making of Turkish Alevi Islam* (Oxford: Oxford University Press, 2013).
23. S. Tejani, *Indian Secularism: A Social and Intellectual History, 1890–1950* (Bloomington: Indiana University Press, 2008).

24. See Lübbe, *Säkularisierung*, 29–31 and 56–59.
25. Needless to say that studies published under the broad umbrella term of 'religious studies', which in some national traditions are part of sociology departments, in others of anthropology or even of theology departments, discussed secular phenomena from their very beginnings. Even though religious studies is a discipline of its own, I subsume and reduce it here for the sake of the argumentation to anthropology and sociology.
26. A.B. Lebner, 'The Anthropology of Secularity beyond Secularism', *Religion and Society: Advances in Research* 6 (2015), 62–74, refers to a statement of Hussein Agrama.
27. M. Wohlrab-Sahr, U. Karstein and T. Schmidt-Lux, *Forcierte Säkularität: Religiöser Wandel und Generationsdynamik im Osten Deutschlands* (Frankfurt/Main and New York: Campus, 2009). See also the fascinating recent study on British humanists by M. Engelke, 'Christianity and the Anthropology of Secular Humanism', *Current Anthropology* 55(10) (2014), 292–301.
28. T. Asad, *Formations of the Secular: Christianity, Islam, Modernity* (Stanford, CA: Stanford University Press, 2003).
29. T. Asad, 'What Might an Anthropology of Secularism Look Like?', in idem (ed.), *Formations of the Secular: Christianity, Islam, Modernity* (Stanford, CA: Stanford University Press, 2003), 35. I am here referring to R. Habermas, 'Piety, Power, and Powerlessness: Religion and Religious Groups in Germany, 1870–1945', in H.W. Smith (ed.), *The Oxford Handbook of Modern German History* (Oxford University Press, 2011), 453–80.
30. For a very similar line of argumentation, emphasizing that during the nineteenth century the notion of religion was already being shaped by the newly invented academic discipline of religious studies, see A.L. Molendijk and P. Pels (eds), *Religion in the Making: The Emergence of the Sciences of Religion* (Leiden: Brill, 1998). Here it is argued that this new scholarly discipline defined religion as an autonomous sphere, clearly to be separated from a secular sphere and more like an inner state of feelings than something that is also interconnected to various sides of economic, political and cultural life.
31. Others showed that the notion of religion itself, and with that the notion of world religion, has only been constructed very recently, mostly by European anthropologists and missionaries; see T. Masuzawa, *The Invention of World Religions, or, How European Universalism Was Preserved in the Language of Pluralism* (Chicago: University of Chicago Press, 2005). Allegedly very old categories such as Hinduism, Buddhism and Fetishism were in fact invented at this time, serving as powerful instruments in the administration of imperialism.
32. Joan W. Scott (*The Politics of the Veil*), for example, brought to light that the use of the secular language in the so-called veil politics of the French state, which not only banned Islamic symbols from French schools but also defined veils and other clothes such as the Burkini as identity markers, defining a group of people from former French colonies as fanatically anti-modern and backward looking. At the same time, politics like the above-mentioned beach actions shaped boundaries between an allegedly modern, democratic and genuinely French space of the secular and a non-European, Islamic and therewith religious space of backwardness. Following this line of argument, it has recently been maintained that the secular realm has sometimes been constructed in a manner 'that implicitly privileges one type of religion, while more or less expressly delegitimizing other sorts of religious engagement'; C. Calhoun, M. Juergensmeyer and J. Vanantwerpen, 'Introduction', in idem (eds), *Rethinking Secularism* (Oxford: Oxford University Press, 2011), 16.

33. This also means that there are multiple secularisms, beyond the established 'European ways of understanding the world'; see R. King, 'Imagining Religions in India: Colonialism and the Mapping of South Asian History and Culture', in M. Dressler and A.-P. S. Mandair (eds), *Secularism and Religion-Making* (Oxford: Oxford University Press, 2011), 39. See for the term 'multiple secularities', see M. Wohlrab-Sahr and M. Burchkardt, 'Multiple Secularities: Toward a Cultural Sociology of Secular Modernities', *Comparative Sociology* 11 (2012), 875–909.
34. Lebner, 'Anthropology of Secularity', 67. Even more, many argued that the concept of secularism as a Western-made ideology is as problematic as Edward Said's book *Orientalism* had been problematic, because instead of a coproduction of ideologies both assume an all too easy picture of a perpetrator on the one side and victims on the other side. Such a perspective is in danger of losing sight of powerful voices of non-European countries as well as dynamics between different parts of the world.
35. Similar arguments were put forward by those more interested in the different ways of negotiating secularism in everyday life beyond the normative setting; see N. Dhawan, 'The Empire Prays Back: Religion, Secularity, and Queer Critique', *boundary 2* 40 (2013), 193. Other scholars such as Rajeev Bhargava asked how many different forms of secularism existed in Europe and North America, emphasizing the main difference between a French model, advocating a state that should be protected from religion, and an American model, separating state and church for the sake of religious liberty; see R. Bhargava, 'How Secular is European Secularism?', *European Societies* 16(3) (2014), 329–36.
36. S. Bruce, 'The Other Secular Modern: An Empirical Critique of Asad', *Religion and Society: Advances in Research* 4 (2013), 79–92, argues that secularism was a product of schismatic actions of religious minorities.
37. Weir, *Secularism and Religion*, 13.
38. The global dimension of religion and of secularity has already been under investigation for some time in anthropology and religious studies, as well as in sociology; see the work of Jose Casanova as well of Charles Taylor, among many others. M. Juergensmeyer and W. Clarke Roof, *Encyclopedia of Global Religion* (Thousand Oaks, CA: Sage, 2012).
39. See R. Habermas, 'Mission im 19. Jahrhundert: Globale Netze des Religiösen', *Historische Zeitschrift* 287(3) (2008), 629–79. A first wave of studies was initiated by J. Comaroff and J. Comaroff, *Of Revelation and Revolution: Vol. 1 – Christianity, Colonialism and Consciousness in South Africa* (Chicago: University of Chicago Press, 1991); Idem, *Of Revelation and Revolution: Vol. 2 – The Dialectics of Modernity on a South African Frontier* (Chicago: University of Chicago Press, 1997). Others, like Patrick Harries, emphasized transnational perspectives showing how missionaries transferred knowledge from South Africa to Switzerland and vice versa: see P. Harries, *Butterflies & Barbarians: Swiss Missionaries & Systems of Knowledge in South-East Africa* (Oxford: Currey, 2007); and see H. Hodacs, *Converging World Views: The European Expansion and Early Nineteenth-Century Anglo-Swedish Contacts* (Uppsala: Uppsala University Press, 2003), on connections between England and Sweden. Also see M. Hill, 'Gender, Culture and the "Spiritual Empire": The Irish Protestant Female Missionary Experience', *Women's History Review* 16(2) (2007), 203–26; K. Rüther, *The Power Beyond: Mission Strategies, African Conversion and the Development of a Christian Culture in the Transvaal* (Münster: LIT, 2001).
40. T. Ballantyne, 'Humanitarian Narratives, Knowledge and the Politics of Mission and Empire', *Social Sciences and Missions* 24 (2011), 233–64, emphasizes the interconnectedness of missionaries with humanitarian narratives. I. Tyrell, *Reforming the World: The*

Creation of America's Moral Empire (Princeton, NJ: Princeton University Press, 2010); and see R. Habermas et al., 'Débat: Reforming the World: The Creation of America's Moral Empire, de Ian Tyrrell', *Monde(s)* 2(6) (2014), 148–68.
41. H. McLeod, *Piety and Poverty: Working-Class Religion in Berlin, London and New York 1870–1914* (New York: Holmes & Meier, 1996). Idem (ed.), *European Religion in the Age of Great Cities 1830–1930* (London: Routledge, 1995).
42. S. O'Brien, 'French Nuns in Nineteenth-Century England', *Past and Present* 154 (1997), 142–80.
43. Masuzawa, *Invention of World Religions*; J.P. Burris, *Exhibiting Religion: Colonialism and Spectacle at International Expositions 1851–1893* (Charlottesville: University Press of Virginia, 2001).
44. P. van der Veer, *Imperial Encounters: Religion and Modernity in India and Britain* (Princeton, NJ: Princeton University Press, 2001), 94.
45. C.A. Bayly, *The Birth of the Modern World, 1780–1914* (Oxford: Blackwell, 2004); J. Osterhammel, *Die Verwandlung der Welt: Eine Geschichte des 19. Jahrhunderts* (Munich: Beck, 2009); S. Conrad and J. Osterhammel (eds), *Geschichte der Welt 1750–1870: Wege zur modernen Welt* (Munich: Beck, 2016).
46. Bayly, *Birth of the Modern World*, 360.
47. Ibid., 328.
48. This perspective is shared by S. Conrad, 'Eine Kulturgeschichte globaler Transformation', in S. Conrad and J. Osterhammel (eds), *Geschichte der Welt 1750–1870: Wege zur modernen Welt* (Munich: Beck, 2016), 565; and Bayly, *Birth of the Modern World*. Osterhammel and Conrad also underline the emergence of 'World Religion' as new category.
49. Osterhammel, *Die Verwandlung der Welt*, 1240. Ibid., 1240–42; Osterhammel speaks of 'verhaltene Säkularisierung Westeuropas' (1250) and of West Europe taking a *Sonderweg* concerning religion (1253); Bayly, *The Birth of the Modern World*, 325.
50. Conrad, 'Eine Kulturgeschichte globaler Transformation', 592.
51. Osterhammel, *Die Verwandlung der Welt*, 1245; Bayly, *The Birth of the Modern World*, 327; Conrad, 'Eine Kulturgeschichte globaler Transformation', 559.
52. Studying history beyond the national frame is a very broad description for a still growing field of different approaches, ranging from transnational history to histoire croisée, from entangled to connected history, and from world to global history. These approaches differ in a number of respects, and many of them are even bound together by open hostilities, accusing each other of Eurocentrism, methodological shortcomings because of their Western bias, or of other forms of blindness, due to their restricted lingual capacities. Without going deeper into these debates, they all share translocal perspectives beyond the nation state, and they leave older theories such as the dependency theory and Wallerstein's world-systems theory behind them, and no longer automatically presume the existence of fixed global or even universal structures or patterns of transformation.
53. There is a much broader field of postcolonial studies critique, which I will not go onto here, but will just name the most prominent critique of D. Chakrabarty, *Provincializing Europe: Postcolonial Thought and Historical Difference* (Princeton, NJ: Princeton University Press, 2000). For a very long time these parts of the world were understudied (which first of all means that English research literature is missing), but this is not true anymore and can therefore not be put forward as a reason of exclusion. See also P. Manning, 'Locating Africans on the World Stage: A Problem in World History', *Journal of World History* 26(3) (2016), 624–25, who writes concerning the exclusion of Africans

in world histories: 'the problem addressed here is the recognition and consultation of that historiography by those writing at a broader level' (623), commenting on Bayly's and Osterhammel's ignoring of Africans. It is worth noting that 'continent' as a spatial entity is a problematical term in respect to 'its historicity, boundary instabilities, and internal differences – if not fragmentations' – A. Dirlik, 'Performing the World: Reality and Representation on the Making of World Histor(ies)', *Journal of World History* 16(4) (2005), 391–410.
54. Manning, 'Locating Africans on The World Stage', 608.
55. This linguistic restriction is of crucial importance in so far as it goes hand in hand with epistemological constraints. It needs further investigation, and is less important for smaller academic cultures than for larger ones such as the French and German, which still rely upon a huge national book market.
56. G.W.F. Hegel, *Die Vernunft in der Geschichte: Einleitung in die Philosophie der Weltgeschichte*, ed. G. Lasson (Leipzig: Felix Meiner, 1917). Even though Hegel also had a very clear and negative picture of America as a continent of savages, the selective perspective of many world histories is very reminiscent of exactly this straightforward construction, which had been at the centre of postcolonial critics.
57. Manning, 'Locating Africans on The World Stage', 616; see also M.-R. Trouillot, *Silencing the Past: Power and Production of History* (Boston: Beacon Press, 1995).
58. Neither Osterhammel nor Bayly refers to these parts of the world. Conrad, in 'Eine Kulturgeschichte globaler Transformation', 617, at least notes that there are 'andere Glaubenssysteme' (other systems of belief).
59. Masuzawa, *The Invention of World Religions*.
60. Conrad, 'Eine Kulturgeschichte globaler Transformation', 617, however mentions that there are broad regions beyond world religion. However, he, as Bayly and Osterhammel, spent many pages on the invention of a 'world religion' system, studying its ordering force.
61. This critique has been brought forward by Dirlik, 'Performing the World', 403. On the contrary, 'world religion', as a category-ordering belief system in terms of more and less civilized, was closely interlinked with colonialism.
62. As Andrew Zimmerman wrote: 'the worldview of imperial history'. A. Zimmerman, 'Africa in Imperial and Transnational History: Multi-sited Historiography and the Necessity of Theory', *Journal of African History* 54(3) (2013), 334.
63. J. Adelman already formulated some of these critical points in his review of global histories: J. Adelman, 'Review: Global History or the History of Globalization?', *Journal of World History* 27(4) (2016), 701–8.
64. For the broad debate on the local and the global, which here is intertwined, see also A. Epple, 'Lokalität und die Dimensionen des Globalen: Eine Frage der Relationen', *Historische Anthropologie* 21 (2013), 4–25.
65. 'The Religious and the Secular – The Kaiserreich Transnational Revisited' was generously sponsored by the VW Stiftung. It was held as part of the Richard von Weizsäcker fellowship, which was sponsored by the VW Stiftung as well. Among the attendees were Ruth Harris (Oxford), Gudrun Krämer (Berlin) and Till van Rahden (Montreal). Their work stimulated the lively debate, and I owe a big thank you to all of them. Gratitude also is due to Hubertus Büschel (Gießen) and David Rechter (Oxford), as well as to Paul Betts (Oxford), contributing as chairs as well as attendees. The volume has been enlarged by articles from Carolin Kosuch, Relinde Meiwes and Paul Michael Kurtz, as well as by

Karolin Wetjen. I am most grateful to all contributors for their patience, and particularly to Paul Betts.
66. Masuzawa, *The Invention of World Religions*; Burris, *Exhibiting Religion*.
67. M. Burchardt and M. Wohlrab-Sahr, 'Multiple Secularities: Religion and Modernity in the Global Age', *International Sociology* 28(6) (2013), 621–28.
68. For the role of missionaries, see Habermas and Hölzl, *Mission Global*; for missionary medias and their impact in Europe, see F. Jensz and H. Acke (eds), *Missions and Media: The Politics of Missionary Periodicals in the Long Nineteenth Century* (Stuttgart: Steiner, 2013). Wetjen, 'Religionspädagogische Resonanzen'; J. Hauser, *German Religious Women in Late Ottoman Beirut: Competing Missions* (Leiden: Brill, 2015).

Bibliography

Adelman, J. 'Review. Global History or the History of Globalization?' *Journal of World History* 27(4) (2016), 701–8.
Anderson, M.L. *Windhorst: A Political Biography*. Oxford: Clarendon Press, 1981.
———. 'Die Grenzen der Säkularisierung', in Hartmut Lehmann (ed.), *Säkularisierung, Dechristianisierung, Rechristianisierung im neuzeitlichen Europa* (Göttingen: Vandenhoeck & Ruprecht, 1997), 194–222.
Asad, T. 'What Might an Anthropology of Secularism Look Like?', in idem, *Formations of the Secular: Christianity, Islam, Modernity* (Stanford, CA: Stanford University Press, 2003), 21–66.
———. *Formations of the Secular: Christianity, Islam, Modernity*. Stanford, CA: Stanford University Press, 2003.
Ballantyne, T. 'Humanitarian Narratives, Knowledge and the Politics of Mission and Empire'. *Social Sciences and Missions* 24 (2011), 233–64.
Bayly, C.A. *The Birth of the Modern World, 1780–1914*. Oxford: Blackwell, 2004.
Bhargava, R. 'How Secular is European Secularism?' *European Societies* 16(3) (2014), 329–36.
Blackbourn, D. *Marpingen: Apparitions of the Virgin Mary in Bismarckian Germany*. Oxford: Clarendon Press, 1993.
Borutta, M. *Antikatholizismus: Deutschland und Italien im Zeitalter der europäischen Kulturkämpfe*. Göttingen: Vandenhoeck & Ruprecht, 2010.
———. 'Genealogie der Säkularisierungstheorie: Zur Historisierung einer großen Erzählung der Moderne'. *Geschichte und Gesellschaft* 36(3) (2010), 347–76.
Bruce, S. 'The Other Secular Modern: An Empirical Critique of Asad'. *Religion and Society: Advances in Research* 4 (2013), 79–92.
Burchardt, M., and M. Wohlrab-Sahr. 'Multiple Secularities: Religion and Modernity in the Global Age'. *International Sociology* 28(6) (2013), 612–28.
Burris, J.P. *Exhibiting Religion: Colonialism and Spectacle at International Expositions 1851–1893*. Charlottesville: University Press of Virginia, 2001.
Calhoun, C., M. Juergensmeyer and J. Vanantwerpen. 'Introduction', in idem (eds), *Rethinking Secularism* (Oxford: Oxford University Press, 2011), 3–31.
Chakrabarty, D. *Provincializing Europe: Postcolonial Thought and Historical Difference*. Princeton, NJ: Princeton University Press, 2000.
Clark, C., and W. Kaiser (eds). *Culture Wars: Secular–Catholic Conflict in Nineteenth-Century Europe*. Cambridge: Cambridge University Press, 2003.

Comaroff, J., and J. Comaroff. *Of Revelation and Revolution: Vol. 1 – Christianity, Colonialism and Consciousness in South Africa*. Chicago: University of Chicago Press, 1991.

———. *Of Revelation and Revolution: Vol. 2 – The Dialectics of Modernity on a South African Frontiers*. Chicago: University of Chicago Press, 1997.

Conrad, S. 'Eine Kulturgeschichte globaler Transformation', in S. Conrad and J. Osterhammel (eds), *Geschichte der Welt 1750–1870: Wege zur modernen Welt* (Munich: Beck, 2016), 411–626.

Conrad, S., and J. Osterhammel (eds). *Geschichte der Welt 1750–1870: Wege zur modernen Welt*. Munich: Beck, 2016.

Dhawan, N. 2013. 'The Empire Prays Back: Religion, Secularity, and Queer Critique'. *boundary 2* 40 (2013), 191–222.

Dirlik, A. 'Performing the World: Reality and Representation on the Making of World Histor(ies)'. *Journal of World History* 16(4) (2005), 391–410.

Dressler, M., and A.-P. Madair. 'Introduction: Modernity, Religion-Making and the Postsecular', in ibid (eds), *Secularism and Religion-Making* (Oxford: Oxford University Press, 2011), 3–36.

Enders, S. *Moralunterricht und Lebenskunde*. Bad Heilbonn: Julius Klinkhardt, 2002.

Engelke, M. 'Christianity and the Anthropology of Secular Humanism'. *Current Anthropology* 55(10) (2014), 292–301.

Epple, A. 'Lokalität und die Dimensionen des Globalen: Eine Frage der Relationen'. *Historische Anthropologie* 21(1) (2013), 4–25.

Evans, R. 'Religion and Society in Modern Germany'. *European Studies Review* 12 (1982), 249–88.

Febvre, L. *Un destin: Martin Luther*. Paris: Rieder, 1928.

Findleyn, C.V. *Turkey, Islam, Nationalism, and Modernity: A History, 1787–2007*. New Haven, CT: Yale University Press, 2010.

Geertz, C. 'Religion als kulturelles System', in idem (ed.), *Dichte Beschreibung: Beiträge zum Verstehen kultureller Systeme* (Frankfurt/Main: Suhrkamp, 1983), 44–95.

Gross, M.B. *The War against Catholicism: Liberalism and the Anti-Catholic Imagination in Nineteenth-Century Germany*. Ann Arbor: The University of Michigan Press, 2005.

Habermas, R. 'Weibliche Religiosität oder: Von der Fragilität bürgerlicher Identitäten', in K. Tenfelde and H.U. Wehler (eds), *Wege zur Geschichte des Bürgertums* (Göttingen: Vandenhoeck & Rupprecht, 1994), 125–48.

———. 'Mission im 19. Jahrhundert: Globale Netze des Religiösen'. *Historische Zeitschrift* 287(3) (2008), 629–79.

———. 'Piety, Power, and Powerlessness: Religion and Religious Groups in Germany, 1870–1945', in H. Walser Smith (ed.), *The Oxford Handbook of Modern German History* (Oxford University Press, 2011), 453–80.

Habermas, R., and R. Hölzl (eds). *Mission Global: Eine Verflechtungsgeschichte seit dem 19. Jahrhundert*. Cologne: Böhlau, 2014.

Habermas, R., et al. 'Débat: Reforming the World: The Creation of America's Moral Empire, de Ian Tyrrell'. *Monde(s)* 2(6) (2014), 148–68.

Harries, P. *Butterflies & Barbarians: Swiss Missionaries & Sytems of Knowledge in South-East Africa*. Oxford: Currey, 2007.

Haupt, H.G., and D. Langewiesche (eds). *Nation und Religion in Europa*. Frankfurt/Main and New York: Campus, 2004.

Hauser, J. *German Religious Women in Late Ottoman Beirut: Competing Missions*. Leiden: Brill, 2015.

Hegel, G.W.F. *Die Vernunft in der Geschichte: Einleitung in die Philosophie der Weltgeschichte*, ed. G. Lasson. Leipzig: Felix Meiner, 1917.

Hill, M. 'Gender, Culture and the "Spiritual Empire": The Irish Protestant Female Missionary Experience'. *Women's History Review* 16(2) (2007), 203–26.

Hodacs, H. *Converging World Views: The European Expansion and Early Nineteenth-Century Anglo-Swedish Contacts*. Uppsala: Uppsala University Press, 2003.

Hölscher, L. 'Die Religion des Bürgers: Bürgerliche Frömmigkeit und protestantische Kirche'. *Historische Zeitschrift* 250 (1990), 595–630.

Jacoby, S. *Freethinkers: A History of American Secularism*. New York: Metropolitan Books, 2004.

Jensen, U. *Gebildete Doppelgänger:* Bürgerliche Juden und Protestanten im 19. Jahrhundert. Goettingen: Vandenhoeck & Ruprecht, 2005.

Jensz, F., and H. Acke (eds). *Missions and Media: The Politics of Missionary Periodicals in the Long Nineteenth Century*. Stuttgart: Steiner, 2013.

Joskowicz, A. *The Modernity of Others: Jewish Anti-Catholicism in Germany and France*. Stanford, CA: Stanford University Press, 2014.

Joskowicz, A., and E.B. Katz (eds). *Secularism in Question: Jews and Judaism in Modern Times*. Philadelphia: University of Pennsylvania Press, 2015.

Juergensmeyer, M., and C.W. Roof (eds). *Encyclopedia of Global Religion*. Thousand Oaks, CA: Sage, 2012.

Kaplan, M. *The Making of the Jewish Middle Class: Women, Family and Identity in Imperial Germany*. New York: Oxford University Press, 1991.

King, R. 'Imaging Religions in India: Colonialism and the Mapping of South Asian History and Culture', in M. Dressler and A.-P. S. Madair (eds), *Secularism and Religion-Making* (Oxford: Oxford University Press, 2011), 37–61.

Larkin, E. 'The Devotional Revolution in Ireland'. *American Historical Review* 77(3) (1972), 625–52.

Lehner, A.B. 'The Anthropology of Secularity beyond Secularism', *Religion and Society: Advances in Research* 6 (2015), 62–74.

Leff, L.M. 'The Jewish Oath and the Making of Secularism in Modern France'. *The Baeck Institute Year Book* 58 (2013), 23–34.

Linse, U. *Geisterseher und Wunderwirker: Heilssuche im Industriezeitalter*. Frankfurt/Main: Fischer Taschenbuch, 1996.

Lübbe, H. *Säkularisierung: Geschichte eines ideenpolitischen Begriffs*. Freiburg: Herder, 1965.

Manning, P. 'Locating Africans on the World Stage: A Problem in World History'. *Journal of World History* 26(3) (2016), 605–37.

Masuzawa, T. *The Invention of World Religions, or, How European Universalism Was Preserved in the Language of Pluralism*. Chicago: University of Chicago Press, 2005.

Matysik, T. 'Secularism, Subjectivity, and Reform: Shifting Variables', in G. Eley, J. Jenkins and T. Matysik (eds), *German Modernities from Wilhelm to Weimar: A Contest of Futures* (London, Oxford and New York: Bloomsbury, 2016), 215–34.

McLeod, H. (ed.). *European Religion in the Age of Great Cities 1830–1930*. London: Routledge, 1995.

———. *Piety and Poverty: Working Class Religion in Berlin, London and New York 1870–1914*. New York: Holmes & Meier, 1996.

Meiwes, R. *'Arbeiterinnen des Herrn': Katholische Frauenkongregationen im 19. Jahrhundert*. Frankfurt/Main: Campus, 2000.

Molendijk, A.L., and P. Pels (eds). *Religion in the Making: The Emergence of the Sciences of Religion*. Leiden: Brill, 1998.
Nipperdey, T. *Religion im Umbruch Deutschland 1870–1918*. Munich: Beck, 1988.
O'Brien, S. 'French Nuns in Nineteenth-Century England'. *Past and Present* 154 (1997), 142–80.
Osterhammel, J. *Die Verwandlung der Welt: Eine Geschichte des 19. Jahrhunderts*. Munich: Beck, 2009.
Prelinger, C.M. *Charity, Challenge, and Change: Religious Dimensions of the Mid-Nineteenth-Century Women*. New York: Greenwood Press, 1987.
Rahden, T. van. *Juden und andere Breslauer: Die Beziehungen zwischen Juden, Protestanten und Katholiken in einer deutschen Großstadt von 1860 bis 1925*. Göttingen: Vandenhock & Rupprecht, 2000.
Ribbat, C. *Religiöse Erregung: Protestantische Schwärmer im Kaiserreich*. Frankfurt/Main: Campus, 1996.
Rüther, K. *The Power Beyond: Mission Strategies, African Conversion and the Development of a Christian Culture in the Transvaal*. Münster: LIT, 2001.
Sawicki, D. *Leben mit den Toten: Geisterglauben und die Entstehung des Spiritismus in Deutschland 1770–1900*. Paderborn: Schöningh, 2002.
Scheer, M., P. Eitler and B. Hitzer. 'Feeling and Faith: Religious Emotions in German History'. *German History* 32(3) (2014), 343–52.
Schieder, W. 'Kirche und Revolution: Sozialgeschichtliche Aspekte der Trierer Wallfahrt von 1844'. *Archiv für Sozialgeschichte* 14 (1974), 419–54.
Schnabel, F. *Deutsche Geschichte im neunzehnten Jahrhundert*, 4 vols. Freiburg: Herder, 1929; repr. Munich: Deutscher Taschenbuchverlag, 1987.
Scott, J.W. *The Politics of the Veil*. Princeton, NJ and Oxford: Princeton University Press, 2007.
Seed, J. '"Secular" and "Religious": Historical Perspectives'. *Social History* 39(1) (2014), 3–13.
Smith, H.W. *Protestants, Catholics and Jews in Germany, 1800–1914*. Oxford: Berg, 2001.
Sperber, J. *Popular Catholicism in Nineteenth-Century Germany*. Princeton, NJ: Princeton University Press, 1984.
Tejani, S. *Indian Secularism: A Social and Intellectual History, 1890–1950*. Bloomington: Indiana University Press, 2008.
Trouillot, M.-R. *Silencing the Past: Power and Production of History*. Boston, MA: Beacon Press, 1995.
Tyrell, I. *Reforming the World: The Creation of America's Moral Empire*. Princeton, NJ: Princeton University Press, 2010.
Veer, P. van der. *Imperial Encounters: Religion and Modernity in India and Britain*. Princeton, NJ: Princeton University Press, 2001.
Walser-Smith, H. *German Nationalism and Religious Conflict: Culture, Ideology, Politics, 1870–1914*. Princeton, NJ: Princeton University Press, 1995.
———. *Protestants, Catholics and Jews in Germany, 1800–1914*, Oxford: Berg, 2001.
Walser-Smith, H., and C. Clark. 'The Fate of Nathan', in H. Walser-Smith (ed.), *Protestants, Catholics and Jews in Germany, 1800–1914* (Oxford: Berg, 2001), 3–29.
Weber, M. 'Wissenschaft als Beruf (1919)', in D. Kaesler (ed.), *Schriften 1884–1922* (Stuttgart: Kröner, 2002), 472–512.
Weir, T.H. *Secularism and Religion in Nineteenth-Century Germany: The Rise of the Fourth Confession*. Cambridge: Cambridge University Press, 2014.

Welter, B. 'The Feminization of American Religion, 1800–1860', in M.S. Hartmann and L. Banner (eds), *Clio's Consciousness Raised: New Perspectives on the History of Women* (New York: Octagon Books, 1976), 137–57.

Wetjen, K. 'Religionspädagogische Resonanzen und die Mission "Christianity Making" im missionarischen Bildungsraum am Ende des 19. Jahrhunderts', in D. Kaebisch and M. Wermke (eds), *Transnationale Grenzgänge und Kulturkontakte: Historische Fallbeispiele in religionspädagogischer Perspektive* (Leipzig: Evangelische Verlagsanstalt, 2016), 23–38.

Wohlrab-Sahr, M., and M. Burchkardt. 'Multiple Secularities: Toward a Cultural Sociology of Secular Modernities'. *Comparative Sociology* 11 (2012), 875–909.

Wohlrab-Sahr, M., U. Karstein and T. Schmidt-Lux. *Forcierte Säkularität: Religiöser Wandel und Generationsdynamik im Osten Deutschlands*. Frankfurt/Main and New York: Campus, 2009.

Zimmerman, A. 'Africa in Imperial and Transnational History: Multi-sited Historiography and the Necessity of Theory'. *Journal of African History* 54(3) (2013), 331–40.

PART I
Religious and Secular
Scientific Debates

1
A Secular Age?

The 'Modern World' and the Beginnings of the Sociology of Religion

Wolfgang Knöbl

A couple of years ago, Guy G. Stroumsa convincingly argued that the emergence of religious studies in seventeenth-century Europe could legitimately be interpreted as an intellectual revolution: the 'discovery' of the New World, the Renaissance with its interest in ancient Greece and Rome, and the so-called wars of religion, had created decisive structural conditions for new ways of thinking about religion.[1] From late antiquity up until that time, religion was usually interpreted as an internalized belief system, as something belonging to the inner life of the believer: 'True religion ... was ... orthodox Christianity, while all other forms of religion were identified as heresies or forms of idolatry and hence false. In many ways, this internalized conception of religion would remain prevalent throughout the Middle Ages'.[2] The new structural conditions just mentioned, however, turned the tables. Contact with non-European cultures opened up the possibility to think about religion other than in terms of a personalist vision, but in terms of conduct, of behaviour, of doing. Stroumsa makes the point that a radical semantic externalization of religion took place, 'its transformation from inner piety to social patterns of behaviour'.[3] As he further elaborates: 'The paradigm of religion emerging in the seventeenth century thus privileged ritual over belief, and abandoned value-judgment for observation as a chief classifier of religious attitudes'.[4]

Stroumsa, at the same time, knows quite well that the development of religious studies was much more than a process of intellectual learning reflecting new structural conditions. Thinking about religion was always, even in the seventeenth century, linked to cultural criticism,[5] and to a critical diagnosis of the society in which the interpreters of religion lived. Thus, writings about 'foreign' societies and their religions often tell us more about the society of the interpreters than about the one under observation, and therefore are occasionally the result of somewhat odd kinds of entanglement. That is certainly true with respect to the nineteenth century, when a new discipline emerged, sociology, which from its very beginning was tremendously interested in religion. None of the so-called founding fathers of the discipline could afford to neglect the religious problems of their time, and the most prominent of them, Emile Durkheim and Max Weber,[6] even put religion, or at least questions closely related to religion, at the very centre of their research.

In contrast to some prejudices and stereotypes (which is why there is a question mark in the title of this chapter), the sociology of religion as it emerged in the second half of the nineteenth century did not come into being because the majority of sociologists then believed in the secularizing effects of processes of social change all over the world.[7] The constellation was more complex. But what is relevant here, and related to Stroumsa's insight concerning the 'critical' character of religious studies, the sociological classics were certainly not disinterested or objective observers of foreign belief systems. Quite the contrary – they often fought in the battles between science and religion raging in their own societies.[8] And, in addition, quite a few of them saw themselves fulfilling a kind of 'national' mission in order to find religion's proper place in their societies, which makes it difficult to link their discourse on religion in an abstract way to the one on the 'modern world',[9] and which also indicates that the concept and idea of secularity/secularism often not only varied between different national contexts but also between different authors within a nation state.

Taking this into consideration, I start by looking into seemingly isolated national contexts. In the first part of this chapter, my focus is on prominent intellectual discourses on religion in France, because that will give us the appropriate background in order to understand the approach taken by Max Weber in the German Kaiserreich in the second part. As will be made clear in the third part, there were rather different ways of theorizing religion. The way it was done in Germany was very much shaped by philosophical developments and political constellations not found anywhere else – developments and constellations, however, that were the result of observations of, and comparisons between, different 'cultures'. The fourth and concluding part of the chapter will reflect on the difficulties the concept of 'religion' created in the past and will continue to create in the future in so far as its origins within the social sciences were to be found in the desperate intellectual attempts to come to terms with a mostly 'non-Western' reality, which was difficult for 'Western' scholars to grasp.

Intellectual Discourses on Religion in France

In 1864, French historian Numa Denis Fustel de Coulanges published his *La Cité antique*, a groundbreaking work on the role of religion in ancient Greece and Rome. What still fascinates readers of this book is Fustel's attempt to explain almost each and every institution of these societies by looking into their religious roots. Doing so he argued that religion for the Greeks and the Romans, in order to make sense of metaphysical mysteries, was not 'a body of dogmas, a doctrine concerning God, a symbol of faith'.[10] Ancient religion was above all a web of ceremonies and rites that bound people to their city or their society, as the Latin origin of the word religion indeed suggests ('ligare', 'religio'). Thus, Fustel analysed religion by emphasizing its cohesive effects, its power to integrate people into a larger community. One might even say that he stressed the political and societal functions of ancient religion by defining it as a community cult.

Fustel had a huge impact on religious studies in France and very much influenced Emile Durkheim,[11] the founder of French sociology, who not only institutionalized the discipline within the French university system but who shaped sociological thinking about religion – at least the one in France.[12] His famous *Les Formes élémentaires de la vie religieuse* [The elementary forms of the religious life], originally published in 1912, indeed sees religion through the perspective of a community cult. One has to emphasize, however, that neither Fustel's nor Durkheim's thinking about religion came out of the blue. On the contrary, as Michel Despland has convincingly argued in his important book on the origins of a French science of religion, their way of theorizing religion could be traced back to the intellectual milieu of post-revolutionary France and the desperate search for order after the rule of Napoleon Bonaparte.[13] In the first decades of the nineteenth century, some counter-revolutionary and reactionary philosophers such as Joseph de Maistre had begun to see religion as a tool to discipline the masses. Yet, it was not until the 1830s and the July Monarchy that a broad academic discourse on religion emerged, one which had different aims from those de Maistre had in mind, but a discourse nevertheless that was very much based on similar arguments and tried to answer the question of how a post-revolutionary, and thus a seemingly rather fragile society, could and should be organized. What made the discourse of this period so interesting, and thus contributed in a fruitful way to a new sociology or a new comparative history of religion, were two interrelated aspects.

Firstly, since the 1820s, mostly German ideas concerning the use and purpose of symbols had become an important topic within French intellectual circles. As Despland explains, the production of symbols was now increasingly interpreted as a constitutive feature of humanity – and this was held to be true for religious symbols as well.[14] Yet the importance of certain German arguments for the French discourse on religion did not lead to a convergence of ideas. On the contrary, whereas in Germany, particularly during the nineteenth century, Eastern religions and their often mystical features became increasingly admired by scholars and intellectuals, French thinkers particularly highlighted the political functions of religion. This, by the way, was one of the reasons why during the July Monarchy the political regime carefully tried to stick to strict neutrality towards the different Christian denominations, because religion was regarded as important per se.[15] Secondly, the aforementioned belief in the central role of symbols had the effect that religion now could be seriously interpreted – that is to say, not interpreted any longer as a useful tool for elites to deceive the masses, as had so often been done by authors of the radical enlightenment (and reactionary authors such as de Maistre). On the contrary, religion now came to be seen as an elementary and important part of the human fabric in general.[16] According to Despland, these two intellectual developments paved the way for the emergence of a true comparative history/sociology of religion – a discipline, however, that was often used to highlight the problems and weaknesses of French society.[17] Fustel's and Durkheim's religious treatises were written in this political and intellectual context,[18] and it was the idea of religion as a cohesive community cult that made their work so fascinating and interesting for contemporary readers who had some doubts about the stability of French society. At the same time, Durkheim's way of thinking permitted reflection on the transformation of religion in the contemporary world, which did not take its secularization as a given. On the contrary, even if important (political) actors within France, influenced by certain anti-clerical arguments originating in the French Revolution of 1789, wanted to keep religion completely separated from the rest of the social fabric, even if it was clear that it became more and more problematic to talk of *one* true religion that could serve as a kind of societal glue, Durkheim's arguments sensitized for the fact that religion might always have a certain place in social life. Indeed, the 'religious' is seen as undergoing continuous transformation and transference to new objects, so that, within the 'modern world' the individual becomes more and more sacralized.[19]

Max Weber on Religion

I am certainly not the first one who has observed the coincidence that in the same year that Fustel's book was published, 1864, the great German sociologist Max Weber was born. And indeed, a mere coincidence it was, because the authors had little in common – at least with regard to the ways they thought about religion.

Max Weber did not invent the sociology of religion, and he was not the first or only one working in this academic field in the German Kaiserreich, with authors such as Georg Simmel and Ernst Troeltsch also playing key roles in its development.[20] But Weber's work was either much more systematic than the oeuvre of most of his colleagues, or his influence on future generations of social scientists interested in religion much greater. So, it is worthwhile to screen *his* arguments and to look into the intellectual milieu of *his* life in order to characterize the beginnings of a sociology of religion in Germany. But this is certainly an invidious task because Weber's work is well known and there is a danger of telling a rather familiar story. Therefore, I have chosen not to start with Weber's systematic arguments but to highlight his somewhat awkward position towards Catholicism before I deal with more general questions.

We nowadays know much[21] about Weber's attitude towards the Catholic Church and Catholicism in general, and his experiences with respect to Catholic milieus. Early in his career, Weber spent some time doing research on the rural areas of Eastern Prussia, when he looked into the living conditions of mostly Polish farmers and laborers; and, more importantly, after his nervous breakdown of 1898–1902 Weber stayed and travelled in Italy for many months. Thus, as a person, who during the *Kulturkampf* was socialized into a Protestant family, and who was intellectually brought up and lived most of the time in a Protestant milieu, Weber must have learned quite a bit about Catholicism. But how correct was this 'knowledge', and what did he 'learn'? Some commentators have argued that Weber was strictly against Catholicism, especially against 'Ultramontanism and political Catholicism'.[22] Although there is some truth in such a statement, it does not encapsulate the nuances of Weber's thought on the matter, because he actually distinguished between different forms of Catholicism, and evaluated them accordingly. There is no doubt, for instance, that one can find much anti-Polish resentment in his infamous Freiburg inaugural lecture on 'The Nation State and Economic Policy', delivered in 1895. In this lecture, as well as in other texts, Weber's contemptuous attitude towards the Polish population expressed traditional German Slavophobia.[23] But anti-Catholicism was in the background too, which obviously made it impossible for Weber to see anything positive in Polish culture.

The case was different with respect to Italy. Weber obviously loved Rome,[24] which was certainly nothing exceptional for a member of the German educated classes at that time; but this love, in Weber's case, must have been somewhat ambivalent because Rome was also the centre of the bureaucracy of the Catholic Church which – according to him – had played such a fateful role in the history of the Western world due to its levelling influence.[25] And yet, as has been pointed out by Dirk Kaesler, Silke Schmitt and others, not all Catholic phenomena, not even the ones close to the papacy, were despised by Weber. He possessed a certain admiration for the Jesuits in the sense that he regarded them as members of a dynamic organization that fought for certain goals, and propagated a systematic and ascetic lifestyle (*Lebensführung*), and – similar to Puritanism – abstained from escaping the world.[26]

Despite these rather positive judgements, however, almost all commentators on Weber's work agree that in the end Weber interpreted Catholicism as a lower form of Christian faith,[27] as it lacked, at least in Weber's eyes, a thorough systematization of the individual lifestyles and ethics of its believers: Catholic theology did not allow the emergence of a certain 'habitus of the personality',[28] which is based on continuous self-control; and Catholicism was shot through with magic, rituals, priestly domination and supervision, and by the central role of confession. In Weber's mind, all of this prevented individual believers from being exclusively responsible for their own 'certitudo salutis' – that is, the use of their own strength to gain salvation.[29]

'Individual strength', 'asceticism', 'personality', 'systematization': these have been the key words used in my brief description of Weber's attitude towards Catholicism. And it is certainly no accident that they can also be found in Manuel Borutta's brilliant characterization of anti-Catholic discourses in Germany and Italy in the second half of the nineteenth century,[30] where he claims that the Catholic 'other' was identified with internationalism, but above all with irrationalism, backwardness, sickness and femininity. It is hard to deny that Weber's terms are quite similar, that they do have a strong 'male' touch (such as individual strength) as well, and that 'personality' and 'systematization' are indeed to be seen as a kind of opposite to 'irrationality' and 'sickness'. In this respect Max Weber's judgement of Catholicism was probably deeply rooted both in national liberalism and in the hegemonic cultural currents within the German Kaiserreich, especially within Cultural Protestantism (*Kulturprotestantismus*). This explains a considerable amount – but certainly not everything – of how Weber built his theoretical edifice in order to study and then evaluate world religions in the way he actually did.

As has been pointed out by historians of the Kaiserreich, the *liberal* understanding of the proper role of religion within politics was something like this: frightened by Catholic social and political movements during the last decades of the nineteenth century, in which women and the lower classes played a decisive role,[31] liberals defined true religion as something that happens within one's personality; it must not be expressed by rituals or other irrational gestures,[32] and therefore can and must go along – in strict separation, however – with the other spheres of society and politics. The liberal vision of a secular state had no problems in defining the appropriate role of religion as long as this secular state looked rather Protestant. That is, secularity – at least in the self-understanding of a Protestant elite – could be guaranteed, as long as religion was above all a question of the inner-self, and each and every person practised his or her religion in this particular way.

Not surprisingly, this political standpoint went along with the '*bildungsbürgerliche*' current, often called 'Cultural Protestantism'. As defined by Gangolf Hübinger, Cultural Protestantism was an anti-clerical 'personalistic and neo-idealistic *Bildungsreligion*'[33] that was explicitly legitimized[34] by the majority of Protestant theologians of that period, who very much emphasized the autonomy of the (Protestant) individual and who stressed that religion in general (and not only Protestantism) essentially postulates a kind of stand-off from the existing world. This somewhat distant position allowed Protestantism a type of cultural critique, which pointed into two directions. Firstly, it was directed against 'the masses', and more specifically it set the proletarian (and female?) masses against the (male?) bourgeois personality. Secondly, it was directed against the pernicious influence of modern science, which seemed to threaten the subjectivity of the bourgeois individual through its dry matter-of-factness. In this way – and this was the point made by Ernst Troeltsch, one of the most eminent representatives of Cultural Protestantism, and a close collaborator and friend of Max Weber –

religion could be interpreted as the only sphere left in a mechanized world in which the soul could blossom.[35] Taking these two criticisms into account, it becomes clear why religion could be understood as the only safe haven for the autonomous individual. It was not that religion was regarded as a kind of glue for a broken social fabric, as was obviously the case in France where students of Fustel and Durkheim dominated the academic and intellectual debate. Religion, as theorized by Weber and other Cultural Protestants, was seen much more as a highly individualistic affair that was supposed to guarantee the survival of certain values in the world, values an autonomous personality cannot live without. And, in this respect, it is certainly revealing that the notion of values (*Werte*), which had been introduced to philosophy by Kant but was made the centre of Hermann Lotze's philosophy not before the 1830s and 1840s,[36] became one of the most important starting points for almost every ethical and even logical debate in the German Kaiserreich – as was so nicely shown by Jürgen Gebhardt.[37] The recourse to values was a means to draw boundaries, quite specific boundaries indeed. And this is one of the decisive reasons why Weber and the German tradition of thinking about religion not so much focused on 'socially undifferentiated community cults' but on '*differentiated* (salvation) religious communities'.[38] Since it was and is the individual's most noble task to choose his or her own values, his or her own gods, a truly overarching horizon of identical values (this is assumed when one theorizes community cults) was not only empirically highly unlikely, but also ethically enormously problematic, since such a horizon always threatens the human condition (i.e. a person's ability to choose between *different* values). According to this perspective, and in contrast to the one proposed by Durkheim and his followers, it was assumed that there is always a tension or a gap between the religious and the secular, a point that – as Gangolf Hübinger argues – was made sense of by Troeltsch's concept of 'secularization' and by Weber's concept of 'rationalization'.[39] A completely secularized world was not something beyond imagination; the question, however, was how humane such a secularized world would turn out to be.

Here is not the place to reflect on the wider theoretical consequences of the two somewhat contradictory perspectives on religion. As has already been pointed out by quite a few interpreters, Fustel's and Durkheim's approach makes it rather difficult to think in a productive way about trends of secularization, because in processes of social change – and due to the assumption that society somehow needs the cohesive effects of religions – each and every religion seems to become immediately transformed into another religion, be it a political or civil religion. It is rather difficult to think about differentiation between societal spheres – for instance, separation between church and state – if one sticks too closely to the idea of religion as a community cult. Thus, Weber's way of thinking seems to be the theoretically more adequate paradigm – at least if one believes that secularization is indeed an irresistible force within the modern world.[40] But praising Weber at this point does *not* mean that one has to agree with the overall architecture of his theoretical approach, which has some costs as well:

they might consist in his highly intellectualist and cognitivist way of framing religion, something which has very deep roots in the German intellectual tradition and can be traced back at least to Immanuel Kant. Weber's work on religion is indeed very much entrenched in the German philosophical tradition so that one wonders whether he really had a chance to build his sociology of religion in a completely different way. As has often been pointed out, even by friendly critics, Weber tried to reduce religion to a kind of intellectual endeavour, since there is – as he claims – a metaphysical need of the human spirit 'to grasp the world as a *meaningful* cosmos',[41] which also means that religion can best be understood by pointing to the subjective life of the believer, a believer who has been granted the ability of reasoning in order to satisfy the aforementioned metaphysical needs. Thus, the individual ability of reasoning was *the* starting point of Weber's sociology of religion – something, in fact, he shared with Kant.

Thinking about Religion – the German Philosophical Tradition

Kant's *Die Religion innerhalb der Grenzen der bloßen Vernunft* [Religion within the boundaries of mere reason], published in 1793, propagated (and sometimes reinforced) the thoughts that later on became so influential within the German context. Kant basically identified religion with (individual) morality as 'knowledge of all our duties as divine commandments'.[42] By doing so he was not only able to reinforce the already well-established distinction between religion and religiosity, but also to distinguish between different forms of religious practices: reading Kant's essay on religion it becomes obvious how much he despised, in an almost Weberian temper, the belief in miracles, which he characterized as 'against reason' ('*vernunftwidrig*');[43] how much he condemned superstition and fetishism 'because tools of nature can never influence the supernatural';[44] how much he almost hated tools of mercy ('*Gnadenmittel*') such as Christian charity and pilgrimage of Muslims to Mecca;[45] how much he tried to get rid of everything within religion that seemed to have a kind of irrational touch, such as 'rituals', which are not compatible with his understanding of religion (rituals as 'morally indifferent deeds', as he called them); and how much he tried to push particularistic features of religion into the background when he, for example, praised Christianity as a universalistic religion in contrast to Judaism, which was a political community at best.[46] Arguing this way, Kant already had a simple tool at hand in order to hierarchize different types of religion: the closer a religion gets to the ideal of a pure religion – one that is truly universalistic and morally strict and clear – the higher it has to be judged. For Kant, there is a clear polar dichotomy between a mechanistic belief in a church and its odd cults on the one side and – to repeat it again – pure religion on the other. Whereas, according to Kant, Judaism celebrates a kind of mechanistic cult, it is only with Christianity that a general history of churches began[47] – which, however, has not yet come to a successful end.

Although Kant's successors tried to modify the Kantian way of thinking about religion, they hardly ever succeeded.[48] Of course, Hegel was sociologically inspired enough to understand that a religion without particularistic traits will not survive, and that Kant obviously forgot to think about a religion of the hearts.[49] But in general Hegel confirms Kant's overall approach by arguing that the purpose of all religion 'is the morality of mankind'.[50] True, and this is often emphasized, Schleiermacher in his *Über die Religion: Reden an die Gebildeten unter ihren Verächtern* [On religion: Speeches to its cultured despisers] almost at the same time sharply turned against Kant's and Hegel's conceptualization of religion; he very much criticized their (and any) attempt to functionalize religion for other purposes, so that he sharply differentiated religion from morality.[51] In this respect, at least, he was very influential in so far as the separation of religion from the other spheres of life became one of the basic assumptions of members of the educated classes in Germany in general, and of Cultural Protestantism in particular.[52] And, this has also to be admitted: for Schleiermacher, religion basically was the non-systematic – it was contemplation ('*Anschauung*') and emotion ('*Gefühl*'),[53] an idea that, more than hundred years later, was accepted by Georg Simmel.[54] In the end, however, and as much as Schleiermacher might have influenced a lay audience interested in religion and – of course – true believers, the systematic and, in a way, rather problematic groundwork done by Kant and Hegel was not disputed by most subsequent authors.

This is even true for Arthur Schopenhauer, the last philosopher to be mentioned here with a particularly strong influence on Weber,[55] a philosopher who had died in 1860 and whose works from the 1870s onwards slowly became the focus of a kind of counterculture within the Kaiserreich, which popularized discourses on non-Western religions.[56] As Christopher Ryan has pointed out, Schopenhauer 'assimilated the ancient religions of India to his own system in order to create a centre of opposition to positivism and materialism, and in order to fill the gap opened up by the decline of Christian institutions in the wake of the increasing awareness of the intellectual indefensibility of historical Christianity'.[57] Again, intellectual and academic writings on religion were not only the results of odd kinds of entanglements, but also had a strong touch of cultural criticism. This criticism, however, could be articulated in very different ways. It was one of his major contributions to the debate, that Schopenhauer interpreted religion not so much by looking into dogmatic texts. His primary concern was the ethic of a religion, its 'evaluatory spirit',[58] and its understanding of the world. According to him, dogmatic texts are only the embodiment of this spirit, they justify the religious ethic and are above all only carriers of a religion's attitude towards the world. With this in mind, Schopenhauer was very much interested in classifying religions according to whether they have a pessimistic or an optimistic stance towards the world.[59]

This can be seen most vividly in Schopenhauer's second volume of *Die Welt als Wille und Vorstellung* [The world as will and representation] (1844). It is not only remarkable how much of the British literature on diverse religions within the Empire this philosopher has read and quoted in this book: Schopenhauer also begins a radical transformation of values, which had been self-evident for Kant, Hegel and Schleiermacher. For example, whereas Kant and Hegel obviously admired the rationality and calmness of Protestant Christianity and hence (as in the case of Kant)[60] generally criticized Protestant sects, or (as in the case of Hegel) Calvinism,[61] Schopenhauer takes the opposite position and praises Protestant sects such as the Shakers who had seemingly found their way back to true Christianity.[62] Schopenhauer was highly critical towards Lutherans, whom he accused of having given up the quintessence of Christianity, which obviously makes it difficult to reconcile Schopenhauer's position with those later propagated by most Cultural Protestants. But with respect to Max Weber and the emergence of the sociology of religion some fifty years later, this is quite remarkable, because Schopenhauer's criticism of Lutheranism was the consequence of an obviously theoretically and ethically highly attractive position (one certainly attractive to Weber), which allowed one to classify and to evaluate all major religions.

Schopenhauer's pessimistic philosophy contrasted the will (and that is: life) on the one side and intellect (representation) on the other. The will is continuous aspiration without any end or goal, hence without satisfaction.[63] Life is always suffering, work, misery, and even death.[64] And religion is a kind of antidote to death,[65] an intellectual antidote, since all the major religions such as Christianity, Brahmanism, Buddhism correctly interpret being in the world as sin; salvation can only be achieved by negating the will and hence life itself. Thus, according to Schopenhauer, asceticism, mysticism and quietism are all closely connected with each other. All religions of the Orient in general, and true Christianity in particular, have a kind of ascetic nature[66] – they all are abnegating the world![67] That is why – as Gerard Mannion explains – Schopenhauer's interest in religions such as Hinduism, Buddhism and Christianity extensively deals with 'renunciation', and not 'resignation',[68] and why he is so interested in mysticism as a means to overcome the world.[69]

All this may sound rather anti-Kantian and even anti-Hegelian – indeed, in many ways it is. But there is certainly a common element uniting Kant, Hegel and Schopenhauer, despite all their differences. In some sense they all see religion as an intellectual or ethical endeavour; religion is essentially an intellectual statement even if it might lead (see Schopenhauer's high opinion of mysticism or asceticism) to anti-intellectual consequences. Taking all these particularities of the German philosophical discourse at the end of the eighteenth and the first half of the nineteenth century into consideration, one should be able to grasp the logic of Weber's sociology of religion, for which terms and dichotomies such as religion and morality, magic vs. true religion, religion and being in the world are crucial. Weber indeed incorporated Kant's profound aversion[70] to magical phenomena in his own analysis, a move which, by the way, seemed to be empirically justified when (in contrast to most of his colleagues) famous British anthropologist William Robertson Smith, in his 1889 'Lectures on the Religion of the Semites: The Fundamental Institutions', also sharply distinguished between magic and religion.[71] Using this distinction as developed within evolutionary anthropology, Weber claimed that magic is still the attempt to force demons and gods to execute the will of the magician ('Gotteszwang') whereas in religion everything being done is in order to serve the Gods, which are too far from the human world to be influenced by human beings – therefore 'Gottesdienst'! This allowed Weber to differentiate between types of beliefs, types even *within* Christianity, by asking whether and how many magical elements had still survived in different belief systems:[72] in Catholicism, according to him, quite a few, which is why Catholicism must be interpreted as a lower form of Christianity[73] in comparison to Calvinism, for instance.

But there is another possibility for putting religions into a (hierarchized) order, namely by making use of Schopenhauer's idea that true religions try to overcome the world. Weber went along with and slightly modified Schopenhauer's position by arguing that all true salvation religions such as Christianity, Judaism, Buddhism and Hinduism grapple with the intellectual problem of the evil on earth, grapple with the theodicy problem, and seek salvation from this miserable world.[74] But how believers of these different religions have to behave in the world is rather specific, because in Protestant sects, for example, the ethic of the believers demands ascetic actions[75] that are directed *towards* the world ('Welt*zugewandtheit*') whereas in Hinduism and Buddhism, for instance, a quietist or mystic escapism *from* the world is often ethically required ('Welt*flucht*'). As the complete title of Weber's famous *Zwischenbetrachtung* reveals [in English: Intermediate reflections: Stages and directions of religious rejection of the world], and as Hans Kippenberg has so nicely put it: 'Weber reduced the historical plurality of religions to a limited number of intellectually grounded statements with respect to the world, and then tried to identify the diverging maxims of a methodical lifestyle'.[76]

Summarizing Weber's overall approach towards the study of religion, one should emphasize that he started from individual action and individual metaphysical needs, so that for him the problem of theodicy became the driving force of the development of religion, an evolutionary development, indeed, leading from magic to so-called salvation religions. Holding such evolutionary assumptions, the idea of religion as a community cult was rather far away from his way of thinking. This was one of the major contrasts to Fustel's and Durkheim's work. Weber, of course, knew quite well that religion *might* have integrative functions and hence could sometimes be regarded as a community cult[77] in which ceremonies and rites play an important role. But his perspective focused on something different – namely, on the emergence, creation and re-creation of socially differentiated religious communities that get their particular shape and form from the arduous work of prophets and intellectuals in solving in a meaningful and somehow rational and systematic way the theodicy problem that has always haunted believers everywhere.[78] It is not that Weber – to repeat it again – disregards particular religious practices such as ceremonies and rites; but they are above all the consequences of an intellectual endeavour called religion, but are not at the very centre of religion itself. And, in addition, Weber, in contrast to Durkheim, from the very beginning of his sociology of religion interprets religion as a separated sphere with its own logic and developmental path – a path that in the end might lead to a complete disenchantment ('*Entzauberung*') of the world that allows even the emergence of a secular age. In this way, he in fact had seemingly more theoretical options in analysing phenomena of the modern world than Durkheim, who always had to look at least for functional equivalents of religion, such as 'civil religions'. It is difficult to imagine a secular world through Durkheimian thought, because it is always needed as a kind of societal glue, and through the process of history the sacred is continuously transferred from object to object.[79] In Weber's approach, by contrast, his acceptance of a sharp distinction between religion and the other spheres of life, between religion and the secular, had its costs as well – and to these I will turn in the conclusion.[80]

Conclusion

It is obvious that each and every way to theorize religion has its own problems – and not only because those theories almost necessarily reflect the assumptions, conflicts and prejudices of the theorists and their societies. One should also be aware that the very term 'religion' is itself highly problematic, so that any attempt to write about religion should at least try to historicize and to contextualize its use. This leads me to three concluding remarks.

My first point is – and here I draw upon the work of Talal Asad – that interpreting religion as an autonomous sphere tends to make it a somehow trans-historical and transcultural phenomenon,[81] which forgets that the term did not come into being until the period of the Protestant Reformation and hence is of Christian origin.[82] Talking about religion in the sense of a separated sphere, at the same time means that one necessarily defines non-religious spheres: counter-terms to the term religion, such as economy, science and polity, are quickly at hand. Thus, the setting apart of religion allows us for the very first time to think about secular spheres that are seemingly 'free' from religion. One wonders whether such a way of thinking is really helpful, if one takes into consideration how heavily such theories of functional differentiation have been criticized over recent decades within the discipline of sociology.[83]

Second, more than fifty years ago, German sociologist Joachim Matthes, writing basically at the same time as Wilfred Cantwell Smith's publication of his famous 'The Meaning and End of Religion' in which he fiercely criticized the use of the term 'religion',[84] asked the disturbing question of why the term 'religion' and its pendant 'secularization' are and will be used as general terms of the social sciences, despite their obvious ethnocentric origins and all their other limitations. Answering his own question, he points to four functions these terms have – functions for different actors. I will use my words and my predilection for ordering Matthes's arguments:[85] (1) if there is a segregated religion then there is invariably someone to defend it (i.e. theologians, orthodox and not so orthodox believers), who are all somehow keen to define the turf they are playing on, and to find and strengthen their identity 'by doing religion' and arguing about it; (2) the creation of a separated religion makes a wonderful research object – academics know where and what to look at, something that Matthes years later called 'the birth of religion from the spirit of research on it';[86] (3) creating the 'religious' and the 'secular' is the only way of asking causal questions; and if one wants to ask causal questions, and many scholars obviously do, one simply has to have a realm called religion as a dependent variable – a variable which, at least theoretically, can be manipulated by changing the independent one; and (4), and most importantly, when one talks about religion and secularization, one is making caesuras between pre-modernity and modernity – and the result will be a wonderful and obviously endless debate not only between scholars but also between lay people concerning the meaning of modernity.[87] In sum, there are quite a few extra-scientific reasons why the obviously problematic concept of 'religion' is still so important within different disciplines.

This brings me to my third and last point: from its very beginning the rather recent term 'religion' has been used both by actors and – as an analytical category – by scholars. It is impossible to disentangle both uses of the term, so that Matthes, Asad and many others are certainly correct in arguing that religion is nothing but a discursive phenomenon difficult to apply to pre-Reformation periods or to those areas not affected by Reformation Christianity. Nowadays, obviously the term religion has proliferated and it is used by lay persons in many Christian and non-Christian parts of the world – not least because of the impact of 'the West'. As Peter van der Veer has pointed out, the general concept 'religion' was created and adopted as an umbrella term for the simple reason to pacify conflicts between different groups in colonial contexts, suggesting they are all part of a similar intellectual or spiritual universe.[88] Be that as it may, within the humanities and the social sciences it obviously was and still is difficult to avoid this term, so that the problematic terminological and conceptual baggage we have inherited from the sociology of religion, either in the French tradition of Fustel and Durkheim, or in the German tradition based around the work of Weber, is still with us today. And, at least in my opinion, those disciplines with an interest in generalized terms and statements will have enormous difficulties in accepting the claim of the discursive construction of their 'object' of research that cannot be treated as a variable. One wonders whether this might be a good starting point for interdisciplinary work, or whether disciplines such as history on the one side and sociology on the other will follow strictly separated paths, particularly now that a more transnational perspective seems to be in vogue.

Wolfgang Knöbl is director of the Hamburg Institute for Social Research, and professor for Political Sociology and Research on Violence at Leuphana University, Lueneburg, Germany. Between 2002 and 2015, he was professor for Comparative Sociology at the University of Göttingen, and during this period also German chair at the University of Toronto, Canada and fellow at the Freiburg Institute for Advanced Studies (FRIAS) and at the Max Weber Centre for Advanced Cultural and Social Studies at Erfurt University. His fields of expertise are political and historical-comparative sociology, the history of sociology, and social theory. Books include *Die Kontingenz der Moderne: Wege in Europa, Asien und Amerika* (Campus, 2007); *Social Theory: Twenty Introductory Lectures* [together with Hans Joas] (Cambridge University Press, 2009), and translated into Russian and Spanish; *War in Social Thought: Hobbes to the Present* [also together with Hans Joas] (Princeton University Press, 2012), and translated into Chinese.

Notes

1. G.G. Stroumsa, *A New Science: The Discovery of Religion in the Age of Reason* (Cambridge: Harvard University Press, 2010), 5.
2. Ibid., 25.
3. Ibid., 27.
4. Ibid., 29.
5. Ibid., 9.
6. F.W. Graf, 'Ursprüngliche Akkumulation ganz anders: Der sehr deutsche Diskurs über die Genese des Kapitalismus um 1900', *Mittelweg* 36, 26(6) (2017/18), 29–44.
7. See H. Joas, *Glaube als Option: Zukunftsmöglichkeiten des Christentums* (Freiburg: Herder, 2012), 30ff.
8. F.H. Tenbruck, 'Die Religion im Maelstrom der Reflexion', in J. Bergmann, A. Hahn and T. Luckmann (eds), *Religion und Kultur: Sonderheft 33 der Kölner Zeitschrift für Soziologie und Sozialpsychologie* (Opladen: Westdeutscher, 1993), 63.
9. Here it should be emphasized that, in contrast to many interpreters, the sociological classics almost never wrote about 'modernity'. Although the word had already existed in different European languages since the 1880s (*modernité, Moderne*, etc.), it was hardly ever used. Most of them talked about the 'modern world', 'die neueste Zeit' etc., but not – to emphasize it again – about 'modernity'. The discourse on modernity did not start until the 1960s; see W. Knöbl, 'The Sociological Discourse on "Modernization" and "Modernity"', *Revue Internationale de Philosophie* 3(281) (2017), 311–29.
10. N.D. Fustel de Coulanges, *The Ancient City: A Study on the Religion, Laws, and Institutions of Greece and Rome* (Kitchener, Ont.: Batoche Books, 2001), 139.
11. Cf. A. Momigliano, 'Der antike Staat des Fustel de Coulanges', in idem (ed.), *Wege in die Alte Welt* (Frankfurt/Main: Fischer, 1995), 271–93.
12. J. Heilbron, *French Sociology* (Ithaca, NY and London: Cornell University Press, 2015), 59–91. J. Salvador, *L'École Française de Socioanthropologie*. Préface de Georges Balandier (Paris: Èditions Sciences Humaines, 2015).
13. M. Despland, *L'émergence des sciences de la religion. La Monarchie de Juillet: un moment fondateur* (Paris and Montreal: L'Harmattan, 1999).
14. Ibid., 281ff.
15. Ibid., 106ff.

16. Ibid., 364.
17. Hartmann Tyrell sees Durkheim's keen interest in the role of religion in order to understand and solve the problems of contemporary France as follows: 'Religion … was indispensable for modern society. Durkheim says this repeatedly, especially where he interprets individualism, the "cult of the individual" as religion of his own time. But what "religion" sociologically stands for is, in relation to society, threefold: first of all the "piety-generating *superiority*" of "society" towards the individuals (just as with Comte); then *unity*: as Rousseau's "general will" or as "social bond"; finally with Kant the *imperative*, the ultimate and unconditional claims to validity, for "society possesses all characteristics of an awe-inspiring moral authority".' – H. Tyrell, 'Von der "Soziologie *statt* Religion" zur Religionssoziologie', in V. Krech and H. Tyrell (eds), *Religionssoziologie um 1900* (Würzburg: Ergon, 1995), 101f., italics in the original; translation by Wolfgang Knöbl. See also the brilliant essay by H. Firsching in the same volume: H. Firsching, 'Die Sakralisierung der Gesellschaft: Émile Durkheims Soziologie der "Moral" und der "Religion" in der ideenpolitischen Auseinandersetzung der Dritten Republik', in V. Krech and H. Tyrell (eds), *Religionssoziologie um 1900* (Würzburg: Ergon, 1995), 159–93.
18. Cf. H.G. Kippenberg, 'Religionsentwicklung', in H.G. Kippenberg and M. Riesebrodt (eds), *Max Webers Religionssystematik* (Tübingen: Mohr Siebeck, 2001), 80.
19. H. Joas, *Die Macht des Heiligen: Eine Alternative zur der Geschichte von der Entzauberung* (Berlin: Suhrkamp, 2017), 120ff.
20. For a brief comparison of the different approaches to religion of Durkheim, Weber and Simmel, see P. Watier, 'Erkenntnisinteressen der klassischen Religionssoziologie: Simmel, Weber, Durkheim', in M. Koenig and J.P. Willaime (eds), *Religionskontroversen in Frankreich und Deutschland* (Hamburg: Hamburger Edition, 2008), 204–36. For the importance of Troeltsch and his ambitious research programme, see H. Joas, 'Gesellschaft, Staat und Religion: Ihr Verhältnis in der Sicht der Weltreligionen', in H. Joas and K. Wiegandt (eds), *Säkularisierung und die Weltreligionen* (Frankfurt/Main: Fischer, 2007), 23f.; Joas, *Die Macht des Heiligen*, 165–277.
21. D. Kaesler, *Max Weber: Preuße, Denker, Muttersohn. Eine Biographie* (Munich: Beck, 2014); S. Schmitt, *Max Webers Verständnis des Katholizismus: Eine werkbiographische Analyse*, Master's thesis (Marburg: Philipps-Universität, 2006); D. Kaesler, 'Sonnig, gegenwartsfroh und katholisch: Max Webers Italien', in F. Schönemann and T. Maassen (eds), *Prüft alles, und das Gute behaltet! Zum Wechselspiel von Kirchen, Religionen und säkularer Welt*. Festschrift für Hans-Martin Barth zum 65. Geburtstag (Frankfurt/Main: Lenbeck, 2004), 271–96; P. Hersche, 'Max Weber, Italien und der Katholizismus', *Quellen und Forschungen aus italienischen Archiven und Bibliotheken* 76 (1996), 362–82; W. Stark, 'The Place of Catholicism in Max Weber's Sociology of Religion', *Sociological Analysis* 29(4) (1968), 202–10.
22. Hersche, 'Max Weber', 373.
23. Schmitt, *Max Webers Verständnis*, 50.
24. 'Above all, he [Weber] thanks the sun and glory of the eternal city for hours saturated with the past, which have now made the meagre present worth living in for almost a year'. M. Weber, *Max Weber: Ein Lebensbild* (Munich: Piper, 1989), 268; translation by Wolfgang Knöbl.
25. Kaesler, *Max Weber*, 511f.
26. Cf. Weber, 'Die protestantische Ethik und der Geist des Kapitalismus', in M. Weber (ed.), *Gesammelte Aufsätze zur Religionssoziologie I*, 9th edn (Tübingen: Mohr Siebeck, 1988), 116, where he characterizes the Jesuits as 'emanzipiert von planloser Weltflucht und

virtuosenhafter Selbstquälerei' ('emancipated from an aimless flight from the world and virtuoso self-torment'); cf. also M. Weber, *Wirtschaft und Gesellschaft, Grundriss der verstehenden Soziologie*, 5th edn (Tübingen: Mohr Siebeck, 1972), 699, where he emphasizes the ascetic features of Jesuitism.

27. Cf., for example, Kaesler, *Max Weber*, 513.
28. Weber, *Wirtschaft und Gesellschaft*, 339.
29. Ibid.
30. M. Borutta, 'Das Andere der Moderne: Geschlecht, Sexualität und Krankheit in antikatholischen Diskursen Deutschlands und Italiens (1850–1900)', in W. Rammert et al. (eds), *Kollektive Identitäten und kulturelle Innovationen: Ethnologische, soziologische und historische Studien* (Leipzig: Leipziger Universitätsverlag, 2001), 62; for a characterization of Heidelberg's anti-Catholic milieu, in which Max Weber happened to live most of the time, see H.W. Smith. 1995. *German Nationalism and Religious Conflict: Culture, Ideology, Politics, 1870–1914* (Princeton, NJ: Princeton University Press, 1995), 104ff. See also G. Hübinger, *Kulturprotestantismus und Politik: Zum Verhältnis von Liberalismus und Protestantismus im wilhelminischen Deutschland* (Tübingen: Mohr Siebeck, 1994), 111.
31. D. Blackbourn, *Marpingen: Apparitions of the Virgin Mary in Nineteenth-Century Germany* (New York: Alfred A. Knopff, 1994), 24ff.
32. A. Heinen, 'Umstrittene Moderne: Die Liberalen und der preußisch-deutsche Kulturkampf', *Geschichte und Gesellschaft* 29 (2003), 144ff.
33. Hübinger, *Kulturprotestantismus und Politik*, 23.
34. Here I simply reproduce the brilliant arguments of F.W. Graf, 'Rettung der Persönlichkeit: Protestantische Theologie als Kulturwissenschaft des Christentums', in R. vom Bruch, F.W. Graf and G. Hübinger (eds), *Kultur und Kulturwissenschaften um 1900: Krise der Moderne und Glaube an die Wissenschaft* (Stuttgart: Steiner, 1989), 125ff.
35. H.G. Kippenberg, 'Die Krise der Religion und die Genese der Religionswissenschaften', in V. Drehsen and W. Sparn (eds), *Vom Weltbildwandel zur Weltanschauungsanalyse: Krisenwahrnehmung und Krisenbewältigung um 1900* (Berlin: Akademie, 1996), 93ff.
36. Cf. H. Schnädelbach, *Philosophie in Deutschland 1831–1933* (Frankfurt/Main: Suhrkamp, 1983), 206–18.
37. 'With Lotze, Windelband, Rickert and Weber, we encounter the experience of the man of culture threatened by chaos, the representative of a German cultural experience, as a leitmotif of thinking. In the face of crisis of a socio-cultural change experienced as a world-historical caesura the educational bourgeois-protestant-liberal professorial culture would like to preserve this intellectual-cultural world by developing the concept of a science of values of historical cultural humanity.' – J. Gebhardt, 'Die Werte', in R. Hofmann, J. Jantzen and H. Ottmann (eds), *Anodos: Festschrift für Helmut Kuhn* (Weinheim: VCH – Acta Humaniora, 1989), 54; translation by Wolfgang Knöbl. Needless to say, mentioning the particularistic or even biased context of the discovery of a concept does not spoil the concept in general; see especially the brilliant book by H. Joas, *The Genesis of Values* (Chicago: University of Chicago Press, 2001).
38. This is obviously Weber's own distinction, the one between '*Gemeindereligiosität*' (Weber, *Wirtschaft und Gesellschaft*, 277) and other forms of religions of '*Vergesellschaftung*'; for clarification see J. Casanova, 'Welche Religion braucht der Mensch? Theorien religiösen Wandels im Zeitalter der Kontingenz', in B. Hollstein, M. Jung and W. Knöbl (eds), *Handlung und Erfahrung: Das Erbe von Historismus und Pragmatismus und die Zukunft der Sozialtheorie* (Frankfurt/Main: Campus, 2011), 169–89; and J. Casanova, 'Rethinking

Secularization: A Global Comparative Perspective', *The Hedgehog Review. Critical Reflections on Contemporary Culture* 8(1/2) (2006), 15.
39. G. Hübinger, 'Erfahrung und Erforschung der "Säkularisierung"', in idem, *Engagierte Beobachter der Moderne: Von Max Weber bis Ralf Dahrendorf* (Göttingen: Wallstein, 2016), 85ff.
40. There are some doubts, however, whether 'secularization' is indeed something that affects the whole world and whether 'differentiation' is a particularly fruitful sociological concept at all.
41. Weber, *Wirtschaft und Gesellschaft*, 304; cf. A. Bienfait, 'Religionen verstehen – eine Einleitung', in idem (ed.), *Religionen verstehen: Zur Aktualität von Max Webers Religionssoziologie* (Wiesbaden: VS Verlag, 2011), 8. See also Kippenberg, 'Die Krise der Religion', 101.
42. I. Kant. 'Die Religion innerhalb der Grenzen der bloßen Vernunft', in Kant, *Werke in Zwölf Bänden. VIII. Schriften zur Ethik und Religionsphilosophie* (Frankfurt/Main: Suhrkamp, 1956), 645–879.
43. Ibid., 745.
44. Ibid., 846f.
45. Ibid., 869.
46. Ibid., 791.
47. Ibid., 792.
48. See E. Feil, *Religio. Vierter Band: Die Geschichte eines neuzeitlichen Grundbegriffs im 18. und frühen 19. Jahrhundert* (Göttingen: Vandenhoeck & Ruprecht, 2007).
49. G.F.W. Hegel, 'Fragmente über Volksreligion und Christentum (1793–1794)', in idem, *Frühe Schriften. Werke 1* (Frankfurt/Main: Suhrkamp, 1986), 19, 25.
50. G.F.W. Hegel, 'Die Positivität der christlichen Religion', in idem, *Frühe Schriften. Werke 1* (Frankfurt/Main: Suhrkamp, 1986), 105.
51. F.D.H. Schleiermacher, *Über die Religion: Reden an die Gebildeten unter ihren Verächtern* (Hamburg: Felix Meiner, 1970), 17.
52. Cf. V. Krech and H. Tyrell, 'Religionssoziologie um die Jahrhundertwende: Zu Vorgeschichte, Kontext und Beschaffenheit einer Subdisziplin der Soziologie', in V. Krech and H. Tyrell (eds), *Religionssoziologie um 1900* (Würzburg: Ergon, 1995), 45.
53. Schleiermacher, *Über die Religion*, 16, 29.
54. G. Simmel, 'Zur Soziologie der Religion', in H.J. Dahme and D.P. Frisby (eds), *Georg Simmel. Gesamtausgabe. Band 5: Aufsätze und Abhandlungen 1894 bis 1900* (Frankfurt/Main: Suhrkamp, 1992), 266–86; G. Simmel, 'Die Religion', in M. Behr, V. Krech and G. Schmidt (eds), *Georg Simmel. Gesamtausgabe. Band 10: Philosophie der Mode (1905). Die Religion (1906/1912). Kant und Goethe (1906/1916). Schopenhauer und Nietzsche* (Frankfurt/Main: Suhrkamp, 1995), 39–118.
55. This influence has been quite correctly emphasized by S. Breuer, 'Die Geburt der Moderne aus dem Geist der Weltablehnung', in idem, *Max Webers tragische Soziologie: Aspekte und Perspektiven* (Tübingen: Mohr Siebeck, 2006), 44ff.
56. S. Marchand, *German Orientalism in the Age of Empire: Religion, Race, and Scholarship* (Washington, DC: Cambridge University Press, 2009), 302. From Marianne Weber's biography (Weber, *Max Weber*, 48) we know that Max Weber had already read Schopenhauer at school.
57. C. Ryan, *Schopenhauer's Philosophy of Religion: The Death of God and the Oriental Renaissance* (Leuven: Peeters, 2010), 62.
58. Ibid., 79.

59. Ibid., 80.
60. Kant, 'Die Religion innerhalb der Grenzen', 848.
61. Hegel, 'Fragmente über Volksreligion', 81.
62. A. Schopenhauer, *Die Welt als Wille und Vorstellung. Zweiter Band, welcher die Ergänzungen zu den vier Büchern des ersten Bandes enthält* (Zurich: Haffmans, 1991), 728.
63. A. Schopenhauer, *Die Welt als Wille und Vorstellung. Erster Band: Vier Bücher, nebst einem Anhange, der die Kritik der Kantischen Philosophie enthält* (Zurich: Haffmans, 1991), 418.
64. Schopenhauer, *Die Welt als Wille und Vorstellung. Zweiter Band*, 680.
65. Ibid., 537.
66. Ibid., 715.
67. 'This fits the ascetic spirit of denial of one's own self and the overcoming of the world, which, like the borderless love of one's neighbour, even of one's enemy, is the basic characteristic which Christianity has in common with Brahmanism and Buddhism, and which certifies its kinship.' (Schopenhauer, *Die Welt als Wille und Vorstellung, Zweiter Band*, 726; translation by Wolfgang Knöbl).
68. G. Mannion, *Schopenhauer, Religion and Morality: The Humble Path to Ethics* (Aldershot: Ashgate, 2003), 28f.
69. Ibid., 78.
70. And, one should add, he was at the same time influenced by Schleiermacher's interpretation of magic, as Peter van der Veer had argued: P. van der Veer, *The Modern Spirit of Asia: The Spiritual and the Secular in China and India* (Princeton, NJ: Princeton University Press, 2014), 127.
71. 'From the earliest times, religion, as distinct from magic or sorcery, addresses itself to kindred and friendly beings, who may indeed be angry with their people for a time, but are always placable except to the enemies of their worshippers or to renegade members of the community.' – R. Smith, *The Religion of the Semites: The Fundamental Institutions* (New York: Meridian Books, 1957), 54; see also G.W. Stocking, *After Tylor: British Social Anthropology 1888–1951* (Madison: University of Wisconsin Press, 1995), 80. Stocking also points to the strong influence of Robertson Smith on Durkheim, especially with respect to Robertson Smith's emphasis on the emotional role of rituals. I have no knowledge of whether Weber read Robertson Smith, but his book was well known in the German context of that time, and at least the arguments therein should have come to Weber's mind because there was already a German translation in 1899.
72. Weber claimed that Judaism was responsible for a break with the Asian culture area in so far as the Jewish prophets for the first time formulated a stringent ethic and thus liberated all ways to salvation from magic – cf. S. Breuer, 'Magie – Religion – Entzauberung', in idem, *Max Webers tragische Soziologie: Aspekte und Perspektiven* (Tübingen: Mohr Siebeck, 2006), 32.
73. Whatever Weber's influence in this aspect, it is remarkable that, for example, Wilhelm Windelband used the same criteria of differentiation between magic and religion by clearly addressing magic as *'Gotteszwang'* – cf. W. Windelband, 'Das Heilige: Skizze zur Religionsphilosophie', in idem, *Präludien: Aufsätze und Reden zur Einleitung in die Philosophie*, 5th edn, vol. 2 (Tübingen: Mohr Siebeck, [1902] 1915).
74. See, above all, M. Weber, 'Zwischenbetrachtung: Theorie der Stufen und Richtungen religiöser Weltablehnung', in idem, *Gesammelte Aufsätze zur Religionssoziologie I*, 9th edn (Tübingen: Mohr Siebeck, 1988), 536–73. As has been argued within the debates on Weber's concept of salvation religion, the term *'Weltablehnung'* was certainly not common within the theological or sociological circles of his time, and nor did it play a role

in the proceedings of the first meeting of the German Sociological Society of 1910 in Frankfurt, in which Weber took part and in which religion was an important topic – cf. H.G. Kippenberg. 2001. 'Meine Religionssystematik', in H.G. Kippenberg and M. Riesebrodt (eds), *Max Webers Religionssystematik* (Tübingen: Mohr Siebeck, 2001), 22. 'The central position of the concept of world rejection for Weber is already attested by the subtitle of the *Zwischenbetrachtung*. At the same time it is noticeable that it is anything but widespread in literature. In none of the current philosophical or theological encyclopedias does it stand out as a keyword, not even today. With Weber himself, the term is subject to a development in the course of which it gains in sharpness.' – B. Jacobsen, 'Hiatus Irrationalis: Der Bruch zwischen Sein und Sollen', in H.G. Kippenberg and M. Riesebrodt (eds), *Max Webers Religionssystematik* (Tübingen: Mohr Siebeck, 2001), 39f.; translation by Wolfgang Knöbl.
75. It should be emphasized here that Weber's sharp distinction between the ethics of Lutheranism and, for example, Calvinism was certainly not only due to Schopenhauer's influence. As has been pointed out by Friedrich Wilhelm Graf, Weber's position was very much shaped by the interpretation of the German theologian Matthias Schneckenburger who had a somewhat idiosyncratic position in this case – F.W. Graf, 'Die "kompetentesten" Gesprächspartner? Implizite Werturteile in Max Webers "Protestantischer Ethik"', in V. Krech and H. Tyrell (eds), *Religionssoziologie um 1900* (Würzburg: Ergon 1995), 225ff.
76. Kippenberg, 'Die Krise der Religion', 101 (my translation).
77. See note 34 where it is emphasized that Weber himself introduced the term 'Gemeindereligion'. Thus, the point is not that Weber had nothing to say with respect to community cults; it is just that in order to analyse the development of religion he had and indeed needed a different focus.
78. H. Tyrell, 'Kulturkämpfe in Frankreich und Deutschland und die Anfänge der Religionssoziologie', in M. Koenig and J.P. Willaime (eds), *Religionskontroversen in Frankreich und Deutschland* (Hamburg: Hamburger Edition, 2008), 152.
79. It has to be emphasized again that this is not a value judgement of mine: Durkheim might be right in assuming that a thoroughly secularized world is indeed unthinkable.
80. As John Milbank has argued, such a – in principle – Protestant understanding of religion has also shaped very recent sociological attempts of theorizing religion; for example, the one by Niklas Luhmann – J. Milbank, *Theology and Social Theory: Beyond Secular Reason* (London: Blackwell, 2001), 132ff. It is indeed astonishing how depricatingly Luhmann – N. Luhmann, *Die Religion der Gesellschaft* (Frankfurt/Main: Suhrkamp, 2002), 12 – talks about the seemingly useless attempts of, for example, phenomenologists of religion without taking into consideration how problematic his own way of theorizing religious communication is. It seems to be highly doubtful whether Luhmann's insistence on the centrality of the distinction between immanence and transcendence (77) really covers all or even the majority of religious phenomena.
81. T. Asad, *Genealogies of Religion: Discipline and Reasons of Power in Christianity and Islam* (Baltimore, MD: Johns Hopkins University Press, 1993), 28.
82. Basically at the same time, this point – if I understand the debate correctly – was made in the German context much more precisely by Joachim Matthes; see J. Matthes, 'Auf der Suche nach dem "Religiösen": Reflexionen zu Theorie und Empirie religionssoziologischer Forschung', *Sociologia Internationalis* 29 (1992), 129–42; J. Matthes, 'Was ist anders an anderen Religionen? Anmerkungen zur zentristischen Organisation des

religionssoziologischen Denkens', in J. Bergmann, A. Hahn and T. Luckmann (eds), *Religion und Kultur* (Opladen: Westdeutscher, 1993), 16–30.
83. Cf., for example, H. Joas, *The Creativity of Action* (Chicago: University of Chicago Press, 1996), 223ff.
84. W.C. Smith, *The Meaning and End of Religion* (New York: Macmillan, 1963).
85. J. Matthes, *Religion und Gesellschaft: Einführung in die Religionssoziologie I* (Reinbek: Rowohlt, 1967), 78ff.
86. Matthes, 'Was ist anders an anderen Religionen?', 26.
87. W. Knöbl, 'Soziologie', in F. Jäger, W. Knöbl and U. Schneider (eds), *Handbuch der Moderneforschung* (Stuttgart: Metzler, 2015), 261–74.
88. Van der Veer, *The Modern Spirit of Asia*, 31.

Bibliography

Asad, T. *Genealogies of Religion: Discipline and Reasons of Power in Christianity and Islam.* Baltimore, MD: Johns Hopkins University Press, 1993.

Bienfait, A. 'Religionen verstehen – eine Einleitung', in idem (ed.), *Religionen verstehen: Zur Aktualität von Max Webers Religionssoziologie* (Wiesbaden: VS Verlag, 2011), 7–17.

Blackbourn, B. *Marpingen: Apparitions of the Virgin Mary in Nineteenth-Century Germany.* New York: Alfred A. Knopff, 1994.

Borutta, M. 'Das Andere der Moderne: Geschlecht, Sexualität und Krankheit in antikatholischen Diskursen Deutschlands und Italiens (1850–1900)', in W. Rammert et al. (eds), *Kollektive Identitäten und kulturelle Innovationen: Ethnologische, soziologische und historische Studien* (Leipzig: Leipziger Universitätsverlag, 2001), 59–75.

Breuer, S. 'Die Geburt der Moderne aus dem Geist der Weltablehnung', in idem, *Max Webers tragische Soziologie: Aspekte und Perspektiven* (Tübingen: Mohr Siebeck, 2006), 33–59.

———. 'Magie – Religion – Entzauberung', in idem, *Max Webers tragische Soziologie: Aspekte und Perspektiven* (Tübingen: Mohr Siebeck, 2006), 13–32.

Casanova, J. 'Rethinking Secularization: A Global Comparative Perspective'. *The Hedgehog Review. Critical Reflections on Contemporary Culture* 8(1/2) (2006), 7–22.

———. 'Welche Religion braucht der Mensch? Theorien religiösen Wandels im Zeitalter der Kontingenz', in B. Hollstein, M. Jung and W. Knöbl (eds), *Handlung und Erfahrung: Das Erbe von Historismus und Pragmatismus und die Zukunft der Sozialtheorie* (Frankfurt/Main: Campus, 2011), 169–89.

Despland, M. *L'émergence des sciences de la religion: La Monarchie de Juillet: un moment fondateur.* Paris and Montreal: L'Harmattan, 1999.

Feil, E. *Religio. Vierter Band: Die Geschichte eines neuzeitlichen Grundbegriffs im 18. und frühen 19. Jahrhundert.* Göttingen: Vandenhoeck & Ruprecht, 2007.

Firsching, H. 'Die Sakralisierung der Gesellschaft: Émile Durkheims Soziologie der "Moral" und der "Religion" in der ideenpolitischen Auseinandersetzung der Dritten Republik', in V. Krech and H. Tyrell (eds), *Religionssoziologie um 1900* (Würzburg: Ergon, 1995), 159–93.

Fustel de Coulanges, N.D. *The Ancient City: A Study on the Religion, Laws, and Institutions of Greece and Rome.* Kitchener, Ont.: Batoche Books, 2001.

Gebhardt, J. 'Die Werte', in R. Hofmann, J. Jantzen and H. Ottmann (eds), *Anodos: Festschrift für Helmut Kuhn* (Weinheim: VCH – Acta Humaniora, 1989), 35–54.

Graf, F.W. 'Rettung der Persönlichkeit: Protestantische Theologie als Kulturwissenschaft des Christentums', in R. vom Bruch, F.W. Graf and G. Hübinger (eds), *Kultur und Kulturwissenschaften um 1900: Krise der Moderne und Glaube an die Wissenschaft* (Stuttgart: Steiner, 1989), 103–31.

———. 'Die "kompetentesten" Gesprächspartner? Implizite Werturteile in Max Webers "Protestantischer Ethik"', in V. Krech and H. Tyrell (eds), *Religionssoziologie um 1900* (Würzburg: Ergon, 1995), 209–48.

———. 'Ursprüngliche Akkumulation ganz anders: Der sehr deutsche Diskurs über die Genese des Kapitalismus um 1900'. *Mittelweg* 36(6) (2017/18), 29–44.

Hegel, G.F.W. 'Fragmente über Volksreligion und Christentum (1793–1794)', in idem, *Frühe Schriften. Werke 1* (Frankfurt/Main: Suhrkamp, 1986), 9–103.

———. 'Die Positivität der christlichen Religion', in idem, *Frühe Schriften. Werke 1* (Frankfurt/Main: Suhrkamp, 1986), 104–229.

Heilbron, J. *French Sociology*. Ithaca, NY and London: Cornell University Press, 2015.

Heinen, A. 'Umstrittene Moderne: Die Liberalen und der preußisch-deutsche Kulturkampf'. *Geschichte und Gesellschaft* 29 (2003), 138–56.

Hersche, P. 'Max Weber, Italien und der Katholizismus', *Quellen und Forschungen aus italienischen Archiven und Bibliotheken* 76 (1996), 362–82.

Hübinger, G. *Kulturprotestantismus und Politik: Zum Verhältnis von Liberalismus und Protestantismus im wilhelminischen Deutschland.* Tübingen: Mohr Siebeck, 1994.

———. 'Erfahrung und Erforschung der "Säkularisierung"', in idem, *Engagierte Beobachter der Moderne: Von Max Weber bis Ralf Dahrendorf* (Göttingen: Wallstein, 2016), 77–96.

Jacobsen, B. 'Hiatus Irrationalis: Der Bruch zwischen Sein und Sollen', in H.G. Kippenberg and M. Riesebrodt (eds), *Max Webers Religionssystematik* (Tübingen: Mohr Siebeck, 2001), 31–50.

Joas, H. *The Creativity of Action*. Chicago: University of Chicago Press, 1996.

———. *The Genesis of Values*. Chicago: University of Chicago Press, 2001.

———. 'Gesellschaft, Staat und Religion: Ihr Verhältnis in der Sicht der Weltreligionen', in H. Joas and K. Wiegandt (eds), *Säkularisierung und die Weltreligionen* (Frankfurt/Main: Fischer, 2007), 9–43.

———. *Glaube als Option: Zukunftsmöglichkeiten des Christentums*. Freiburg: Herder, 2012.

———. *Die Macht des Heiligen: Eine Alternative zur Geschichte von der Entzauberung*. Berlin: Suhrkamp, 2017.

Kaesler, D. 'Sonnig, gegenwartsfroh und katholisch: Max Webers Italien', in F. Schönemann and T. Maassen (eds), *Prüft alles, und das Gute behaltet! Zum Wechselspiel von Kirchen, Religionen und säkularer Welt. Festschrift für Hans-Martin Barth zum 65. Geburtstag.* (Frankfurt/Main: Lenbeck, 2004), 271–96.

———. *Max Weber: Preuße, Denker, Muttersohn. Eine Biographie*. Munich: Beck, 2014.

Kant, I. 'Die Religion innerhalb der Grenzen der bloßen Vernunft', in Kant, *Werke in Zwölf Bänden. VIII: Schriften zur Ethik und Religionsphilosophie* (Frankfurt/Main: Suhrkamp, 1956), 645–879.

Kippenberg, H.G. 'Die Krise der Religion und die Genese der Religionswissenschaften', in V. Drehsen and W. Sparn (eds), *Vom Weltbildwandel zur Weltanschauungsanalyse: Krisenwahrnehmung und Krisenbewältigung um 1900* (Berlin: Akademie, 1996), 89–102.

———. 'Meine Religionssystematik', in H.G. Kippenberg and M. Riesebrodt (eds), *Max Webers Religionssystematik* (Tübingen: Mohr Siebeck, 2001), 13–30.

———. 'Religionsentwicklung', in H.G. Kippenberg and M. Riesebrodt (eds), *Max Webers Religionssystematik* (Tübingen: Mohr Siebeck, 2001), 77–99.

Knöbl, W. 'Soziologie', in F. Jäger, W. Knöbl and U. Schneider (eds), *Handbuch der Moderneforschung* (Stuttgart: Metzler, 2015), 261–74.

———. 'The Sociological Discourse on "Modernization" and "Modernity"', *Revue Internationale de Philosophie* 3(281) (2017), 311–29.

Krech, V., and H. Tyrell. 'Religionssoziologie um die Jahrhundertwende: Zu Vorgeschichte, Kontext und Beschaffenheit einer Subdisziplin der Soziologie', in V. Krech and H. Tyrell (eds), *Religionssoziologie um 1900* (Würzburg: Ergon, 1995), 11–78.

Luhmann, N. *Die Religion der Gesellschaft*. Frankfurt/Main: Suhrkamp, 2002.

Mannion, G. *Schopenhauer, Religion and Morality: The Humble Path to Ethics*. Aldershot: Ashgate, 2003.

Marchand, S. *German Orientalism in the Age of Empire: Religion, Race, and Scholarship*. Washington, DC: Cambridge University Press, 2009.

Matthes, J. *Religion und Gesellschaft: Einführung in die Religionssoziologie I*. Reinbek: Rowohlt, 1967.

———. 'Auf der Suche nach dem "Religiösen": Reflexionen zu Theorie und Empirie religionssoziologischer Forschung'. *Sociologia Internationalis* 29 (1992), 129–42.

———. 'Was ist anders an anderen Religionen? Anmerkungen zur zentristischen Organisation des religionssoziologischen Denkens', in J. Bergmann, A. Hahn and T. Luckmann (eds), *Religion und Kultur* (Opladen: Westdeutscher, 1993), 16–30.

Milbank, J. *Theology and Social Theory: Beyond Secular Reason*. London: Blackwell, 2001.

Momigliano, A. 'Der antike Staat des Fustel de Coulanges', in idem (ed.), *Wege in die Alte Welt* (Frankfurt/Main: Fischer, 1995), 271–93.

Ryan, C. *Schopenhauer's Philosophy of Religion: The Death of God and the Oriental Renaissance*. Leuven: Peeters, 2010.

Salvador, S. *L'École Française de Socioanthropologie*. Préface de Georges Balandier. Paris: Èditions Sciences Humaines, 2015.

Schleiermacher, F.D.H. *Über die Religion: Reden an die Gebildeten unter ihren Verächtern*. Hamburg: Felix Meiner, 1970.

Schmitt, S. 'Max Webers Verständnis des Katholizismus: Eine werkbiographische Analyse'. Master's thesis. Marburg: Philipps-Universität, 2006.

Schnädelbach, H. *Philosophie in Deutschland 1831–1933*. Frankfurt/Main: Suhrkamp, 1983.

Schopenhauer, A. *Die Welt als Wille und Vorstellung. Erster Band: Vier Bücher, nebst einem Anhange, der die Kritik der Kantischen Philosophie enthält*. Zurich: Haffmans, 1991.

———. *Die Welt als Wille und Vorstellung. Zweiter Band, welcher die Ergänzungen zu den vier Büchern des ersten Bandes enthält*. Zurich: Haffmans, 1991.

Simmel, G. 'Zur Soziologie der Religion', in H.J. Dahme and D.P. Frisby (eds), *Georg Simmel. Gesamtausgabe. Band 5: Aufsätze und Abhandlungen 1894 bis 1900* (Frankfurt/Main: Suhrkamp, 1992), 266–86.

———. 'Die Religion', in M. Behr, V. Krech and G. Schmidt (eds), *Georg Simmel. Gesamtausgabe. Band 10: Philosophie der Mode (1905). Die Religion (1906/1912). Kant und Goethe (1906/1916). Schopenhauer und Nietzsche* (Frankfurt/Main: Suhrkamp, 1995), 39–118.

Smith, H.W. *German Nationalism and Religious Conflict: Culture, Ideology, Politics, 1870–1914*. Princeton, NJ: Princeton University Press, 1995.

Smith, R. *The Religion of the Semites: The Fundamental Institutions*. New York: Meridian Books, 1957.

Smith, W.C. *The Meaning and End of Religion*. New York: Macmillan, 1963.

Stark, W. 'The Place of Catholicism in Max Weber's Sociology of Religion'. *Sociological Analysis* 29(4) (1968), 202–10.
Stocking, G.W. *After Tylor: British Social Anthropology 1888–1951*. Madison: University of Wisconsin Press, 1995.
Stroumsa, G.G. *A New Science: The Discovery of Religion in the Age of Reason*. Cambridge: Harvard University Press, 2010.
Tenbruck, F.H. 'Die Religion im Maelstrom der Reflexion', in J. Bergmann, A. Hahn and T. Luckmann (eds), *Religion und Kultur: Sonderheft 33 der Kölner Zeitschrift für Soziologie und Sozialpsychologie* (Opladen: Westdeutscher, 1993), 31–67.
Tyrell, H. 'Von der "Soziologie *statt* Religion" zur Religionssoziologie', in V. Krech and H. Tyrell (eds), *Religionssoziologie um 1900* (Würzburg: Ergon, 1995), 79–127.
———. 'Kulturkämpfe in Frankreich und Deutschland und die Anfänge der Religionssoziologie', in M. Koenig and J.P. Willaime (eds), *Religionskontroversen in Frankreich und Deutschland* (Hamburg: Hamburger Edition, 2008), 97–181.
Veer, P. van der. *The Modern Spirit of Asia: The Spiritual and the Secular in China and India*. Princeton, NJ: Princeton University Press, 2014.
Watier, P. 'Erkenntnisinteressen der klassischen Religionssoziologie: Simmel, Weber, Durkheim', in M. Koenig and J.P. Willaime (eds), *Religionskontroversen in Frankreich und Deutschland* (Hamburg: Hamburger Edition, 2008), 204–36.
Weber, M. *Wirtschaft und Gesellschaft: Grundriss der verstehenden Soziologie*. Tübingen: Mohr Siebeck, 1972.
———. 'Die protestantische Ethik und der Geist des Kapitalismus', in idem, *Gesammelte Aufsätze zur Religionssoziologie I* (Tübingen: Mohr Siebeck, 1988), 17–206.
———. 'Zwischenbetrachtung: Theorie der Stufen und Richtungen religiöser Weltablehnung', in idem, *Gesammelte Aufsätze zur Religionssoziologie I* (Tübingen: Mohr Siebeck, 1988), 536–73.
———. *Max Weber: Ein Lebensbild*. Munich: Piper, 1989.
Windelband, W. 'Das Heilige: Skizze zur Religionsphilosophie', in idem, *Präludien: Aufsätze und Reden zur Philosophie und ihrer Geschichte* (Tübingen: Mohr Siebeck, [1902] 1915), 295–332.

2

The Silence on the Land

Ancient Israel versus Modern Palestine in Scientific Theology

Paul Michael Kurtz

> The peaceful crusade has begun. Jerusalem must become ours.
> —Titus Tobler, *Palästina*[1]

In any myth of origins, the where is often as important as the when. These 'wheres' can then provide the grounds for other claims of space – material and intellectual alike. If historians have discerned a 'reformulation of the sacred within a desacralized discourse' or 'secularization of Lutheranism' for modern German history in general, and a 'Protestantization of the national' for the Kaiserreich in particular, a narrative of Christian genealogy spirited conceptions of cultural heritage from Europe further eastward, deep in the Ottoman Empire, to Palestine.[2] Alongside Rome and Athens stood Jerusalem. As the Lutheran biblical scholar Hermann Gunkel once declared, '[t]his is the religion on which we depend, from which we have ever to learn, on whose foundations our whole civilization is built; we are Israelites in religion even as we are Greeks in art and Romans in law'.[3] Such a mental mapping therefore annexed a diversity of pasts to the self-understanding of a European (Christian) identity. As a religion from ancient Palestine occupied the thoughts of modern Germans, this imagined patrimony displaced other claims to continuity, not only with that past but also with that place.

This essay examines an intellectual irony in the German Empire. Protestant biblical scholars, Semitists, and early church historians – often housed in faculties of theology – could spend their entire lives studying Palestine and yet show little, if any, interest in the dynamic, even tumultuous events in contemporaneous Palestine. Through the voluminous historiography of ancient Israel composed in libraries at home, and the burgeoning efforts of geography, ethnography and archaeology in new-found institutes abroad, academic labour on the Holy Land constructed and reinforced a genealogy that connected ancient Israel to 'Western' civilization via Christianity, which suggested the ancient past of Palestine belonged to the history of Christian Europe, not that of other peoples in the land. As Lorenzo Kamel writes of the British context, '[t]his enormous production [of books, private diaries, and maps], alongside a wide range of phenomena such as evangelical tourism, generated the idea of a meta-Palestine, an imaginary place devoid of any history except that of biblical magnificence'.[4] This chapter considers a so-called 'biblical orientalism' in the German Empire, probing the production of knowledge in academic theology. Focused less upon intention than effect, it explores how a concern for the ancient, biblical past, on the one hand, and a disregard for material, geographical and ethnic continuities, on the other, ultimately effected an appropriation of Palestine's past and present alike – a colonization of history that obscured current events on the ground.

The first section of the chapter scrutinizes how 'their' history became 'ours'. Analysing especially Protestant histories of ancient Israel as a historiographical corpus, it discerns two fundamental claims: a rift between Israel and Judaism and the culmination of Israelite history and religion in the Christian faith, which then moved towards Europe. Whatever the real divergences apparent in this corpus – from the beginning or end of Israel's history, to the value of certain sources, to interpretations of specific biblical texts – the genealogy of Israel and Christianity remained a constant. This section further demonstrates the true tenacity of these claims. In an age of heavy positivism and philological science, the results of theoretical, methodological and empirical challenges in general, and of historical criticism in particular, may have led to a drastic rewriting of ancient Israelite history, but the thrust of this formulation, of coupling and decoupling Israel, Judaism and Christianity, still held good. In fact, the very connection of Israel to Christianity operated as a major justification for Old Testament study to persist in theological faculties. Notably, public universities accommodated these institutions of Christian theology. Rigorous scrutiny of this scholarship – of the practices employed, the epistemologies warranting them, the conclusions therefore reached, and the conditions that kindled questions and inflamed them into debates – thus reveals the powerful draw of the biblical past and the persistence of Christian claims in historiographical work, whose hefty empiricism often shrouded the underlying commitments. The volume itself speaks volumes, with continued translations and editions manifesting the imposing presence of an ancient, distant world.

The second section of this chapter investigates the explorations in the land. At the turn of the twentieth century, the study of Palestine swelled. If an interest in the Bible and religion pushed any number of scientists and settlers, pilgrims and missionaries thither, then new possibilities in the land itself – opened by increased globalization and imperial ambition – pulled them there. Starting with the institutionalization of researches abroad – amidst the foundation of foreign institutes, the establishment of publication organs and the contest among nations – the chapter investigates how the religious dimensions were part and parcel of these developments. It concentrates on the objectives and operations of the Deutscher Verein zur Erforschung Palästina's, or Deutscher Palästina-Verein (DPV, the German Society for the Exploration of Palestine) and the Deutsches Evangelisches Institut für Altertumswissenschaft des Heiligen Landes (DEIAHL, the German Protestant Institute for Ancient Study of the Holy Land). These leading German institutes, their funders, directors and members, undertook sundry ventures with a strong orientation towards the ancient world. Such investigations, especially of the archaeological and ethnographic kind, could betray an even more specific drive: the places dug and people observed functioned as a window into the specifically biblical past. Furthermore, these labours often reproduced the genealogy of Christian origins in Palestine, and the limited interest in the land for any sake of its own. Modern Palestine, a museum, provided access to the ancient, holy past.

In conclusion, the chapter considers how the historiography of Israel and the work of institutes abroad factored into transformations of the sacred and the secular and, furthermore, contributed to building colonial knowledge. It locates the discourse of these endeavours within several larger discussions: the construction of *Wissenschaft* itself, where religious preoccupations, priorities and practices were inscribed into an allegedly neutral science for inquiry into the past; the colonization of Jewish history, where Christian authors arrogated unto themselves the historiography of Christian origins and antique Judaism; the issue of a 'deep orientalism', where claims already advanced in ancient sources echoed in modern historiography; and the process of transfer and non-transfer in knowledge production, where a silencing occurred. This appropriation of Palestine's ancient past for the history of Christian Europe, together with this attraction to the modern land expressly for the sake of the biblical past, dissolved the integrity of past and present and ultimately obstructed a view of contemporary space. Through such creation of knowledge, the past eclipsed the present.

Ancient People, Modern Faith

'Of making many books there is no end', declares the book of Ecclesiastes, 'and much study is a weariness of the flesh'.[5] At the time of the German Empire, the making undoubtedly applied to work on ancient Israel, although the weariness may pertain less to the indefatigable efforts then than to reading them today. From the 1880s onwards, decennia of philological inquiry into the biblical texts gave way to larger reconstructions of the history of Israel, with acribic analysis leading to broader synthesis. On top of the conclusions reached by literary criticism (i.e. internal analysis of the biblical texts themselves), which could carry scandalizing implications for reconstruction of the past, decipherment of other ancient languages, finds from excavations, advances in psychology, developments in anthropology and ventures in comparative religion, all contributed to a reappraisal of what happened in antiquity, for Palestine in particular and the Middle East in general.[6] As a measure of the booming production in this cottage industry, between 1898 and 1917 Wilhelm Nowack alone reviewed for the *Theologische Rundschau* over 250 studies on 'the history of Israelite religion'.[7] The distant past of ancient Israel was indeed a present one.

The historiographical drive into that past could steer towards any number of more specific directions, depending on the author's interest and his (usually his) aim. Long accessed almost exclusively via sacred texts, however, the history of Israel often mapped onto the history of religion – as recounted in biblical literature.[8] The Venn diagram of these histories was oft at risk of total collapse. Accordingly, Rudolf Smend suggested that the history of Israel and the Jews corresponded to the history of 'Old Testament Religion', even more so than the history of the Romans to that of Roman law.[9] (In fact, one prolific writer praised the prophets for recognizing 'religion itself is history, the history of God with his people and, moreover, even the history of God with the individual person' – an understanding that 'no non-Christian religion is capable of teaching like [that of] the Old Testament'.[10]) One conventional claim asserted the relative insignificance of ancient Israel, historically, in things political, commercial, architectural, agricultural and the like, but emphasized its import in religion, further stressing that the nation would have fallen into oblivion without it, as it had ultimately united the people over time and, furthermore, endured into the present.[11] Some investigations did aim to disentangle histories – religious, cultural and political.[12] Nonetheless, as Mario Liverani has diagnosed, histories of Israel have long represented 'a sort of paraphrase of the Biblical text'.[13] So, too, Jean Louis Ska discerns, '[w]e have, so to speak, an Old Testament rewritten and – practically – without oracles and miracles'.[14] The Hebrew Bible thus supplied the blueprint as architects of antiquity aimed to reconstruct the past.

As for the narrative of this biblical tradition, it construed the history of Israel as a special, sacred one. Having created the cosmos, the deity planted the first humans in a garden and uprooted them when they disobeyed. As future generations continued in their wayward ways, the creator destroyed his earth by deluge and then sought to start anew, with Noah and his family. He promised Abraham a nation and to that nation a land. Thus, Abraham fathered Isaac, Isaac sired Jacob, whose name was changed to Israel, and Jacob spawned twelve sons, whose offspring were enslaved in Egypt. God appointed Moses to spirit his people into Palestine, the land of Canaan pledged to their progenitor. En route, the deity endowed Moses with a code of law for his people, including monolatry. (Set at this point in the narrative, the book of Deuteronomy claims to be that very code, accenting a centralization of the cult, stressing a subordination of the king to God's election and to the law as safeguarded by the priesthood and emphasizing a divine promise of blessing for compliance, and curses for defiance.) The people of Israel conquered Canaan and massacred its inhabitants. After an era of judges – a cycle of lapse and restoration – God granted the nation a king.

Having first selected Saul, the deity elected David as his chosen one. While David united the kingdom, his son Solomon built the temple. Upon the latter's death, the kingdom divided in two, with Israel in the north, Judah in the south. Varied in their virtue, these kingdoms' monarchs came and went, sometimes with support, other times with censure from the prophets. One king, Josiah, found in the temple the law of Moses – long consigned to oblivion – and sought to re-enact it. In the end, the people of Israel were passed from one empire to the next: Assyria exterminated Israel while Babylon obliterated Judah, demolishing the temple; but after Persia conquered Babylon, the deported population was permitted to return. The returnees Ezra and Nehemiah thus hoped to rebuild the temple, reinstate the law and revive the Jewish people (i.e. those from Judah). Other prophetic figures prognosticated a coming saviour who would restore the kingdom again.

A descendant of Judaism, the Christian religion aimed to add itself to this narrative, forging a continuity to ancient Israel. According to the New Testament, Jesus of Nazareth – a peripatetic Jewish preacher and the saviour long promised to his people – worked miracles in the Roman province of Judea. Although welcomed by the masses, he was spurned by religious authorities, who convinced the Roman government to crucify him as an insurrectionist. Certain that he had risen from the dead, his disciples journeyed far and wide to proselytize, expanding the community to include non-Jews as well. These adherents expected Jesus to return and establish a kingdom for his followers.

With this design in hand, biblical scholars went to work on reconstructing a past set in Palestine. The repetition of this genealogy could rise on the level of structure, with the history of Israel including that of Christianity. If the title of August Klostermann's account suggested a conclusion with the 'restoration' under Ezra and Nehemiah, the story sprang ahead, on the final page, to close with Jesus and the church.[15] Bernhard Stade's massive *Geschichte des Volkes Israel* also encompassed the rise of Christianity.[16] Covering much the same material, Eduard König called his work *Geschichte des Reiches Gottes bis auf Jesus Christus*, which ended as promised by its title.[17] Yet such a chronological horizon did more than merely demonstrate a sensitivity to the real genealogy of a Christianity stemming from Judaism, itself rooted in Israel and Judah. Rather, this very structure betrayed two fundamental claims operative throughout the historiographic corpus as a whole, which became manifest in content: the rift between Israel and Judaism, and the culmination of Israelite history and religion in the Christian faith.

First, the underlying narrative advanced across these histories marked two essential periods for the past of ancient Israel, a juxtaposition once formulated as Hebraism vis-à-vis Judaism.[18] Although the standard periodization came to contrast Hebrews, Israelites and Jews, the more freighted segmentation split the latter two: the political autonomy of the two kingdoms (Israel and Judah) versus the religious community of post-state Judaism.[19] Rudolf Kittel therefore argued a work devoted to the era after deportation would properly constitute a history of the Jews and hence demand a corresponding title.[20] Yet more than nomenclature divided ancient Israel from later Judaism. As another writer wrote, '[t]he history of Judaism thus begins not with Moses but with the Babylonian captivity. However, Judaism is not merely the continuation of Israelite history but a churchly construct [*Gebilde*] on the basis of a nationality [*Volkstum*] artificially animated once again'.[21] Channelling the biblical texts themselves, a third even called the downfall of the southern kingdom the 'death' of the people of Israel.[22] So came the crucial moment of separation for this historiography.

Any number of arguments could sever the tie between these Israelites and Jews. Data frequently mustered to demonstrate a disruption included, inter alia, the vernacular transition from Hebrew to Aramaic, and a quantitative shift in the standards for measures, weights and calendars.[23] Further still, a different dissevering assertion divided the people from the place, stressing the disconnection of geography for the Jews. 'Quite literally the ground had been snatched from beneath the feet of the nation', contended Carl Heinrich Cornill, of Königsberg, 'which was therefore obliged to seek another ground and foundation, and this was necessarily religious'.[24] Centred on the separation of nation and land, and a related revolution during exile, one major line of inquiry thus examined the representation of feasts and sacrifices in the Hebrew Bible, arguing that Judaism fractured the natural bond of people and religion to the land, to the rhythm of seasons and agriculture.[25] While the elimination of a national-political autonomy and the collateral expulsion from Palestine tore the continuity between Israel and Judaism, Persian and especially Hellenistic influence sundered it even further, transforming Judaism all the more.[26]

If the basic plot remained the same across this corpus, the chronological and geographical scope of the narration could still exhibit variation. The history of Israel could commence – in structure and/or content – with the conquest of Palestine or exodus from Egypt,[27] the Hebrew/pre-Israelite period or its prehistory,[28] the Palaeolithic[29] or even the (biblical) cosmogony.[30] By the same token, this history could conclude – and therefore that of Judaism start – with deportations by the Neo-Babylonian Empire under Nebuchadnezzar II, when the Kingdom of Judah became the Province of Yehud (ca. 586 BCE),[31] the return of deportees during the Achaemenid Empire (ca. 539 BCE),[32] the conquest of Alexander the Great and rise of Hellenism (ca. 330 BCE),[33] the occupation of Jerusalem and destruction of the second temple under Titus (70 CE),[34] the Siege of Masada (73 CE)[35] or the expulsion of Jews by Hadrian following the Third Jewish–Roman War, in the Bar Kokhba Revolt (132–135 CE).[36] Consequently, the scope extended several centuries at both extremities. Such variance notwithstanding, these accounts shared a centre of attraction in the connection of the people to the land, from the political consolidation under the monarchy to the downfall of the southern kingdom. Whatever the cut-off for the upper limit, this historiography cut Judaism off from Israel in the end.

Second, a claim across this corpus connected early Christianity to ancient Israel. Far more than mere descendent – one element among others in a series –

the Christian religion constituted its apotheosis. In his history of Israel, which extended through the Jewish–Roman Wars, Hermann Guthe redescribed Jesus as 'the consummator of the divine content of the Israelite religion'.[37] In the preface to his volume on ancient Israel, from its origins up to exile, delivered in the framework of the American Lectures on the History of Religion, Karl Budde also tied the two:

> If the shortest possible line was to be drawn between the starting point and the goal, it must be all the clearer that this line is a straight one, that the way by which the unique development of the religion of Israel progressed, notwithstanding all apparent deflections and zigzags, really led consistently, necessarily, wisely, and triumphantly upward, and at the point where these lectures stop already opens a vista of the consummation in the Gospel of Jesus Christ.[38]

Whether or not the question of Christian origins fell within the chronological confines of a given historiographic venture, this trajectory oft emerged explicitly – and persisted as a presupposed conviction, even when not expressed. As a result, the Christian religion was deeply intertwined with that of Israel.

But standing between ancient Israel and formative Christianity was early Judaism. Whatever the juncture assigned, the eventual severance of Israelites and Jews, of Judah and Judaism, helped to facilitate the fusion of the Christian faith to the history of Israel. As one distinguished scholar asserted, Judaism 'is full of new impulses, and has an entirely different physiognomy from that of Hebrew antiquity, so much so that it is hard even to catch a likeness', whereas '[t]he Gospel develops hidden impulses of the Old Testament, but it is a protest against the ruling tendency of Judaism'.[39] Instead of a direct continuation, a progressive development or a step in the same direction, formative Christianity nourished itself – according to this telling – on an older source of inspiration: (early) prophetic religion. Karl Marti thus concluded, 'Jesus passed over the later form of the Jewish religion in the law, and went back to the prophets. He recognized in them living religion and His spiritual kindred'.[40] Despite divergence in delineation of this lineage – whether through or more around the Jewish community – the Christian faith was bound to the best of ancient Israel. At the *fin de siècle*, a number of scholars began to grant greater attention to continuities between Christianity and Judaism; nevertheless, the narrative of going backwards to go forwards – as well as higher – still prevailed. Even a major proponent of this venture to disentangle the exact relationship between early Jewish and Christian communities could dedicate a volume to pursuing such entanglement, declaring Judaism 'the real matrix of the gospel', and nonetheless maintain that '[t]he gospel possessed by the earliest community is a fresh sprout from the old, all-but-withered root of Old Testament prophecy'.[41] This conflict of historicist and theological values in accessing the past proved endemic to the study of Christian origins.

These two claims proved powerful indeed, directing the overall narrative of such writings on the past, which remained impervious to assaults from empirical data and theoretical innovation. If the specific course of ancient Israel could change in presentation – as the latest results from newer sources and reappraisals of the old were brought to bear on reconstruction of the past – the final destination stayed consistent. Ultimately, the history of Israel produced a universalized, ethical monotheism, not least through inspired prophetic individuals, which represented the highest form of religion among contemporaneous peoples and saw revival, much later, in the person of Jesus and formative Christianity. Among the numerous impediments that forced a redirecting of the historiographical path to arrive at this one endpoint ranked conclusions reached through an internal, literary criticism of the biblical texts themselves. The ability of these fundamental claims to endure even radical reconstructions reveals their true tenacity – these theological pretensions being less rewritten than written around.

The finds of historical criticism increasingly supported a developmental, rather than degenerative, account of ancient Israel. Integrating decades of research in that venerable tradition of *philologia sacra*, critical work on biblical texts exploited any number of tensions, omissions and repetitions to separate their underlying sources and rearrange them in a chronological order of composition. Instead of setting the so-called priestly law at the dawn of antique Israel, one disruptive thesis placed it at the twilight – succeeding the 'classical' prophets – and maintained that the biblical tradition, with its claims and jeremiads of continued transgression and correction, had in fact betrayed a retrojection of later ideals onto an imagined, counterfactual, still more ancient past. Julius Wellhausen, who wrought the classic formulation of this theory along with its effects for reconstructing the past, posed the problem thus: 'whether that law [of Moses] is the starting point for the history of ancient Israel, or rather not for that of Judaism, i.e. of the religious communion which survived the destruction of the nation by the Assyrians and Chaldæans'.[42] The thesis *lex post prophetas*, which had already circulated in the upper echelons of international scholarship during the 1860s, gained forceful traction by the 1880s, as more descriptive histories of Israel appeared. As the theory quickly took hold, this new account of the biblical literature yielded a new one of the biblical past – one that denied the fundamental narrative of the biblical tradition itself and claimed, instead, the emergence of the priestly law only towards Israel's very end. Reaching beyond the ivory tower's highest chambers of textual dissection, reserved for specialists, it first scandalized the public.

No matter this reshuffling of sources and the dramatic rewriting of Israel's past that it occasioned, the essential Christian narrative reigned supreme. The kind of literary criticism deployed by liberal theology did indeed destabilize a number of assertions set forth in the Hebrew Bible, deducing a discrepancy between the past as it 'really' was and as distorted by tradition, but the grander course of history stayed intact by preservation of certain elemental claims: namely, the distinctiveness of Israelite religion and its perpetuation, nay perfection, through the Christian faith. This new rendering of early Israel recounted the gradual rise of a primitive people, not its fall from a holy law. These more anthropological accounts envisioned a Semitic people tied to language, land and god. Invoking the noted German philologist transplant to Oxford Friedrich Max Müller, the Swiss Alfred Bertholet quoted, '[W]hat constitutes the ideal unity of a nation lies far more in the intellectual factors, in religion and language, than in common descent and common blood', and then expanded on this notion, also operative in Israel, 'that binds the god to a land and to a people'.[43] True, the prophets in this revised narration of the past did dissolve a natural union of deity and people, 'sever[ing] the natural bond between them, and put in its place a relation depending on conditions, conditions of a moral character', which made them 'the spiritual destroyers of the old Israel'.[44] Yet, as Bernhard Duhm declared, 'The entire content of the prophetic religion is quintessentially expressed, positively, in the formula: Israel, the people of Yahweh and Yahweh, the people of God'.[45] The connection of religion to morality became the hallmark of this ancient people. Furthermore, this ethical innovation – promoted by great inspired personalities – applied to the individual as well. 'In the prophetic age, the longer, the more decisively', opined another exegete, 'Israel's faith becomes an ethically purifying and renewing power for the life of the nation and the individual'.[46] Olden prophecy, so this historiography, supplied the firm foundation for Jesus and his movement – on the other side of Judaism. In the demise of a national-political autonomy and the rise of a religious community, historicizing philologists discerned three major trends: a consolidation of the law, a promotion of individual piety and an extension of universalistic perspective. This nexus then provided raw materials for the development of Judaism as well as Christianity, which allowed for affirmation of the Christian narrative, with its revival of ancient Israel's true religion – that of the prophets. Universalism, piety and law thus protruded from the rubble of ancient Israel, the building blocks for the subsequent developments of early Judaism and, some half millennium later, formative Christianity.

Whether explicit, intended or not, the design of these endeavours paved the way for Israel to run into Christianity – even if the new arrangement of sources did alter the course of Israelite history itself. The theological components of inner piety and universalist perspective supported a heavy load in this regard. By contrast, Judaism reportedly came to consist almost entirely of the law, an object of scorn for many a Protestant, anti-Catholic scholar. Significantly, the arguments advanced to detach a prophetic (mostly pre-exilic) ancient Israel from the later Jewish community – the change in vernacular from Hebrew to Aramaic, the geographical disconnection from land, the want of an independent political existence and the separation of religion and nature through an expanded cultic apparatus – provided little disruption for the connection of that same Israel to an early Christianity, a religion reliant on Greek, detached from specific geography, lacking a political manifestation and disengaged from nature. (Ethnicity also bound Israelites to Jews, though not to many Christians.) In this way, the criteria for separating pre-exilic Israel from post-exilic Judaism did not remain in force for uniting it to Christianity. Rather, the 'spirit' of Israel at its best – in the form of prophetic religion – lived on in the Christian faith. Uriel Tal thus observes 'the general theological tendency of scholarly research in that period that Christianity was the legitimate successor of ancient Israel, with all its claims and prerogatives, charged with the task of developing and preserving the ethical elements in the religion of the prophets and in the psalms, the finest flower of the Israelite religion before it degenerated'.[47] Even with a relocation of 'the law' in reconstructions – and the dramatic retelling of an ancient past that came with it – the distinctiveness of Israel stood strong, as did its legacy in Christianity.

In fact, historiographers employed this genealogy to warrant the very study of ancient Israel. Not only did *Alttestamentler* increasingly have to vindicate their ventures as a properly historical endeavour, but they also felt compelled to defend its import for theology, as a discipline and enterprise.[48] A long line of Christian thought had proved ambivalent, if not hostile, to the Hebrew scriptures, a position tracing back to antiquity itself. This debate would reach a high point in the early 1920s, when the formidable church historian Adolf von Harnack recommended their removal from the canon altogether. The New Testament should thus become the lone source of Christian theology, thereby excluding Jews and Israelites from any equal status even in the study of the past – a programme that breathed new life into the ghost of Marcion, a second-century 'heretic', whom Harnack himself examined in an 1870 essay and a 1921 tome.[49]

Decades earlier, however, specialists in the field perceived the need to plead a case for such pursuits. Identifying the history of Israelite religion with the theology of the Old Testament, declaring the task of such a 'discipline' to be description of the religious and ethical content of the Old Testament locating the correlate of this assignment in description of that of the New Testament, and equating the two in tandem with 'the history of the biblical religion' or 'biblical theology', Marti deemed these inquiries essential to Christian preachers.[50] More than merely accent the importance of ancient Israel's religion for the Apostles and Reformers, he further emphasized the gospel as its product and 'the consummate end point of the entire religious development of Israel', which meant the New Testament was only comprehensible with a knowledge of the Old.[51] In the same way, Stade grounded such scholarship in its contribution to an understanding of Christian history.[52] The most immediate – or at least nominal – interest in Israel depended on its connection to Christianity.

In the end, this historiographic corpus affirmed the line of succession from Israel to Christianity – at the expense of Judaism. For the time of the German Empire, no matter the diachronic change in empirical data, methodological approach or theoretical framework introduced to the long tradition of writing Israel's past, on the one hand, and in spite of the synchronic variance in delimiting the purview of that history or in reconstructing finer details, on the other, the thrust of these accounts reinforced the separation between ancient Israel and the Jewish people, and upheld the realization of Israelite history in the Christian faith. The spiritual patrimony of Israel became loosed from ethnic people and physical place. Accordingly, Cornill could conclude his *History of the People of Israel* with a view of Israel surviving domination and transcending time and space, even becoming 'the heir of Rome'.[53] By pinning the past of ancient Israel to that of its religion, identifying the essence of that religion with individual piety as preached by inspired prophetic personalities and divesting Israel of its ethnic, political and geographic properties, these Protestant Europeans therefore made 'their' history into 'ours'. This genealogy then justified the study of an ancient oriental culture. The connection of this old Semitic people to a transnational Christian faith – as a means of understanding origins, comprehending scripture and improving an ethical life – created a stake in that past of millennia prior. As the world changed rapidly at the *fin de siècle*, both in the German Empire and abroad, this interest in ancient Israel led beyond the imagined world of texts to a real one – that of modern Palestine.

Palestine Past in the Present

A sacred history had drawn pilgrims to the holy lands for centuries. Even at the *fin de siècle*, well into the supposed age of secularization, a deep and abiding religious concern with the *terra sancta* pushed attention of Christian writers thither, as expanding opportunities for travel, knowledge and experience exerted a pull upon them thence. But it was a Palestine past that often drove this interest. A biblical past – the origins of 'our history' and 'our civilization' – captured this imagination. 'Whoever discerns in holy scripture the history of God's revelation for our salvation', announced the tenth edition of *Biblische Geographie für Schulen und Familien*, 'must indeed also have an interest in the lands in which this history took place'.[54] Frants Buhl, the Danish Semitist at Leipzig, may have distinguished his more technical, ancient geography from the biblical sort and popular kind, yet he still hoped it might offer an aid to readers of the Bible to visualize the land of holy history.[55] Via a vivid description of this place as encountered in travel, wrote another, 'many an otherwise dark word of scripture appears, on its own, in an entirely new light'.[56] The animating interest in Palestine oft concerned its ancient days. A present place thus promised access to that past.

At the turn of the twentieth century, the literature on the land exploded. A vast bibliographic undertaking counted nigh three thousand publications on things Palestine, printed in many lands and languages, between 1895 and 1909 alone.[57] Topics ranged from history (from antiquity into the modern period) alongside historical geography and topography through archaeology, epigraphy and numismatics beyond contemporaneous politics, customs, religions, languages and colonies to geology, climatology, meteorology, zoology, botany, cartography and travel. Showing a continuity in the land's religious lure, some of these explorations reckoned pilgrims to their forebears as they outlined the history of the field. A common account of the grand trajectory in contributions made to the knowledge of Palestine moved rather quickly from antiquity (beginning with the Egyptian Amarna letters of the second millennium BCE) through the early Byzantine period into the Crusades until it emphasized the import of the Reformation – with the incipient 'scientific' interest engendered in things biblical – and then stressed the significance of European expeditions in the second half of the eighteenth and first half of the nineteenth centuries, all before marking the transition from individuals to institutions as the movers and shakers of research in the final third of that same century.[58] In fact, some reports even evoked a sense of rediscovery. 'Nearly half a century has passed by', said Guthe in 1903, 'since Palestine was delivered from the oblivion into which it had fallen for trade and transit, and was once again moved into the horizon of Western peoples'.[59] Information on the land had, of course, come down since antiquity, largely via travelogues. Reinhold Röhricht, for example, published a comprehensive bibliography spanning from 330 to 1878 that included thousands of entries.[60] However, transformations both qualitative and quantitative did indeed occur in such literature as the nineteenth became the twentieth century: whether produced atop the hills of Jerusalem or underneath the lindens of Berlin, these publications did proliferate and diffuse throughout the German Empire and beyond.

Across the genres of geography and compendium, of treatise and handbook, much of the German-speaking work on Palestine reinforced the same theological narrative – one not only reflected in but also constituted by the aforementioned ventures in the history of ancient Israel and that of the Hebrew Bible. The heritage of faith – biblical history – had since resumed in Christianity and made its way to Europe. Even a researcher so devoted to the place as Peter Thomsen could nonetheless maintain that 'Christianity, the succession of Jesus, consists not in confinement at certain localities, in their veneration, which so easily turns into superstition, but in life according to his example, in his spirit, and such life is divorced from time and space'.[61] In the same way, Hugo Gressmann conjured up a Jesus 'who belongs not to the Jews but to humanity, not to Palestine but to the world. His essence [*Wesen*] is above space and time and not absorbed by the narrow and bounded circumstances of his land or of his era'.[62]

The effect had further consequences. Such a realignment through religious genealogy – a historical cohesion begun in Palestine yet transferred to Christian Europe – fractured other continuities back in the eastern Mediterranean, in materiality, geography, ethnicity and the like. Furthermore, the idea of stasis – where social classes, ethnic groups or allegedly isolated areas had missed the boat of progress, whether that progress be seen as sociological or technological, economic or religious – suggested these entities could offer penetrating insight into archaic ages passed, stuck in the past as they were. In fact, a long theological tradition had sought to overcome temporal distance with the geographic kind.[63] The land's stated significance thus often lay in its historical connection to a specifically European Christianity and its hermeneutical power for understanding the biblical past. This conception of a living past in the present kindled a blaze of scientific inquiry into peoples and place alike: the objects lying underneath the ground together with the people treading on it were of more significance for what they said about the Palestine of yore, about the biblical world.

If Napoleon Bonaparte's invasion of Egypt, in 1798, had opened a new phase in relations between the Middle East and Europe, the opening of the ground in Palestine for archaeological excavations began a new chapter in the production of knowledge on the land. Whatever the preferred heuristic benchmarks for dividing the history of Palestine in this period (the Ottoman–Egyptian Wars, the Treaty of Paris, etc.), the foundation of the Palestine Exploration Fund (PEF), in 1865, surely marked a new depth of research – a transition from individuals to institutions and from what the eye could spy to what the spade could strike.[64] A number of foreign institutes were opened and expeditions launched in Palestine itself from this point onwards, with many supporting bodies established back in the mother countries: they included the British Society of Biblical Archaeology (1870), which folded into the Royal Asiatic Society of Great Britain and Ireland after the Great War; the short-lived American Palestine Exploration Society (1870); the DPV (1877); the Russian Imperial Orthodox Palestine Society (Императорское Православное Палестинское Общество, 1882); the French Dominican École pratique d'études bibliques, since renamed the École biblique et archéologique française de Jérusalem (1890); the American School for Oriental Study and Research in Palestine, later called the American School of Oriental Research, now the W.F. Albright Institute of Archaeological Research (1900); and the DEIAHL (ca. 1900).[65] Besides cooperation, these efforts also generated contest, a sense of needing to keep up with the Indiana Joneses: 'Today a delightful [*erfreulich*] competition of all nations prevails for the exploration of the Holy Land', Thomsen rhapsodized.[66]

Like the Little Corporal's earlier campaign, the empirical enterprise as promoted by these institutes implied political ambitions, economic interests and visions of national glory – a venture further enmeshed in the not dissociated rise of archaeology as a discipline, for both the classical and Near Eastern lands, as well as in the larger specialization and professionalization of scholarship more broadly.[67] These international dynamics affected national exploits abroad, turning fellow foreign citizens in Palestine into colleagues as well as competitors. Defending the progress of German-speaking scholarship in 1881, for instance, the Swiss orientalist at Tübingen, Albert Socin, noted the more restricted focus of the French on archaeology and art history, as opposed to, say, the domains of natural science or geography.[68] But the British furnished greater competition. He explained the many contributions of the English (and Americans) through their marked devotion to the Bible. Unlike much of this underdeveloped, popularizing literature on Palestine, however, which frequently neglected the fruits of other nations' labours, German exploits – so Socin – proudly prioritized that crucial trait of *Wissenschaftlichkeit*, or scientificness.

By no means unrelated to questions of general interest or perceived religious relevance, financing, as always, also played a central role. 'Now, Germany is certainly no land of the Lords and Ladies', another added pithily.[69] Guthe, too, permitted a bit of publicity in his volume *Palästina*, arguing more support would be required to determine just how much the study of modern Palestine could reveal about the ancient history of the land, especially with reference to the Bible.[70] Capital the everlasting question, an expressed concern for funding to assist in subsidizing such activities abroad came in the first remarks of the very first issue of *Zeitschrift des Deutschen Palästina-Vereins*' (*ZDPV*), and remained a constant theme thereafter.[71] The same society continuously sought to strike a balance with its publisher between 'purer' science and pecuniary alongside popular concerns.[72] Of course, no small amount of cynicism may have been involved as well, using the Good Book to sell other ones and secure the necessary funds. But religious matters did act as a powerful force for such pursuits in Palestine. After all, millenarians and missionaries undertook the antecedent antiquarian efforts in that land which they deemed holy.[73]

Indeed, the germanophone institutes and individuals also had a religious stake in the real estate of holy history. With the British PEF as both role model and rival, the Germans, together with Swiss associates, founded the DPV, a society that had its roots in the Deutsche Morgenländische Gesellschaft (DMG), itself derived from the Versammlung der Deutschen Philologen und Schulmänner.[74] As Sabina Mangold has observed, '[i]n contrast to the DMG, the DPV was less a "self-help" society of scholars than an association of small and large "patrons" for support of scholarly ventures in a field that appeared to be of vital interest not only scientifically but also culturally and with regard to (foreign) political affairs'.[75] Despite close ties between the two, the DPV consumed a greater slice of non-academia from the start, including any number of teachers, pastors, civil servants, publishers and merchants. Although perhaps more muted than that of its anglophone counterparts, a religious tenor echoed here as well. The British and American equivalents certainly signalled a bold biblical drive. Hence, the very motto of the PEF, already announced in its first printed periodical, read, 'A society for the accurate and systematic investigation of the archaeology, topography, geology and physical geography, natural history, manners and customs of the Holy Land, for biblical illustration'.[76] Likewise, in the American Palestine Exploration Society's earliest statement, the chairman argued that its work 'appeals to the religious sentiment of the Christian and the Jew alike; it is of interest to the scholar in almost every branch of linguistic, historical, or physical investigation; but its supreme importance is for the illustration and defense of the Bible'.[77]

Yet the DPV did not play coy about its own allegiance, even if the express ends were less apologetic. The very founding of the institution placed a premium on the link between its labours and the Bible. Created 'to promote the scientific exploration of Palestine in all its connections and to disperse participation therein among wider circles' (§2), the statutes of the DPV directed two separate operations for fulfilment of its aims: the publication of a journal (§3a) and academic inquiries into Palestine itself (§3b).[78] In addition to reviews of the relevant literature, domestic and foreign alike (§4b), and both statistical and political updates on the current state of Palestine (§4c), the journal was tasked with printing 'scientific treatises on topographical, ethnographical, natural-scientific, historical and archaeological questions from the field of the exploration of Palestine and of the adjoining lands insofar as they come into consideration for the promotion of the study of the Bible [*Bibelkunde*]' (§4a). For execution of its second operation, the statutes recommended the recruitment of German residents already in the land, the activation of academic interests amongst travellers to Palestine and the collection of resources for it to sponsor expeditions (§5). A decennium after the DPV's foundation, amidst the struggle over the journal's proper contents, the executive committee [*der geschäftsführende Ausschuss*] alluded to these statutes with their dual devotion to scientific inquiry and support for a better understanding of the Bible: 'But the latter can only be fostered through serious scientific work in the true sense', it maintained.[79] Ten years later, the committee once again affirmed – in a plea for further support – the primary place of a biblical learning among its other objectives.[80] Certainly, any number of topics came into view, whether the recent history of Jerusalem, the state of Jewish colonies, past and present precipitation in Palestine, a travel report from ca. 1600 or the meaning of *eretz Israel*.[81] The early call for a *Palästinabibliothek* was intended to house such a range of material.[82] Nevertheless, alongside geography and topography the literature published in the journal largely skewed towards the ancient past in general, and the biblical one in particular, thereby mostly concealing matters of contemporaneous Palestine.[83] The Bible not only sparked initial interest in the land but continued to fan the flames of exploration, too.

In the DEIAHL, that fire burned all the brighter. With the consecration, on Reformation Day 1898, of the Lutheran Church of the Redeemer – which also featured none other than the Kaiser – came the expressed desire for a centre devoted to Protestant study of the Holy Land in the Holy City itself.[84] If the DPV was rather non-exclusive, both confessionally and nationally, and yet still flowed within the stronger currents of a liberal theology along with cultural Protestantism, the DEIAHL was a specifically, confessedly, German Lutheran institution. The records of the Protestant church conference that established the institute explicitly referred to the work conducted by Catholics along with the 'inter-confessional' kind undertaken by the DPV, which then made grounding such a centre 'a duty of honour for the German Lutheran Church'.[85] Founded 'to foster, encourage and direct, in the domain of biblical and churchly ancient studies, the connections between the sites of holy history and between scholarly research and the interest of Christian piety in the Protestant church', this venture represented a joint effort by the German regional churches, aimed at supporting 'young theologians' in particular.[86] Evoking the Reformation, the first director drew a straight line from the translation of Holy Scripture to its original languages, and then extended the logic from a knowledge of those languages to a knowledge of the land.[87] The DEIAHL, complete with library and museum, was thus designed to organize trips, orchestrate lectures and coordinate classes.[88] Alongside any scientific dividends, it placed emphasis on the transfer of knowledge and experience back to the motherland, stressing a practical exploitation in schools and churches, and accenting the popular dimension for any publishable papers.[89] Even more so than with the DPV, the DEIAHL set its sights on a Palestine of the 'Christian' past.[90]

These two institutions often worked in tandem. As early as 1904, studies from the DEIAHL started appearing in the *ZDPV*, while the latter reviewed the former's yearbook from 1907 onwards. Institutionally, the statutes of the DEIAHL specified that a member of its board be a (Protestant) member on that of the DPV as well, and though not directed by its resolutions, the DPV pulled the director of the DEIAHL onto its own grand committee in 1903.[91]

Perhaps unsurprisingly, the archaeological endeavour had a principal attraction to a past related to the Bible. Rather than, say, the Byzantine period or even the Roman one, the earliest German-speaking excavations in the land mostly sought to unearth information on the more ancient Israel.[92] Once the missionary, modeller and architect Conrad Schick happened upon the Siloam Tunnel inscription (1880), the DPV-sponsored excavations in Jerusalem by the Leipzig Old Testament scholar and Palestine specialist Guthe (1881) and – with further support from the Kaiser as well as the Deutsche Orient-Gesellschaft (DOG) – in Megiddo (Tell el-Mutesellim) by the Templer settler, cartographer, architect and engineer Gottlieb Schumacher (1903–5). Such efforts also encompassed research on synagogue ruins in Galilee by Carl Watzinger and architects Ernst Hiller and Heinrich Kohl, funded by the DOG (1905–7). Exceptionally, the Catholic priest Paul Karge pursued prehistory at Tell el-'Oreimeh/Tel Kinrot (Khirbat al-Minya), thanks to financial assistance from the Görres-Gesellschaft zur Pflege der katholischen Wissenschaften (1911).[93] After the nominal end of the First World War, this so-called 'biblical archaeology' would flourish in Mandatory Palestine – albeit less by Austrians and Germans than through the British and Americans.

Apart from that which rested underneath the soil, what stood upon its surface acted as a window to the ancient, biblical world. Gustaf Dalman, *né* Marx, director of the DEIAHL, described the Holy Land as 'overabundant in instruction for whoever grasps [how] to learn, who knows to see the characteristic in things great and small, [to see] the old in the new, to wander in the Arabic land the paths of the patriarchs, of Moses, and of the prophets and of the Son of God'.[94] Bursting with a miscellany of drawings and descriptions, of photographs and maps, the Bible atlas edited by Ludwig Johannes Frohnmeyer and Immanuel Benzinger declared the relative constancy between the plant and animal worlds of Palestine, past and present, which justified the juxtaposition of representations and biblical references.[95] Side by side with flora and fauna, geology and geography, topography and climate, works on Palestine could also set people for observation.[96] While some such overviews did encompass Europeans – particularly German Jewish and Christian colonists – in grander histories of the land or updates on recent developments, the gaze mostly gravitated towards Arabs, Bedouin and peasants for leverage on the ancient past. 'It is almost as though the tide of time has in these lands rushed past without a trace', wrote Gressmann; 'The Canaanites disappeared, the Jews were killed or deported, the Arabs took their place, and yet much has stayed as it was since time immemorial'.[97] If the past was a foreign country, in the German view of modern Palestine they did things quite the same there.

Two separable lines of sight allowed this ethnographic eye to look at the present and see the distant past: the 'Semitic' and the 'primitive'. Although frequently conflated, these two categories represented distinct epistemological premises. Operative, often powerfully, in the historiographic corpus on ancient Israel, the logic supporting the comparison of Semitic peoples past and present proceeded from a principle of genealogical relations, whereby an ontological 'type' shared common properties in ethnicity, language and cultural practice. Such a postulate thus resided in the realm of biology or homology, not analogy or parallels.[98] Even in literature on Palestine whose scope extended far beyond the ancient history of Israel, this dual claim of Semitic peoples bearing an essential unity and, further, doing so through all time could see explicit formulation.[99] The second rationale for watching people of the land to visualize antiquity derived from a notion of primitivity. Accordingly, a theory of universal stages in development warranted the equation of peoples absent genealogical relations. A relative place on the imagined ladder of human progress then permitted comparison, often irrespective of chronology or geography. As explained by the aforementioned atlas, 'on so many points, the Orient has stood still across the centuries, and many institutions of the farmers and Bedouin are here so primitive that they could hardly have been more primitive in ancient times, and the depiction of the Bible fits many customs and practices so splendidly that we may quite safely presuppose them as similar in ancient times'.[100] The same supposition thus accounted for the claim, quite prominent in (Protestant) histories of Israel, that since antiquity 'the Jewish religion has never altered; its essential character has remained unaffected by any changes'.[101] Through a sort of synergy, these conceptions meant that a walk through Palestine could constitute, with some qualification, a step into the biblical world itself.

In fact, complaints consistently arose throughout this literature for all the transformations in the land from recent years. A sense of urgency set in: the dynamic Occident would soon sully a static Orient. The first prospectus of the PEF, issued in 1869, diagnosed in consequence, 'Many of the ancient and peculiar customs of Palestine are fast vanishing before the increasing tide of Western manners, and in a short time the exact meaning of many things which find their correspondences in the Bible will have perished'.[102] Max Löhr, professor in Breslau and early collaborator with Dalman at the DEIAHL, criticized civilizing missions for not promoting the local inhabitants' knowledge of their own history, language and culture, which generated 'a regrettable youth, a spiritual hybrid race [*Zwittergeschlecht*], no longer Arabs and yet not Europeans by a long shot'.[103] Alongside this anxiety of Western influence on the East, another source of worry faulted the locals themselves for a ruination of antiquity's preservation in the present. A third commentator – who had noted a steady decline in 'the spiritual [*geistige*] culture of the Orient' over the past four hundred years, which fell to its nadir in the nineteenth century – censured the 'illegitimate excavations' of domestic antiquities dealers, while Thomsen decried a populace that 'stands over and against them [sc. monuments and discoveries] blankly or even hostilely, and uses them without compunction for their purposes (new buildings, illicit excavation for sale to foreigners)'.[104] The museum that was contemporary Palestine was therefore quickly crumbling, and in need of conservation.

Jews could pose a problem for these dichotomies, however, whether they were considered either like or unlike their ancient ancestors or native to the land. (Similarly, Eastern Orthodox Christians occupied an ambiguous position between Orient and Occident, between 'them' and 'us'.) Jews themselves could serve as objects of classification. Guthe, for instance, offered an overview of their migration to Palestine, and included not only physical descriptions but also pictures of different types of Jews, from Russia, Poland, Morocco, Yemen, Romania, Bulgaria, Bukhara and from Palestine itself.[105] This side of Jewish history – including the causes of emigration since the Middle Ages, though primarily the nineteenth century – drew no little attention in these works on Palestine. Yet the same history did occasion doubt as to their value for a purchase on the past. Supplying an ethnographic survey of the peoples found in Palestine, Gustav Hölscher argued that ancient Palestinian Judaism had disappeared long ago, and further reasoned, in light of such migration history, that European Jews were no longer 'pure Semites but a mixed race [*Mischrasse*]', which then limited their value for providing insight on the past.[106] Bauer likewise deemed the Jews of Palestine 'less descendants of the original Israelite population than immigrants from Europe'.[107] Nowack struck a more precise balance when he contended, consonant with much of the historiography of antique Israel and early Judaism, that contemporaneous Jews preserved the religious qualities of old but had undergone at least some alteration in other habits and customs through assimilation among other peoples.[108] In consequence, the ancient biblical past may indeed have long lain at the ready, for the perspicacious viewer, in present Palestine, but that past was vanishing, under threat by both foreign and local elements, with misleading lines of sight along the way. The prospect of this view drew no few spectators, be it in person or through publications.

Of course, not each and every individual and institute active in Southwest Asia set as its ultimate aim an extraction of information from modern Palestine – whether from its soil or its citizens – on the strictly biblical past, let alone a confirmation of the Bible's claims. While the multiplex constellation of enterprises, figures and institutions ensured a dissonance of ends and means, an interest in the Holy Land was not, of necessity, a sacred one: it was not purely religious, cultural, national, geopolitical or economic, as though these analytical categories allowed such sharp delineation. Nonetheless, religion, particularly in its more sanitized manifestation as a component of cultural identity or the genealogy of Western civilization, not only energized the imagination of Germans – Jewish, Catholic, Protestant and other – already primed by a knowledge of the Bible and a perceived stake in theological debates, but it also exerted a galvanizing force for action on such concerns.[109] As the controversial cuneiformist Friedrich Delitzsch saw it:

> What is the object of these labours in distant, inhospitable and dangerous lands? ... Why this rivalry among nations for the purpose of securing, each for itself, these desolate hills – and the more the better – in which to excavate? And from what source, on the other hand, is derived the self-sacrificing interest, ever on the increase, that is shown on both sides of the ocean, in the excavations in Babylonia and Assyria? To either question there is one answer, which, if not exhaustive, nevertheless to a great extent tells us the cause and aim: it is *the Bible*.[110]

In a similar fashion, Hiller recommended the establishment (or re-establishment) of a research institute in Syria-Palestine similar to the branches of the German Imperial Archaeological Institute in Rome and Athens, since those already running in Jerusalem – whether German, French, Italian or Russian – 'are all led in a one-sidedly theological manner and, despite the great services they have rendered thus far, do not seem to be in the position to perform the task in a perfect way'.[111] These two statements testify to the durable strength of that genealogical cord, manufactured over generations and tightened by a globalizing world, which interwove the strands of cultural identity and religious belonging – a tie that bound together East and West, past and present, and pulled both learned and laity to Palestine. Its import lay in the past, a past continued in Europe's Christianity.

The Colonization of Place and Past

As the national was Protestantized, so the religious was scientificized. Now, liberal theologians in particular had often seen 'theology' and 'science' as entirely compatible, an intellectual defence against the challenges posed by other ways of knowing.[112] Theological questions could, should and would find their answers through secular science. Yet even ostensibly unrelated or allegedly areligious academic explorations could bear the mark of theological concerns: secular research animated, at times unwittingly, by the spirit of religion. While 'the Protestant church became identified with the German state and thereby became part of the secular realm', theological modalities – tied as they were to the state and the history of knowledge – had constructed the apparatus of *Wissenschaft* itself, and structured other, secular disciplines as well.[113] Beyond the clear entanglement in a far older tradition of Christian and humanistic learning – of biblical and classical erudition – the models and the methods, pursuits and practices characteristic of such interests were diffused across, or built into, the human sciences more broadly. Linguistic explorations sought relationships both between and among 'Hamitic', 'Semitic' and 'Japhetic' languages through a biblical lens of monogenesis and degeneration; literary study concentrated on hermeneutics based on in-depth interpretation of meaning, mind and spirit; and textual criticism promised to recover lost archetypes, if not original texts themselves. For this reason, historians have noted the religious freight borne by research on mythology and even history itself.[114] In work on ancient Palestine, similar frames of reference determined which texts qualified for philological treatment, which sites merited archaeological excavation and which pasts deserved their stories told – even in public, non-confessional, historicist endeavours. The legacy of especially Protestant learning therefore disciplined supposedly non-religious fields, becoming the unmarked epistemology in the world of German science. These secular spheres of knowledge – philology, archaeology, history – then found themselves, in turn, deployed to validate religious claims and ventures.

As Christian theologians, church historians, biblical scholars and orientalists – even (perhaps especially) of the undogmatic, liberal, cultural Protestant variety – laboured in the past of Israel and Judah, they seized it for themselves. While some historiographers did draw bold, hard lines running from antique Israel directly into a culminating account of Christianity, others detailed only single chapters in the periods preceding Christian origins, yet even they mostly left the larger sketch implicit, through their portraits of prophecy and law, individuals and ethics, nation and the Greeks. Together, they split Israel from Judaism and spliced it with Christianity – a genealogy of religion achieved by categorical transition, from ethnicity (Semites) via nation (Israelites and Judahites) through ancestry (Jews) to spirit (Christians). In fact, Harnack extended the narrative even further, to reach its apex in Protestantism.[115] However, Judaism hindered any genealogy of a progressive, self-contained history so quickly transferred onto 'European culture'. This living, if marginal(ized), religion reminded of other pretenders to Israel's legacy and of Christianity's oriental origins. Indeed, other historiographical roads went untaken. Susannah Heschel has thus dissected counterhistories of the ancient past, first by Christian scholars writing on ancient Judaism and then – as a counter to those counters – by Jewish scholars writing on Christian origins.[116] Focusing on the figure of Abraham Geiger, she availed herself of postcolonial theory to reveal the reversal of power relations – of viewer and viewed in 'the theological gaze' – as Jews began to write in earnest on the subject. Like the contested relationship between Jesus and Judaism, the debate over Israel's true inheritor emerged in the reviewed historiography, representing another episode in the clash of rival claims to construct the past and to align it with the present. This arrogation of antiquity, which turned 'their' past into 'ours', supplies a further example of history's workability – the power of historical narratives to maintain continuities and discontinuities, to encompass and exclude.[117]

Yet even ancient texts could construct this genealogy. 'We have been led to God through this crucified Christ,' wrote Justin Martyr, in the second century

CE, 'and we are the true spiritual Israel, and the descendants of Judah, Jacob, Isaac and Abraham'.[118] Although Justin represents the first extant writer to designate Christians 'Israel', even in the New Testament Paul himself had sought to reconcile Israel and non-Jews.[119] More than articulations of Christians as the new Israel in a spiritual sense, however, some early texts went so far as to deploy 'ethnic reasoning' for a definition of 'Christianness'.[120] Determining the precise relationship between 'Greeks' and 'Jews' – themselves unstable, contested categories – had remained a persistent, often intense preoccupation of theological reflection for many centuries, long before the nineteenth century. As the modern writers of history under scrutiny read select ancient sources for the historiographic venture, they followed perennial questions, used canonical texts and found answers bequeathed by a long tradition of Christian thought. In this way, theological imperatives, or at least conditions, directed the historical endeavour. Furthermore, these Christian historians reproduced specific claims if not always advanced by, then at least advanceable through, the ancient texts themselves, albeit in altered form. Rather than merely project a narrative of Christianity succeeding Israel (and displacing Judaism in the process) onto some blank, even surface of their sources – the *imprimatura* of the Flemish Masters' panels – they inscribed it atop an existent materiality with its own textures, shades and contours. To switch metaphors, these histories resembled a sort of palimpsest, an over- or re-writing of pretences in the form of ancient history, within the limits of what lay before. Ultimately, such academic ventures rationalized theological pretensions through their interpretive readings of biblical texts and empirical constructions of the past, translating a Christian narrative into hard philological science. The religious became scientificized. This religious self-understanding – reinscribed as the result of unmarked, secular historiography – was then taught especially in faculties of theology at public universities by employees of the German state, who graduated students based upon this knowledge.

The question of these ancient claims reverberating in modern historiography bears on that which Sheldon Pollock has named a 'deep orientalism', where later discourse recapitulates that of an earlier time.[121] In this sense, the histories in question displayed a deeper genealogy – the narrative of Christianity's relationship to Israel – by reflecting assertions already embedded in the ancient texts themselves, which they then readapted or reshaped, but in the end reproduced. Of course, the collection of sources produced, preserved and privileged did not arise outside tradition: not only the what but also the how of interpretation were governed by determinative, if not unquestioned, parameters. If these scholars proved willing to challenge or even upend certain fundamental claims advanced in biblical texts, others doubtless lay beyond dispute. The historicity of the patriarchs, an extensive exodus from Egypt and eisodus into Palestine, original monotheism among the Israelites and Mosaic authorship of the Pentateuch could therefore all come into doubt, whereas the uniqueness of Israel, the statecraft of David or the morality of the prophets – to say nothing of revelation itself, however vaguely construed – did not succumb to disbelief. As Colin Kidd has shown for the Bible and concepts of race, '[t]he human imagination is equally capable of interpreting the Christian scriptures in a racialist as in an anti-racialist manner. It often depends less, it seems, on the logic of the scriptures than on the objectives of the interpreter, or indeed on the logic of the system developed conjointly out of the scriptures and their theological accompaniment'.[122] A wider potential in the ancient texts thus saw later, more restricted activation.

If the historiography of ancient Israel appropriated the past, a proliferating literature on Palestine then colonized a present place by imagination. Whether coming from the libraries of the motherland or from the tells of the holy one, specific forms of knowledge were produced by German researchers, no matter the -ology (phil-, archae-, the-) or -ography (top-, ge-, ethn-). Even the work assembled and assessed, published and patronized through the institutes in Jerusalem betrayed a precious interest in the present for the sake of the past, and in the past for the sake of the present: while the value of modern Palestine lay largely in the insight it afforded into the biblical past, that biblical past then found its worth in connection to the modern Christian, whether in German society at home or civilizing missions abroad. Furthermore, the empirical efforts of excavation and ethnography colonized place as well – perhaps, in the German case, less the physical and more the imagined kind. Such undertakings often overlooked the readily apparent in favour of the conjured. The very landscape itself, whatever rested hidden underneath it and whoever trod upon it, constituted a museum: the biblical past preserved in a present Palestine.

Although certainly not without crucial distinctions, these dimensions of writing about the past and accessing it through the present correspond to Bernard Cohn's investigation of colonial knowledge in India – specifically, his formulation of the historiographic, observational/travel, survey and museological modalities.[123] Cohn has described the occupation of an 'epistemological space' interpreted and rendered significant through categories already to hand. Conceptualizing 'a kind of living fossil bed of the European past', 'a "case" of an earlier civilisation, or a museum of ancient practices, from which earlier stages of universal world history could be recovered', the British not only identified, described and classified ancient ruins and local practices, but also determined the value and meaning of objects – those worth preserving on site, displaying in museums and trading on the market.[124] Even more, Cohn discerns a discourse that centred on India's 'double lack of a history': 'Since it has no documents, dateable records, chronicles, the kinds of materials out of which the West constructed a history of itself, the British were called upon to provide India with a history. In a second sense India had no history as it has not progressed'.[125] This historiography hinged on the binaries of progress and regress, development and degeneration, dynamicity and staticity. If the British sought to navigate the foreign land of India with bearings from the classical and biblical worlds, the later Germans who wrote on Palestine had an orientation still more obvious, drawn as they were to the lands of biblical history, ones with classical connections as well. The attribution of value, to present people or past places, was perhaps all the more pronounced – or uncontested – for this reason. Consequently, the conception of a museum harmonized with the melody of a genealogy of the West. Whether the local populace of Palestine or the Jewish minority back at home, German Christians cast them in supporting roles for their own inquiries, which were directed by a specific view of the past, and with certain implications for the present.

Knowledge production and transfer were selective, their propagation and predominance powered by government support, institutional advantage, financial contributions, social capital and even perceived consensus. Yet the actuality of transfer and production corresponds to the potentiality of their opposites: what was not produced or transferred. This intellectual, and frequently physical, labour united the modern West to the ancient East and, in doing so, divided other potential continuities, be they ethnic, geographic, religious or the like: the past overtook the present. Like renewed reflections on space, which have challenged its conceptualization as neutral, empty or apolitical, recent rumination on silence has analysed it as something other than absence, lack or non-existence. Jay Winter, for example, has theorized 'the category of socially constructed silence' and 'the socially sanctioning activity of silencing'.[126] Closer to the Kaiserreich and Palestine, Rebekka Habermas has bound together transfer and non-transfer to interrogate the structure of relationships between colony and metropole, probing further implications of suppression or 'not-knowing'.[127] Regardless of intentionality, the heavy empirical industry in things Palestine that boomed – from historiography through ethnography to archaeology – amplified certain discourses while also muting others. An ancient past could concern the modern present. The conceived relationships of lauded Hellenes from antiquity to contemporary Greeks, or of exalted Aryans to later Indians, for example, did (and indeed still do) imply consequences, especially around the War of Independence and in the British Empire, respectively.[128] Historiographic ventures – whether they bound or broke connections to the past – carried political, national and economic implications; at the same time, political, national and economic ventures carried historiographic implications. By conceptually incorporating the Eastern Mediterranean into Christian Europe by way of 'history', the production and non-production or the transfer and non-transfer of knowledge on Palestine could allow a present space to disappear. As one of many repercussions, the past drowned out the present.

Intention and effect, however, differ. As this cluster of experts on Palestine – a company of archaeologists and philologists, theologians and church historians, biblical scholars and Semitists, whose lives often showed the fuzzy boundaries between such classifications – sought to build a bridge into 'their' past, whether at home or abroad, be it through texts or tells, they showed slender interest in the doings or drives of empire. Their work left little trace of any aspiration to advance such visions, ambitions or efforts, or to further the kind of colonialism so often caricatured – even if they themselves may have enabled or profited from these pursuits or prejudices. More than anyone else, Suzanne Marchand has detailed – unaccompanied by any aim at blanket exculpation – the complexities, textures and nuances of German orientalist scholarship, including in its relation to imperialism, along the way exploring a frequent aversion to usefulness and also underscoring a 'sympathetic historicism'.[129] Those who devoted themselves to the study of Palestine fit within this matrix. True, Bauer may have enumerated less than flattering qualities of the natives' 'national character' (*der Volkscharakter*), but he painted an appreciative portrait as well, contending that Europeans were often too judgmental in their appraisal of the East, and even inconsistent, since they themselves betrayed a tendency to become 'oriental' after spending time abroad.[130] The Baedeker travel guide edited by Benzinger likewise spent a substantial amount of time exploring the rich diversity of locals' histories, customs and languages. Notwithstanding his problematic attempts at proselytizing, Dalman spent much of his life studying texts, periods and languages outside the standard fare of Old Testament research, leading expeditions all through Palestine, and documenting the minutiae of everyday local life, especially by photography.[131] Although perhaps implicated in the enterprise of empire, such figures were rarely nefarious in their labours, drawn, more often than not, to the land because of its supposed holy history and its place in their own religion. Rather, they were the ones who bothered to dwell in dusty libraries and learn the ancient languages, or left the comforts of home to dig into the earth. These scholars of Palestine may merit, then, a more sympathetic assessment. After all, in view of current events across the globe – from political through economic to social exploitation – we historians who devote ourselves to the past (ancient and modern alike) might also run the risk of silencing the present, and therefore will appreciate a more gracious scrutiny from our own successors a hundred years from now.

Paul Michael Kurtz is a Marie Skłodowska-Curie individual fellow at the University of Cambridge and a postdoctoral research associate at Queens' College, Cambridge. His work centres on the study of the ancient world and its religions in nineteenth- and twentieth-century Germany. In support of his research, Kurtz has received generous funding from the Fulbright Program, German Academic Exchange Service (DAAD), Research Foundation – Flanders (FWO) and American Schools of Oriental Research. His first book, *Kaiser, Christ, and Canaan: The Religion of Israel in Protestant Germany, 1871–1918*, was recently published by Mohr Siebeck.

Notes

I must express my gratitude to Rebekka Habermas for her invitation to contribute to this volume, as well as her insight on the endeavour. For helpful suggestions at the conceptual stages of this project, I am grateful to Suzanne Marchand, Dan Pioske, Harald Samuel, Emiliano Urciuoli and Rebecca Van Hove. I am also obliged to Hermann Spieckerman and Reinhard Kratz for their generous support of this research. Such an inquiry would have been nigh impossible without the tremendous digitalization efforts across the globe; Catherine Bronson supplied me with access to many of these sources. Where possible, the translation comes from official versions; otherwise, I render the German myself.

1. T. Tobler, *Palästina: Nebst anhang der vierten wanderung* (Berlin: Reimer, 1868), 322. The line was added for this reprint: cf. idem, 'Analekten aus Palästina. 9: Meine vierte Wanderung im Jahr 1865', *Das Ausland. Ueberschau der neuesten Forschungen auf dem Gebiete der Natur-, Erd- und Völkerkunde* 39 (1866), 273.
2. A.J. La Vopa, *Fichte: The Self and the Calling of Philosophy, 1762–1799* (Cambridge: Cambridge University Press, 2001), 13; R. Habermas, 'Piety, Power and Powerlessness: Religion and Religious Groups in Germany, 1870–1945', in H.W. Smith (ed.), *The Oxford Handbook of Modern German History* (Oxford University Press, 2001), 459.
3. H. Gunkel, *Israel and Babylon: The Influence of Babylon on the Religion of Israel [A Reply to Delitzsch]*, trans. E.S.B. (Philadelphia, PA: McVey, 1904), 48 [German Original: *Israel und Babylonien: Der Einfluss Babyloniens auf die israelitische Religion* (Göttingen: Vandenhoeck & Ruprecht, 1903)].
4. L. Kamel, *Imperial Perceptions of Palestine: British Influence and Power in the Late Ottoman Times* (London: I.B. Tauris, 2015), 2; see further, inter alia, E. Bar-Yosef, *The Holy Land in English Culture, 1799–1917: Palestine and the Question of Orientalism* (Oxford: Clarendon Press, 2005).
5. Ecclesiastes 12:12, New Revised Standard Version (NRSV).
6. For the history of orientalist scholarship in general, see S.L. Marchand, *German Orientalism in the Age of Empire: Religion, Race, and Scholarship* (Cambridge: Cambridge University Press, 2009); for changes within research on ancient Israel in particular, see P.M. Kurtz, *Kaiser, Christ, and Canaan: The Religion of Israel in Protestant Germany, 1871–1918* (Tübingen: Mohr Siebeck, 2018).
7. The subheadings, all listed beneath 'Altes Testament', varied from 'Geschichte der israelitischen Religion' through 'Religionsgeschichte' to 'israelitische Religionsgeschichte' and 'Religionsgeschichte Israels'. The net was rather wide, and did include a relatively small number of foreign works.
8. The descriptor Hebrew Bible represents a more neutral designation for the literature elsewhere denominated the Old Testament or Tanakh, though these corpora are not strictly synonymous in the context of their respective traditions: cf. J.D. Levenson, *The Hebrew Bible, the Old Testament, and Historical Criticism: Jews and Christians in Biblical Studies* (Louisville, KY: Westminster/John Knox Press, 1993), 1–32.
9. R. Smend, *Lehrbuch der alttestamentlichen Religionsgeschichte*, Sammlung theologischer Lehrbücher: Alttestamentliche Theologie (Freiburg: Mohr Siebeck, 1893), 6 n. 1.
10. A. Bertholet, *Die Eigenart der alttestamentlichen Religion: Eine akademische Antrittsrede* (Tübingen: Mohr Siebeck, 1913), 24–25. The equation of revelation with the course of history itself became a standard claim of liberal theology.
11. So, inter alia, S. Oettli, *Die Geschichte Israels*, Vol. 1: *Geschichte Israels bis auf Alexander den Großen* (Calw: Verlag der Vereinsbuchhandlung, 1905), 7–16; cf. B. Stade, *Geschichte des Volkes Israel*, Vol. 1: *Geschichte Israels unter der Königsherrschaft oder Geschichte des Volkes Israel von Beginn der Königsherrschaft bis zur Zerstörung Jerusalems durch die Babylonier*, Allgemeine Geschichte in Einzeldarstellungen 1/6 (Berlin: Grote, 1887), 1–8; K. Marti, *Geschichte der Israelitischen Religion*, 4th edn (Strasbourg: Bull,

1903), 3. Oettli, Swiss Old Testament professor at Greifswald, completed this undertaking in tandem with a New Testament professor at Tübingen, a compatriot also born in St Gallen. Marti's work started as the second edition of August Kayser's *Die Theologie des Alten Testaments*, which became *Geschichte der Israelitischen Religion* beginning with the third edition.

12. Cf., e.g., H. Winckler, *Geschichte Israels in Einzeldarstellungen*, 2 vols., Völker und Staaten des alten Orients 2–3 (Leipzig: Pfeiffer, 1895, 1900), Vol. 1, 4–11; the forewords of A. Köhler, *Lehrbuch der Biblischen Geschichte Alten Testamentes*, 2 vols. (Erlangen: Deichert, 1875, 1884); Marti, *Geschichte der Israelitischen Religion*, 1–15.
13. M. Liverani, *Israel's History and the History of Israel*, trans. C. Peri and P.R. Davies (London: Equinox, 2007), xv.
14. J.L. Ska, 'The "History of Israel": Its Emergence as an Independent Discipline', in M. Sæbø (ed.), *Hebrew Bible/Old Testament: The History of Its Interpretation*, Vol. 3/1: *The Nineteenth Century* (Göttingen: Vandenhoeck & Ruprecht, 2013), 343.
15. A. Klostermann, *Geschichte des Volkes Israel bis zur Restauration unter Esra und Nehemia* (Munich: Beck, 1896), 268; cf. also C.F.F. Lehmann-Haupt, *Israel: Seine Entwicklung im Rahmen der Weltgeschichte* (Tübingen: Mohr Siebeck, 1911), 285.
16. Stade, *Geschichte des Volkes Israel*; O. Holtzmann, Vol. 2.2: *Das Ende des jüdischen Staatswesens und die Entstehung des Christenthums*, Allgemeine Geschichte in Einzeldarstellungen 1/6 (Berlin: Grote, 1888).
17. E. König, *Geschichte des Reiches Gottes bis auf Jesus Christus*, Grundrisse der Theologie, Sammlung der theologischen Wissenschaften 2/1 (Braunschweig: Wollermann, 1908).
18. Although anticipated by others, this formulation by Wilhelm Martin Leberecht de Wette became a powerful lens for subsequent histories: see W.M.L. de Wette, *Lehrbuch der christlichen Dogmatik in ihrer historischen Entwickelung dargestellt*, Vol. 1: *Biblische Dogmatik Alten und Neuen Testaments, Oder kritische Darstellung der Religionslehre des Hebraismus, des Judentums und Urchristenthums, Zum Gebrauch akademischer Vorlesungen* (Berlin: Realschulbuchhandlung, 1813).
19. In 1843, Heinrich Ewald argued this triad corresponded to three distinct epochs, 'because the people itself becomes a different one with each of these changes [*Wendungen*]': H. Ewald, *Geschichte des Volkes Israels bis Christus*, vol. 1 (Göttingen: Dieterich, 1843), 14.
20. R. Kittel, *A History of the Hebrews*, 2 vols., trans. J. Taylor, H.W. Hogg and E.B. Speirs, Theological Translation Library 3–4 (London: Williams and Norgate, 1895, 1896), 1:viii, cf. 2:395, although he indicated the two fell beneath the broader history of Israel (cf. 1:4, 2:v) [German Original: *Geschichte der Hebräer*, 2 vols., Handbücher der alten Geschichte 1/3 (Gotha: Perthes, 1888, 1892]; cf. also W. Nowack, *Lehrbuch der hebräischen Archäologie*, 2 vols., Sammlung theologischer Lehrbücher (Freiburg: Mohr Siebeck, 1894), 1:2, 106. The heavily revised second edition appeared as *Geschichte des Volkes Israel*, 2 vols. (Gotha: Perthes, 1909, 1912); in that second edition, Kittel altered the second volume's final conclusion to declare 'the people of Israel' – rather than 'the people of the Hebrews' – ended with the fall of Judah, also adding the end of the state and of the people was only ostensibly that of the nation. The third volume only appeared much later – Vol. 3: *Die Zeit der Wegführung nach Babel und die Aufrichtung der neuen Gemeinde*, 2 parts. (Stuttgart: Kohlhammer, 1927, 1929).
21. M. Haller, *Das Judentum: Geschichtsschreibung, Prophetie und Gesetzgebung nach dem Exil*, Die Schriften des Alten Testaments 2/3 (Göttingen: Vandenhoeck & Ruprecht, 1914), x.

22. H. Guthe, *Geschichte des Volkes Israel*, Grundriss der Theologischen Wissenschaften 2/3 (Freiburg: Mohr Siebeck, 1899), 227. He ultimately argued that a new Israel – but not a new people – resulted (229).
23. I. Benzinger, *Hebräische Archäologie*, Grundriss der Theologischen Wissenschaften 2/1 (Freiburg: Mohr Siebeck, 1894), 80–83.
24. C.H. Cornill, *History of the People of Israel from the Earliest Times to the Destruction of Jerusalem by the Romans, Written for Lay Readers*, trans. W.H. Carruth (Chicago: Open Court Publishing Company, 1898), 147 [German Original: *Geschichte des Volkes Israel von den ältesten Zeiten bis zur Zerstörung Jerusalems durch die Römer* (Leipzig: Harrassowitz, 1898)]. He, too, stated that 'there is accomplished in the Babylonian exile, and as a consequence of it, that remarkable transformation which makes the Judean state a Jewish church, of the Israelitish people a Jewish religious congregation. For the history of religion there is perhaps no other period in the history of the people of Israel of equal importance or significance with the half century of the Babylonian exile, from 586 to 537 BC' (English Translation: 147–48).
25. See, e.g., J. Wellhausen, *Prolegomena to the History of Israel, with a reprint of the article Israel from the 'Encyclopædia Britannica'*, trans. J.S. Black and A. Menzies (Edinburgh: Adam & Charles Black, 1885), esp. 100–4 [German Original: *Prolegomena zur Geschichte Israels*, 2nd edn (Berlin: Reimer, 1883), whereas the first edition appeared as *Geschichte Israels*, Vol. 1 (Berlin: Reimer, 1878), and the second volume came as *Israelitische und jüdische Geschichte* (Berlin: Reimer, 1894)]. This separation from the land then turned the Jews into a 'trading people' (English Translation: 108). Wellhausen wrote that 'the word "Canaanite" (like "Jew" in German) was used in the sense of "trader"', although the German gloss was removed from the reprinted version – cf. 'Israel', in *Encyclopædia Britannica*, 9th edn, 25 vols. (Edinburgh: Adam and Charles Black, 1875–89), 13: 408, reprinted in *Prolegomena to the History of Israel*, 465.
26. The interface of Judaism and Hellenism received much attention at the turn of the twentieth century, with the precise relationship between 'Hellenistic' and 'Palestinian' Judaisms becoming a point of much debate: cf., e.g., A. Bertholet, *Das religionsgeschichtliche Problem des Spätjudentums*, Sammlung gemeinverständlicher Vorträge und Schriften aus dem Gebiet der Theologie und Religionsgeschichte 55 (Tübingen: Mohr Siebeck, 1909) [English Translation: 'The Religious-Historical Problem of Later Judaism', in *Transactions of the Third International Congress for the History of Religions*, 2 vols. (Oxford: Clarendon Press, 1908), 1:272–80].
27. E. Sellin, *Beiträge zur israelitischen und jüdischen Religionsgeschichte*, 2 vols. (Leipzig: Deichert [Böhme], 1896, 1897), 1:60, 135–38.
28. König, *Geschichte des Reiches Gottes*, 38–40; idem, *Geschichte der Alttestamentlichen Religion kritisch dargestellt* (Gütersloh: Bertelsmann, 1912), 26–27.
29. Kittel, *Geschichte des Volkes Israel*, 1:24–27; A. Bertholet, *Kulturgeschichte Israels* (Göttingen: Vandenhoeck & Ruprecht, 1919), 19–20.
30. Köhler, *Lehrbuch der Biblischen Geschichte Alten Testaments*, 1:21; Klostermann, *Geschichte des Volkes Israel bis zur Restauration unter Esra und Nehemia*, 6–18.
31. Smend, *Lehrbuch der alttestamentlichen Religionsgeschichte*, 263–64; K. Budde, *Religion of Israel to the Exile*, American Lectures on the History of Religions, Fourth Series, 1898–1899 (New York: G.P. Putnam's Sons, 1899), 217–18 [German Translation: *Die Religion des Volkes Israel bis zur Verbannung*, Amerikanische religionswissenschaftliche Vorlesungen 4 (Gissen: Ricker, 1900)].

32. E. Sellin, *Serubbabel: Ein Beitrag zur Geschichte der messianischen Erwartung und der Entstehung des Judentums* (Leipzig: Deichert [Böhme], 1898), 1–2; cf. idem, *Studien zur Entstehungsgeschichte der jüdischen Gemeinde nach dem babylonischen Exil*, 2 vols. (Leipzig: Deichert [Böhme], 1901), 2:160–62.
33. I. Benzinger, *Geschichte Israels bis auf die griechische Zeit*, Sammlung Göschen (Leipzig: Göschen, 1904). Notably, Holtzmann argued, 'The greatest achievement of Alexander's triumphs is without a doubt that Alexander prepared the way on which the religion of Israel in its Christian transformation could be transmitted to the Western civilized world [*die Religion Israels in ihrer christlichen Umgestaltung der abendländischen Culturwelt übermittelt werden konnte*]' (*Das Ende des jüdischen Staatswesens und die Entstehung des Christenthums*, 274).
34. Cornill, *Geschichte des Volkes Israel von den ältesten Zeiten bis zur Zerstörung Jerusalems durch die Römer*, 17; cf. A. Bertholet, *Das Ende des jüdischen Staatswesens: Sechs populäre Vorträge* (Tübingen: Mohr Siebeck, 1910), 1–2, 164.
35. Stade, *Geschichte Israels unter der Königsherrschaft*, 10; Holtzmann, *Das Ende des jüdischen Staatwesens und die Enstehung des Christenthums*, 673–74.
36. Guthe, *Geschichte des Volkes Israel*, 316; Lehmann-Haupt, *Israel: Seine Entwicklung im Rahmen der Weltgeschichte*, 241–42; A. Schlatter, *Israels Geschichte von Alexander dem Großen bis Hadrian*, Reiche der Alten Welt 3 (Calw: Verlag der Vereinsbuchhandlung, 1901). Schlatter's second edition appeared as *Die Geschichte Israels*, vol. 2: *Geschichte Israels von Alexander dem Großen bis Hadrian* (Calw: Verlag der Vereinsbuchhandlung, 1906); cf. Oettli, *Die Geschichte Israels*, vol. 1: *Geschichte Israels bis auf Alexander den Großen*.
37. Guthe, *Geschichte des Volkes Israel*, 302; with his description of the Samaritans, Guthe had already thinned the herd of prophetic religion (ibid., 266); cf. König, *Geschichte des Reiches Gottes*, 328.
38. Budde, *Religion of Israel to the Exile*, xvi. This course of lectures expressly corresponded to those delivered the previous year by T.K. Cheyne, *Jewish Religious Life after the Exile*, American Lectures on the History of Religions, Third Series, 1897–1898 (New York: G.P. Putnam's Sons, 1898).
39. Wellhausen, 'Israel', in *Prolegomena to the History of Israel*, 508–9.
40. K. Marti, *The Religion of the Old Testament: Its Place Among the Religions of the Nearer East*, ed. W.D. Morrison, trans. G.A. Bienemann, Crown Theological Library 19 (New York: G.P Putnam's Sons, 1907), 243–44 [German Original: *Die Religion des Alten Testaments unter den Religionen des vorderen Orients* (Tübingen: Mohr Siebeck, 1906)]; cf. idem, *Geschichte der Israelitischen Religion*, 196.
41. H. Gunkel, *The Influence of the Holy Spirit: The Popular View of the Apostolic Age and the Teaching of the Apostle Paul*, trans. R.A. Harrisville and P.A. Quanbeck II (Philadelphia, PA: Fortress Press, 1979), 12–13 [German Original: *Die Wirkungen des heiligen Geistes, nach der populären Anschauung der apostolischen Zeit und nach der Lehre des Apostels Paulus: Eine biblisch-theologische Studie* (Göttingen: Vandenhoeck & Ruprecht, 1888)].
42. Wellhausen, *Prolegomena to the History of Israel*, 1.
43. A. Bertholet, *Die Stellung der Israeliten und der Juden zu den Fremden* (Freiburg: Mohr Siebeck, 1896), 66–67, 68. Bertholet cited F.M. Müller's Essays, Vol. 4: *Aufsätze hauptsächlich sprachwissenschaftlichen Inhalts enthaltend*, trans. R. Fritzsche (Leipzig: Engelmann, 1876), 114, a translation of *Chips from a German Workshop*, Vol. 4.1: *Essays Chiefly on the Science of Language* (London: Longmans, Green, and Co., 1875), 222.
44. Wellhausen, *Prolegomena to the History of Israel*, 417; 'Israel', in ibid., 491.

45. B. Duhm, *Die Theologie der Propheten als Grundlage für die innere Entwicklungsgeschichte der israelitischen Religion dargestellt* (Bonn: Marcus, 1875), 96. While Wellhausen often sees credit for the formulation, Duhm has in the very least literary priority.
46. Oettli, *Die Geschichte Israels*, Vol. 1: *Geschichte Israels bis auf Alexander den Großen*, 12.
47. U. Tal, *Christians and Jews in Germany: Religion, Politics, and Ideology in the Second Reich, 1870–1914*, trans. N.J. Jacobs (Ithaca, NY: Cornell University Press, 1975), 199.
48. As the *fin de siècle* saw an erosion of cultural institutions, those traditional bastions of theology and classics then began to crumble: see S.L. Marchand, 'From Liberalism to Neoromanticism: Albrecht Dieterich, Richard Reitzenstein, and the Religious Turn in *Fin-de-Siècle* German Classical Studies', in M. Ruehl and I. Gildenhard (eds), *Out of Arcadia: Classics and Politics in Germany in the Age of Burckhardt, Nietzsche and Wilamowitz* (London: Institute of Classical Studies, School of Advanced Studies, University of London, 2003), 129–60.
49. A. von Harnack, *Marcion: Der moderne Gläubige des 2. Jahrhunderts, der erste Reformator: Die Dorpater Preisschrift (1870)*, ed. F. Steck, Texte und Untersuchungen zur Geschichte der altchristlichen Literatur 149 (Berlin: de Gruyter, 2003); idem, *Marcion: Das Evangelium vom fremden Gott, eine Monographie zur Geschichte der Grundlegung der katholischen Kirche*, Texte und Untersuchungen zur Geschichte der altchristlichen Literatur 45 (Leipzig: Hinrichs, 1921); cf. idem, *Neue Studien zu Marcion*, Texte und Untersuchungen zur Geschichte der altchristlichen Literatur 44/4 (Leipzig: Hinrichs, 1923); see further W. Kinzig, *Harnack, Marcion und das Judentum, nebst einer kommentierten Edition des Briefwechsels Adolf von Harnacks mit Houston Stewart Chamberlain* (Leipzig: Evangelische Verlagsanstalt, 2004).
50. Marti, *Geschichte der israelitischen Religion*, 1.
51. Ibid.
52. B. Stade, *Biblische Theologie des Alten Testaments*, Vol. 1: *Die Religion Israels und die Entstehung des Judentums*, Grundriss der Theologischen Wissenschaften 2/2.1 (Tübingen: Mohr Siebeck, 1905), 1–20.
53. Cornill, *History of the People of Israel*, 300, 301, cf. esp. 3.
54. I. Frohnmeyer, *Biblische Geographie für Schulen und Familien*, 10th edn (Calw: Verlag der Vereinsbuchhandlung, 1883), 1, cf. 2. Frohnmeyer, among others, also noted its importance for 'the orthodox [*altgläubig*] Israelite' and 'the Mohammedan'. The first edition came from the pen of Gottlob Ludwig Hochstetter (1836), which accompanied Christian Gottlieb Barth's *Biblische Naturgeschichte für Schule und Familien*.
55. F. Buhl, *Geographie des alten Palästina*, Grundriss der Theologischen Wissenschaften 2/4 (Freiburg: Mohr Siebeck, 1896), v–vi. In a similar circumscription, Otto Procksch employed the (recorded) history of ancient Israel to determine the peoples for consideration in his volume on Palestine: cf. idem, *Die Völker Altpalästinas*, Das Land der Bibel: Gemeinverständliche Hefte zur Palästinakunde 1/2 (Leipzig: Hinrichs, 1914), 3–5.
56. (K.)R. Schramm, *Geographie von Palästina: Zum Gebrauch in Seminaren, beim Katechumenen-Unterricht und für Lehrer*, 2nd edn, ed. K. Furrer (Bremen: Heinsius, 1882), iv.
57. P. Thomsen, *Systematische Bibliographie der Palästina-Literatur auf Veranlassung des Deutschen Vereins zur Erforschung Palästinas bearbeitet*, Vol. 1: *1895–1904* (Leipzig: Haupt, 1908).
58. Cf. the thorough H. Guthe, *Palästina*, Land und Leute: Monographien zur Erdkunde 21 (Bielefeld: Velhagen & Klasing, 1908), 3–16; Buhl, *Geographie des alten Palästina*, 1–8; G. Hölscher, *Landes- und Volkskunde Palästinas*, Sammlung Göschen (Leipzig:

Göschen, 1907), 8–9, 114, cf. 120–25; P. Thomsen, *Palästina und seine Kultur in fünf Jahrtausenden: Nach den neuesten Ausgrabungen und Forschungen dargestellt*, Aus Natur und Geisteswelt: Sammlung wissenschaftlich-gemeinverständlicher Darstellungen 260 (Leipzig: Teubner, 1909), 1–11; idem, *Kompendium der palästinischen Altertumskunde*, 3–8; O. Ankel, *Grundzüge der Landesnatur des Westjordanlandes: Entwurf einer Monographie des westjordanischen Palästina, mit einem Vorworte von Prof. Dr. Th. Fischer* (Frankfurt: Verlag der Jaeger'schen Buch- & Landkarten-Handlung, 1887), 4–23.

59. Guthe, *Palästina*, 101. Alongside rediscovery, a sense of recovery could also emerge in literature on Palestine. Prefacing a volume on the ventures undertaken by the British Palestine Exploration Fund, one commentator wrote: 'It is hoped, therefore, that the adoption for its title of the old Crusading watchword, the "Recovery of Jerusalem", will be thought germane to the general object of the Society under whose auspices it was put forth. That old cry pointed to the land as well as to the City, and may fairly be used for the purpose of the new Crusade': W. Morrison, 'Editor's Preface', in C.W. Wilson et al. (eds), *The Recovery of Jerusalem: A Narrative of Exploration and Discovery in the City and the Holy Land*, 2 vols. (London: Bentley, 1871), vii–viii.

60. R. Röhricht, *Bibliotheca Geographica Palaestinae: Chronologisches Verzeichniss der auf die Geographie des Heiligen Landes bezüglichen Literatur von 333 bis 1878 und Versuch einer Cartographie herausgegeben* (Berlin: Reuther, 1890).

61. P. Thomsen, *Denkmäler Palästinas aus der Zeit Jesu*, Das Land der Bibel: Gemeinverständliche Hefte zur Palästinakunde 2/1 (Leipzig: Hinrichs, 1916), 6.

62. H. Gressmann, *Palästinas Erdgeruch in der israelitischen Religion*, Kultur und Leben 8 (Berlin: Curtius, 1909), 5.

63. For more on this epistemological endeavour, see P.M. Kurtz, 'Of Lions, Arabs, & Israelites: Some Lessons from the Samson Story for Writing the History of Biblical Scholarship', *Journal of the Bible and its Reception* 5(1) (2018), 31–48.

64. The foundation of the PEF in particular, and this turn towards archaeology in general, served as a major reference point for histories of research at the time (cf., e.g., Thomsen, *Kompendium der palästinischen Altertumskunde*, 3–4); on the wider institutionalization of German orientalist scholarship, see S. Mangold, *Eine 'weltbürgerliche Wissenschaft' – Die deutsche Orientalistik im 19. Jahrhundert* (Stuttgart: Steiner, 2004); L. Hanisch, *Die Nachfolger der Exegeten: Deutschsprachige Erforschung des Vorderen Orients in der ersten Hälfte des 20. Jahrhunderts* (Wiesbaden: Harrassowitz, 2003); U. Wokoeck, *German Orientalism: The Study of the Middle East and Islam from 1800 to 1945* (London: Routledge, 2009).

65. With roots reaching back to 1901, the *Studium Biblicum Franciscanum* blossomed in 1924. The British School of Archaeology in Jerusalem (recently restructured as the Kenyon Institute) was set in motion during the British Mandate (1919). Locally, the Society for the Reclamation of Antiquities – subsequently styled the Jewish Palestine Exploration Society and currently the Israel Exploration Society – launched in 1914. I am grateful to Paul Allen for his kind help on the Russian institute.

66. Thomsen, *Palästina und seine Kultur in fünf Jahrtausenden*, 10.

67. See esp. M. Díaz-Andreu, *A World History of Nineteenth-Century Archaeology: Nationalism, Colonialism, and the Past* (Oxford: Oxford University Press, 2007), 131–66; S.L. Marchand, *Down from Olympus: Archaeology and Philhellenism in Germany, 1750–1970* (Princeton, NJ: Princeton University Press, 1996); B. Kuklick, *Puritans in Babylon: The Ancient Near East and American Intellectual Life, 1880–1930* (Princeton, NJ: Princeton University Press, 1996); cf. further E.D. Corbett, *Competitive Archaeology*

in Jordan: Narrating Identity from the Ottomans to the Hashemites (Austin: University of Texas Press, 2014); M.T. Bernhardsson, *Reclaiming a Plundered Past: Archaeology and Nation Building in Modern Iraq* (Austin: University of Texas Press, 2005).
68. A. Socin, 'Bericht über neue Erscheinungen auf dem Gebiete der Palästinaliteratur 1880', *Zeitschrift des Deutschen Palästina-Vereins (ZDPV)* 4 (1881), 127–28.
69. Ankel, *Grundzüge der Landesnatur des Westjordanlandes*, 14, referring to the aforementioned article. The British expressed similar concerns. In an early progress report, the Palestine Exploration Fund warned, 'To abandon these works at such a moment [for lack of funds] would be most lamentable; it would be to proclaim to America, to Germany, and to France, that England – the country where the Bible has been most loved and most studied – will not from her great wealth spare a few thousands yearly to carry on the work of elucidating and explaining the Bible history' ('Quarterly Statement of Progress', *Palestine Exploration Fund Quarterly Statement* 1 [1869], 8).
70. Guthe, *Palästina*, 16.
71. E. Kautzsch, 'Vorwort', *ZDPV* 1 (1878), 1–9, at 9.
72. Cf. U. Hübner, 'Der Deutsche Verein zur Erforschung Palästinas: seine Vorgeschichte, Gründung und Entwicklung bis in die Weimarer Zeit', in U. Hübner (ed.), *Palaestina exploranda: Studien zur Erforschung Palästinas im 19. und 20. Jahrhundert anläßlich des 125jährigen Bestehens des Deutschen Vereins zur Erforschung Palästinas* (Wiesbaden: Harrassowitz, 2006), 18–19, 22–24.
73. See H. Goren, '*Zieht hin und erforscht das Land*': *Die deutsche Palästinaforschung im 19. Jahrhundert*, trans. A.C. Naujoks (Göttingen: Wallstein, 2003); R. Hallote, *Bible, Map, and Spade: The American Palestine Exploration Society, Frederick Jones Bliss, and the Forgotten Story of Early American Biblical Archaeology* (Piscataway: Gorgias Press, 2006). For further insights extractable through the history of missions, cf., e.g., R. Habermas, 'Mission im 19. Jahrhundert: Globale Netze des Religiösen', *Historische Zeitschrift* 287(3) (2008), 629–79; U. Makdisi, 'Reclaiming the Land of the Bible: Missionaries, Secularism, and Evangelical Modernity', *American Historical Review* 102(3) (1997), 680–713.
74. Mangold, *Eine 'weltbürgerliche Wissenschaft'*, 217–25; Goren, '*Zieht hin und erforscht das Land*', 317–44.
75. Mangold, *Eine 'weltbürgerliche Wissenschaft'*, 224, cf. 223. Similarly, Gabriele Fassbeck has observed the Deutsche Orient-Gesellschaft (DOG), founded in 1898, showed a stronger attraction to the more spectacular finds from the ancient Near East, found mostly outside Palestine, to fill museums (G. Fassbeck, '"The Longer, the More Happiness I Derive from This Undertaking": James Simon and Early German Research into Galilee's Ancient Synagogues', in G. Fassbeck and A.E. Killebrew (eds), *Viewing Ancient Jewish Art and Archaeology: VeHinnei Rachel – Essays in Honor of Rachel Hachlili* [Leiden: Brill, 2016], 101–20); on the DOG within the larger context of German archaeological endeavours, see Marchand, *Down from Olympus*, esp. 209–20.
76. *Palestine Exploration Fund Quarterly Statement* 1 (1869), front matter.
77. J.P. Thompson, 'Concluding Appeal', *Palestine Exploration Society, First Statement* (1871), 34; see further W.J. Moulton, 'The American Palestine Exploration Society', *The Annual of the American Schools of Oriental Research* 8 (1926–27), 55–78; F.J. Cobbing, 'The American Palestine Exploration Society and the Survey of Eastern Palestine', *Palestine Exploration Quarterly* 137 (2005), 9–21.
78. 'Statuten des Deutschen Vereins zur Erforschung Palästina's', *ZDPV* 1 (1878), 1–4; repr. in Hübner, *Palaestina exploranda*, 322–34.

79. H. Guthe, 'Rechenschaftsbericht über das Vereinsjahr 1886', *ZDPV* 10 (1887), x.
80. K. Furrer et al., 'Die Arbeiten des Deutschen Vereins zur Erforschung Palästina's von 1878–1897', *Mittheilungen und Nachrichten des Deutschen Palaestina-Vereins* 3 (1897), Supplement, 1–5.
81. P. Wolff, 'Zur neueren Geschichte Jerusalems: Von 1843–1884', *ZDPV* 8 (1885), 1–15; G. Dalman, 'Gegenwärtiger Bestand der jüdischen Colonien in Palästina', *ZDPV* 16 (1893), 193–201; cf. idem, 'Gegenwärtiger Bestand der jüdischen Colonien in Palästina: Nachträgliche Correcturen und Ergänzungen', *ZDPV* 17 (1894), 301–2; J. Press, 'Die jüdischen Kolonien Palästinas', *ZDPV* 35 (1912), 161–85; H. Hilderscheid, 'Die Niederschlagsverhältnisse Palästinas in alter und neuer Zeit', *ZDPV* 25 (1902), 1, 3, 5–105; F. Mühlau, 'Martinus Seusenius' Reise in das heilige Land i.J. 1602/03', *ZDPV* 26 (1903), 1–92; L. Köhler, 'Eine Frage betreffs des Ausdrucks "Erez Israel"', *ZDPV* 33 (1910), 46; S. Klein, '"Erez Israel" im weiteren Sinne', *ZDPV* 33 (1910), 221–24; S. Krauss, '"Erez Israel" im weiteren Sinne', *ZDPV* 33 (1910), 224–25.
82. H. Guthe et al., 'Aufruf zur Gründung einer Palästinabibliothek', *ZDPV* 1 (1878), 238–39.
83. See further, Goren, *'Zieht hin und erforscht das Land'*, 328–39.
84. Cf. G. Dalman, 'Entstehung und bisherige Entwicklung des Instituts', *Palästinajahrbuch des Deutschen evangelischen Instituts für Altertumswissenschaft des heiligen Landes zu Jerusalem* 1 (1905), 14–20; H.-J. Zobel, 'Geschichte des Deutschen Evangelischen Instituts für Altertumswissenschaft des Heiligen Landes von den Anfängen bis zum Zweiten Weltkrieg', *ZDPV* 97 (1981), 1–11.
85. 'Protokolle der xxiv. deutschen evangelischen Kirchen-Konferenz, am 14. bis 20. Juni 1900', cited in H. Guthe, 'Das deutsche evangelische Institut für Alterthumswissenschaft des heiligen Landes', *Mittheilungen und Nachrichten des Deutschen Palaestina-Vereins* 8 (1902), 82.
86. 'Urkunde über Errichtung der deutschen evangelischen Stiftung für Altertumswissenschaft des heiligen Landes', *Palästinajahrbuch des Deutschen evangelischen Instituts für Altertumswissenschaft des heiligen Landes zu Jerusalem* 1 (1905), 1, 3.
87. Dalman, 'Entstehung und bisherige Entwicklung des Instituts', 14.
88. 'Mitteilungen und Ratschläge für die Mitglieder des Instituts', *Palästinajahrbuch des Deutschen evangelischen Instituts für Altertumswissenschaft des heiligen Landes zu Jerusalem* 1 (1905), 9–13. In fact, a separate committee had already instituted *Das Deutsche Palästina-Museum* in 1875 (cf. H. Guthe, 'Rechenschaftsbericht über das Vereinsjahr 1883', *ZDPV* 7 [1884], vii–xi; see also Goren, *'Zieht hin und erforscht das Land'*, 216–18, 352).
89. Goren, *'Zieht hin und erforscht das Land'*, 10; G. Dalman, 'Foreword', *Palästinajahrbuch des Deutschen evangelischen Instituts für Altertumswissenschaft des heiligen Landes zu Jerusalem* 1 (1905), i. Similar to the DPV, the DEIAHL struggled to balance scientific and popular concerns in its publications: see J. Männchen, 'Gustaf Dalman und der Deutsche Verein zur Erforschung Palästinas', in U. Hübner (ed.), *Palaestina*, 230–31.
90. See 'Urkunde über Errichtung der deutschen evangelischen Stiftung für Altertumswissenschaft des heiligen Landes', 3, §5; 'Mitteilungen und Ratschläge für die Mitglieder des Instituts', 9 bis; cf. Dalman, 'Entstehung und bisherige Entwicklung des Instituts', 20.
91. 'Urkunde über Errichtung der deutschen evangelischen Stiftung für Altertumswissenschaft des heiligen Landes', 2, §2.3; 'Geschäftliche Mitteilungen', *Mittheilungen und Nachrichten des Deutschen Palaestina-Vereins* 9 (1903), 87.

92. For the background of these early undertakings, see especially Goren, *'Zieht hin und erforscht das Land'*, 271–316; cf. M. Kirchhoff, *Text zu Land: Palästina im wissenschaftlichen Diskurs 1865–1920* (Göttingen: Vandenhoeck & Ruprecht, 2005).
93. On these excavations, see the relevant essays in Hübner, *Palaestina exploranda*; the second edition of Thomsen, *Palästina und seine Kultur in fünf Jahrtausenden*, 8–11; idem, *Kompendium der palästinischen Altertumskunde* (Tübingen: Mohr, 1913), 3–8; P. Karge, *Die Resultate der neueren Ausgrabungen und Forschungen in Palästina*, 3rd edn, Biblische Zeitfragen 3/8–9 (Münster: Aschendorff, 1912), 7–20; although imprecise at times, cf. also L. Nigro, 'In the Shadow of the Bible: Archaeological Investigations by the *Deutsche [sic!] Palästina Verein* before the First World War: Taanek, Megiddo, Jericho, Schechem', in V. Krings and I. Tassignon (eds), *Archéologie dans l'Empire Ottoman Autour de 1900: Entre Politique, Économie et Science* (Brussels: Belgisch Historisch Instituut te Rome, 2004), 215–29.
94. G. Dalman, 'Jahresbericht nebst Mitgliederverzeichnis', *Palästinajahrbuch des Deutschen evangelischen Instituts für Altertumswissenschaft des heiligen Landes zu Jerusalem* 2 (1906), 3.
95. L.J. Frohnmeyer and I. Benzinger, *Bilderatlas zur Bibelkunde: Ein Handbuch für den Religionslehrer u. Bibelfreund* (Stuttgart: Benzinger, 1905), 166.
96. Hölscher, *Landes- und Volkskunde Palästinas*; Guthe, *Palästina*; cf. also L. Bauer, *Volksleben im Lande der Bibel*, 2nd edn (Leipzig: Wallmann, 1903); M. Löhr, *Volksleben im Lande der Bibel*, Wissenschaft und Bildung: Einzeldarstellungen aus allen Gebieten des Wissens 7 (Leipzig: Quelle & Meyer, 1907).
97. Gressmann, *Palästinas Erdgeruch in der israelitischen Religion*, 7. Gressmann's work described the disappointment often felt by travellers to Palestine, and therefore sought to lower expectations.
98. See esp. Stade, *Geschichte Israels unter der Königsherrschaft*, 108–26. Nowack, for example, drew a quick yet explicit distinction between these lines of inquiry: *Lehrbuch der hebräischen Archäologie*, 101–2.
99. So, e.g., Thomsen, *Palästina und seine Kultur in fünf Jahrtausenden*, 2nd edn, 3.
100. Frohnmeyer and Benzinger, *Bilderatlas zur Bibelkunde*, 133; cf. Bauer, *Volksleben im Lande der Bibel*, v–vii.
101. Marti, *The Religion of the Old Testament*, 186, cf. 187.
102. 'Extract from the Original Prospectus', *Palestine Exploration Fund, Quarterly Statement* 1 (1869), 1.
103. Löhr, *Volksleben im Lande der Bibel*, 119.
104. Hölscher, *Landes- und Volkskunde Palästinas*, 112, 120; Thomsen, *Kompendium der palästinischen Altertumskunde*, 2.
105. Guthe, *Palästina*, 125–26; cf. also K. Baedeker, *Palästina und Syrien: Die Hauptrouten Mesopotamiens und Babyloniens und die Insel Cypern: Handbuch für Reisende*, 7th edn, ed. I. Benzinger (Leipzig: Baedeker, 1910), lxxxiii–lxxxix [English Translation: *Palestine and Syria, with Routes through Mesopotamia and Babylonia and the Island of Cypris: Handbook for Travellers*, 5th edn (New York: Scribner's Sons, 1912), lx]. The question of original inhabitants also arose in the literature, and some commentators suggested Indogermanic, rather than Semitic, peoples may have first occupied the land (cf. Kittel, *Geschichte des Volkes Israel*, 1:27–33; Thomsen, *Kompendium der palästinischen Altertumskunde*, 12–13). This line of inquiry required only a short step to reach that of the Aryan Jesus: see further, S. Heschel, *The Aryan Jesus: Christian Theologians and the Bible in Nazi Germany* (Princeton, NJ: Princeton University Press, 2008).

106. Hölscher, *Landes- und Volkskunde Palästinas*, 69–70, 103; see also idem, *Die Geschichte der Juden in Palästina seit dem Jahre 70 nach Chr.: Eine Skizze* (Leipzig: Hinrichs, 1909), 64.
107. Bauer, *Volksleben im Lande der Bibel*, 2.
108. Nowack, *Lehrbuch der hebräischen Archäologie*, 2.
109. For an overview of the diversity among Jewish movements, see, e.g., W. Laqueur, *A History of Zionism: From the French Revolution to the Establishment of the State of Israel*, repr. edn (New York: Schocken Books, 2003).
110. F. Delitzsch, *Babel and Bible: Two Lectures, Delivered before the Members of the Deutsche Orient-Gesellschaft in the presence of the German Emperor*, ed. and trans. C.H.W. Johns, Crown Theological Library (London: Williams and Norgate, 1903), 2–3; italics present in the English but not the original German [German Original: *Babel und Bibel: Ein Vortrag* (Leipzig: Hinrichs, 1902)].
111. E. Hiller, *Die archäologische Erforschung Palästinas*, Gesellschaft für Palästina-Forschung (Vienna: Schwarzinger, 1910), 20.
112. See further J. Zachhuber, *Theology as Science in Nineteenth-Century Germany: From F.C. Baur to Ernst Troeltsch*, Changing Paradigms in Historical and Systematic Theology (Oxford: Oxford University Press, 2013).
113. Habermas, 'Piety, Power, and Powerlessness', 459.
114. E.g. G.S. Williamson, *The Longing for Myth in Germany: Religion and Aesthetic Culture from Romanticism to Nietzsche* (Chicago: The University of Chicago Press, 2004); T.A. Howard, *Religion and the Rise of Historicism: W.M.L. de Wette, Jacob Burckhardt, and the Theological Origins of Nineteenth-Century Historical Consciousness* (Cambridge: University of Cambridge Press, 2000).
115. As Harnack wrote, 'And just as Eastern Christianity is rightly called Greek, and the Christianity of the Middle Ages and of Western Europe is rightly called Roman, so the Christianity of the Reformation may be described as German, in spite of Calvin. ... Through the Reformation the Germans mark a stage in the history of the Universal Church': A. von Harnack, *What is Christianity? Lectures Delivered at the University of Berlin during the Winter-Term 1899–1900*, trans. T.B. Saunders, 2nd edn (New York: G.P. Putnam's Sons, 1902), 302–3 [German Original: *Das Wesen des Christentums: Sechzehn Vorlesungen vor Studierenden aller Facultäten im Wintersemester 1899/1900 an der Universität Berlin gehalten* (Leipzig: Hinrichs, 1900)].
116. S. Heschel, *Abraham Geiger and the Jewish Jesus* (Chicago: The University of Chicago Press, 1998); see also C. Wiese, *Challenging Colonial Discourse: Jewish Studies and Protestant Theology in Wilhelmine Germany*, trans. C. Wiese and B. Harshav (Leiden: Brill, 2005).
117. By contrast, Yael Zerubavel has explored the malleability of Jewish antiquity in Zionist representations of history: see idem, *Recovered Roots: Collective Memory and the Making of Israeli National Tradition* (Chicago: University of Chicago Press, 1995).
118. J. Martyr, *Dialogue with Trypho*, trans. T.B. Falls, rev. ed. T.P. Halton and M. Slusser (Washington, DC: The Catholic University of America Press, 2003), 21.
119. Cf. D. Boyarin, *A Radical Jew: Paul and the Politics of Identity* (Berkeley: University of California Press, 1997), 73–76.
120. See D.K. Buell, *Why This New Race: Ethnic Reasoning in Early Christianity* (New York: Columbia University Press, 2005); cf. also J.M. Lieu, *Christian Identity in the Jewish and Graeco-Roman World* (Oxford: Oxford University Press, 2004).

121. S. Pollock, 'Deep Orientalism? Notes on Sanskrit and Power beyond the Raj', in C.A. Breckenridge and P. van der Veer (eds), *Orientalism and the Postcolonial Predicament: Perspectives on South Asia* (Philadelphia: University of Pennsylvania Press, 1993), 76–133.
122. C. Kidd, *The Forging of Races: Race and Scripture in the Protestant Atlantic World, 1600–2000* (Cambridge: Cambridge University Press, 2006), 271.
123. B.S. Cohn, *Colonialism and Its Forms of Knowledge: The British in India*, Princeton Studies in Culture/Power/History (Princeton University Press, 1996).
124. Ibid., 79, 53–54, cf. esp. 48, 77, 80, 81.
125. Ibid., 93.
126. Cf. J. Winter, 'Thinking about Silence', in J. Winter, E. Ben-Ze'ev and R. Ginio (eds), *Shadows of War: A Social History of Silence in the Twentieth Century* (Cambridge: Cambridge University Press, 2010), 8, 10.
127. R. Habermas, 'Lost in Translation: Transfer and Nontransfer in the Atakpame Colonial Scandal', *The Journal of Modern History* 86 (2014), 47–80. She hence prescribes for historians today: '[s]cholarly historical analysis ought to analyse and not duplicate the processes of forgetting and the emergence of the historically significant. But this can only occur when attention is paid to forgetting and/or ignorance' (ibid., 80).
128. See, e.g., S. Gourgouris, *Dream Nation: Enlightenment, Colonization, and the Institution of Modern Greece* (Stanford, CA: Stanford University Press, 1996); T. Ballantyne, *Orientalism and Race: Aryanism in the British Empire* (Basingstoke: Palgrave Macmillan, 2002); cf. also the genealogical constructions of British Israelism in Kidd, *The Forging of Races*, 203–18.
129. As Marchand writes, '[t]o think of themselves as simply learning how to do things contemporary society needed done would have been to do violence to both the concept of *Bildung* and that of *Wissenschaft*' (*German Orientalism*, 333); cf. also idem, 'Georg Ebers, Sympathetic Egyptologist', in A. Blair and A.-S. Goeing (eds), *For the Sake of Learning: Essays in Honor of Anthony Grafton*, 2 vols. (Leiden: Brill, 2016), 917–32.
130. Bauer, *Volksleben im Lande der Bibel*, 20–21; cf. also 17, 226; Axel was less admiring (*Grundzüge der Landesnatur des Westjordanlandes*, 126–29).
131. Cf. T. Willi. 'Mission among the Jews, Holy Land and Aramaic Studies: The Case of Gustaf Dalman', in I. Provan and M.J. Boda (eds), *Let us Go up to Zion: Essays in Honour of H.G.M. Williamson on the Occasion of his Sixty-Fifth Birthday*, Supplements to Vetus Testamentum 153 (Leiden: Brill, 2012), 17–29.

Bibliography

Ankel, O. *Grundzüge der Landesnatur des Westjordanlandes: Entwurf einer Monographie des westjordanischen Palästina, mit einem Vorworte von Prof. Dr. Th. Fischer*. Frankfurt: Verlag der Jaeger'schen Buch- & Landkarten-Handlung, 1887.

Baedeker, K. *Palästina und Syrien: Die Hauptrouten Mesopotamiens und Babyloniens und die Insel Cypern: Handbuch für Reisende*, 7th edn, ed. I. Benzinger. Leipzig: Baedeker, 1910.

Ballantyne, T. *Orientalism and Race: Aryanism in the British Empire*. Basingstoke: Palgrave Macmillan, 2002.

Bar-Yosef, E. *The Holy Land in English Culture, 1799–1917: Palestine and the Question of Orientalism*, Oxford English Monographs. Oxford: Clarendon Press, 2005.

Bauer, L. *Volksleben im Lande der Bibel*, 2nd edn. Leipzig: Wallmann, 1903.
Benzinger, I. *Hebräische Archäologie*, Grundriss der Theologischen Wissenschaften 2/1. Freiburg: Mohr Siebeck, 1894.
———. *Geschichte Israels bis auf die griechische Zeit*, Sammlung Göschen. Leipzig: Göschen, 1904.
Bernhardsson, M.T. *Reclaiming a Plundered Past: Archaeology and Nation Building in Modern Iraq*. Austin: University of Texas Press, 2005.
Bertholet, A. *Die Stellung der Israeliten und der Juden zu den Fremden*. Freiburg: Mohr Siebeck, 1896.
———. *Das religionsgeschichtliche Problem des Spätjudentums*, Sammlung gemeinverständlicher Vorträge und Schriften aus dem Gebiet der Theologie und Religionsgeschichte 55. Tübingen: Mohr Siebeck, 1909.
———. *Das Ende des jüdischen Staatswesens: Sechs populäre Vorträge*. Tübingen: Mohr Siebeck, 1910.
———. *Die Eigenart der alttestamentlichen Religion: Eine akademische Antrittsrede*. Tübingen: Mohr Siebeck, 1913.
———. *Kulturgeschichte Israels*. Göttingen: Vandenhoeck & Ruprecht, 1919.
Boyarin, D. *A Radical Jew: Paul and the Politics of Identity*. Berkeley: University of California Press, 1997.
Budde, K. *Religion of Israel to the Exile*, American Lectures on the History of Religions, Fourth Series, 1898–1899. New York: G.P. Putnam's Sons, 1899.
Buell, D.K. *Why This New Race: Ethnic Reasoning in Early Christianity*. New York: Columbia University Press, 2005.
Buhl, F. *Geographie des alten Palästina*, Grundriss der Theologischen Wissenschaften 2/4. Freiburg: Mohr Siebeck, 1896.
Cheyne, T.K. *Jewish Religious Life after the Exile*, American Lectures on the History of Religions, Third Series, 1897–1898. New York: G.P. Putnam's Sons, 1898.
Cobbing, F.J. 'The American Palestine Exploration Society and the Survey of Eastern Palestine'. *Palestine Exploration Quarterly* 137 (2005), 9–21.
Cohn, B.S. *Colonialism and Its Forms of Knowledge: The British in India*, Princeton Studies in Culture/Power/History. Princeton, NJ: Princeton University Press, 1996.
Corbett, E.D. *Competitive Archaeology in Jordan: Narrating Identity from the Ottomans to the Hashemites*. Austin: University of Texas Press, 2014.
Cornill, C.H. *History of the People of Israel from the Earliest Times to the Destruction of Jerusalem by the Romans, Written for Lay Readers*, trans. W.H. Carruth. Chicago: Open Court Publishing Company, 1898 [German Original: *Geschichte des Volkes Israel von den ältesten Zeiten bis zur Zerstörung Jerusalems durch die Römer*. Leipzig: Harrassowitz, 1898].
Dalman, G. 'Entstehung und bisherige Entwicklung des Instituts'. *Palästinajahrbuch des Deutschen evangelischen Instituts für Altertumswissenschaft des heiligen Landes zu Jerusalem* 1 (1905), 14–20.
———. 'Foreword'. *Palästinajahrbuch des Deutschen evangelischen Instituts für Altertumswissenschaft des heiligen Landes zu Jerusalem* 1 (1905), i.
———. 'Jahresbericht nebst Mitgliederverzeichnis'. *Palästinajahrbuch des Deutschen evangelischen Instituts für Altertumswissenschaft des heiligen Landes zu Jerusalem* 2 (1906), 1–12.
de Wette, W.M.L. *Lehrbuch der christlichen Dogmatik in ihrer historischen Entwickelung dargestellt*, Vol. 1: *Biblische Dogmatik Alten und Neuen Testaments, Oder kritische Darstellung der Religionslehre des Hebraismus, des Judentums und Urchristenthums, Zum Gebrauch akademischer Vorlesungen*. Berlin: Realschulbuchhandlung, 1813.

Delitzsch, F. *Babel and Bible: Two Lectures, Delivered before the Members of the Deutsche Orient-Gesellschaft in the presence of the German Emperor*, ed. and trans. C.H.W. Johns, Crown Theological Library. London: Williams and Norgate, 1903 [German Original: *Babel und Bibel: Ein Vortrag*. Leipzig: Hinrichs, 1902].

Díaz-Andreu, M. *A World History of Nineteenth-Century Archaeology: Nationalism, Colonialism, and the Past*, Oxford Studies in the History of Archaeology. Oxford: Oxford University Press, 2007.

Duhm, B. *Die Theologie der Propheten als Grundlage für die innere Entwicklungsgeschichte der israelitischen Religion dargestellt*. Bonn: Marcus, 1875.

Ewald, H. *Geschichte des Volkes Israels bis Christus*, vol. 1. Göttingen: Dieterich, 1843.

Fassbeck, G. '"The Longer, the More Happiness I Derive from This Undertaking": James Simon and Early German Research into Galilee's Ancient Synagogues', in G. Fassbeck and A.E. Killebrew (eds), *Viewing Ancient Jewish Art and Archaeology: VeHinnei Rachel – Essays in Honor of Rachel Hachlili*, Supplements to the Journal for the Study of Judaism 172 (Leiden: Brill, 2016), 101–20.

Frohnmeyer, I. *Biblische Geographie für Schulen und Familien*, 10th edn. Calw: Verlag der Vereinsbuchhandlung, 1883.

Frohnmeyer, L.J., and I. Benzinger. *Bilderatlas zur Bibelkunde: Ein Handbuch für den Religionslehrer u. Bibelfreund*. Stuttgart: Benzinger, 1905.

Furrer, K. et al. 'Die Arbeiten des Deutschen Vereins zur Erforschung Palästina's von 1878–1897'. *Mittheilungen und Nachrichten des Deutschen Palaestina-Vereins* 3 (1897), Supplement, 1–5.

Goren, H. *'Zieht hin und erforscht das Land': Die deutsche Palästinaforschung im 19. Jahrhundert*, trans. A.C. Naujoks, Schriftenreihe des Instituts für deutsche Geschichte der Universität Tel Aviv 23. Göttingen: Wallstein, 2003.

Gourgouris, S. *Dream Nation: Enlightenment, Colonization, and the Institution of Modern Greece*. Stanford, CA: Stanford University Press, 1996.

Gressmann, H. *Palästinas Erdgeruch in der israelitischen Religion*, Kultur und Leben 8. Berlin: Curtius, 1909.

Gunkel, H. *Israel and Babylon: The Influence of Babylon on the Religion of Israel [A Reply to Delitzsch]*, trans. E.S.B. Philadelphia, PA: McVey, 1904 [German Original: *Israel und Babylonien: Der Einfluss Babyloniens auf die israelitische Religion*. Göttingen: Vandenhoeck & Ruprecht, 1903].

———. *The Influence of the Holy Spirit: The Popular View of the Apostolic Age and the Teaching of the Apostle Paul*, trans. R.A. Harrisville and P.A. Quanbeck II. Philadelphia, PA: Fortress Press, 1979 [German Original: *Die Wirkungen des heiligen Geistes, nach der populären Anschauung der apostolischen Zeit und nach der Lehre des Apostels Paulus: Eine biblisch-theologische Studie*. Göttingen: Vandenhoeck & Ruprecht, 1888].

Guthe, H. *Geschichte des Volkes Israel*, Grundriss der Theologischen Wissenschaften 2/3. Freiburg: Mohr Siebeck, 1899.

———. *Palästina*, Land und Leute: Monographien zur Erdkunde 21. Bielefeld: Velhagen & Klasing, 1908.

Guthe, H., et al. 'Aufruf zur Gründung einer Palästinabibliothek'. *ZDPV* 1 (1878), 238–39.

Habermas, R. 'Piety, Power and Powerlessness: Religion and Religious Groups in Germany, 1870–1945', in H.W. Smith (ed.), *The Oxford Handbook of Modern German History* (Oxford University Press, 2001), 453–80.

———. 'Mission im 19. Jahrhundert: Globale Netze des Religiösen'. *Historische Zeitschrift* 287(3) (2008), 629–79.

———. 'Lost in Translation: Transfer and Nontransfer in the Atakpame Colonial Scandal'. *The Journal of Modern History* 86 (2014), 47–80.

Haller, M. *Das Judentum: Geschichtsschreibung, Prophetie und Gesetzgebung nach dem Exil*, Die Schriften des Alten Testaments 2/3. Göttingen: Vandenhoeck & Ruprecht, 1914.

Hallote, R. *Bible, Map, and Spade: The American Palestine Exploration Society, Frederick Jones Bliss, and the Forgotten Story of Early American Biblical Archaeology*. Piscataway: Gorgias Press, 2006.

Hanisch, L. *Die Nachfolger der Exegeten: Deutschsprachige Erforschung des Vorderen Orients in der ersten Hälfte des 20. Jahrhunderts*. Wiesbaden: Harrassowitz, 2003.

Harnack, A. von. *Marcion: Der moderne Gläubige des 2. Jahrhunderts, der erste Reformator. Die Dorpater Preisschrift (1870)*, ed. F. Steck, Texte und Untersuchungen zur Geschichte der altchristlichen Literatur 149. Berlin: de Gruyter, 2003.

———. *What is Christianity? Lectures Delivered in the University of Berlin during the Winter Term 1899–1900*, 2nd edn, trans. T.B. Saunders. New York: G.P. Putnam's Sons, 1902 [German Original: *Das Wesen des Christentums: Sechzehn Vorlesungen vor Studierenden aller Facultäten im Wintersemester 1899/1900 an der Universität Berlin gehalten*. Leipzig: Hinrichs, 1900].

———. *Marcion: Das Evangelium vom fremden Gott, eine Monographie zur Geschichte der Grundlegung der katholischen Kirche*, Texte und Untersuchungen zur Geschichte der altchristlichen Literatur 45. Leipzig: Hinrichs, 1921.

———. *Neue Studien zu Marcion*, Texte und Untersuchungen zur Geschichte der altchristlichen Literatur 44/4. Leipzig: Hinrichs, 1923.

Heschel, S. *Abraham Geiger and the Jewish Jesus*, Chicago Studies in the History of Judaism. Chicago: The University of Chicago Press, 1998.

———. *The Aryan Jesus: Christian Theologians and the Bible in Nazi Germany*. Princeton, NJ: Princeton University Press, 2008.

Hiller, E. *Die archäologische Erforschung Palästinas*, Gesellschaft für Palästina-Forschung. Vienna: Schwarzinger, 1910.

Hölscher, G. *Landes- und Volkskunde Palästinas*, Sammlung Göschen. Leipzig: Göschen, 1907.

———. *Die Geschichte der Juden in Palästina seit dem Jahre 70 nach Chr.: Eine Skizze*. Leipzig: Hinrichs, 1909.

Holtzmann, O. *Geschichte des Volkes Israel*, Vol. 2.2: *Das Ende des jüdischen Staatswesens und die Entstehung des Christenthums*, Allgemeine Geschichte in Einzeldarstellungen 1/6. Berlin: Grote, 1888.

Howard, T.A. *Religion and the Rise of Historicism: W.M.L. de Wette, Jacob Burckhardt, and the Theological Origins of Nineteenth-Century Historical Consciousness*. Cambridge: Cambridge University Press, 2000.

Hübner, U. 'Der Deutsche Verein zur Erforschung Palästinas: seine Vorgeschichte, Gründung und Entwicklung bis in die Weimarer Zeit', in U. Hübner (ed.), *Palaestina exploranda: Studien zur Erforschung Palästinas im 19. und 20. Jahrhundert anläßlich des 125jährigen Bestehens des Deutschen Vereins zur Erforschung Palästinas*, Abhandlungen des Deutschen Palästina-Vereins 34 (Wiesbaden: Harrassowitz, 2006), 1–52.

Kamel, L. *Imperial Perceptions of Palestine: British Influence and Power in the Late Ottoman Times*. London: I.B. Tauris, 2015.

Karge, P. *Die Resultate der neueren Ausgrabungen und Forschungen in Palästina*, 3rd edn, Biblische Zeitfragen 3/8–9. Münster: Aschendorff, 1912.

Kidd, C. *The Forging of Races: Race and Scripture in the Protestant Atlantic World, 1600–2000*. Cambridge: Cambridge University Press, 2006.

Kinzig, W. *Harnack, Marcion und das Judentum, nebst einer kommentierten Edition des Briefwechsels Adolf von Harnacks mit Houston Stewart Chamberlain*, Arbeiten zur Kirchen- und Theologiegeschichte 13. Leipzig: Evangelische Verlagsanstalt, 2004.

Kirchhoff, M. *Text zu Land: Palästina im wissenschaftlichen Diskurs 1865–1920*, Schriften des Simon-Dubnow-Instituts 5. Göttingen: Vandenhoeck & Ruprecht, 2005.

Kittel, R. *A History of the Hebrews*, 2 vols., trans. J. Taylor, H.W. Hogg and E.B. Speirs, Theological Translation Library 3–4. London: Williams and Norgate, 1895, 1896 [German Original: *Geschichte der Hebräer*, 2 vols., Handbücher der alten Geschichte 1/3. Gotha: Perthes, 1888, 1892].

———. *Geschichte des Volkes Israel*, 2nd edn, 2 vols. Gotha: Perthes, 1909, 1912.

———. *Geschichte des Volkes Israel*, 3rd edn, Vol. 3: *Die Zeit der Wegführung nach Babel und die Aufrichtung der neuen Gemeinde*, 2 parts. Stuttgart: Kohlhammer, 1927, 1929.

Klostermann, A. *Geschichte des Volkes Israel bis zur Restauration unter Esra und Nehemia*. Munich: Beck, 1896.

Köhler, A. *Lehrbuch der Biblischen Geschichte Alten Testamentes*, 2 vols. Erlangen: Deichert, 1875, 1884.

König, E. *Geschichte des Reiches Gottes bis auf Jesus Christus*, Grundrisse der Theologie, Sammlung der theologischen Wissenschaften 2/1. Braunschweig: Wollermann, 1908.

———. *Geschichte der Alttestamentlichen Religion kritisch dargestellt*. Gütersloh: Bertelsmann, 1912.

Kuklick, B. *Puritans in Babylon: The Ancient Near East and American Intellectual Life, 1880–1930*. Princeton, NJ: Princeton University Press, 1996.

Kurtz, P.M. *Kaiser, Christ, and Canaan: The Religion of Israel in Protestant Germany, 1871–1918*, Forschungen zum Alten Testament I/122. Tübingen: Mohr Siebeck, 2018.

———. 'Of Lions, Arabs, & Israelites: Some Lessons from the Samson Story for Writing the History of Biblical Scholarship'. *Journal of the Bible and its Reception* 5(1) (2018), 31–48.

La Vopa, A.J. *Fichte: The Self and the Calling of Philosophy, 1762–1799*. Cambridge: Cambridge University Press, 2001.

Laqueur, W. *A History of Zionism: From the French Revolution to the Establishment of the State of Israel*, repr. ed. New York: Schocken Books, 2003.

Lehmann-Haupt, C.F.F. *Israel: Seine Entwicklung im Rahmen der Weltgeschichte*. Tübingen: Mohr Siebeck, 1911.

Levenson, J.D. *The Hebrew Bible, the Old Testament, and Historical Criticism: Jews and Christians in Biblical Studies*. Louisville, KY: Westminster/John Knox Press, 1993.

Lieu, J.M. *Christian Identity in the Jewish and Graeco-Roman World*. Oxford: Oxford University Press, 2004.

Löhr, M. *Volksleben im Lande der Bibel*, Wissenschaft und Bildung: Einzeldarstellungen aus allen Gebieten des Wissens 7. Leipzig: Quelle & Meyer, 1907.

Makdisi, U. 'Reclaiming the Land of the Bible: Missionaries, Secularism, and Evangelical Modernity'. *American Historical Review* 102(3) (1997), 680–713.

Mangold, S. *Eine 'weltbürgerliche Wissenschaft': Die deutsche Orientalistik im 19. Jahrhundert*, Pallas Athene: Beiträge zur Universitäts- und Wissenschaftsgeschichte 11. Stuttgart: Steiner, 2004.

Männchen, J. 'Gustaf Dalman und der Deutsche Verein zur Erforschung Palästinas', in U. Hübner (ed.), *Palaestina exploranda: Studien zur Erforschung Palästinas im 19. und 20. Jahrhundert anläßlich des 125jährigen Bestehens des Deutschen Vereins zur Erforschung Palästinas*, Abhandlungen des Deutschen Palästina-Vereins 34 (Wiesbaden: Harrassowitz, 2006), 227–34.

Marchand, S.L. *Down from Olympus: Archaeology and Philhellenism in Germany, 1750–1970.* Princeton, NJ: Princeton University Press, 1996.

———. 'From Liberalism to Neoromanticism: Albrecht Dieterich, Richard Reitzenstein, and the Religious Turn in *Fin-de-Siècle* German Classical Studies', in M. Ruehl and I. Gildenhard (eds), *Out of Arcadia: Classics and Politics in Germany in the Age of Burckhardt, Nietzsche and Wilamowitz,* Bulletin of the Institute of Classical Studies Supplement 79 (London: Institute of Classical Studies, School of Advanced Studies, University of London, 2003), 129–60.

———. *German Orientalism in the Age of Empire: Religion, Race, and Scholarship*, Publications of the German Historical Institute. Cambridge: Cambridge University Press, 2009.

———. 'Georg Ebers, Sympathetic Egyptologist', in A. Blair and A.-S. Goeing (eds), *For the Sake of Learning: Essays in Honor of Anthony Grafton,* 2 vols. (Leiden: Brill, 2016), 917–32.

Marti, K. *Geschichte der Israelitischen Religion,* 4th edn. Strasbourg: Bull, 1903.

———. *The Religion of the Old Testament: Its Place Among the Religions of the Nearer East,* ed. W.D. Morrison, trans. G.A. Bienemann, Crown Theological Library 19. New York: G.P. Putnam's Sons, 1907 [German Original: *Die Religion des Alten Testaments unter den Religionen des vorderen Orients.* Tübingen: Mohr Siebeck, 1906].

Morrison, W. 'Editor's Preface', in C.W. Wilson et al. (eds), *The Recovery of Jerusalem: A Narrative of Exploration and Discovery in the City and the Holy Land,* 2 vols. (London: Bentley, 1871), v–viii.

Moulton, W.J. 'The American Palestine Exploration Society'. *The Annual of the American Schools of Oriental Research* 8 (1926–27), 55–78.

Nigro, L. 'In the Shadow of the Bible. Archaeological Investigations by the *Deutsche* [*sic!*] *Palästina Verein* before the First World War: Taanek, Megiddo, Jericho, Schechem', in V. Krings and I. Tassignon (eds), *Archéologie dans l'Empire Ottoman Autour de 1900: Entre Politique, Économie et Science,* Studies over Oude Filologie, Archeologie en Geschiedenis 40 (Brussels: Belgisch Historisch Instituut te Rome, 2004), 215–29.

Nowack, W. *Lehrbuch der hebräischen Archäologie,* 2 vols., Sammlung theologischer Lehrbücher. Freiburg: Mohr Siebeck, 1894.

Oettli, S. *Die Geschichte Israels,* Vol. 1: *Geschichte Israels bis auf Alexander den Großen.* Calw: Verlag der Vereinsbuchhandlung, 1905.

Pollock, S. 'Deep Orientalism? Notes on Sanskrit and Power beyond the Raj', in C.A. Breckenridge and P. van der Veer (eds), *Orientalism and the Postcolonial Predicament: Perspectives on South Asia* (Philadelphia: University of Pennsylvania Press, 1993), 76–133.

Procksch, O. *Die Völker Altpalästinas,* Das Land der Bibel: Gemeinverständliche Hefte zur Palästinakunde 1/2. Leipzig: Hinrichs, 1914.

Röhricht, R. *Bibliotheca Geographica Palaestinae: Chronologisches Verzeichniss der auf die Geographie des Heiligen Landes bezüglichen Literatur von 333 bis 1878 und Versuch einer Cartographie herausgegeben.* Berlin: Reuther, 1890.

Schlatter, A. *Israels Geschichte von Alexander dem Großen bis Hadrian,* Reiche der Alten Welt 3. Calw: Verlag der Vereinsbuchhandlung, 1901.

———. *Die Geschichte Israels,* 2nd edn, Vol. 2: *Geschichte Israels von Alexander dem Großen bis Hadrian.* Calw: Verlag der Vereinsbuchhandlung, 1906.

Schramm, (K.)R. *Geographie von Palästina: Zum Gebrauch in Seminaren, beim Katechumenen-Unterricht und für Lehrer,* 2nd edn, ed. K. Furrer. Bremen: Heinsius, 1882.

Sellin, E. *Beiträge zur israelitischen und jüdischen Religionsgeschichte,* 2 vols. Leipzig: Deichert [Böhme], 1896, 1897.

———. *Serubbabel: Ein Beitrag zur Geschichte der messianischen Erwartung und der Entstehung des Judentums*. Leipzig: Deichert [Böhme], 1898.

———. *Studien zur Entstehungsgeschichte der jüdischen Gemeinde nach dem babylonischen Exil*, 2 vols. Leipzig: Deichert [Böhme], 1901.

Ska, J.L. 'The "History of Israel": Its Emergence as an Independent Discipline', in M. Sæbø (ed.), *Hebrew Bible/Old Testament: The History of Its Interpretation*, vol. 3/1: *The Nineteenth Century* (Göttingen: Vandenhoeck & Ruprecht, 2013), 307–45.

Smend, R. *Lehrbuch der alttestamentlichen Religionsgeschichte*, Sammlung theologischer Lehrbücher: Alttestamentliche Theologie. Freiburg: Mohr Siebeck, 1893.

Socin, A. 'Bericht über neue Erscheinungen auf dem Gebiete der Palästinaliteratur 1880'. *Zeitschrift des Deutschen Palästina-Vereins* 4 (1881), 127–56.

Stade, B. *Geschichte des Volkes Israel*, Vol. 1: *Geschichte Israels unter der Königsherrschaft oder Geschichte des Volkes Israel von Beginn der Königsherrschaft bis zur Zerstörung Jerusalems durch die Babylonier*, Allgemeine Geschichte in Einzeldarstellungen 1/6. Berlin: Grote, 1887.

———. *Biblische Theologie des Alten Testaments*, Vol. 1: *Die Religion Israels und die Entstehung des Judentums*, Grundriss der Theologischen Wissenschaften 2/2.1. Tübingen: Mohr Siebeck, 1905.

Tal, U. *Christians and Jews in Germany: Religion, Politics, and Ideology in the Second Reich, 1870–1914*, trans. N.J. Jacobs. Ithaca, NY: Cornell University Press, 1975.

Thomsen, P. *Systematische Bibliographie der Palästina-Literatur auf Veranlassung des Deutschen Vereins zur Erforschung Palästinas bearbeitet*, Vol. 1: *1895–1904*. Leipzig: Haupt, 1908.

———. *Palästina und seine Kultur in fünf Jahrtausenden: Nach den neuesten Ausgrabungen und Forschungen dargestellt*, Aus Natur und Geisteswelt: Sammlung wissenschaftlich-gemeinverständlicher Darstellungen 260. Leipzig: Teubner, 1909 [2nd edn, 1917].

———. *Kompendium der palästinischen Altertumskunde*. Tübingen: Mohr, 1913.

———. *Denkmäler Palästinas aus der Zeit Jesu*, Das Land der Bibel: Gemeinverständliche Hefte zur Palästinakunde 2/1. Leipzig: Hinrichs, 1916.

Tobler, T. *Palästina: Nebst anhang der vierten wanderung*. Berlin: Reimer, 1868.

Wellhausen, J. *Prolegomena to the History of Israel, with a reprint of the article* Israel *from the 'Encyclopædia Britannica'*, trans. J.S. Black and A. Menzies. Edinburgh: Adam & Charles Black, 1885 [German Original: *Prolegomena zur Geschichte Israels*. Berlin: Reimer, 1883. 1st edn published as *Geschichte Israels*, Vol. 1. Berlin: Reimer, 1878].

———. *Israelitische und jüdische Geschichte*, 1st edn. Berlin: Reimer, 1894.

Wiese, C. *Challenging Colonial Discourse: Jewish Studies and Protestant Theology in Wilhelmine Germany*, trans. C. Wiese and B. Harshav. Leiden: Brill, 2005.

Willi, T. 'Mission among the Jews, Holy Land and Aramaic Studies: The Case of Gustaf Dalman', in I. Provan and M.J. Boda (eds), *Let us Go up to Zion: Essays in Honour of H.G.M. Williamson on the Occasion of his Sixty-Fifth Birthday*, Supplements to Vetus Testamentum 153 (Leiden: Brill, 2012), 17–29.

Williamson, G.S. *The Longing for Myth in Germany: Religion and Aesthetic Culture from Romanticism to Nietzsche*. Chicago: The University of Chicago Press, 2004.

Winckler, H. *Geschichte Israels in Einzeldarstellungen*, 2 vols., Völker und Staaten des alten Orients 2–3. Leipzig: Pfeiffer, 1895, 1900.

Winter, J. 'Thinking about Silence', in J. Winter, E. Ben-Ze'ev and R. Ginio (eds), *Shadows of War: A Social History of Silence in the Twentieth Century* (Cambridge: Cambridge University Press, 2010), 3–31.

Wokoeck, U. *German Orientalism: The Study of the Middle East and Islam from 1800 to 1945*, Culture and Civilization in the Middle East. London: Routledge, 2009.

Zachhuber, J. *Theology as Science in Nineteenth-Century Germany: From F.C. Baur to Ernst Troeltsch*, Changing Paradigms in Historical and Systematic Theology. Oxford: Oxford University Press, 2013.

Zerubavel, Y. *Recovered Roots: Collective Memory and the Making of Israeli National Tradition*, Chicago: University of Chicago Press, 1995.

PART II
Religious and Secular
Public Debates

3
What Does It Mean To Be 'Secular' in the German Kaiserreich?

An Intervention

Lucian Hölscher

The German Kaiserreich was a 'secular' society, but not in the sense that many use the word today. For at the same time it was a religious society, but again not in the sense that many today call things 'religious'. Both statements seem to be contradictory, because when speaking of 'secularity', many people are used to thinking of something very much opposed to religion. But this is a deficient understanding of secularity, not only in reference to the society of the Kaiserreich, but also to our present time. In fact, the concepts of 'secular' and 'religious' are much more entangled in modern times than most people are aware of. The following chapter will demonstrate this by giving attention to: (1) the changing meaning of the term 'secular' in modern times; (2) the very important relation of confession and liberty in the German discourse about religion and secularity in the German Kaiserreich; and (3) the emergence of what can be called a German Protestant version of 'civil religion'.

Some Opening Remarks on Conceptional History

One of the most basic insights of conceptional history is the hypothesis that language is an expression of the society that makes use of it. That means, for conceptional historians, that language is bound to certain times and regions, at the same time representing and shaping the institutions and ideas of that society. But this does not mean that the contemporary existence of a word is a necessary precondition for using that word today in referring to things of that time; historical objects differ from their contemporary perception when they are perceived by another time and society, hence it makes sense to label them in a different way and by different terms. Nevertheless, it is useful to reflect on the fact that a concept did not exist in a past period, and ask the question why.[1] This is the reason it makes sense to start with some observations about conceptual questions.

In dealing with historical concepts, the historian should be aware of the differences of languages: the English 'secular' is not the same concept as the German *säkular*. It may also be translated by *weltlich*, as much as *weltlich* can be translated into English by using other words such as 'mundane' or 'temporal' (which again finds its equivalent in the German *zeitlich*). In a purely linguistic discourse, such overlapping semantic fields may be of minor importance, but in historical discourses they become relevant in pointing to different discursive structures. That is why I employ the words in their original (German) language, adding the English translation for the reader who is not familiar with the German terms.

In the period of the German Kaiserreich (1871–1918), the term *säkular* was not a key concept for long-term historical developments; it did not even exist in today's established meaning of 'the opposite of religious'. The nearest German equivalent to the English 'secular' was *weltlich*, but it is doubtful whether *weltlich* had the same meaning, since the term was used in the political sense of 'belonging to the sphere of state or community'.[2]

The same can be said of the term 'secularization': there was a German term *Säkularisation* in the nineteenth century derived from Latin *saecularisatio* pointing to the juridical concept of transmitting a good from the church to the temporal power of the state. However, the modern idea of secularization, invented in England in the 1840s by the group around the freethinker George J. Holyoake (1817–1906), was not introduced to the German academic discourse until the turn of the century, and only became popular after the First World War.[3] For the interpretation of the Kaiserreich it is an alien concept, as far as the discourse of the time is concerned. But this does not mean that it does not make sense to use the terms 'secularity' and 'secularization' for analysing the religious landscape of Germany in the late nineteenth and early twentieth centuries. Rather we should ask whether they are appropriate to the religious situation of Germany at this time.

In dealing with the problem of secularity in the German Kaiserreich I shall speak, with Pierre Bourdieu, of a 'religious field'.[4] But I use this concept in a slightly different sense: not as a container concept for certain objects, which may be called 'religious' or 'secular', but as a set of antithetic semantic structures used in political debates for organizing the reality.[5] The relation of the terms 'religious' and 'secular' is one of them, but not the only one, nor even the most important one, structuring the religious field of German discourses in the late nineteenth and early twentieth centuries. Discussing problems related to what we today call 'secularity', concepts such as 'religion' (*Religion*) and 'state' (*Staat*), 'science' (*Wissenschaft*) and 'confession' (*Konfession*), 'freedom' (*Freiheit*) and 'hierarchy' (*Hierarchie*) were much more prominent and familiar at the time.

Semantic structures are mobile: they are, often at one and the same time, set by various partners in different ways and they change over time. It is exactly this changing framework of historical semantics that interests the conceptional historian. Hence what we may call 'secular' in the German Kaiserreich differs from contemporary England, France and the United States as much as from secularity in the Weimar Republic or in the first half of the nineteenth century. And even in the German society of the Kaiserreich various meanings of the same semantic structure were in circulation.

The main reason for being so scrupulous about using the concepts 'religion' and 'secularity' is that the contemporary usage of the terms can lead us to characteristic features of the contemporary discourse, which again reproduced mental and social structures of that time. By the time of the Kaiserreich, religion and secular society were seen as opposites only by a minority of people in Germany. Most people would have agreed to what we may call a secular understanding of religion or a religious understanding of secularity. Hence, it makes more sense to speak of religion and secularity not in terms of opposition, but in terms of convergence – that is, as a relationship full of tensions but aiming at certain balances.

Semantic Changes: From 'Spiritual/Temporal' to 'Religious/Secular'

In the mid nineteenth century, a new political and semantic pattern began to occupy the religious discourse of Western Europe: the rejection of religion and the Christian churches by large parts of society.[6] The same can be said of large parts of the Jewish population who became alienated from traditional features of the Jewish faith. All those enlightened people who, in defining themselves as deists, pantheists, Unitarians, liberals, and so on, had described the world in terms of rational discourse and liberal ethics, now began to reject religion altogether in favour of science, liberty and republicanism, leaving the concept of 'religion' to the theistic orthodoxy and to the conservatives in Christian and Jewish institutions who supported authoritarian governments.[7] Some scholars date the beginning of modern secularism back to the seventeenth and eighteenth centuries, but the semantic patterns only changed definitely by the mid nineteenth century.[8] It was only then that the cooperation of the spiritual and the temporal power, which had occupied late medieval and early modern societies for so long, gave way to an antagonistic confrontation of secular and religious powers – not in all parts of society, but in a growing number of radical discourses. As a consequence, secular societies began to develop their own secular worldview, called 'secularism' in England, *laïcité* in France,[9] and *Wissenschaft* (science) in Germany. In response, the churches developed a broad network of social institutions, thought of as a kind of spiritual alternative and substitute for the supposed 'atheistic' nature of secular society.[10]

Gradually the German term *weltlich* as much as the English 'secular' began to change their meaning in the second half of the nineteenth century: up to that time, when institutions were called 'secular' (*weltlich*), this was an indicator that they were run by 'temporal' authorities such as kings and princes. But this did not mean that they were opposed to religion. The Prussian government, for instance, established *weltliche Schulen* ('secular' primary schools) in the 1770s, but such schools of course included religious teaching. The term *weltlich* referred to the fact that these schools were established and run by state authorities, not by the churches. Nobody would have assumed that they were opposed to religion as such.

This understanding of the concept *weltliche Schulen* continued to be the normal usage, at least up to the First World War. But when in 1891 the Social Democratic party programme of Erfurt asked for the *Weltlichkeit der Schule* (secularity of schools), the term *Weltlichkeit* had another meaning: it asked for religious teaching to be excluded from primary schools altogether. Schools should not only be directed by state authorities (instead of ecclesiastical bodies as before), but they should also exclude religious instruction from teaching – as much in the subject *Religionsunterricht* as in the humanities and all natural sciences.[11]

Only after 1900 was the term *weltlich* – in the new radical sense of 'anti-religious' –gradually substituted by the new term *säkular*. The word as such was well established already, but with the meaning 'temporal'. It pointed to the turn of a century for instance (*Säkularfeiern*), but not the sphere of state and society in opposition to the church or religious issues. And even when its use became more and more popular after the First World War, the term *säkular* (unlike *weltlich*) kept to a critical understanding of the secularization process. Only in the 1950s, under the influence of the secular theology of Friedrich Gogarten, did a positive understanding of secularity and secularization begin to revolutionize the relationship of state and church, religion and secular society.[12]

But to come back to the period of the late Kaiserreich, the term *weltlich* ('secular') was not unclear but ambivalent and contested: it was ambiguous in referring to state authority (as opposed to church authority) and to the rejection of religion at the same time; and so was the attitude of contemporaries. However, in pointing to the new understanding of 'secularity' around 1900, three facts should be kept in mind: first, the demands of social democrats and radical liberals – such as the Society for Ethical Culture, the Monistenbund and even the so-called Weimarer Kartell, a forum of all progressive groups, established in 1908 – were not representative of German society as a whole, even if we include the orthodox parts of the churches who spoke of *Weltlichkeit* in terms of atheism and political revolution. Second, in the semantic transformation of the term *weltlich*, Jews played a major role, both as emancipated citizens being interested in pushing back the influence of religious tradition and as prominent members of liberal and socialist organizations. Finally, even in these left-wing groups, secularism in the sense of an anti-religious feeling was not a 'culture', a positive way of understanding the world and society, but rather the negation and denial of a religious (Christian or Jewish) culture.

In Kaiserreich Germany, it was not easy to speak of secularity in terms of a positive culture at all. For expressing what they believed in, liberals and socialists would rather go for terms such as *Wissenschaft* (science), *Vernunft* (reason) and *Freiheit* (liberty), than for *Weltlichkeit* (secularity). To give some examples: Otto von Bismarck, protestant chancellor of Germany, was well known for his animosity to church orthodoxy (Protestant and Catholic), but nevertheless he was a religious person, deeply rooted in both Hegelian deism and Lutheran pietism; and the 'materialistic' scholar and politician Rudolf von Virchow, although engaged in opposing Christianity as an irrational myth, he was a humanist and as such was religious in a broader sense. Many social democrats, like Friedrich Engels, believed in the coming of a future society called 'socialism', in much the same way as Christians believe in the coming realm of God. Even Karl Marx, Karl Kautsky, Eduard Bernstein and other Jewish members of the Social Democratic party believed in the teleological development of history, transforming the Jewish religious figure of the coming Messiah into the idea of a happy communist future. Also, the biologist Ernst Haeckel, founder of the German Monist League in 1906, asserted his monism to be a 'religion'.[13]

Calling all these people and belief systems 'secular' only makes sense if we take the term 'secular' for addressing religious attitudes, which combine their natural understanding of the world with some kind of religious or transcendent idea. The only institution that resisted this was the Catholic church. Already in 1864, Pope Pius IX in his *Syllabus errorum* condemned eighty liberal and anti-Christian sentences that were considered to support a secular understanding of the world and of society. Many Catholics did not support this 'anti-modernist' position of the Holy Seat, but in following 'secular' ideas they did not rely on religious Church traditions as much as Protestants and Jews.

Catholic semantics did not allow defining a 'secular' understanding of state and society beyond religion, but they opened a wide range of activities and responsibilities beyond the church. For example, Ludwig Windthorst, leader of the Catholic centre party in the Reichstag and an ardent opponent against Bismarck's state Protestantism, insisted on political independence of the centre party from directives of the Pope in secular affairs as much as from the *Reichskanzler*; he cooperated with Protestant parties and accepted the secular equality of all religions and denominations. 'We again and again act according to our convictions only, and even the bishops of Germany have no influence on our decisions whatsoever', he declared in 1875 when the government had suspended the liberty of the churches to elect their own staff. Following the doctrine of infallibility, he underlined in a speech before the members of parliament on April 19th that the Pope had no secular powers, but only a spiritual ones.[14] In many aspects of civil life, Catholics felt much freer than Protestants to follow their secular convictions without mingling them with religious ideas and concepts.

Confession and Liberty

To get a deeper understanding of religious conflicts in late nineteenth-century German society, it is useful to turn to another key concept of the time, that of *Konfession*. In the German language *Konfession* is a much broader concept than the English 'confession', as it not only covers 'profess' and 'faith' but also 'avowal', 'commitment' and 'denomination'.[15] Taken as a general concept for religious bodies (Lutheran, Reformist and Catholic churches) the concept was created around 1800.[16] It turned out to be a most useful tool for the religious pacification at the time of the political rearrangement of Germany after 1800, when Catholic and Protestant regions were united in one country and subordinated to the power of sovereign princes without losing their status of public institutions.[17]

From that time onwards, in most German countries, all the three Christian denominations (*Konfessionen*) that had been recognized as public religions in 1648 (i.e. Lutheran, Catholic and the Reformed Church), were taken as being equal in public and private affairs. Different from France under Napoleon, the 'confessional churches' (*Konfessionskirchen*) themselves were accepted as 'public corporations' – despite being under the control of the state (seen as a neutral body above all religious matters and bodies).[18] This did much to pacify the conflict between the spiritual and the temporal powers.

But the peacekeeping function of the newborn concept *Konfession* was soon threatened, as in the 1830s *Konfessionalismus* (confessionalism) began to change the religious field once more. A new structure of religious dispute arose, first among Protestant groups; questioning the denominational formation of religious bodies (such as Catholics, Lutherans and Reformed Churches), 'enlightenment', 'rationality' and 'culture' were accepted as the new criteria for religious groups. Hence those who argued for going back to the pre-enlightened foundations of the reformation were called *Konfessionalisten* (confessionalists), their opponents *Rationalisten* (rationalists) or *Liberale* (liberals). By the 1840s, a new competition for *wahre Religion* (true religion) emerged, cutting through all denominations, just at a time when the juridical war between the old denominations had begun to be pacified. Even the Jews were included in the number of *Konfessionen*, but not the Moslems or other non-Christian groups.

'True religion', the confessionalists would argue from now on, could only be 'confessional' Christendom (*konfessionelles Christentum*). At the time of the Kaiserreich the animosity between 'confessionalists' and 'liberals' within all denominations was much higher than between Catholic and Protestant confessionalists respectively liberals. This became most apparent in the 1870s, when Bismarck's liberal government fought the *Kulturkampf*: for instance, when the liberal government installed civil marriage as an obligatory act for all citizens in 1876, they had to face opposition from confessionalists of all denominations. A similar coalition among confessionalists of both denominations happened to come together in the 1890s, when the Prussian government established confessionalist primary schools (*Konfessionsschulen*), which was strongly opposed by both Catholic and Protestant liberals.

Later, many historians declared the *Kulturkampf* to be a fight between Protestants and Catholics, but this was not true: it was a fight between 'confessionalist' Catholicism, called 'ultramontan' and supported by confessionalist Protestants on the one side, and 'liberal' Protestantism, centred around the Free Conservative, National Liberal and the left Liberal parties, and supported by liberal Catholics. Accusing the other side of subverting the religious foundations of state and society, each side began to blast open the concept of 'religiosity': free religious authors, such as David Friedrich Strauss in his bestseller of 1872 *Der alte und der neue Glaube*, would rely on the concept of 'religion' as much as orthodox conservatives such as Pope Pius IX.

In the Prussian *Kulturkampf* a new formation of the religious field developed: 'liberty', 'freedom of thought', 'science' and 'culture' were opposed to 'confession', not so much to 'religion' as such. For radical opponents such as social democrats, 'confession' and 'religion' became more or less the same, Christianity a 'confessional religion' altogether. This is the semantic background from 1900 up to the 1930s, when both left- and right-wing critics of the churches defined 'confessional Christendom' to be the enemy. But this was true also for confessionalists: by the 1920s they began to see 'secularity' as the enemy of religion, and both sides were seen as belonging to one another.[19] But for the Kaiserreich this is a view *ex post*, not appropriate to the time before the war.

Aspects of Secularity in the German Kaiserreich

Turning away from the contemporary usage of concepts to those aspects of secularity that can only be seen from our time, one may ask: how much secularism can be attached to the German Kaiserreich, if we take the term as an expression of secular concerns?

Substantial parts of the urban society of the Kaiserreich were most secular in neglecting religious and church obligations. By the mid nineteenth century, even in rural districts, church practices such as regular attendance at Sunday services had dropped to less than 50 per cent, not to speak of the big cities, where attendance dropped to under 10 per cent.[20] Only a small minority of Protestants prayed regularly outside church. Protestant religion became rapidly diversified in various forms, such as reform movements, '*Bildungsreligionen*' – cults of 'classical' authors (Goethe, Schiller, Nietzsche, Wagner etc.), later '*völkische*', and

'Arian' religions.[21] Within the regional Protestant churches (*Landeskirchen*) various religious branches (liberals, modernists, positives, mediatorials, and others) fought against each other, leaving it to individual free choice to decide how much belief in traditional doctrines, such as the personality of God and the resurrection of Jesus Christ, he would accept. There was a broad attachment to some kind of religiosity, but Christendom no longer embraced all of them as a unifying factor or organization.

There was strong competition between Christian denominations, in the homeland of Germany as much as in missionary activities outside of Europe. But the Christian denominations began to close ranks: first, by excluding their nominal members, who seemed to be too secular (*weltlich*), and too inclined to blur the denominational borders; and later, by fighting the common enemy, socialism and atheism, which turned out to be a perfect way to keep down the traditional animosity between Catholics and Protestants.[22]

Among those who may be called 'secular' according to the understanding of the term today, we may discern several groups: first, there was the small group of freethinking atheists – most of them socialist and radical liberals – sometimes called 'secularists' in analogy to the followers of Holyoake in England,[23] who in 1880 had melded with materialists and radical republicans in the International Freethought Federation; second, a broader group of people coming from all social strata who without quitting church membership looked for other inspirations to replace or to complement the Christian doctrine by scientific worldviews, religious ideas from sources beyond Christendom such as Buddhism and Confucianism, and projects of social reform such as vegetarianism and socialism; and finally, a growing number of people who did not care for religion any more, being convinced that they had no need for any religious orientation whatsoever. Despite their fundamental differences, these groups came together in their opposition to church politics and in the hope that the secularization of society would lead to a peaceful arrangement of people with different convictions. As long as this belief was not shattered by the totalitarian aspirations of communism after the First World War, the concept of 'secularity' was a utopian vision for at least a strong minority in Germany.

Comparing the social institutions of Protestant Germany with other Protestant countries such as England, Scandinavia and the United States of America, it is remarkable how secular liberal German institutions were in general. Universities, schools of higher education, clubs, journals and many other institutions had no religious character in their practical work anymore.[24] In the higher ranks of bourgeois institutions, religious topics or perspectives were less present than in England and the United States, but perhaps more present than in the *laïque* educational system of France. Among liberals, a rather distant view of religious cultures in other parts of the world was so common that religious interests survived only as a subculture of religious minorities, such as the Jesuits or the Pietists on the Protestant side.

The German Model of 'Civil Religion'

Taking all this together, one may speak of Christian liberalism in Germany, especially in the Protestant north of the country, as a Prussian type of civil religion. The German 'civil religion' is different from the French and the American type: it is not based on a fierce opposition to Christianity as in the French '*laïcité*', but rather on a pretty conventional Protestant anti-Catholicism. The Prussian God is a Protestant God, national and enlightened at the same time, fighting for his 'chosen people'.[25] This is not so different from the American civil religion, which had an anti-Catholic and nationalist bias, too. However, the Prussian model of Protestant-biased civil religion differs from the American in its anti-deistic character. There was little space for an acknowledgement of equal rights for many religious cults, if they did not fit to norms of modern Protestant culture – Lutheranism, Calvinism, even Roman Catholicism and Judaism were accepted, but only under the condition of being loyal to the Prussian monarchy and open to modern cultural standards, which were described mainly in terms of Protestant ethics (*Sittlichkeit*).

In the *Kulturkampf* of the 1870s, for example, Catholic students were asked to pass a so-called *Kulturexamen* in order to make sure that teachers trained by the churches were familiar with the foundations of modern philosophy and hermeneutics, education and aesthetics, such as the writings of Immanuel Kant, Johann Heinrich Pestalozzi and Friedrich Schleiermacher. In politics as much as in science and morals, religion had to keep silent. And if the Christian character of state and society was attacked, tolerance had an end.

Different from American civil religion, many members of the Prussian upper class had a very distant relationship to the religious culture of their churches altogether. This was a strong heritage of the time of state building in the seventeenth and eighteenth centuries, when higher civil servants, and above all officers of the Prussian army, fostered prejudices against the church and Christian religion.[26] Up to the First World War, many noblemen still took the role of patrons in their community, but they lost contact with the ecclesiastical culture and piety of that community. There was little warm religiosity, but sometimes much concern for secular humanity.[27] Prussian virtues such as honourable behaviour, punctuality, courage and dutifulness were taken as moral standards that substituted the Christian virtues.

After the revolution of 1848, broad strata of the new middle classes, enlightened people such as physicians, lawyers and teachers had joined the anti-ecclesiastical camp. Many of them lived a private Christianity, with a kind of humanitarian religiosity, represented by spiritual heroes such as Goethe, Nietzsche and Schopenhauer. But in general, the higher classes were concerned to not make too much fuss about religion. For many it was a question of decency that their religion would not be too 'noisy'. This seems to be characteristic for the German model of civil religion, at least up to the 1960s, if not until today.

Lucian Hölscher, born in 1948, is a German historian, who held a chair for Modern German History and Theory of History at the Ruhr University Bochum in Germany from 1991 to 2014. His work focuses on conceptual history ('Contradictory Concepts: An Essay on the Semantic Structure of Religious Discourses', *Contributions to the History of Concepts* 10, 2015), historical future research ('The Discovery of the Future', in Peter Gollwitzer et al. [eds], *The Psychology of Thinking about the Future*, Guilford Press, 2017) and religious history ('The Religious and the Secular: Semantic Reconfigurations of the Religious Field in Germany from the Eighteenth to the Twentieth Centuries', in Lucian Hölscher and Marion Eggert (eds), *Religion and Secularity: Transformations and Transfers of Religious Discourses in Europe and Asia*, Brill, 2013), as well as theory of historical times ('5. Time Gardens. Historical Concepts in Modern Historiographie', *History and Theory* 53, 2014).

Notes

1. Cf. L. Hölscher, 'The Concept of Conceptual History (Begriffsgeschichte) and the "Geschichtliche Grundbegriffe"', *Concept and Communication* 1(2) (2008), 179–98; R. Koselleck, *Begriffsgeschichten: Studien zur Semantik und Pragmatik der politischen und sozialen Sprache* (Frankfurt/Main: Suhrkamp, 2008).
2. L. Hölscher, 'The Religious and the Secular: Semantic Reconfigurations of the Religious Field in Germany from the Eighteenth to the Twentieth Centuries', in L. Hölscher and M. Eggert (eds), *Religion and Secularity: Transformations and Transfers of Religious Discourses in Europe and Asia* (Leiden: Brill, 2013), 35–58.
3. It is true, the terms *Säkularisation*, *Säkularisierung* and *Verweltlichung* are much older, going back to at least the early nineteenth century, and in certain exceptional cases even to the seventeenth century. But it was only in the late nineteenth century that *Säkularisierung* adopted the character of a key concept for long-term historical developments. Cf. H. Lübbe, *Säkularisierung: Geschichte eines ideenpolitischen Begriffs* (Freiburg: Alber, 1965); U. Barth, 'Säkularisierung I', in G. Müller and H. Balz (eds), *Theologische Realenzyklopädie* (Berlin: De Gruyter, 1998), 603–33; H.W. Strätz and H. Zabel, 'Säkularisation, Säkularisierung', in O. Brunner et al. (eds), *Geschichtliche Grundbegriffe* (Stuttgart: Klett-Cotta, 1984), 789–830. The English expression 'secularization' can be translated to German by two words: *Säkularisation* and *Säkularisierung*. Today most authors use *Säkularisation* when referring to the legal aspect, and *Säkularisierung* when referring to the cultural process, but in the past both aspects were addressed by both terms; cf. H. Lehmann, 'Säkularisation und Säkularisierung: Zwei umstrittene historische Deutungskategorien', in H. Lehmann (ed.), *Säkularisierung: Der europäische Sonderweg in Sachen Religion* (Göttingen: Wallstein, 2004), 36–56.
4. P. Bourdieu, 'Genesis and Structure of the Religious Field', *Comparative Social Research* 13 (1991), 144; E. Dianteill, 'Pierre Bourdieu and the Sociology of Religion', *Theory and Society* 32 (2003), 529–49.
5. Cf. L. Hölscher, 'Contradictory Concepts: An Essay on the Semantic Structure of Religious Discourses', *Contributions* 10(1) (2015), 69–88.

6. H. McLeod, *Secularisation in Western Europe, 1848–1914* (London: Macmillan, 2000); C. Brown, *The Death of Christian Britain: Understanding Secularisation 1800–2000* (London: Routledge, 2001); L. Hölscher, 'Europe in the Age of Secularisation', in C. Brown and M. Snape (eds), *Secularisation in the Christian World: Essays in Honour of Hugh McLeod* (Farnham: Ashgate, 2010), 197–204.
7. F.W. Graf, *Die Politisierung des religiösen Bewusstseins. Die bürgerlichen Religionsparteien im deutschen Vormärz: Das Beispiel des Deutschkatholizismus* (Stuttgart: Frommann-Holzboog, 1978).
8. H. Roetz, 'The Influence of Foreign Knowledge on Eighteenth-Century European Secularism', in L. Hölscher and M. Eggert (eds), *Religion and Secularity: Transformations and Transfers of Religious Discourses in Europe and Asia* (Leiden: Brill, 2013), 9–34; Hölscher, 'The Religious and the Secular'.
9. For a history of the French concept of '*laïcité*', cf. S. Le Grand-Ticchi, 'The Origin of the Concept of "Laïcité" in Nineteenth-Century France', in L. Hölscher and M. Eggert (eds), *Religion and Secularity: Transformations and Transfers of Religious Discourses in Europe and Asia* (Leiden: Brill, 2013), 59–76; idem (ed.), *La laïcité en question: Religion, État et société en France et en Allemagne du 18e siècle à nos jours* (Villeneuve d'ascq: Presses universitaires du septentrion, 2008).
10. L. Hölscher, *Geschichte der protestantischen Frömmigkeit* (Munich: Beck, 2005).
11. R. Lachmann and F. Schweitzer (eds), *Geschichte des evangelischen Religionsunterrichts in Deutschland* (Neukirchen-Vluyn: Neukirchener, 2007); Hölscher, 'The Religious and the Secular', 45–52.
12. L. Hölscher, 'Kirche im Zeitalter der Säkularisierung', *Zeitschrift für evangelische Ethik*. Sonderheft 52 (2007), 3–11; idem, 'Die Säkularisierung der Kirchen: Sprachliche Transformationsprozesse in den langen 1960er Jahren', in W. Damberg (ed.), *Soziale Strukturen und Semantiken des Religiösen im Wandel: Transformationen in der Bundesrepublik Deutschland 1949–1989* (Essen: Klartext, 2011), 203–14.
13. E. Haeckel, *Die Welträtsel: Gemeinverständliche Studien über monistische Philosophie, chapter 18: Unsere monistische Religion* (Bonn: Strauss, 1899).
14. E. Hüsgen, *Ludwig Windhorst: Sein Leben, sein Wirken* (Cologne: J.P. Bachem, 1911), 169. Cf. H. Kues, 'Gesellschaft braucht Orientierung: Ein Plädoyer für eine engagierte Kirche', in W. Erbacher (ed.), *Entweltlichung der Kirche? Die Freiburger Rede des Papstes* (Freiburg: Herder, 2012), 170.
15. The various meanings were adopted at different times: the ideas of 'profess' and 'avowal' were the oldest ('profess' going back to the middle ages, and 'avowal' to the time of the Protestant reformations of the sixteenth century), while 'denomination' was the youngest; cf. L. Hölscher, 'Konfessionspolitik in Deutschland zwischen Glaubensstreit und Koexistenz', in idem (ed.), *Baupläne der sichtbaren Kirche: Sprachliche Konzepte religiöser Vergemeinschaftung in Europa* (Göttingen: Wallstein, 2007), 11–52.
16. From the sixteenth century onwards, Protestant assemblies used the term 'confessio' for written documents – like the 'confessio Augustana' (1530) or the 'confessio Helvetica' (1536). Before the end of the eighteenth century it was not used for religious groups and their faith. Cf. L. Hölscher, *Protestantische Frömmigkeit zwischen Reformation und säkularer Gesellschaft* (Freiburg: Herder, 2017), 61.
17. Hölscher, 'Konfessionspolitik in Deutschland'.
18. S. Weichlein, 'Von der Staatskirche zur religiösen Kultur: Die Entstehung des Begriffs der "Körperschaft des öffentlichen Rechts" mit Blick auf die Kirchenartikel der Weimarer

Reichsverfassung', in L. Hölscher (ed.), *Baupläne der sichtbaren Kirche: Sprachliche Konzepte religiöser Vergemeinschaftung in Europa* (Göttingen: Wallstein, 2007), 90–116.
19. T. Weir, *Secularism and Religion in Nineteenth-Century Germany: The Rise of the Fourth Confession* (New York: Cambridge University Press, 2014); idem, 'A European Culture War in the Twentieth Century? Anticatholicism and Antibolshevism between Moscow, Berlin and Rome 1922 to 1933', *Journal of Religious History* 39(2) (2015), 175–331.
20. L. Hölscher (ed.), *Datenatlas zur religiösen Geographie im protestantischen Deutschland von der Mitte des 19. Jahrhunderts bis zum Zweiten Weltkrieg* (Berlin: De Gruyter, 2003); Hölscher, *Geschichte der protestantischen Frömmigkeit*, 181–207.
21. Hölscher, *Geschichte der protestantischen Frömmigkeit*, 330–400.
22. Weir, *Secularism and Religion*.
23. *Kirchenlexikon*. 1895. 2nd edition, edited by Joseph Cardinal Hergenröther and continued by Dr Franz Kaulen, vol. 9, Freiburg, 1535–1536: Säcularismus.
24. F. Paulsen, *Geschichte des gelehrten Unterrichts auf den deutschen Schulen und Universitäten vom Ausgang des Mittelalters bis zur Gegenwart: Mit besonderer Rücksicht auf den klassischen Unterricht* (Berlin: Verein Wissenschaftlicher Verleger, [1920] 1960).
25. G. Krumeich and H. Lehmann (eds), *Gott mit uns: Nation, Religion und Gewalt im 19. und frühen 20. Jahrhundert* (Göttingen:Vandenhoeck & Ruprecht, 2000).
26. R.N. Bellah, 'Civil Religion in America', *Daedalus. Journal of the American Academy of Arts and Sciences* 96(1) (1967), 1–21; R. Schieder, *Civil Religion: die religiöse Dimension der politischen Kultur* (Gütersloh: Gütersloher Verlagshaus Mohn, 1987); L. Hölscher, 'Civil Religion and Secular Religion', in G. Motzkin and Y. Fischer (eds), *Religion and Democracy in Contemporary Europe* (London: Alliance Publishing Trust, 2008), 55–62.
27. Hölscher, *Geschichte der protestantischen Frömmigkeit*, 305–6.

Bibliography

Barth, U. 'Säkularisierung I', in G. Müller and H. Balz (eds), *Theologische Realenzyklopädie* (Berlin: De Gruyter, 1998), 603–33.
Bellah, R.N. 'Civil Religion in America'. *Daedalus. Journal of the American Academy of Arts and Sciences* 96(1) (1967), 1–21.
Bourdieu, P. 'Genesis and Structure of the Religious Field'. *Comparative Social Research* 13 (1991), 1–44.
Brown, C. *The Death of Christian Britain: Understanding Secularisation 1800–2000*. London: Routledge, 2001.
Dianteill, E. 'Pierre Bourdieu and the Sociology of Religion'. *Theory and Society* 32 (2003), 529–49.
Graf, F.W. *Die Politisierung des religiösen Bewusstseins. Die bürgerlichen Religionsparteien im deutschen Vormärz: Das Beispiel des Deutschkatholizismus*. Stuttgart: Frommann-Holzboog, 1978.
Haeckel, E. *Die Welträtsel: Gemeinverständliche Studien über monistische Philosophie, chapter 18: Unsere monistische Religion*. Bonn: Strauss, 1899.
Hölscher, L. (ed.). *Datenatlas zur religiösen Geographie im protestantischen Deutschland von der Mitte des 19. Jahrhunderts bis zum Zweiten Weltkrieg*. Berlin: De Gruyter, 2003.
———. *Geschichte der protestantischen Frömmigkeit*. Munich: Beck, 2005.

———. 'Kirche im Zeitalter der Säkularisierung', *Zeitschrift für evangelische Ethik*. Sonderheft 52 (2007), 3–11.

———. 'Konfessionspolitik in Deutschland zwischen Glaubensstreit und Koexistenz', in idem (ed.), *Baupläne der sichtbaren Kirche: Sprachliche Konzepte religiöser Vergemeinschaftung in Europa* (Göttingen: Wallstein, 2007), 11–52.

———. 'The Concept of Conceptual History (Begriffsgeschichte) and the "Geschichtliche Grundbegriffe"'. *Concept and Communication* 1(2) (2008), 179–98.

———. 'Civil Religion and Secular Religion', in G. Motzkin and Y. Fischer (eds), *Religion and Democracy in Contemporary Europe* (London: Alliance Publishing Trust, 2008), 55–62.

———. 'Europe in the Age of Secularisation', in C. Brown and M. Snape (eds), *Secularisation in the Christian World: Essays in Honour of Hugh McLeod* (Farnham: Ashgate, 2010), 197–204.

———. 'Die Säkularisierung der Kirchen: Sprachliche Transformationsprozesse in den langen 1960er Jahren', in W. Damberg (ed.), *Soziale Strukturen und Semantiken des Religiösen im Wandel: Transformationen in der Bundesrepublik Deutschland 1949–1989* (Essen: Klartext, 2011), 203–14.

———. 'The Religious and the Secular: Semantic Reconfigurations of the Religious Field in Germany from the Eighteenth to the Twentieth Centuries', in L. Hölscher and M. Eggert (eds), *Religion and Secularity: Transformations and Transfers of Religious Discourses in Europe and Asia* (Leiden: Brill, 2013), 35–58.

———. 'Contradictory Concepts: An Essay on the Semantic Structure of Religious Discourses'. *Contributions* 10(1) (2015), 69–88.

———. *Protestantische Frömmigkeit zwischen Reformation und säkularer Gesellschaft*. Freiburg: Herder, 2017.

Hüsgen, E. *Ludwig Windhorst: Sein Leben, sein Wirken*. Cologne: Bachem, 1911.

Koselleck, R. *Begriffsgeschichten: Studien zur Semantik und Pragmatik der politischen und sozialen Sprache*. Frankfurt/Main: Suhrkamp, 2008.

Krumeich, G., and H. Lehmann (eds). *Gott mit uns: Nation, Religion und Gewalt im 19. und frühen 20. Jahrhundert*. Göttingen:Vandenhoeck & Ruprecht, 2000.

Kues, H. 'Gesellschaft braucht Orientierung: Ein Plädoyer für eine engagierte Kirche', in W. Erbacher (ed.), *Entweltlichung der Kirche? Die Freiburger Rede des Papstes* (Freiburg: Herder, 2012), 168–76.

Lachmann, R., and F. Schweitzer (eds). *Geschichte des evangelischen Religionsunterrichts in Deutschland*. Neukirchen-Vluyn: Neukirchener, 2007.

Le Grand-Ticchi, S. 'The Origin of the Concept of "Laicité" in Nineteenth-Century France', in L. Hölscher and M. Eggert (eds), *Religion and Secularity: Transformations and Transfers of Religious Discourses in Europe and Asia* (Leiden: Brill, 2013), 59–76.

———. (ed.). *La laïcité en question: Religion, État et société en France et en Allemagne du 18e siècle à nos jours*. Villeneuve d'ascq: Presses universitaires du septentrion, 2008.

Lehmann, H. 'Säkularisation und Säkularisierung: Zwei umstrittene historische Deutungskategorien', in H. Lehmann (ed.), *Säkularisierung: Der europäische Sonderweg in Sachen Religion* (Göttingen: Wallstein, 2004), 36–56.

Lübbe, H. *Säkularisierung: Geschichte eines ideenpolitischen Begriffs*. Freiburg: Alber, 1965.

McLeod, H. *Secularisation in Western Europe, 1848–1914*. London: Macmillan, 2000.

Paulsen, F. *Geschichte des gelehrten Unterrichts auf den deutschen Schulen und Universitaeten vom Ausgang des Mittelalters bis zur Gegenwart: Mit besonderer Rücksicht auf den klassischen Unterricht*. Berlin: Verein Wissenschaftlicher Verleger, (1920) 1960.

Roetz, H. 'The Influence of Foreign Knowledge on Eighteenth-Century European Secularism', in L. Hölscher and M. Eggert (eds), *Religion and Secularity: Transformations and Transfers of Religious Discourses in Europe and Asia* (Leiden: Brill, 2013), 9–34.

Schieder, R. *Civil Religion: die religioese Dimension der politischen Kultur*. Gütersloh: Gütersloher Verlagshaus Mohn, 1987.

Strätz, H.W., and H. Zabel. 'Säkularisation, Säkularisierung', in O. Brunner et al. (eds), *Geschichtliche Grundbegriffe* (Stuttgart: Klett-Cotta, 1984), 789–830.

Weichlein, S. 'Von der Staatskirche zur religiösen Kultur: Die Entstehung des Begriffs der "Körperschaft des öffentlichen Rechts" mit Blick auf die Kirchenartikel der Weimarer Reichsverfassung', in L. Hölscher (ed.), *Baupläne der sichtbaren Kirche: Sprachliche Konzepte religiöser Vergemeinschaftung in Europa* (Göttingen: Wallstein, 2007), 90–116.

Weir, T. *Secularism and Religion in Nineteenth-Century Germany: The Rise of the Fourth Confession*. New York: Cambridge University Press, 2014.

———. 'A European Culture War in the Twentieth Century? Anticatholicism and Antibolshevism between Moscow, Berlin and Rome, 1922 to 1933'. *Journal of Religious History* 39(2) (2015), 175–331.

4
Secularism in the Long Nineteenth Century between the Global and the Local

Rebekka Habermas

Searching for notions such as secular or secularism – understood literally – in the long nineteenth century is not something I would recommend as a pastime. The 'secular' is indeed barely explicitly mentioned in documents. If one consults encyclopaedia such as the *Brockhaus Konversations-Lexikon* or the *Meyers Konversations-Lexikon*, say from 1817, from 1847, and from 1878, and looks for (the word) 'secular', written with a 'c' or a 'k', the result is always the same[1] – there are no entries.[2]

However, this absence of the secular from contemporary encyclopaedias does not mean that there was no interest in the concept. On the contrary, the writings of Max Weber, Rudolf Virchow and other liberal academics, as well as those of many unknown men of the so-called *Innere Mission* (the contemporary umbrella term for an ever-growing number of charity associations, dealing with the battle against 'moral decline', which they understood as a negative outcome of secularization), prove how intense and almost ubiquitous these debates were in the nineteenth century. Moreover, leaving official and more prominent statements aside while focusing on everyday discussions in journals such as *Die Gartenlaube*, we realize that the absence of a discourse concerning the secular does not indicate disinterest or ignorance. On the contrary, many articles, even though they rarely engaged in an open debate on secularism or the secular, and almost never named it as such, can be read as statements referring exactly to phenomena that belong – at least from the standpoint of contemporaries – to a world seemingly becoming more and more secular. Various articles address phenomena that stretch beyond the common belief systems. They depict the decline of church attendance among the working class, freethinker rituals, alcohol abuse due to a lack of moral convictions, freemasonry, spiritual meetings, and African fetish customs.[3] I argue that these articles, while not directly referring to terms such as secular, actually address what at that time became to be known as secular, judged by contemporaries either positively or negatively, even though its exact meaning was anything but clear or even stable. What is more, these articles treat the secular in a sort of hidden and even secret way whilst openly dealing with religious, superstitious or non-European phenomena, very often by using a highly emotional language. They were written with anger, formulated in an aggressive, sometimes even cynical and openly hostile tone. In short, although often only indirectly addressed and imprecisely defined, the secular in the long nineteenth century raised tremendous interest and caused profoundly emotional reactions, either openly or in a more hidden form.

Situational Secularity

But how to study the making and unmaking of the secular? Apart from the early work of Hermann Lübbe, who studied the writings of, among others, Hegel, Treitschke, Marx and Troeltsch,[4] historical research on secularism is very rare.[5] He underlines that the secular is more than a lack of religion, and more than freedom from belief systems. Yet, the overwhelming majority of historical studies seem to assume that the secular is self-evident and not worth studying, because it is no more than a lack of religion, and thus a phenomenon of mere absence. This widely shared understanding is probably due to the very history of the discipline, whose origin is itself part of a genuinely secular project closely related to the emergence of the modern state and nineteenth-century intellectual trends.

Only recently has this disciplinary blindness been openly addressed, and historians like Todd H. Weir have begun to develop a more substantial understanding of what it meant to be secular in the Kaiserreich. His book *Secularism and Religion in Nineteenth-Century Germany*, published in 2014, studied those associations founded in nineteenth-century Germany that proclaimed to put forward a secular ideology. Weir argues that two groups defined as secular can be distinguished: the 'worldview secularists and advocates of state secularization', with 'the former being more lower class and politically radical, the latter being more middle class and liberal'.[6] He thereby refers on the one hand to groups such as the social democrats and working-class freethinker associations as for instance the 'Zentralverband proletarischer Freidenkervereine', and on the other hand to people like Rudolf Virchow and Ernst Häckel, both prominent liberals and natural scientists, engaged in freethinker societies, and other members of the 'Deutsche Gesellschaft für ethische Kultur' for instance.[7] He furthermore defines the ideas put forward by these groups as 'fourth confession', competing for religious goods such as salvation, patronage or sinecures, rejecting confessionalism and supporting the separation of church and state.[8] Even though Weir must be praised for opening up the field of secular studies in history, offering a range of new insights, his approach also has its shortcomings. Without denying the existence of these two groups and the differences between them,[9] which are of the utmost importance if one wants to get an idea of the broad field of monists, atheists, freethinkers, social and life reformers, and many other groups, I want to argue that there were a lot more people to be found outside of these associations, who were being defined and defining themselves as secular, at least at certain moments of their life. Even though these individuals did not pronounce a clear-cut worldview in the sense of Weir's fourth confession, they are extremely important if one wishes to examine what exactly was meant by the term secular in the long nineteenth century, and particularly around 1900.

Many of these men, who neither attended freethinker meetings, nor read articles from Häckel or other celebrities of the monist movement, but nevertheless claimed to be secular, can be traced in journals like *Die Gartenlaube*, addressing the average middle-class public. There were numerous nameless and unorganized men of the middle class, criticizing exorcism in the name of scientific research into mental illness,[10] making fun of nuns, orthodox Jews and so-called pagan rituals. They were neither well-known men like Virchow, who gave a number of prominent speeches, denouncing belief in miracles, and claiming only natural science can deliver reliable proofs,[11] nor had they necessarily read Ernst Häckel's bestseller *Das Welträtsel* ('The Riddle of Universe'), which sold over 300,000 copies and resembled a form of secular manifesto.[12] Many who defined themselves as men without religious convictions and openly pronounced the unique value of a worldview based on the insights of the natural sciences, might not even have heard of these associations. Others were involved in occult movements like those in Berlin affiliated with more than six hundred mediums in 1900,[13] or were members of theosophist associations believing in the supranational, but they would nevertheless always think of themselves as Christians.

However, if we expand the definition beyond the small group of freethinker and other similar organizations, it becomes clear that Weir's notion of 'fourth faith' is also misleading, because it assumes the existence of a well-defined set of ideas. The opposite is true, as most contributions to this debate do not contain straightforward or clear-cut arguments, but ones full of contradictions, far from easy to grasp. What this huge and heterogeneous group put forward is more like a bricolage than a consistent ideology. Some of them shared a monist worldview, denying the freethinker's mantra that science holds the key to solve modern society's most vexing issues,[14] while they nevertheless, at least in some moments of their life, uttered clear-cut religious arguments. Others, like the well-known medical expert Krafft-Ebing, openly related celibacy to forms of mental illness and thereby labelled the Catholic Church a pathological institution.[15] Still others were openly propagating cremation as a '*Culturfortschritt*'[16] (cultural progress) which would help to overcome religious and supposedly non-hygienic forms of burials. Another group of people, who themselves regularly attended church, was propagating elements of anti-Catholic polemics, arguing that all forms of pilgrimage, the appearances of the Virgin Mary, and Catholic devotions were nothing but superstition,[17] and thereby arguing in favour of a semi-Protestant and semi-secular worldview. However, anti-Catholicism was propagated by a variety of groups and did not necessarily reflect atheistic sentiment.[18] Among the most prominent anti-Catholics were militant Protestants, hardcore natural scientists and Jews, who, in the aftermath of the so-called 'anti-Semitism war' of the late 1870s had converted to Protestantism, although they defined themselves as no longer believing in a religion.[19] Then there were socialists claiming that 'Religion ist Privatsache' (religion belongs to the private sphere),[20] and thereby putting forward at least some elements of what one could call a secular worldview, even though this was a perspective shared by almost all Protestants at that time, Schleiermacher being a key influence. In addition, there were members of the socialist party claiming that the *Heilsarmee* (Salvation Army) and theosophism were 'superstitious' institutions,[21] and should be prohibited because they constitute a threat to a neutral and scientific perspective, even though the Salvation Army was, first and foremost, a charitable organization.[22] Then there were writers like the North German Allmers, who initiated a vital debate about new forms of baptismal rituals in *Die Gartenlaube*. He did not claim to be secular; on the contrary, he wrote: 'If someone provides proof for even a single thought contrary to the spirit of Christianity in my poetry, I am immediately ready to recant everything'.[23] Nonetheless, he was accused by others of being a '*Götzendiener*' (an idolater), and it is undeniable that there were several secular elements in his proposal. Ernst Häckel, the founder of a freethinking society, and the most prominent monist in Germany, claimed religious grounds for his ethical principles, underlining our difficulties of definition.[24]

I could go on with similar statements by numerous men not belonging to those rather small and often not very influential freethinker clubs. But these few citations already make it crystal clear that there were more than one or two well-defined secular groups, asserting clear-cut conceptions of the secular, which can be defined as a 'fourth faith'. Instead, there were countless individuals, typically lacking in any collective organization, asserting at some time of their life some bits and pieces of very often contradictory ideas or practices one can easily call secular. They should not be understood as people with a straightforwardly secular perspective, nor does that necessarily mean that they avoided church attendance or even eschewed an open Christian engagement. They were representatives of a 'situative secularism', referring to Till van Rahden's notion of 'situative ethnicity', which he used in order to describe German Jewishness in the late nineteenth century.[25] Most of them underlined a secular element, only to deny it a few minutes later in another situation. Instead of following an outspoken agenda, their daily lives were full of moments of 'situative secularity' as well as of moments of 'situative religiosity'. This means as well that very different forms of secularities could be observed.

This brings me back to the beginning of this section and the question of how to study the secular in Germany's long nineteenth century. Perhaps current debates in anthropology, where unlike academic history, a rich field of secular studies has steadily grown over the last twenty years, might deliver some suggestions on how to proceed. And indeed, even though many of these secular studies concentrate on state policies and what Talal Asad calls secularism, understood as a governance practice and an ideological policy,[26] there are also less state-centred and therefore for us more appropriate perspectives. Particularly fruitful for a historical analysis is Markus Dressler's and Arvind-Pal Mandair's fascinating book on *Secularism and Religion-Making*[27]. They introduced the term 'religion-making', which indeed gives some hint about how to examine what exactly was understood by the term 'secular' in the Kaiserreich. They define religion-making and the making of the secular as two sides of one coin, 'as the way in which certain social phenomena are configured and reconfigured within the matrix of a world-religion(s) discourse … the notion refers to the reification and institutionalization of certain ideas, social formations, and practices as "religious" and "secular"'.[28] The essence of the secular itself, as they argue, is rather fluid, always changing and not without contradictions. Moreover, following their line of argumentation, the secular as well as the religious should be understood as relational terms, steadily made and remade and not only by people defining themselves as either secularists or as believers. They have also been shaped and reshaped in numerous debates, especially in controversial debates among people claiming to be secular and those pretending to be believers, be they Protestants, Catholics or Jews.[29]

What does that imply for a study of the secular in the German Empire? First of all, we have to turn away from the small circle of freethinker associations and extend our focus to all utterances made in debates about issues related to questions of the secular and the religious, regardless of whether they are in favour or against a secular worldview. Thus, we have to enclose statements from liberal middle-class men, such as the well-known social and medical expert Virchow as well as those of religious groups, fighting against them – associations such as the Catholic *Volksverein*, Protestant working-class associations, and women's charity groups.[30]

Yet, a study of the secular in the Kaiserreich needs more than everyday sources from different strata of the population, including those openly arguing against everything defined as secular. As the aforementioned, almost hopeless, search for notions like secular or secularism in encyclopaedia has proven, it also requires a very close look at a whole range of debates, even though they do not openly address phenomena that contemporaries would call secular. As numerous studies have shown, anti-Catholic polemics, typical for Germany during the entirety of the long nineteenth century, are primarily suited for such an enterprise. Furthermore, a broader contextualization of these debates is needed in order to be able to distinguish the different layers and levels of meaning at stake. Such a contextualization, as I will argue in more detail later, brings to light that these debates were intermingled with a whole range of other negotiations taking place at that time.[31] This means that our search for a more precise and simultaneously more general meaning of the secular in the long nineteenth century will neither concentrate on a particularly secular group nor on specifically secular texts, but on controversial debates about the secular. This search for negotiations of the secular will proceed in two steps: first I will look for features attributed to the secular, which at that time were more or less undisputed; then I will turn to the more controversial elements of what is understood by the term secular.

However, even though the main purpose of this chapter is to find out what was understood by the term secular, we have to depart from at least some definitions, however broad and loose, of the secular. I will start with a definition of secular as describing something or somebody questioning faith as a given.[32] We thereby have to keep in mind that questioning faith is anything but a clearly formulated concept. It can better be described as a state of mind, open to questioning elements of Protestant, Catholic as well as Jewish doctrine, belief and practice.[33]

Who Is Secular? Common Sense and Its Entanglements: Male and of Caucasian Race

The most uncontroversial, almost basic assumption shared by many, if not almost all, engaged in debates on secular phenomena or on ideas defined as secular, is that secular individuals are mostly men. People marked as representatives of the secular in cartoons, for instance, may be of middle- or lower-class background, they may be socialists, liberals or sometimes even conservatives, but they were always depicted as male. Being female and secular seemed to be a *contradictio in adiecto*.

That masculinity and secularity were deemed to be intertwined comes as no surprise in the light of the emerging contemporary notion of hegemonic masculinity. As Isabel Hull has shown, hegemonic masculinities in the course of the eighteenth century turned away from noble ideals, as described by Baldasare Castiglione in his *Libro de Cortegano*, to the new concept of a masculine achiever – a man in a dark suit, symbolizing austerity, modesty, sobriety and authority, as well as reason and self-discipline.[34] According to these mainstream gender stereotypes emerging around 1800, and fully established by the end of the nineteenth century, men could also be identified with being less and less connected to a domestic and pious space, whereas religion became more and more ascribed to a female, and thus private, sphere.

This seemingly natural interconnectedness of masculinity and the secular becomes even more obvious when we turn to the other side of the coin, and notice that an increasingly close identification of femininity with the religious was developing in contemporary minds. In contrast to the already mentioned nearly complete lack of studies on the secular, and its identification with manliness, the female, and therefore religious, side of the coin has systematically been explored and is now known under the umbrella term of 'feminization of religion'.[35] This term refers to a broad contemporary discourse, constructing women as beings of higher sensibility, particularly regarding religion. It was widely believed that women were more susceptible to religion, and that all sorts of female activities, particularly in the private sphere, were religion-centred. Women at that time were described as being engaged in what scholars today call a 'privatization of piety', emphasizing their internal reflections and relationship to God.[36] Their gender identity thereby became closely connected to the religious sphere.[37] Not only novels but also medical manuals and advice books depicted women as deeply involved in religious matters. And by increasingly relegating religion and women to the realm of the private, religious women were accurately separated from the public of secularism.[38] Even though we have to be very cautious not to misunderstand the wide range of female activities in associations only loosely connected to religious institutions as signs of deep religious devotion, it is obvious that the normative as well as imaginative side of middle-class gender boundaries were rearranged according to the poles of the religious and the secular. This becomes even more obvious in particularly intense situations of religious confrontation, as described by Michael B. Gross in his book on anti-Catholicism. He shows that a particular anti-Catholic mapping of gender boundaries even extended to depicting Jesuits as particularly feminized representatives of a dangerous religious worldview. The same can be observed in the culture wars of the 1870s, when priests were depicted as feminized.[39]

If we now put these numerous studies on the female side in one frame with the rare insights we have from male identification with the secular, we could rename the well-known phenomenon of 'feminization of religion' and call it the 'masculinization of the secular'.[40] Moreover, it becomes obvious that symbols of femininity and masculinity were crucial for the making and unmaking of the secular. This gendering of the secular as a specific male sphere is something that could be observed in all layers of society, even though it might have been more dominant in the middle than in the lower classes, and in urban than in rural areas.

However, following the long and intense debate initiated by scholars such as Catherine Hall and Leonore Davidoff concerning the gendering of private and public in nineteenth-century Britain and continental Europe, showing the ambivalent and anything but exclusively negative effect this new mapping had for women, we must not draw all too easy conclusions from this kind of gendering of the religious and the secular. For example, we have to keep in mind that the restriction of women to the private sphere was subverted and used for their own purposes. Women described as experts in the religious, and therefore as beings beyond the secular, used these attributions to gain new societal positions beyond the dichotomies of the secular and the religious. Or to take up an argument of Rebecca Ayako Bennette, Catholic women could draw on the imaginary of the strong woman Mary as an actor in her own right, even beyond the religious sphere, and thus leave their privileged private sphere using religious arguments.[41]

In addition to the widely shared definition of the secular as something belonging to a male sphere, most contemporaries thought of the secular as something particularly European, or at least as a phenomenon characteristic of the so-called 'civilized' world. As a number of postcolonial studies have already emphasized, the secular at that time was defined as something that could supposedly only be found among people of the Caucasian race.[42] In particular, it is noteworthy that contemporaries defined a Western identity as *conditio sine qua non* for being secular. That also meant that people of non-Caucasian race were almost devoid of any possibility of ever entering the secular sphere. In Germany, the identification of being secular and of being of Caucasian race can best be observed *ex negative* in the huge media world of the missionaries reporting from African colonies. Even though it is quite ironic that the religious men and women of the missions were the first to complain about the lack of secular attributes such as rationality and soberness within 'the heathen world', it was these missionaries who openly spoke about a world separated into Europeans who had access to a secular sphere, and non-Europeans who relied on obscure magic beliefs. They emphasized that people belonging to the so-called fetish religions and 'Heiden-Neger'[43] of Africa could not be part of the secular world. This common understanding can be observed not only among missionaries, but also among colonial experts dominating the German media and in the Reichstag, deploring in dozens of debates the problems of the 'civilizing' mission in Africa.[44] At the same time, articles on world fairs, where the latest inventions, technical innovations and scientific explorations of the German Empire were displayed, constructed Europe as the heart of the secular.[45] Similar processes of translating cultural difference as 'religious' or 'secular' in the Western imagination can be observed in more academic debates, such as are analysed in David Chidester's fascinating book on *Inventing Religion in Africa*, where he investigates how phenomena have been classified as religious, magic or secular by anthropologists and other academic and non-academic experts in South Africa.[46]

Although other non-European continents such as Asia were also marked as spaces lacking almost all secular elements, these parts of the world were more often described as belonging to the so-called 'World Religions'.[47] The notion of 'World Religion' leads us to another observation: the close connection between the making of an exclusively European secular masculinity and the invention of the concept of a 'World Religion'. As Tomoko Masuzawa has shown in her seminal study, this term came into being among philological academic circles and missionaries towards the end of the nineteenth century. This notion allowed a straightforward ordering of a world that, at least for many Europeans, seemed to become more and more chaotic, populated by hundreds if not thousands of different ethnicities, or 'tribes' – to use the contemporary wording – all practising different religious customs and rituals.[48] The idea of a system of only five so-called 'World Religions' follows a strictly hierarchical civilizational model, placing Christianity at the peak of an imagined scale, and the so-called 'Nature Religions', described as 'polydaemonistic magical religions under the control of Animism', or so-called 'Tribal Religion' practised by 'savages and uncivilized people' on the other end, with 'Ethical Religions' such as Taoism, Confucianism and a third category, the 'universalistic religious communities', the so-called World Religions, founded on a law or Holy Scripture starting from principles and maxims, such as Buddhism, Christianity and Mohammedanism in the middle.[49] This powerful invention, which slowly took shape on the basis of dozens of writings from various authors, arranging 'disparate evidence from all over the world into a single, uniform temporal sequence, from primitive to civilized, that claimed to represent the universal history of humanity',[50] also helped to foster the idea that the secular can only, if at all, be found in Europe, where Christian faith was already at the edge of being transformed into a state of believing in rational and well-proofed, as well as written down and universally valuable norms.

In short, even though we do not know exactly who thought of him- or herself as a secular person, or even who developed a secular identity with any particular outlook, one can at least grasp two uncontroversial, almost basic, necessary prerequisites attributed to the secular realm at that time: it was supposed to be a sphere of male whiteness.

Who Is Secular? The Contested Ground of Temporal, Political, Cognitive, Emotional and Moral Dimensions

Besides this basic shared understanding of who could, and who could not, claim to have access to the secular realm, other features of the secular were more controversial. Questions about whether particular ethical qualities could be attributed to the secular, or whether secular people shared specific political assumptions, or possessed certain cognitive as well as emotional abilities that were lacking in religious people, were open to debate. Even more importantly, over the course of the long nineteenth century, debates surrounding the notion of a secular concept of time, and appropriate moral standards, became more and more lively. And again, many of these debates were part of, or started as, anti-Catholic polemics and then turned into a broader debate.

Some of these contentious issues can be traced back to the eighteenth century, when French revolutionaries and the founding fathers of the *Encyclopédie* developed anti-clerical, anti-Catholic and even atheistic arguments, on a whole range of political topics, often revisited in the culture wars of the late nineteenth century.[51] Other debates in exclusively Protestant regions, as shown by Jonathan Sheehan,[52] and evolving around 1800 concerning the value of the Bible, ended up reconstituting the authority of the Bible less as a religious text, but more as a cultural and historical one, and thereby gave birth to what was later called *Kulturprotestantismus*, and its very particular concept of the secular. And then there were the debates among anthropologists and other scholars throughout the nineteenth century about whether all non-Europeans have a religion, or whether only civilized people are able to develop religious customs and moral values, which in the end led to a new notion of the religious, and thereby of the secular.[53] Each of these debates developed arguments, which were used and reused at one or another occasion, attributing positive or negative characteristics to the secular or the religious.

However controversial and contradictory these debates were, some rough lines of conflict as well as some crucial topics can be detected. At least five topics seem to have been particularly popular around the turn of the century, namely, the temporal dimension of the secular, as well as its political, cognitive, emotional and in particular moral sides. Starting with the temporal aspects, many defined it as something linked to a very recent past, agreeing that it had just emerged and must therefore be regarded as an essential component of modernity. The secular was conceived as something modern. Rudolf Virchow's speech 'Die Freiheit der Wissenschaft', delivered in front of the Versammlung deutscher Naturforscher in 1877, presented such a straightforward narrative drawing a sharp line between the past, mainly the Middle Ages as a time marked by a lack of freedom and the dominance of the Catholic religion, the present, as a period of progress, natural science, 'Denken ohne Autorität' (thinking without authority),[54] and the future, full of further heroic secular promises. The same temporal definition of the secular as something new and modern can be found in debates among socialists referring to Marxist models of history and religious development.[55] Articles published for instance in *Die Neue Zeit* defined the nineteenth century as an increasingly secular time, finally having left behind the dark time of the religions. We must also remember that Max Weber defined the secular as a quintessentially modern phenomenon, and shared assumptions about the alleged 'backwardness' of Catholics, something very common among those identifying with secular ideas. And even those openly criticizing secular ideas fully subscribed themselves to this narrative about the temporal feature of the secular. Yet, they sharply rejected the positive evaluation of this modernity and instead defined this new secular time as an epoch of moral decline and loss of security by warning against the fall from faith and the attendant political as well as economic instability.

A second important and no less controversial feature ascribed to the secular was its political dimension.[56] In a positive view, the secular was identified with liberty and freedom, while the religious, let alone the magical and superstitious, was associated with oppression, bondage,[57] and the dominance of the Catholic clergy, to paraphrase a well-known trope from the *Kulturkampf*, directly relating to the French Revolution. The *Neue Zeit* even saw the 'katholische Kirche … [als] eine Seelenfängerin von diabolischer Geschicklichkeit' (the Catholic Church as seducing poor souls with an almost diabolic ability).[58] A secular person seen from this perspective was identified as somebody fighting for liberally understood notions of liberty and freedom from constraints imposed by outside powers such as religious institutions and political tyranny.[59] The images of priests keeping people ignorant in order to oppress their liberty of movement and opinion are, of course, myths. However, this perspective was strongly criticized by all those engaged in the, at that time, very popular Christian associations such as the Catholic *Volksverein*, the Protestant workers' associations and far beyond these groups, claiming that inner and outer freedom could only be found in Christian belief whereas modern economy and liberal political systems led to the tyranny of materialism. Their highly critical stance towards the political dimension of the secular emphasized the danger of anarchy instead of the will to liberty, fearing both the loss of authority and tradition, and the despotism of individualism beyond all sacred laws.

The cognitive dimension positively attributed to the secular can also be drawn back to the mid eighteenth century, where the dichotomous narrative of reason versus stupidity and stultification became very popular in the early Enlightenment as well as in the conspiratorial societies of the pre-revolutionary and revolutionary period, meticulously studied by Robert Darnton.[60] In the nineteenth century, this cognitive dimension can best be observed in debates about so-called superstitious customs such as 'Geisterbeschwörung' and 'Spiritualismus',[61] which fascinated a growing public, beginning with Goethe's *Eine Gespenstergeschichte* and finally leading to Karl May's vivid experience of spiritualistic sessions.[62] At the end of the nineteenth century, liberal as well as social democratic newspapers were full of reports describing famous spiritualistic mediums with a mixture of fascination and disdain, underlining the superiority of 'natural' explications for the supposedly supernatural.[63] Similar dichotomies between rational/secular and irrational/religious can be observed in anti-Catholic and, above all, anti-Jesuit propaganda, denouncing Catholicism as irrational and Jesuits as only superficially erudite, following a papal order and not the logic of true science.[64]

At the same time, a growing number of journals began to report about non-European customs such as witchcraft and fetish ceremonies. These articles were full of superstitious and magical pieces, while strongly emphasizing the advantages of a worldview based on the latest discoveries of the natural sciences. It goes without saying that this dichotomous narrative connected secular identity once again with the well-known hegemonic concepts of masculinity on the one hand, and with the values of the middle class on the other.[65] Needless to say, this identification of the secular with reason gave rise to protest not only from those who were now defined as seduced, dumb, extremely superstitious creatures, even though a straightforward counter-narrative is hard to find.

Closely connected to this definition of the cognitive dimension of the secular was an even more disputed narrative concerning the emotional side. Those who were in favour of secular perspectives were convinced that an imagined scale measuring the intensity of emotions would clearly indicate that secular individuals per se had considerably fewer emotions than people of religious faith, who were always in danger of being overwhelmed by their emotions. This was understood as a lack of self-control, and condemned as a condition devoid of all rationality, ultimately leading to a danger of being easily seduced. Yet more strikingly, contemporary scholars like Georg Simmel went so far as to understand religion as mere emotion.[66] This downright identification of religion with emotion can best be observed during the *Kulturkampf*. Especially in that period, countless articles were printed depicting highly emotional scenes of young women crying and shouting (almost out of rage) for the only reason that a priest had been prohibited from praying. Numerous novels proposed an excellent idea of how to sell passionate devotion,[67] while psychiatrists like Krafft-Ebing wrote about 'spermatorrhea panic', almost exclusively attributed to priests. Caricatures printed in the *Kladderadatsch* showed pilgrims on their journey marked by either pain or joy, but always in a highly emotional state of mind. Articles depicting rituals of exorcism were illustrated with emotional scenes of horror and fear as well as of hope and religious zeal.[68] Belief in witches, condemned as being of either Catholic or heathen origin, was described in pathological terms such as hysteria, thereby insinuating a highly emotional mindset.[69] Fanaticism was a notion that was often evoked in the context of Islam, arguing that Muslims per se tend to have a fanatical character.[70] One also spoke of 'appalling tortures'[71] when describing specific rituals in the non-European mission field or in cases of local exorcisms. And missionaries were depicted in bright colours in the magical world of heathen dances in remote African villages, becoming increasingly ecstatic, beyond any cognitive control. Whereas European sects, as well as so-called tribal religious groups, and even members of the Salvation Army, were labelled as uncivilized and wild, tending to be overwhelmed by their religious emotions.[72]

It then was only logical that the secular was defined as a state almost devoid of any emotion, as pure rationality und neutrality. The socialist journal *Die Neue Zeit* praised the secular to be of absolute neutrality, of having no feelings and being totally indifferent towards whatever religion.[73] Even more, its emotional world was supposed to be almost non-existent, or at least very controlled. The secular self-understanding can be characterized as something that highly appreciates a world of general disenchantment, as it was described by Max Weber. In this world, feelings such as fear have been overcome due to technical superiority, whereas positive emotions seem to be common among those defined as secular, but only as long as the emotions are kept at a low, always controlled level. '*Nüchtern*' (sober) is a word often used for self-description.[74] Secular people were supposed to be of a reserved nature, guided by their sharp and controlling mastery and intelligence.

It is obvious that these concepts gave rise to strong protests, not only from those now judged as having 'spermatorrhea panic', tending to fanaticism, and being overwhelmed by their feelings and thus beyond any cognitive control. This secular narrative was also disputed by those praising classical Christian emotional techniques of cognition, practised by famous mystics such as Theresa von Avila, whose way to a deeper understanding of the world was based on strong emotions. A secular perspective constructing emotion and cognition as almost mutually exclusive principles, and reducing a state of overwhelming emotions to hovering dangerously on the brink of the irrational instead of opening up the door to spiritual dimensions, surely was a declaration of war against a very long Christian tradition of mysticism.

No less disputed was the fifth, the ethical dimension ascribed to the religious as well as to the secular. Those in favour of the secular assumed that the secular went hand in hand with a particular morality and secular ethics. They equated the secular with values such as authenticity, trueness and sincerity, 'Wahrhaftigkeit'. These values had already played a role in Enlightenment debates as well as in the anti-Catholic campaigns of the late eighteenth century. They had also been of crucial importance to debates about middle-class identity, which can be observed in novels, very popular at the time, such as *Pamela*, where unprincipled and dishonest noblemen tried to seduce innocent middle-class girls, hence negotiating the new middle-class values of trueness and sincerity. In brief, a positively judged secular person, understood in ethical terms, was defined as a human being who is devoid of hypocrisy and devoted to 'Wahrhaftigkeit'. He, or sometimes in this case even she, belonged to the opposite group of those who were supposed to commit fraud and lie, as the Catholic Church is said to do by making people believe in miracles. Jesuits played the role of veritable anti-heroes in these debates, or as Roisin Healy has put it, they were 'a-moral supermen', sinister, luxury loving and powerful.[75] Another contrast to these ethical dimensions of a secular identity was seen in men, but mostly women, lacking reason who allegedly were inclined to be victims of hypocrites and who at the same time were said to be hypocrites themselves.[76] Even worse things were said about Jesuits, beings of supposedly pathological immorality as well as individuals whom nobody could trust.[77]

Naturally, a critical or outrightly hostile perspective towards secular ideas, arguing from religious grounds, heavily rejected these kinds of correlations and instead emphasized a narrow link between high ethical standards and religious faith. Some downplayed values such as authenticity and trueness, and rather praised values like the ability to empathize. Others understood trueness and authenticity as genuine religious virtues. Hence the huge number of charity associations that were unified under the umbrella of the so-called *Innere Mission* all shared the basic assumption that ethically grounded practices could only be of religious origin.

If we summarize this rather rough sketch of how temporal, cognitive, political, emotional and ethical ideas were negotiated as either secular or religious, it becomes clear that these debates were linked to several other discussions of crucial importance at that time. First of all the positively judged dimensions of the secular were closely linked to what has extensively been discussed under the umbrella term '*Bürgerlichkeit*', as middle-class values, which were made and remade simultaneously within a group of men and women, rarely exceeding 10 to 15 per cent of the population, but somehow influential far beyond the middle class itself.[78] Furthermore, the features positively defined as secular, such as rationality, sobriety, emotionless neutrality, liberty, modernity and sincerity, versus those negatively defined as non-secular, such as emotionality, hypocrisy, and the loss of self-control, bear some similarities to what was discussed in advice books as well as novels distinguishing a female from a male sphere. These debates then remind us of academic models discussed in the emerging disciplines of anthropology, criminology and many others, as well as in travel descriptions and public lectures concerning questions of how to understand the evolution of more and less 'civilized' cultures, and how to draw boundaries between 'us and them'. Finally, these debates recall arguments well known from political debates. These were the issues at stake when liberals defended their platforms with reference to notions such as freedom, 'progress' and 'rationality', underlining that they were hard-headed decision makers, controlling irrational and all too emotional feelings. They were of crucial importance as well to the more conservative repertoire of politicians from the Catholic centre party, referring to the danger of moral decline for decisions not grounded on a deeply Christian, and therefore per se ethical, set of norms. Last but not least, very similar arguments were put forward by those in favour of the new welfare state agenda of chancellor Bismarck, underlining the success of a modern state having freed itself from religious constraints. On the contrary, others argued for a Christian fight against poverty, emphasizing the deeply felt pity and compassion based on the example of biblical figures such as Lazarus. In short, this strongly contested battlefield of arguments, sentiments, beliefs and concepts referring to what one could call a secular identity, is part of a much bigger picture and describes only one aspect in a very broad range of what, in the nineteenth century, constituted the hottest and most debated topics.

I do not want to exaggerate the historian's work of contextualization, or for the concept of the secular to totally disappear or dissolve itself into the bigger picture of ongoing negotiations about how to give meaning to the challenges of modernity. And these negotiations not only took place in debates concerning questions of the secular and the religious, they can be observed in many more discussions and were narrowly intermingled with negotiations about many other issues, among them gender, class and race. Having said that, it also becomes obvious that even the values most often assigned to the secular, such as liberty, freedom, rationality and emotional control, cannot claim to describe specific qualities exclusively attributed to the secular.[79] The contrary is true.

Contested Grounds and Emotions

Following the line of argument so far, it has become clear that the secular in nineteenth-century Germany was constructed as something more than a lack of religion or a freedom from religion, and as something that was debated beyond freethinking societies. Even though we could not get to the bottom line of who exactly marked him- or herself in which moments of his or her life as secular, it could be observed that contemporaries agreed on two necessary preconditions for those being depicted as secular: being male and being white. All other features ascribed to the secular, concerning ethical, cognitive, emotional, political and temporal issues, were, at least when it came to judging them, subject to controversial debates. Only very vague notions, imprecise concepts and fuzzy ideas of the secular as a sober, almost emotionless state of authenticity, full of liberties and rationalities, located in the present and in the future but not in the past, could be singularized. However vague such ideas were, the topics associated with the secular and the religious formed a crucial battleground involving an ever-growing public and media, which was narrowly linked to other issues, not easily or perhaps not at all to be understood separately from these.

Nevertheless, the secular has a specific and significant quality which must be clearly designated. This particular capacity comes to light when we once again turn to the emotional side of debates on the secular.[80] Despite the decidedly clear secular ideal of controlled emotions and disinterested objectivity, the tone among all the participants in these debates, be they self-fashioned as secular or as religious, was anything but sober and neutral. Instead, the choice of words revealed strong emotions. Still more, the exact wordings in these texts seemed to reveal an imminent danger of losing control, provoked by strong feelings of disgust, anger and fear. The texts, particularly of those pretending to open up a genuine secular, and with that emotionless space, are paradoxically full of violence, aggression, disdain and disgust. The caricatures to be found, for example, in the well-known satirical magazine *Kladderadatsch* criticizing pilgrimages to Marpingen, from an openly secular point of view, convey violent and hateful fantasies.[81] Furthermore, the *Gartenlaube* openly and quite harshly accuses religious men and women, such as the pietists, of being hypocritical and seductive as well as cruel, with even more openly aggressive metaphors. Other articles provoked harsh reactions on behalf of those who pretended not to criticize the so-called Orthodoxy, and at the same time accusing them in innumerable letters, most of them full of anger, inspired by almost religious zeal of idolatry ('*Götzendienst*').[82] Most comments on pilgrims, spiritualists or 'heathens', written by people defining themselves as secular, were full of biting irony[83] and of disgust aroused by the veneration of relics[84] or other religious rituals. Many resembled polemical hate speech rather than rational argumentation. And, as Roisin Healy has stated, many anti-Jesuit members of the cultural-Protestant elite, feeling themselves haunted by Jesuits, 'revealed themselves to be less rational than they believed'.[85]

To put it briefly, debates on religious and secular topics had a very strong emotional side in nineteenth-century Germany, laying bare a hidden commonality of the supposedly sober secular and the so-called dishonest and non-rational religious. What is more, the tone in these debates opened up a field of emotional outburst almost at the edge of hate speech. It was in these moments that the contrast between religion, as an inner state of feeling, and the secular, as an objective common ground for rational decisions, became thin and brittle.[86]

These moments of intense emotionality give very clear proof that the making of the secular in all its interconnectedness with the making of the middle class, a new gender order and shifting concepts of race, was something contemporaries judged with a lot of emotions. The debates about secular and religious phenomena – be that a belief in miracles, a baptismal ritual, far away tribal religious customs, or a cremation – took place in an extremely passionate atmosphere on a battleground where many feared to get injured.

This highly emotionalized tone can best be seen when we look at the debate about the secular beyond the so-called freethinker associations, in the contexts of organizations fighting against everything associated with the secular, be it the so-called *Volksverein*, with more than 800,000 members,[87] or a Catholic association with the aim of fighting what they labelled as the atheism of German social democrats – to quote from their programme. A similar association was established by Protestants, aiming 'to awaken and promote the evangelical consciousness', which principally meant 'to raise moral elevation and general education',[88] but actually aimed at offering counter-narratives to a rhetoric that was quite successful, especially among young workmen in the Ruhr region. Then hundreds of Catholic Jünglings- und Gesellenvereine engaged in a restless battle against the same supposedly atheistic working class as the Protestant *Jungfrauenvereine* of the Innere Mission.[89] Meanwhile, so-called *Kulturprotestanten* organized media campaigns against Jesuits, and some even spoke of veritable outbursts of Jesuitphobia.[90] And, as Anthony Steinhoff's book on Protestantism in Strasbourg showed, numerous groups of the *Innere Mission*, fighting against social evils such as drunkenness in a very aggressive pitch, went hand in hand with dozens of other religious associations, all engaged in an anything but secular battle for a new city politics.[91] At the same time, church reformers encouraged religious, spiritual as well as charitable activities, and printed leaflets, booklets and newspapers propagating Christian ideas, often full of hostile rhetoric. To be brief, the secular was debated in a highly emotional, violent tone. I would even argue that secularism in nineteenth-century Germany was defined much less by its own rhetoric of liberty, sobriety, masculinity and rationality, than by precisely this highly emotional state, which played just as influential a role in this context as it did for contemporary notions of the religious and the sacred.

Out of these controversies about secular issues emerged emotional outbursts comparable to what we can observe today, for instance, in the debates concerning cartoon portrayals of the prophet Muhammad, published in a Danish newspaper in 2006.[92] Saba Mahmood has shown that, for many contemporary Muslims, there are moral injuries at stake, with some perceiving these cartoons as personal insults, deeply offensive not only to what we call 'religious feelings', but a very personal relationship, hence a much more private belief. Something very similar seems to have been the case in nineteenth-century debates about the secular and the religious.

My search for traces of the secular in nineteenth-century Germany began with the silences of the *Brockhaus* and has ended with emotional outbursts of some angry members of religious as well as liberal, left-wing or even scientific associations. It contains a number of loose ends and has probably raised more questions than delivered satisfactory answers to existing problems. However, the making and unmaking of the secular should primarily be understood as something that took place on a contested battleground, where a large number of people, well beyond the ranks of freethinking associations, engaged in highly emotional and controversial disputes on a whole range of issues. The secular was emphatically more charged than a simple plea for less religion.

Against this background, a description of the secular during nineteenth-century Germany can take inspiration from Charles Taylor's arguments. He claims that an understanding of the phenomenon as an intellectual process of questioning faith is misleading, because it silences the violence at stake between those who disagreed on the interpretation, seeing the secular as an option, and those who defined secularism as a surplus of freedom. This definition is also misleading because it overlooks how closely and inseparably this debate was related to other issues of crucial importance to almost all layers of German society at that time, such as class and gender, let alone race.

Hence, Asad's perspective is also too narrow, because debates about the secular in nineteenth-century Germany concerned much more than ideological state policies or legal issues. A huge number of men and women, and dozens of associations, fought against each other over a wide range of topics, most of them touching on other highly charged subjects. And finally, no one single, uncontested kind of secularism emerged out of these debates. Instead many different secularities were negotiated in highly emotional debates, often going hand in hand with veritable hate speech towards religious communities. Some adherents – mostly men – tended to espouse a specific form of secularism only at particular moments of their life cycles, and thus practised a kind of 'situative secularity'.

Rebekka Habermas is professor for modern German history at the University of Göttingen, and has been Richard von Weizsäcker Professor at Oxford and Theodor Heuss Professor at the New School in New York. She has authored several books on nineteenth-century German history, among others *Frauen und Männer des Bürgertums: Eine Familiengeschichte* (Vandenhoeck & Ruprecht, 2000); *Thieves in Court: The Making of the German Legal System in the Nineteenth Century* (Cambridge University Press, 2016); *Skandal in Togo: Ein Kapitel deutscher Kolonialherrschaft* (Fischer, 2016).

Notes

I am grateful for the very helpful readings of Annika Dörner (Göttingen). An earlier version of this chapter was presented at the conference 'Secular Bodies, Affects and Emotions', organized by Monique Scheer in Tübingen in 2016. I owe many new insights into the growing field of secular studies to this conference, and particularly to Monique Scheer (Tübingen). Antonie

Habermas (Munich) has been of enormous help concerning questions of translation. I finally have to thank the reviewers for helpful advice on how to clarify the main arguments.
1. I studied the *Brockhaus Konversations-Lexikon 1809, 1817, 1847, 1854, 1867, 1892* and *1908*, as well as the *Meyers Konversations-Lexikon* of 1866 and 1889. Only the 1878 *Brockhaus* edition has a glossary entry 'Säcularisation' on page 949 of volume 12. The others were checked, but no entries could be found.
2. However, if we enlarge the searching mask and include the eighteenth-century *Zedler*, the famous Universallexikon of the time, we can find the verb '*secularisiern*', and the noun '*Secularisierung, Secularisation*' with the following explanation: 'bedeutet ... nichts anderes, als gewisse Sachen oder Güter, so erst geistlich gewesen, weltlich machen'; see H. Zabel, W. Conze and H.W. Strätz, 'Säkularisation, Säkularisierung', in O. Brunner, W. Conze and R. Koselleck (eds), *Geschichtliche Grundbegriffe: Historisches Lexikon zur politisch-sozialen Sprache in Deutschland*, Vol. 5 (Stuttgart: Klett-Cotta, 2004), 803. The notion 'secularisation' – see H. Lübbe, *Säkularisierung: Geschichte eines ideenpolitischen Begriffs* (Freiburg: Alber, 1965), 23 – refers to a legal act of transferring a kind of control from the church to the state, be it a building, an entire state (as happened in 1803 with a number of church states that were turned into secular states) or something else, even human beings – for instance, Catholic priests, who during the French Revolution were paid by the French revolutionary government and forced to teach the ideals of *liberté*, *égalité* and *fraternité*, and praising the être suprême instead of the Christian God and the ten commandments.
3. See for this discourse A. Przyrembel, *Verbote und Geheimnisse: Das Tabu und die Genese der europäischen Moderne (1784–1913)* (Frankfurt/Main: Campus, 2011). Related to this is a debate among social democrat and other left groups on moral issues arguing from a more anti-religious perspective, see: R. Habermas, 'Wie Unterschichten nicht dargestellt werden sollten: Debatten um 1890 oder "Cacatum non est pictum!"', in R. Lindner and L. Musner (eds), *Unterschicht: Kulturwissenschaftliche Erkundungen der 'Armen' in Geschichte und Gegenwart* (Freiburg: Rombach, 2008), 97–122; R. Habermas, 'Piety, Power, and Powerlessness: Religion and Religious Groups in Germany, 1870–1945', in H.W. Smith (ed.), *The Oxford Handbook of Modern German History* (Oxford University Press, 2011), 453–80. The notion secular in its exact wording plays a role in a debate about civil marriage, the 'Zivilehe', which is introduced in 1874; it again is a stake in a debate taking place around 1892 and 1905 in Prussia when a new law concerning elementary school is decided, and some controversies about the role of religious education arise. See S. Enders, *Moralunterricht und Lebenskunde* (Bad Heilbronn: Julius Klinkhardt, 2002). But in both cases the debate was about issues of secularization (about the institutional relationship between church and state) and not about the secular.
4. Lübbe, *Säkularisierung*.
5. For the growing number of books studying anti-Catholicism in the German Empire and thus also addressing secular phenomena, although in a rather indirect way, see the Introduction of this volume.
6. T.H. Weir, 'Germany and the New Global History of Secularism: Questioning the Postcolonial Genealogy', *The Germanic Review* 90 (2015), 13. Besides his book, Weir published a number of articles elaborating his crucial arguments, underlining not only that there are different freethinker groups but that they develop in different directions. Liberal freethinkers fall silent after 1877 because they feared being confused with the social democrat wing. Another divide concerns those like Tönnies, looking for alliances

with the Protestant church, and those like Häckel, fighting against the church as such (ibid., 16).
7. See Enders, *Moralunterricht*, 55–82, as well as for some forerunner religious movements relating to the Deutsche Gesellschaft für ethische Kultur and other *Freidenker* groups. S. Paletschek, *Frauen und Dissens: Frauen im Deutschkatholizismus und in den freien Gemeinden 1841–1852* (Göttingen: Vandenhoeck & Ruprecht, 1990).
8. T.H. Weir, *Secularism and Religion in Nineteenth-Century Germany: The Rise of the Fourth Confession* (Cambridge: Cambridge University Press, 2014), 18. He follows Bourdieu's definition of a religious field, where one is competing for religious goals. This concept is, I would argue, too static; it essentializes religion instead of investigating how the secular and the religious are constantly shaped and reshaped.
9. Cf. J.-C. Kaiser, *Arbeiterbewegung und organisierte Religionskritik: Proletarische Freidenkerverbände in Kaiserreich und Weimarer Republik* (Stuttgart: Klett-Cotta, 1981), 96, who stresses that the two groups were increasingly critical of each other and finally chose separate paths. While the social democrats adopted the formula 'freethought is class struggle' (ibid., 98), the bourgeois liberals were opponents of the social democrat party.
10. E. Kr., 'Ein preußischer Bischof als Teufelsbanner', *Die Gartenlaube* 24(45) (1872), 740–43.
11. R. Virchow, *Ueber Wunder: Rede, gehalten in der ersten allgemeinen Sitzung der 47. Versammlung deutscher Naturforscher und Aerzte zu Breslau am 18. September 1874* (Breslau: Morgenstern, 1874).
12. Weir, *Secularism and Religion*, 258.
13. Cf. C. Treitel, *A Science for the Soul: Occultism and the Genesis of the German Modern* (Baltimore, MD: Johns Hopkins University Press, 2004), 57.
14. Weir, *Secularism and Religion*, 255, underlines the importance of monism, which 'constituted the essential worldview of nineteenth-century German secularism'.
15. See the excellent article of T. Verhoeven, 'Harmful or Benign? Transnational Medical Networks and the Celibacy of Priests', *Journal of Religious History* 39(2) (2015), 244–60, which studies a number of medical experts who openly engaged in pathologizing religious lifestyle.
16. C. Reclam, 'Die Feuerbestattung', *Die Gartenlaube* 26(19) (1874), 308–13.
17. 'An der Gnadenstätte von Marpingen', *Die Gartenlaube* 29(45) (1877), 666–69. Concerning anti-Catholic campaigns, see B. Gross, *The War against Catholicism: Liberalism and the Anti-Catholic Imagination in Nineteenth-Century Germany* (Ann Arbor: University of Michigan Press, 2005); and M. Borutta, *Antikatholizismus: Deutschland und Italien im Zeitalter der europäischen Kulturkämpfe* (Göttingen: Vandenhoeck & Ruprecht, 2010); R. Healy, *The Jesuit Specter in Imperial Germany* (Boston: Brill, 2003).
18. Anti-Catholicism in many respects offered a shared symbolic language as a unifying other, and could also be a way to express secular arguments. See Y.M. Werner and J. Harvard, 'European Anti-Catholicism in Comparative and Transnational Perspective. The Role of a Unifying Other: An Introduction', *European Studies* 31 (2013), 13–22, in a transnational comparative view on European anti-Catholicisms. See L. Dittrich, 'European Connections, Obstacles and the Search for a New Concept of Religion: The Freethought Movement as an Example of Transnational Anti-Catholicism in the Second Half of the Nineteenth Century', *Journal of Religious History* 39(2) (2015), 261–79, arguing that anti-Catholicism was 'dominated by the battle about true religion and right belief' (ibid., 275), and 'that anti-Catholicism is not anti-religious' (ibid., 279). I would add that, even though it is not necessarily anti-religious, it might be due to a secular worldview. Cf. the

fascinating study of A. Joskowicz, *The Modernity of Others: Jewish Anti-Catholicism in Germany and France* (Stanford, CA: Stanford University Press, 2014), 3, which studies how Jews 'employed anti-Catholicism to articulate their own vision of modernity, national belonging, and proper forms of religion'.

19. See U. Jensen, *Gebildete Doppelgänger:* Bürgerliche Juden und Protestanten im 19. Jahrhundert (Göttingen: Vandenhoeck & Ruprecht, 2005), for the complex debate within the different parties engaged in the anti-Semitism war.
20. G. Roller, 'Partei und Religion', *Die Neue Zeit* 24(51) (1906), 846–48. See Kaiser, *Arbeiterbewegung und organisierte Religionskritik,* for the anti-religious battle of the social democrats.
21. C. Bonnier, 'Wissenschaft, Kunst, Religion', *Die Neue Zeit* 13(2) (1895), 325–30. For the discourse criticizing the Salvation Army and the so-called swarmers, see C. Ribbat, *Religiöse Erregung* (Frankfurt/Main: Campus, 1996).
22. Others even replaced religion by science, claiming that 'Wissenschaft für uns Religion geworden [ist]', cf. R. Virchow, *Ueber die nationale Entwicklung und Bedeutung der Naturwissenschaften: Rede, gehalten in der zweiten allgemeinen Sitzung der Versammlung deutscher Naturforscher und Aerzte zu Hannover am 20. September 1865* (Berlin: Hirschwald, 1865), 18. An author writing in *Die Neue Zeit* claimed that only social democrats are beyond a Christian confession, meanwhile all other parties, among them the national liberals, are part of a religious group: P. Göhre, 'Kirchenaustrittsbewegung und Sozialdemokratie', *Die Neue Zeit* 32(14) (1914), 498.
23. H. Allmers, 'Ein Wort zum Wehren und Klären', *Die Gartenlaube* 26(14) (1874), 234: 'So jemand in meiner Dichtung auch nur einen einzigen Gedanken nachweist, der mit dem Geist des Christentums im Widerspruch steht, bin ich sofort bereit alles zu widerrufen.'
24. For monism and Ernst Häckel, see Enders, *Moralunterricht,* 67–69. She writes that monism was more defined by distinctions, namely, against orthodoxy in theology and philosophy.
25. T. van Rahden, *Juden und andere Breslauer: Die Beziehungen zwischen Juden, Protestanten und Katholiken in einer deutschen Großstadt von 1860 bis 1925* (Göttingen: Vandenhoeck & Ruprecht, 2000), 20. See as well, G. Starrett, 'The Varieties of Secular Experience', *Comparative Studies in Society and History* 52(3) (2010), 626–52, which states that 'the categorization of the world into the secular and the religious is a peculiar kind of practice that serves as a purpose for particular kinds of people … expressing the political position of notable men' (646).
26. Talal Asad himself focused almost exclusively on questions of secularism, arguing that secularism as political ideology is more about control and constraint than about freedom of belief and practice, and that it never lived up to its promises to keep religion out of politics, because it was anything but politically neutral. Without denying the tremendous merits of Asad's writing, his focus on state policies and elite discourse has its shortcomings. His approach is in danger of neglecting other aspects such as the day-to-day negotiations among a whole range of groups inflicted by state policies, and shaping and reshaping them at the same time. At least if one is more interested in studying a particular historical situation at the end of the nineteenth century rather than in explaining constellations of the secular today, a closer look into the forces on the historical ground is needed. There are a huge number of authors criticizing Talal Asad for his concentration on state policies, most convincingly from an anthropological standpoint: A.B. Lebner, 'The Anthropology of Secularity beyond Secularism', *Religion and Society: Advances in Research* 6 (2015), 62–74; see also S. Bruce, 'The Other Secular Modern: An Empirical Critique

of Asad', *Religion and Society: Advances in Research* 4 (2013), 79–92, who assumes that secularism arose out of a competition between different religious groups, and that it was not the state taking the lead. Concerning the German situation, Weir, 'Germany and the New Global History of Secularism', 6–20, argues against Talal Asad, that a closer study of liberal German humanists shows that 'the assumption that state secularization was a singular, global process with local variations' can be questioned (ibid., 19).

27. M. Dressler and A.S. Mandair (eds), *Secularism and Religion-Making* (Oxford: Oxford University Press, 2011).
28. Ibid., 3.
29. Joskowicz, *The Modernity of Others*, 12, studies Jewish anti-Catholicism in, as he calls it, 'polemical secularism' and thus follows a similar approach, because, as he writes: 'Polemics … made secularism'.
30. Having laid out my less state-focused perspective and my particular interest in a broader public, it goes without saying that both the new governance policy of secularism as well as the philosophical and academic debates have to be seriously taken into account in order to come to a full understanding of the broader meanings of the secular. For the broad field of associations engaged in this debate, see Habermas, 'Piety, Power, and Powerlessness', 461–63.
31. To put it the other way around, I think that a full understanding of the secular in nineteenth-century Germany cannot be left only to anthropologists and sociologists, to whom we owe so many fruitful insights into theoretical questions of how to understand the secular as well as into actual societies. However, they are not historical experts and therefore are not concerned with a deeper understanding of historical phenomena. They thus are in danger of overseeing important elements of the bigger historical picture, mostly due to the fact that they tend to overestimate legal procedures and elite discourses. Although a large number of studies has proved that there is no such thing as the secularism and the secular, but rather an enormous variety of different forms of secularism – among the most intensively studied twentieth- and twenty-first-century varieties are the Turkish, French, American, English and Egyptian as well as the German varieties [R. Bhargava, 'How Secular Is European Secularism?' *European Societies* 16(3) (2014), 329–36; M. Burchardt, M. Wohlrab-Sahr and U. Wegert, 'Multiple Secularities: Postcolonial Variations and Guiding Ideas in India and South Africa', *International Sociology* 28(6) (2013), 612–28] – most studies seem to assume that there is only one path to this modern variety of secular and non-secular phenomena in European countries. At least, studies influenced by either Charles Taylor or Talal Asad mostly share, explicitly or not, the assumption of a European secular genealogy without great varieties. For the debate in postcolonial studies, see H.A. Agrama, 'Reflections on Secularism, Democracy, and Politics in Egypt', *American Ethnologist* 39 (2012), 26–31; A.R. Mufti, *Enlightenment in the Colony: The Jewish Question and the Crisis of Postcolonial Culture* (Princeton, NJ: Princeton University Press, 2009); A.R. Mufti, 'Critical Secularism: A Reintroduction for Perilous Times', *boundary 2* 31(2) (2004), 1–9. J. Butler, 'Sexual Politics, Torture and Secular Time', *The British Journal of Sociology* 59 (2008), 1–23, has drawn our attention to the interesting point that 'diversity of secularisms often gain their definition by the nature of the break they make with specific religious inheritances' (ibid., 13).
32. This definition refers to Charles Taylor's seminal work, whose underlying assumption is, that 'we live in a condition where we cannot help but be aware that there are a number of different construals, views which intelligent … people … can and do disagree on …

living our faith also in a condition of doubt and uncertainty' – see C. Taylor, *A Secular Age* (Cambridge, MA: Harvard University Press, 2007), 11.

33. This was more like a perspective shared by only a small elite exploring own and other identities in an ongoing negotiation with much larger groups. Dittrich, 'European Connections', 261–79, makes this argument concerning the freethinker movement.
34. I. Hull, *Sexuality, State, and Civil Society in Germany 1700–1815* (Ithaca, NY: Cornell University Press, 1996), has created this concept of middle-class masculinity. Even though there is indeed some evidence for a withdrawal of middle-class men from church institutions, as shown by numerous studies on church attendance, this identification of manliness and the secular can first of all be observed on the level of vivid ongoing debates. For church attendance in general, see L. Hölscher, *Datenatlas zur religiösen Geographie im protestantischen Deutschland: Von der Mitte des 19. Jahrhunderts bis zum Zweiten Weltkrieg*, 4 vols (Berlin: de Gruyter, 2001).
35. Beginning with the article of Barbara Welter, 'The Cult of True Womanhood: 1820–1860', *American Quarterly* 18(2) (1966), 151–74, the field soon exploded. It has become obvious that terms such as 'female religiosity' have to be understood in relation to male religiosity, as well as on the backdrop of denominational boundaries.
36. As well as newspapers and paintings linking religion to the female, normative literature also established a narrow link between domesticity, religion and women, arguing that middle-class women at their best were furnishing their homes with sacred symbols. Catherine Hall and others even speak of a sacralization of the private as one of the main female duties. The importance of religious practice being firmly embedded within the family was emphasized in prayers and novels, as well as in all sorts of guidebooks; see the seminal study of C. Hall and L. Davidoff, *Family Fortunes: Men and Women of the English Middle Class 1780–1850* (London: Routledge, 1992). Cf. M. Mommertz and C. Opitz-Belakhal (eds), *Das Geschlecht des Glaubens: Religiöse Kulturen Europas zwischen Mittelalter und Moderne* (Frankfurt/Main: Campus, 2008).
37. 'Auf welche Weise in gegenwärtiger Zeit noch Wallfahrtsorte entstehen!', *Die Gartenlaube* 24(24) (1872), 398; and 'Ueber die neue Wallfahrt unweit Würzburg', *Die Gartenlaube* 24(31) (1872), 514.
38. Finally, religion itself became the object of research, and the study of religion turned into a scholarly discipline; cf. A.L. Molendijk and P. Pels (eds), *Religion in the Making: The Emergence of the Sciences of Religion* (Leiden: Brill, 1998).
39. Gross, *The War against Catholicism*, 186–220. A number of studies underlined the assignement of a status to Catholics as private/feminine, and to Protestants liberals as public/male, cf. Borrutta, *Antikatholizismus*; R.A. Bennette, *Fighting for the Soul of Germany: The Catholic Struggle for Inclusion after Unification* (Cambridge, MA: Harvard University Press, 2012), 96–121. Bennette emphasized that the alleged feminity excluded Catholics from the national community.
40. Apart from a few exceptions, such as N. Dhawan, 'The Empire Prays Back: Religion, Secularity, and Queer Critique', *boundary 2* 40 (2013), 191–222, one could speak of a certain gender blindness in secular studies.
41. Bennette, *Fighting for the Soul of Germany*, 107.
42. Even though a detailed study of race in the context of secularization concepts around 1900 in the writings of, e.g., Max Weber, Ernst Troeltsch and Emile Durkheim is still missing.
43. 'Sclavenfang in Afrika', *Die Gartenlaube* 24(21) (1872), 343–46.

44. For the broader context and a much deeper analysis of missionary perspectives, see R. Habermas, *Skandal in Togo: Ein Kapitel deutscher Kolonialherrschaft* (Frankfurt/Main: S. Fischer, 2016).
45. H. Cunow, 'Religionsgeschichtliche Streifzüge', *Die Neue Zeit* 29(35) (1910), 457–66. Heinrich Cunow gives a detailed overview of the developmental ideas in the history of religion and criticizes Marx, although without leaving the contemporary spatial map of the secular and religious.
46. D. Chidester, *Savage Systems: Colonialism and Comparative Religion in Southern Africa* (Charlottesville: University of Virginia Press, 1996); R. King, 'Imagining Religions in India: Colonialism and the Mapping of South Asian History and Culture', in M. Dressler and A.S. Mandair (eds), *Secularism and Religion-Making* (Oxford: Oxford University Press, 2011), 43, whom I am rephrasing here.
47. The Dutch professor of history of religion, Petrus Tiele, was one of the first, compiling many studies from missionaries and scholars into his *Outlines of the History for Religion to the Spread of the Universal Religion*, published in 1876.
48. T. Masuzawa, *The Invention of World Religions: Or, How European Universalism Was Preserved in the Language of Pluralism* (Chicago: University of Chicago Press, 2005).
49. Cf. Masuzawa, *The Invention of World Religions*, 110ff.; and M. Dressler and A.S. Mandair, 'Introduction: Modernity, Religion-Making, and the Postsecular', in idem, *Secularism and Religion-Making* (Oxford: Oxford University Press, 2011), 12ff. It goes without saying that this system, based on the work of hundreds of missionaries and other religious experts, was anything but a neutral fixation of what scholars and missionaries had found.
50. Chidester, *Savage Systems*, 3. Cf. C. Bayly, *The Birth of the Modern World, 1780–1914: Global Connections and Comparisons* (Oxford: Blackwell, 2004), 328, who stresses that reform movements within Buddhism, Confucianism and Hinduism at that time emphasized the rational, 'condemning superstition, … magical beliefs'. Cf. King, 'Imagining Religions in India', 37–61.
51. In recent decades, a rich literature on anti-Catholicism has evolved; for the German and European context: Gross, *The War against Catholicism*; Borutta, *Antikatholizismus*; Dittrich, 'European Connections, Obstacles and the Search for a New Concept of Religion'; Werner and Harvard, 'European Anti-Catholicism in Comparative and Transnational Perspective'; C. Clark and W. Kaiser (eds), *Culture Wars: Secular–Catholic Conflict in Nineteenth-Century Europe* (Cambridge: Cambridge University Press, 2003). Most of these studies emphasize that the boundaries between anti-Catholic, atheistic, secular, freethinker or merely pro-Protestant arguments were fluid.
52. J. Sheehan, *The Enlightenment Bible: Translation, Scholarship, Culture* (Princeton, NJ: Princeton University Press, 2005).
53. J. and J. Comaroff (eds), *Of Revelation and Revolution: Christianity, Colonialism and Consciousness in South Africa*, Vol. 1 (Chicago: Chicago University Press, 1991); and idem (eds), *Of Revelation and Revolution: The Dialectics of Modernity on a South African Frontier*, Vol. 2 (Chicago: Chicago University Press, 1997).
54. Virchow, *Ueber die nationale Entwickelung und Bedeutung der Naturwissenschaften*, 20.
55. Ari Joskowicz argues in the same direction in his book on Jewish anti-Catholicism, when he writes: '[F]or many Jews, anti-Catholicism structured their sense of historical time, with a medieval, unemancipated "before", and a modern, increasingly emancipated "now"' (Joskowicz, *The Modernity of Others*).

56. Cf. debates on the political sphere in the work of Joskowicz, *The Modernity of Otherness*, 197–228. In this chapter he studies how secularism emerged in the French and German parliaments as anti-Catholic polemic, and the role that Jews played here.
57. Virchow, *Ueber die nationale Entwickelung und Bedeutung der Naturwissenschaften*, 20; and Virchow, *Ueber Wunder*, 18.
58. J. Meerfeld, 'Kirche und Sozialdemokratie', *Die Neue Zeit* 32(16) (1914), 580. Also pietists are – this is a very popular assumption – allegedly very dominant, cf. 'Sonntagszwang', *Die Gartenlaube* 29(2) (1877), 40; F. Dannemann, 'Das Wupperthal als Hort der Orthodoxie', *Die Gartenlaube* 29(3) (1877), 46–48; and H. Schulz, 'Religion und Volksschule', *Die Neue Zeit* 23(30) (1905), 123–27.
59. J. Casanova, 'The Religious Situation in Europe', in H. Joas and K. Wiegandt (eds), *Secularization and the World Religions* (Liverpool: Liverpool University Press, 2009), 219.
60. R. Darnton, *Literaten im Untergrund: Lesen, Schreiben und Publizieren im vorrevolutionären Frankreich* (Munich: Hanser, 1985).
61. 'Eine Todtenbeschwörung im Kloster. Aus den Erinnerungen eines sechzigjährigen Landpredigers'. 1872. *Die Gartenlaube* 24(48), 790–91.
62. A. Krieger, 'Die Beurteilung des 'Blumenmediums' Anna Rothe im Jahr 1903 und die Diskussion der Schuldfrage bei Spiritisten, Sachverständigen und der Tagespresse', Master's thesis (University of Göttingen, 2014). cf. Treitel, *A Science for the Soul*.
63. D. Sawicki, *Leben mit den Toten: Geisterglauben und die Entstehung des Spiritismus in Deutschland 1770–1900* (Paderborn: Schöningh, 2002), 299–353.
64. Healy, *The Jesuit Specter*, 179.
65. Cf. Casanova, 'The Religious Situation in Europe', 219.
66. A. Pannekoek, 'Das Wesen der Religion', *Die Neue Zeit* 52(25) (1907), 872–79.
67. Borutta, *Antikatholizismus*.
68. Kr., 'Ein preußischer Bischof als Teufelsbanner'.
69. M. von Humbracht, 'Aus der guten alten Zeit. Der Hexenthurm im Dorfe Lindheim', *Die Gartenlaube* 26(5) (1874), 77–79.
70. R. Habermas, 'Wissenstransfer und Mission. Sklavenhändler, Missionare und Religionswissenschaftler', *Geschichte und Gesellschaft* 36(2) (2010), 257–84.
71. Von Humbracht, 'Aus der guten alten Zeit', 78.
72. Ribbat, *Religiöse Erregung*, 224.
73. Göhre, 'Kirchenaustrittsbewegung und Sozialdemokratie', 497–507.
74. H. Simon, 'Aus der Stadt des ersten protestantischen Bündnisses: Das Lutherhaus in Schmalkalden', *Die Gartenlaube* 26(14) (1874), 230–33. Following this secular perspective, having strong emotions might quickly turn into a sentimental chaos.
75. Healy, *The Jesuit Specter*, 3. They furthermore were depicted as being 'soft on sins', cf. ibid., 151.
76. 'Der Geist der preußischen Schulregulative', *Die Gartenlaube* 24(19) (1872), 316; 'Der Somnambulisten- und Spiritistenschwindel', *Die Gartenlaube* 26(35) (1874), 570; 'Eine Todtenbeschwörung im Kloster', 790–91; C. Sterne, 'Die Aachener Reliquien', *Die Gartenlaube* 26(44) (1874), 708–10; and ibid., 26(47) (1874), 760–62, 764; S.T. Stein, 'Der Spiritismus, eine geistige Verirrung unserer Zeit', *Die Gartenlaube* 28(1) (1876), 16–19; and ibid., 28(3) (1876), 48–50; 'An der Gnadenstätte von Marpingen', 666–69.
77. Haily, *The Jesuit Specter*, 144.
78. Studies on nineteenth-century German middle class can hardly be overlooked anymore – see the still very instructive overview of M. Hettling and S.-L. Hoffmann, *Der Bürgerliche Wertehimmel* (Göttingen: Vandenhoeck & Ruprecht, 2000). Borutta (*Antikatholizismus*,

373) stresses that secularism had been the 'Selbstbeschreibung der progressiven männlichen Elite'(self-description of the progressive male elite).The same can be said concerning the organized social democratic workers.
79. See Habermas, 'Piety, Power, and Powerlessness', 457–60: '"Religious" was a negative category in so far as it included everything that ran counter to a modern bourgeois notion of society: superstition, adherence to traditions, religious practices such as pilgrimages that were denounced as "irrational", and other public forms of prayer, processions, or spiritual exercises, or as it was called at the time, all that "cloying flirtation"'.
80. Against the backdrop of the expanding literature on the history of emotions, such as the seminal works of Ute Frevert, and particularly in the field of religious and secular studies of Monique Scheer, I should mention M. Scheer, P. Eitler and B. Hitzer, 'Feeling and Faith: Religious Emotions in German History', *German History* 32(3) (2014), 343–52.
81. D. Blackbourn, *Wenn ihr sie seht, fragt wer sie sei: Marienerscheinungen in Marpingen – Aufstieg und Niedergang des Deutschen Lourdes* (Reinbek: Rowohlt, 1997), 451–82.
82. Allmers, 'Ein Wort zum Wehren und Klären', 233–35.
83. E.g. 'Der Beitrag zum Volksaberglauben', *Die Gartenlaube* 26(33) (1874), 537–38; and 'Der Beitrag zum Volksaberglauben', *Die Gartenlaube* 26(37) (1874), 601–2.
84. Sterne, 'Die Aachener Reliquien', 708.
85. Healy, *The Jesuit Specter*, 2.
86. King, 'Imagining Religions in India', 40.
87. The *Volksverein* was an association founded in 1890 and aiming to fight the atheism of the social democrat party: see G. Klein, *Der Volksverein für das katholische Deutschland 1890–1933* (Paderborn: Schöningh, 1996). For the Catholic workers' associations targeting as well what they understood as atheism, see M. Bachem-Rehm, *Die katholischen Arbeitervereine im Ruhrgebiet* (Stuttgart: Kohlhammer, 2004).
88. N. Friedrich, 'Zwischen allen Stühlen? Zur Geschichte der protestantischen Arbeiterbewegung zwischen Kaiserreich und früher Bundesrepublik', in C. Hiepel and M. Ruff (eds), *Christliche Arbeiterbewegung in Europa 1850–1950* (Stuttgart: Kohlhammer, 2003), 43.
89. A. Liedhegener, *Christentum und Urbanisierung: Katholiken und Protestanten in Münster und Bochum 1830–1933* (Paderborn: Schöningh, 1997).
90. Gross, *The War against Catholicism*, 39.
91. Anthony J. Steinhoff, *The Gods of the City: Protestantism and Religious Culture in Strasbourg, 1870–1914* (Leiden: Brill, 2008).
92. S. Mahmood, 'Religious Reason and Secular Affect: An Incommensurable Divide?' *Critical Inquiry* 35 (2009), 836–62.

Bibliography

Agrama, H.A. 'Reflections on Secularism, Democracy, and Politics in Egypt'. *American Ethnologist* 39 (2012), 26–31.
Allmers, H. 'Ein Wort zum Wehren und Klären'. *Die Gartenlaube* 26(14) (1874), 234.
'An der Gnadenstätte von Marpingen'. *Die Gartenlaube* 29(45) (1877), 666–69.
'Auf welche Weise in gegenwärtiger Zeit noch Wallfahrtsorte entstehen!'. *Die Gartenlaube* 24(24) (1872), 398.

Bachem-Rehm, M. *Die katholischen Arbeitervereine im Ruhrgebiet.* Stuttgart: Kohlhammer, 2004.
Bayly, C. *The Birth of the Modern World, 1780–1914: Global Connections and Comparisons.* Oxford: Blackwell, 2004.
Bennette, R.A. *Fighting for the Soul of Germany: The Catholic Struggle for Inclusion after Unification.* Cambridge, MA: Harvard University Press, 2012.
Bhargava, R. 'How Secular Is European Secularism?'. *European Societies* 16(3) (2014), 329–36.
Blackbourn D. *Wenn ihr sie seht, fragt wer sie sei: Marienscheinungen in Marpingen – Aufstieg und Niedergang des Deutschen Lourdes.* Reinbek: Rowohlt, 1997.
Bonnier, C. 'Wissenschaft, Kunst, Religion'. *Die Neue Zeit* 13(39) (1895), 325–30.
Borutta, M. *Antikatholizismus: Deutschland und Italien im Zeitalter der europäischen Kulturkämpfe.* Göttingen: Vandenhoeck & Ruprecht, 2010.
Bruce, S. 'The Other Secular Modern: An Empirical Critique of Asad'. *Religion and Society: Advances in Research* 4 (2013), 79–92.
Burchardt, M., M. Wohlrab-Sahr and U. Wegert. 'Multiple Secularities: Postcolonial Variations and Guiding Ideas in India and South Africa'. *International Sociology* 28(6) (2013), 612–28.
Butler, J. 'Sexual Politics, Torture and Secular Time'. *The British Journal of Sociology* 59 (2008), 1–23.
Casanova, J. 'The Religious Situation in Europe', in H. Joas and K. Wiegandt (eds), *Secularization and the World Religions* (Liverpool: Liverpool University Press, 2009), 206–28.
Chidester, D. *Savage Systems: Colonialism and Comparative Religion in Southern Africa.* Charlottesville: University of Virginia Press, 1996.
Clark, C., and W. Kaiser (eds). *Culture Wars: Secular–Catholic Conflict in Nineteenth-Century Europe.* Cambridge: Cambridge University Press, 2003.
Comaroff, J., and J. Comaroff (eds). *Of Revelation and Revolution: Christianity, Colonialism and Consciousness in South Africa*, Vol. 1. Chicago: Chicago University Press, 1991.
———. (eds). *Of Revelation and Revolution: The Dialectics of Modernity on a South African Frontier*, Vol. 2. Chicago: Chicago University Press, 1997.
Cunow, H. 'Religionsgeschichtliche Streifzüge'. *Die Neue Zeit* 29(35) (1910), 457–66.
Dannemann, F. 'Das Wupperthal als Hort der Orthodoxie'. *Die Gartenlaube* 29(3) (1877), 46–48.
Darnton, R. *Literaten im Untergrund: Lesen, Schreiben und Publizieren im vorrevolutionären Frankreich.* Munich: Hanser, 1985.
'Der Beitrag zum Volksaberglauben'. *Die Gartenlaube* 26(33) (1874), 537–38.
'Der Beitrag zum Volksaberglauben'. *Die Gartenlaube* 26(37) (1874), 601–2.
'Der Geist der preußischen Schulregulative'. *Die Gartenlaube* 24(19) (1872), 316.
'Der Somnambulisten- und Spiritistenschwindel'. *Die Gartenlaube* 26(35) (1874), 570.
Dhawan, N. 'The Empire Prays Back: Religion, Secularity, and Queer Critique'. *boundary 2* 40 (2013), 191–222.
Dittrich, L. 'European Connections, Obstacles, and the Search for a New Concept of Religion: The Freethought Movement as an Example of Transnational Anti-Catholicism in the Second Half of the Nineteenth Century'. *Journal of Religious History* 39(2) (2015), 261–79.
Dressler, M., and A.S. Mandair (eds). *Secularism and Religion-Making.* Oxford: Oxford University Press, 2011.

———. 'Introduction: Modernity, Religion-Making, and the Postsecular', in idem, *Secularism and Religion-Making* (Oxford: Oxford University Press, 2011), 3–37.

'Eine Todtenbeschwörung im Kloser: Aus den Erinnerungen eines sechszigjährigen Landpredigers'. *Die Gartenlaube* 24(48) (1872), 790–91.

Enders, S. *Moralunterricht und Lebenskunde*. Bad Heilbrunn: Klinkhardt, 2002.

Friedrich, N. 'Zwischen allen Stühlen? Zur Geschichte der protestantischen Arbeiterbewegung zwischen Kaiserreich und früher Bundesrepublik', in C. Hiepel and M. Ruff (eds), *Christliche Arbeiterbewegung in Europa 1850–1950* (Stuttgart: Kohlhammer, 2003), 42–63.

Göhre, P. 'Kirchenaustrittsbewegung und Sozialdemokratie'. *Die Neue Zeit* 32(14) (1914), 497–507.

Gross, B. *The War against Catholicism: Liberalism and the Anti-Catholic Imagination in Nineteenth-Century Germany*. Ann Arbor: University of Michigan Press, 2005.

Habermas, R. 'Piety, Power, and Powerlessness: Religion and Religious Groups in Germany, 1870–1945', in H.W. Smith (ed.), *The Oxford Handbook of Modern German History* (Oxford University Press, 2011), 453–80.

———. *Skandal in Togo: Ein Kapitel deutscher Kolonialherrschaft*. Frankfurt/Main: S. Fischer, 2016.

———. 'Wie Unterschichten nicht dargestellt werden sollten: Debatten um 1890 oder "Cacatum non est pictum!"', in L. Musner and R. Lindner (eds), *Unterschicht: Kulturwissenschaftliche Erkundungen der 'Armen' in Geschichte und Gegenwart* (Freiburg: Rombach, 2008), 97–122.

———. 'Wissenstransfer und Mission: Sklavenhändler, Missionare und Religionswissenschaftler'. *Geschichte und Gesellschaft* 36(2) (2010), 257–84.

Hall, C., and L. Davidoff. *Family Fortunes: Men and Women of the English Middle Class 1780–1850*. London: Routledge, 1992.

Healy, R. *The Jesuit Specter in Imperial Germany*. Boston: Brill, 2003.

Hettling, M., and S.L. Hoffmann. *Der Bürgerliche Wertehimmel*. Göttingen: Vandenhoeck & Ruprecht, 2000.

Hölscher, L. *Datenatlas zur religiösen Geographie im protestantischen Deutschland: Von der Mitte des 19. Jahrhunderts bis zum Zweiten Weltkrieg*, 4 vols. Berlin: de Gruyter, 2001.

Hull, I. *Sexuality, State, and Civil Society in Germany 1700–1815*. Ithaca, NY: Cornell University Press, 1996.

Humbracht, M. von. 'Aus der guten alten Zeit: Der Hexenthurm im Dorfe Lindheim'. *Die Gartenlaube* 26(5) (1874), 77–79.

Jensen, U. *Gebildete Doppelgänger: Bürgerliche Juden und Protestanten im 19. Jahrhundert*. Göttingen: Vandenhoeck & Ruprecht, 2005.

Joskowicz, A. *The Modernity of Others: Jewish Anti-Catholicism in Germany and France*. Stanford, CA: Stanford University Press, 2014.

Kaiser, J.-C. *Arbeiterbewegung und organisierte Religionskritik: Proletarische Freidenkerverbände in Kaiserreich und Weimarer Republik*. Stuttgart: Klett-Cotta, 1981.

King, R. 'Imagining Religions in India: Colonialism and the Mapping of South Asian History and Culture', in M. Dressler and A. S. Mandair (eds), *Secularism and Religion-Making* (Oxford: Oxford University Press, 2011), 37–61.

Klein, G. *Der Volksverein für das katholische Deutschland 1890–1933*. Paderborn: Schöningh, 1996.

Kr., E. 'Ein preußischer Bischof als Teufelsbanner'. *Die Gartenlaube* 24(45) (1872), 740–43.

Krieger, A. 'Die Beurteilung des 'Blumenmediums' Anna Rothe im Jahr 1903 und die Diskussion der Schuldfrage bei Spiritisten, Sachverständigen und der Tagespresse'. Master's thesis. University of Göttingen, 2014.

Lebner, A.B. 'The Anthropology of Secularity beyond Secularism'. *Religion and Society: Advances in Research* 6 (2015), 62–74.

Liedhegener, A. *Christentum und Urbanisierung: Katholiken und Protestanten in Münster und Bochum 1830–1933*. Paderborn: Schöningh, 1997.

Lübbe, H. *Säkularisierung: Geschichte eines ideenpolitischen Begriffs*. Freiburg: Alber, 1965.

Mahmood, S. 'Religious Reason and Secular Affect: An Incommensurable Divide?' *Critical Inquiry* 35 (2009), 836–62.

Masuzawa, T. *The Invention of World Religions: Or, How European Universalism Was Preserved in the Language of Pluralism*. Chicago: Chicago University Press, 2005.

Meerfeld, J. 'Kirche und Sozialdemokratie'. *Die Neue Zeit* 32(16) (1914), 578–83.

Molendijk, A.L., and P. Pels (eds). *Religion in the Making: The Emergence of the Sciences of Religion*. Leiden: Brill, 1998.

Mommertz, M., and C. Opitz-Belakhal (eds). *Das Geschlecht des Glaubens: Religiöse Kulturen Europas zwischen Mittelalter und Moderne*. Frankfurt/Main: Campus, 2008.

Mufti, A.R. 'Critical Secularism: A Reintroduction for Perilous Times'. *boundary 2* 31(2) (2004), 1–9.

———. *Enlightenment in the Colony: The Jewish Question and the Crisis of Postcololonial Culture*. Princeton, NJ: Princeton University Press, 2009.

Paletschek, S. *Frauen und Dissens: Frauen im Deutschkatholizismus und in den freien Gemeinden 1841–1852*. Göttingen: Vandenhoeck & Ruprecht, 1990.

Pannekoek, A. 'Das Wesen der Religion'. *Die Neue Zeit* 52(25) (1907), 872–79.

Przyrembel, A. *Verbote und Geheimnisse: Das Tabu und die Genese der europäischen Moderne (1784–1913)*. Frankfurt/Main: Campus, 2011.

Rahden, T. van. *Juden und andere Breslauer: Die Beziehungen zwischen Juden, Protestanten und Katholiken in einer deutschen Großstadt von 1860 bis 1925*. Göttingen: Vandenhoeck & Ruprecht, 2000.

Reclam, C. 'Die Feuerbestattung'. *Die Gartenlaube* 26(19) (1874), 308–13.

Ribbat, C. *Religiöse Erregung*. Frankfurt/Main: Campus, 1996.

Roller, G. 'Partei und Religion'. *Die Neue Zeit* 24(51) (1906), 846–48.

Sawicki, D. *Leben mit den Toten: Geisterglauben und die Entstehung des Spiritismus in Deutschland 1770–1900*. Paderborn: Schöningh, 2002.

Scheer, M., P. Eitler and B. Hitzer. 'Feeling and Faith: Religious Emotions in German History'. *German History* 32(3) (2014), 343–52.

Schulz. H. 'Religion und Volksschule'. *Die Neue Zeit* 23(30) (1905), 123–27.

'Sclavenfang in Afrika'. *Die Gartenlaube* 24(21) (1872), 343–45.

Sheehan, J. *The Enlightenment Bible: Translation, Scholarship, Culture*. Princeton, NJ: Princeton University Press, 2005.

Simon, H. 'Aus der Stadt des ersten protestantischen Bündnisses: Das Lutherhaus in Schmalkalden'. *Die Gartenlaube* 26(14) (1874), 230–33.

'Sonntagszwang'. *Die Gartenlaube* 29(2) (1877), 40.

Starrett, G. 'The Varieties of Secular Experience'. *Comparative Studies in Society and History* 52(3) (2010), 626–51.

Stein, S.T. 'Der Spiritismus, eine geistige Verirrung unserer Zeit'. *Die Gartenlaube* 28(1) (1876), 16–19; and 28(3) (1876), 48–50.

Steinhoff, Anthony J. *The Gods of the City: Protestantism and Religious Culture in Strasbourg, 1870–1914*. Leiden: Brill, 2008.
Sterne, C. 'Die Aachener Reliquien'. *Die Gartenlaube* 26(44) (1874), 708–10; and 26(47) (1874), 760–62, 764.
Taylor, C. *A Secular Age*. Cambridge, MA: Harvard University Press, 2007.
Treitel, C. *A Science for the Soul: Occultism and the Genesis of the German Modern*. Baltimore, MD: Johns Hopkins University Press, 2004.
'Ueber die neue Wallfahrt unweit Würzburg'. *Die Gartenlaube* 24(31) (1872), 514.
Verhoeven, T. 'Harmful or Benign? Transnational Medical Networks and the Celibacy of Priests'. *Journal of Religious History* 39(2) (2015), 244–60.
Virchow, R. *Ueber die nationale Entwickelung und Bedeutung der Naturwissenschaften: Rede, gehalten in der zweiten allgemeinen Sitzung der Versammlung deutscher Naturforscher und Aerzte zu Hannover am 20. September 1865*. Berlin: Hirschwald, 1865.
———. *Ueber Wunder: Rede, gehalten in der ersten allgemeinen Sitzung der 47. Versammlung deutscher Naturforscher und Aerzte zu Breslau am 18. September 1874*. Breslau: Morgenstern, 1874.
Weir, T.H. *Secularism and Religion in Nineteenth-Century Germany: The Rise of the Fourth Confession*. Cambridge: Cambridge University Press, 2014.
———. 'Germany and the New Global History of Secularism: Questioning the Postcolonial Genealogy'. *The Germanic Review* 90 (2015), 6–20.
Welter, B. 'The Cult of True Womanhood: 1820–1860'. *American Quarterly* 18(2) (1966), 151–74.
Werner, Y.M., and J. Harvard. 'European Anti-Catholicism in Comparative and Transnational Perspective. The Role of a Unifying Other: An Introduction'. *European Studies* 31 (2013), 13–22.
Zabel, H., W. Conze and H.W. Strätz. 'Säkularisation, Säkularisierung', in O. Brunner, W. Conze and R. Koselleck (eds), *Geschichtliche Grundbegriffe: Historisches Lexikon zur poltisch-sozialen Sprache in Deutschland*, Vol. 5 (Stuttgart: Klett-Cotta, 2004), 789–829.

PART III
Religious and Secular
Negotiating Boundaries

5

Retrieving Tradition?

The Secular–Religious Ambiguity in Nineteenth-Century German-Jewish Anarchism

Carolin Kosuch

In 1907, Maximilian Harden's literary-political weekly *Die Zukunft* released an essay entitled 'People and Land: Thirty Socialist Theses', written by the influential German-Jewish publisher and anarchist Gustav Landauer (1870–1919).[1] The essay campaigned for a clear distinction of 'state' on the one hand, and 'nation, community and people' on the other. While it condemns the former as an artificial construct and sheer functional unit without grounding in language and tradition, it emphasizes a culturally based understanding of the latter. It further criticized the state and the continuous use it made of the nation for its own credibility, which is why, according to Landauer, conflicts between states are inevitably intermingled with it. From his point of view, a nation without governmental repression clearly leads to self-organizing communities, not to state structures.[2]

In his essay, Landauer revealed a specific notion of 'nation' composed of two major elements: the homeland, construed as a naturally grown unit, virtually the 'body' of a community, made up of soil, landscape, climate and geology; and the 'spirit' of this community, which he believed was embedded in language. Following Landauer's reading, this spiritual part of the nation, condensed in poetry, literature and philosophy, could transgress the physical limits of the homeland.[3] Deeply inspired by the idea of a '*Kulturnation*', Landauer furthermore seized 'nation' as an integral and 'authentic' notion, living in the people beyond the state and its interests. In his age though, he bemoaned, the genuine nation no longer exists. As a consequence, he constantly transfigured his nostalgia into a longing for a future stateless, but 'truly' nation-based society.

Both the neo-romantic as well as idealistic shading suffusing Landauer's work reflect his intimate knowledge of philosophers like Fichte and Herder,[4] just as his organic reasoning reminds one of the ambiguity that is typical of the numerous contemporary groups constituting the *Lebensreform*.[5] Basically forward-looking and hypermodern, this transnational social movement no other than anarchism contained traits of cultural pessimism oriented towards a glorified bygone natural state.[6] That being said, Landauer's essay seems to bundle many aspects and influences of his political philosophy. Its underlying concept is clearly a transnational one, leaving out the state as an intermediate instance, uniting the local – landscape, people and tradition – with the global through language. Although influenced by the writings of Bakunin, Kropotkin, Proudhon and Tolstoy,[7] Landauer, with this set of ideas, added his very own contribution to the multifold spectrum of modern anarchisms.[8]

But Landauer's anarchism not only seems to have advocated for the transnational.[9] Even more, it promoted the secular, unveiled by its harsh critique of institutional Christianity and its clergy, the almost unlimited support for the conceptions of socialization, self-determination, free association and by its avowal for pluralism in a coming age of diversity.[10] Within anarchism, church and state – interpreted as two sides of a coin – were frequently labelled as instruments of oppression and exploitation, which inevitably would have to be abolished in favour of a future society based on the liberty and independence of the individual.[11] Landauer shared this conviction:

> I agree with the fine American essayist Ralph Waldo Emerson …, who has said that anyone who wants to be a man has to be a dissident. 'Oh,' I can see the reader think, 'here is an anarchist agenda: to leave the national church!' Yes, we do want to leave the national church, but we want to leave much more: the state and all forced associations; the traditions of private property, of possessive marriage, of familial authority, of privileged labour divisions, of national exclusivity, and of arrogance.[12]

Such an explicit agenda raises the question of whether its call to leave the church points to a general criticism of religion in Landauer's anarchism. If secularization involves 'differentiation, rationalization [and] worldliness',[13] one question that needs to be asked is whether Landauer's affiliation with a radical political anti-clerical philosophy, enforcing heterogeneity and the transnational, make him inevitably a secular agent with a secular political teaching that strives for a strict distance from any religious conviction or connotation. Is religion in his anarchism thus overwritten if not replaced by politics? Could Steve Bruce's research, which traces the ongoing marginalization of religion back to a spreading egalitarian notion causing religious relativism, provide insight also into the case of German-Jewish anarchism?[14] Or, on the other hand, should we follow Shmuel Eisenstadt in his reasoning on the 'multiple modernities', in which the sacred has not vanished but is only subjected to a radically new interpretation?[15] If we do so, the idea of 'multiple secularities', building upon Eisenstadt's notion of 'multiple modernities', might help us to explore how exactly the secular was negotiated in the case of German-Jewish anarchism, and how it related to the religious. The underlying assumption here is that 'the way secularity figures within configurations of modernity is fundamentally shaped by the long durée of civilizational history, by the way religion affects local cosmologies and spiritual ontologies ... and is related to authority and forms of organization'.[16]

This is where the paper ties in: it critically examines the secular and the religious in German-Jewish anarchism of the nineteenth century, drawing attention not only to Landauer, but also to some of his political companions, especially Erich Mühsam (1878–1934). It begins by shedding light on the historical background and biographical specifics of the mentioned anarchists, and raises the question of how anarchism came to be their focal point. Subsequently, the secular and the religious in their transnational anarchist concepts, implemented in Landauer's 'Socialist League' among other places, are scrutinized. The league found the support of Erich Mühsam as well as Martin Buber (1878–1965), and questions the assumption that transnational secular ideologies are inevitably worldly in character. Rather, as part three of the paper suggests, a careful differentiation is essential here, assessing what the religious and the secular in the modern age indicated in each particular case. Within this balancing, a transformed religious notion might prove to be part of nineteenth- and early twentieth-century anarchism, a transnationally oriented and seemingly secular ideology.

From Acculturation to Crisis: The Secular as a Precondition for Anarchism

With their philosophy and undertakings, German Jews like Gustav Landauer and Erich Mühsam stood at the crossroads of Jewish history. Born in the last quarter of nineteenth-century Western Europe to well-off bourgeois families, their generation was the first to grow up in a seemingly completed setting of Jewish emancipation.[17] While diaspora Jews of the pre-Enlightenment era had preserved local autonomy and a somewhat group-specific consciousness based on religion and culture despite their spatial dispersion,[18] the nineteenth-century policy of emancipation had accomplished legal equality, full citizenship and a noticeable removal of social, educational and professional barriers. After several setbacks, an environment of integration and acculturation[19] seemed to have been generated, wiping away the last excluding differences.[20] Previous generations had struggled for this emancipatory scenario to come true: in 1865, Landauer's family had left the small village of Buttenhausen in Swabia, where many of their relatives continued to live in traditional ways, for Karlsruhe.[21] On the city's main promenade, Hermann Landauer, Gustav Landauer's father, ran a flourishing shoe shop. Reflecting on his childhood, Landauer could not remember any stress his parental home had put on religion. Rather, his father had been eager to provide an academic higher education for his three sons.[22] Just like many other German

Jews of the time, the Landauer family obviously adapted to a bourgeois lifestyle, its social and educational values as well as its habits and aims.[23]

The Mühsam family took the same route: already the great-great-grandfather, Pinkus Seligmann Pappenheim (1737–1807), had worked for the advancement of his kin. He served the Prussian king in the Seven Years' War as a loyal soldier, and finally was rewarded with permission to settle in the Silesian city of Byczyna, and to bear the surname Mühsam ('arduous') because of his tenacity.[24] The story of the family continued to be one of acculturation and success, ending with Erich Mühsam's father who, under severe personal and economic hardships, had studied pharmacy in Wrocław. Later, he moved to Berlin and Lübeck, and managed to run his own pharmacies. In his spare time, he actively took part in associations and clubs – not explicitly Jewish, but bourgeois ones such as masonic lodges and charitable or professional associations.[25] Erich Mühsam's sister remembered: 'My parents both originated from traditional, albeit non-orthodox Jewish families. They adapted our way of life to the habits of our non-Jewish environment. Except during holidays, when they visited the synagogue, nothing particularly Jewish became apparent in our daily life'.[26] However, German-Jewish families like the Mühsams and Landauers had not simply been absorbed into an already existing modern bourgeois society. In fact, they had helped to build it, together with non-Jews who likewise had just recently gained entry to the middle class.[27]

While their fathers and grandfathers had been working hard for the advancement and economic well-being of their families and were committed to the credo of acculturation, the generation of German Jews born in the 1870s could no longer neglect the contradictions, having been somewhat hidden behind the notions of prosperity and national unification in the period of promoterism.[28] On the one hand, the young German nation state had imposed a homogenizing identity on all of its subjects through legal equality;[29] but, on the other hand, both growing anti-Semitism[30] and the development of a Jewish cultural revival ensured notions of German-Jewish identity that remained contested. This ongoing problematic dynamic was rooted in the character of the German national state itself, which remained Christian, with the Protestantism of the Hohenzollern dynasty its leading confession. Hence, despite enjoying equality under the law, Jewish citizens were increasingly accused of national disloyalty and subjected to forms of discrimination: they could still neither enter civil service nor hold high military ranks. Besides, their path to a PhD or a professorship continued to be blocked within German academia:[31] 'Although there ceased to be specific restrictions, there were implicit ones, subject to individual interpretation, shifting Jewish emancipation from a legal to a sociopolitical sphere, which in its long and drawn out development was in itself largely responsible for the revival of anti-Jewish debates'.[32]

Having been constitutive for the era of the fathers, the heyday of liberalism had peaked by the last third of the nineteenth century. Subsequently, it underwent a severe crisis.[33] One of its most obvious signs could be found in an intensified anti-Semitism, especially in the politically charged atmosphere that the 'Antisemitismusstreit' of the late 1870s and the 1880s generated.[34] Against this backdrop, Landauer, Mühsam and their generation grasped acculturation no longer as a given social and economic advancement, but with scrutinized bourgeois values and lifestyle at their core.[35] Thus, in the years to come, both these anarchists started to search for a way to implement the enlightened credo of their education, truly and without compromise. This attitude and longing to change society according to their conviction moved them – irrespective of their greater distance from the Jewish tradition – close to the maskilic programme of Jewish Enlightenment, dating back to the late eighteenth century, and its aim to renew and to heal a sickened age by means of culture, knowledge and education.[36] To some extent, Landauer's and Mühsam's anarchisms therefore completed the circle. Their political convictions marked the endpoint of a decisive and highly influential trend of the long nineteenth century: the entry of Jews into wider German society.

Due to their attitudes, the two young men rose in revolt against their bourgeois fathers.[37] Landauer, the former student of philology and national economy, dropped out of university. He composed Nietzschean dramas, joined theatre, writer and independent socialist associations, and quickly became a leading figure in Berlin's radical left-wing circles, fighting authoritarianisms in both monarchy and social democracy.[38] Moreover, he married a non-Jewish seamstress, not befitting his social rank and without the blessing of his parents – a decision, which, together with his recurring imprisonments for civil disobedience and political provocation, deepened the family disputes over his renegade lifestyle.[39] His rebellion was also an expression of the anarchism he had become familiar with in the bohemian-naturalistic writer community of Friedrichshagen,[40] located on Berlin's periphery. While the community's deeply political character crystallized in its predominantly countercultural way of life, the provocative outward appearance of the circle's members, the topics of their work, discussion and the canon of literature they shared,[41] the primary sources of their anarchism (for Landauer too) had been artistic and philosophical texts. Among them were Ibsen's critique of a bigoted society, Nietzsche's and Schopenhauer's philosophy, Proudhon's and Stirner's anarchic concepts, and even Wagner's romantic longings.[42] Landauer merged these influences and created a political programme which he published in the monthly *Der Sozialist*, a journal he temporarily edited as organ of the Association of Independent Socialists. In one of his articles he claimed that the proletariat still had to free itself from its philistine attitude and become what it had already claimed to be: an actual promoter of free ideas and science.[43] Contrary to what this rhetoric might suggest, Landauer did not join workers' associations, but stayed independent most of the time, initiating loose networks of his own.

Erich Mühsam likewise joined Berlin's landscape of free associations and short-living poet societies after he had tried in vain to fit into the bourgeois way of life his father had designated for him as his prospective successor in pharmacy. He became acquainted with Landauer in the writers' community 'Neue

Gemeinschaft', and was quickly attracted by his anarchism.[44] While Landauer bridged the gap between literature, politics and rebellion, and opted for a somewhat conventional way of life after his divorce and a new marriage to Jewish poet and teacher Hedwig Lachmann (1865–1918), Mühsam entered Berlin's coffee house circles and adopted a Bohemian character. The Bohemian, he argued, was a proper, authentic anarchist because of his 'disdain of all centralist organization' and his sheer inability to exist or feel the way 'the masses' did.[45]

In vindication of his theory, Mühsam's whole appearance and habit reflected revolution: his sexual promiscuity; his constant flirtations with bankruptcy; his excessive coffee, cigarette and alcohol consumption; his ever-changing domestic circumstances in mouldy rooms; his uncut hair and shabby clothes; and his taunting as well as radical poetry – these were the elements that helped to generate the image of the rebellious anti-bourgeois.[46]

In truth, this character appears staged, because Mühsam, despite constant quarrels especially with his father about his way of life, always received financial subsidies covering his basic needs on the part of his family. On these grounds he never completely cut the cord from bourgeois society, not least because it was his main source of friction – vital for his self-stylization as 'outsider'.[47] Therefore, he remained the heretic of the bourgeoisie, not its apostate, also on 'Monte Verità', the centre of *Lebensreform*, where he spent some time trying to recruit vegetarians and followers of Otto Gross's unconventional psychoanalysis for anarchism.[48]

Implementing their rebellious attitudes into practice, experience and writing, Mühsam and Landauer grappled with the crisis of acculturation that, in a broader sense, coincided with a general crisis expressed in the *fin de siècle* atmosphere. Yet, notwithstanding their critique of social conditions,[49] the existing order based on a social and cultural secular opening was the essential precondition for their anarchism, and the ways of life both had chosen. They literally stood on a secular ground. But they went further, took seriously the diversity and plurality the secular had envisioned, and acted as advocates for a society still to come: 'Instead of both the national state and the world state that the social democrats dream of, we anarchists want a free order of multiple, intertwined, colorful associations and companies. This order will be based upon the principle that all individuals are closest to their own interests, and that their shirts are closer to them than their jackets'.[50] No way led back to a time before the secular had fundamentally pluralized and individualized society – rather, Landauer's and Mühsam's own history and their political theory were an integral part of this transition.

Seeking Traces: The Religious in the Secular

The secular thus seems to have constituted the main pillar securing Landauer's and Mühsam's existence. It was present in the social advancement of their fathers and grandfathers, as well as in the process of acculturation itself, just as in the eventual accomplishment of legal equality for Jews as citizens. Moreover, the possibility of gaining access to the rich diversity of flourishing associations, groups and clubs bore witness to the secular. Mühsam's life as a Bohemian was utterly secular, since the sheer possibility of living the way he did indicated that bourgeois society opened up small spaces for heterogeneity, though still endangered by governmental repression, especially in bustling cities like Berlin. The secular, finally, was mirrored in the augmentation of possibilities, the variety of potential courses of action and the freedom to choose who and where to be, irrespective of origin and background – at least in part, and for privileged educated sons of affluent fathers like Mühsam and Landauer.[51]

Growing up in a secular setting implied in both cases also the withdrawal from religious institutions like the synagogue and the Jewish body of law in general.[52] However, in their writings, Landauer and Mühsam broadly reflect the religious, which seems surprising only at first glance. In fact, the religious in the modern age – an integral part of social reality – did not vanish, but, together and side-by-side with society as a whole, underwent transformational processes. Consequently, the secular involved diversification both on a social and religious level, resulting in varieties of faith and individual as well as personalized or critical concepts of religion.[53] Additionally to this trend, Landauer's and Mühsam's notion of religion in general and of the Jewish tradition in particular, was shaped by the implications of Jewish acculturation and its orientation towards a Protestant-dominated bourgeois culture. Neither therefore, and very much in line with the idea of 'multiple secularities', ever experienced Jewish tradition unaffected by this religiously grounded focal point of Jewish social advancement within the secular transition.

Hence, even though their bourgeois education had considered Judaism in the sense of institutions and the Halakha only ephemerally, it continued to be Jewish in a modern way, intermingled with Protestant bourgeois values. Its main elements consist of education, culture, literacy and social commitment, as well as family bonds. Visiting the synagogue – reduced to high holidays – for instance, became a bourgeois family ritual.[54] Another example of this transfer could be given regarding the religious education of the Mühsam children, which was limited to some Hebrew reading and the memorization of a few prayers to avoid conflicts between the orthodox rabbinate of Lübeck and the religious liberal stance of the Mühsams. But just like the Landauers, the Mühsams put a lot of effort into a profound secondary education for their children. Although its form and content ceased to be Jewish in a traditional sense, it nonetheless met the bourgeois Jewish appreciation of '*Bildung*'.[55] This shift is also reflected in a widely read novel written by Siegfried Seligman Mühsam commemorating and idealizing the Jewish Shtetl with its tight social bonds and inhabitants of exemplary commitment. Here again the protagonists not only met Jewish standards, but bourgeois ones as well. And just like his book had portrayed, Siegfried Seligman Mühsam demanded the same decency, willingness to help and the utmost morality from his children – and made no exception even for himself. Despite his endeavours to avoid any affiliation too close to the Jews in public, he supported the Jewish community and its efforts on behalf of orphans.[56]

Taking over these patterns of their socialization, the literary oeuvres of Landauer and Mühsam likewise intermingled Jewish and Christian elements in a secular interpretation: God in Mühsam's poems acts the way his earthly father did. Throughout the verses, he misconceives, ignores and even punishes the speaker, no other than Mühsam had remembered his father's attitude towards himself.[57] As a logical consequence, the lyrical Jesus equals Mühsam in his sonship. The poems portray him as a fraternal figure who attempts in vain to strengthen the poor – expelled and desperate in gin palaces – with hope,[58] just like the poet himself had tried hard to prop up the 'Lumpenproletariat' in speakeasies with his anarchistic credo of equality, brotherhood and acceptance.[59] In addition, Caine, the fratricide of the Genesis who gave the name to Mühsam's monthly, is cherished in the poems because of his apostasy from the (bourgeois) majority, its rules and morale, and therein equals Mühsam in his own deviance.[60] In one of his first dramatic attempts, the young Landauer echoed this interpretation of an actual positive Caine figure, who, in contrast to his obedient parents, strikes out on his own to claim back paradise from God.[61] Finally, the sequence of biblical personalities whom Landauer and especially Mühsam referred to in a renewed interpretation was completed by Moses – in their writings a desperately disappointed, longing visionary, a warrior and romantic idealist, no other than them who once truly believed God's Promised Land would be close.[62]

Hence, the re-appropriation of religious contents seems to have been decisive for Mühsam's and Landauer's secularity and its 'iteration'. In the course of reinterpretation, the former meaning of this knowledge partly dissolved. But it outlived in a secular shape, precisely because of this process of interpretative rebalancing.[63] From socio-critical literary writing it was only a small step to politics: even the young Landauer's essay 'Through Separation to Community' (1901), which made Mühsam become a devoted reader of anarchist literature in the first place, is already marked by the constant balancing between secular and religious terms. The essay could be understood as a programmatic roadmap for the aims of the 'Neue Gemeinschaft' (New Community) founded in 1900 as a writers' community by the brothers Hart, both devoted to Stirner's radical philosophy of individualization.[64] It combines such disparate influences as the writings of Meister Eckhart, Goethe, Nietzsche and the philosophy of language that Fritz Mauthner, Landauer's friend and promoter, had published shortly after 1900. In his text, Landauer calls for a new spiritually-grounded libertarian existence:

> [T]here is a young generation that has become sceptical of tradition. We can categorize its members if we want to: we have socialists and anarchists, atheists and gypsies, nihilists and romantics. ... I was among those who had gone to the masses. Now I and my comrades have returned. ... We have come to a realization that took pains to reach: we are too far ahead to be understood. ... Away from the state, as far as we can get! Away

from goods and commerce! Away from the philistines! Let us – us few who feel like heirs to the millennia, who feel simple and eternal, who are Gods – form a small community in joy and activity. Let us create ourselves as exemplary human beings. Let us express all our desires … There is no other way for us![65]

The 'Neue Gemeinschaft' also attracted the young Martin Buber, who, unlike Mühsam and Landauer, had been raised at his grandfather's house in Lviv in an environment that was rich in Jewish textual and religious traditions.[66] Yet, his grandfather, the entrepreneur Salomon Buber, had been an autodidact. His reading of the Jewish canon was not traditional, but modern, reflecting the accomplishments of Haskala, the Jewish enlightenment. With this orientation he guided the mindset of his grandson, just as Martin Buber's father, whom the young Martin had visited frequently during holidays in the Bukovina, had triggered his lifelong occupation with Hasidism.[67] Due to this background, and thanks to the influence Martin Buber had on his comrades of the 'Neue Gemeinschaft', their interest in Judaism intensified. By appealing to a partly forgotten tradition, he answered their neo-romantic longing and underlined their particularity as German Jews, just as he shared their critical stance towards society and craved change together with them.[68] Mühsam remembered the young Buber speaking like a priest about Jewish mysticism in a modern way and lost in thought during his time with the 'Neue Gemeinschaft'.[69] The Jew, echoed Landauer elsewhere, could learn from Buber's writings what he no longer knew innately, but had to be reminded of from an external source.[70] While Buber stated that the eternal in Judaism still had to prove its value for a troubled present,[71] Landauer cherished Judaism's binding forces uniting a group of individuals to a community. For him, decision, change and action constituted the crucial elements that Christianity had adopted from Judaism.[72]

In this fashion, and also due to the influence of Hedwig Lachmann, daughter of a Jewish cantor, Judaism, and the attributes Landauer ascribed to it, became a cornerstone of his anarchism, nourishing his attempts to overcome the existing order. However, his paradigm for a coming stateless age also made use of the Christian heritage, especially the idealized Middle Ages with their communal, artisan and local tradition, which he rediscovered in Kropotkin's writings:[73]

[T]he Christian era represents a cultural level where multiple mutually exclusive social institutions existed side by side, were permeated by a unifying spirit, and constituted a union of many sovereign elements that came together in liberty. We call this principle of the Middle Ages the *principle of ordered multiplicity* in contrast to the *principle of centralism and state power* that always occurs where the common spirit has been lost. … It was only church and theological teachings that began to distinguish between symbols and letters, and robbed Christendom of its life by focusing on the latter and insisting on literal interpretations of the traditions and dogmas. This is how all true Christians turned into mystics, heretics, and then revolutionaries – while stupidity took hold of the Church.[74]

This 'principle of ordered multiplicity' was a decisive aspect of the 'Socialist League' that Landauer founded in 1908. Supported by Mühsam and Buber with various written appeals and leaflets, Landauer's league strived to unite all those willing to realize socialism in the capitalist present.[75] The withdrawal from bourgeois society was conceived as an active general strike[76] of those working together to create cooperatives and independent self-sustaining settlements in the countryside:

> We want to directly link the production of consumer goods to the needs of the people. We want to create the basic form of a new, real, socialist, free, and stateless society – in other words, a *community*. However, we could use the help of everyone who desires socialism, even if they are not able to separate from the current social conditions as thoroughly as we are. They can find ways to support us even if they – at least for now – stay in their parties, unions, and cooperatives. They can help us create the example that we want to create.[77][

Until the First World War, which caused the dissolution of the undertaking, several hundred people followed Landauer's call and established subsections of the 'Socialist League' in the German Empire and Switzerland.[78] Moreover, Landauer's call had an effect on the Zionist-Socialist youth organization Hashomer Hatzair and the Kibbutzim, especially through Buber's lecturing.[79] What kept the single sections together was the league's organ *Der Sozialist*, published anew by Landauer. Only a few of the groups actually opted for settlement, and neither Landauer, nor Buber, nor Mühsam were among those leaving for the countryside. Rather, Landauer accompanied the league as a sometimes quite dominant consultant.[80] Mühsam, on the other hand, according to the family value of social commitment, tried to agitate the poor in his own groups.[81]

The diversity of the groups, their agenda and the notion of a society based on free association clearly reflected the league's secularity. Its global character was present in the idea that humankind, people, groups and individuals were held together loosely and solely because they shared a common interest. Once fulfilled, those groups of interest could regroup – or be maintained, if further purposes of their concern required it. The draft neither foresaw the state, nor a world parliament, but emphasized radical self-determination, advocating for collectivism solely in response to actual needs and necessities.[82] Still, the religious in its modern and eclectic reading constitutes an essential element shaping the concept of the league, because the original pattern for Landauer's libertarian society based on communities was borrowed from his reading of the Christian and Jewish heritage. In this sense, Landauer made use of the 'Bund' recalling the biblical covenants of both the Torah and the New Testament. Moreover, he utilized the term 'Geist', which likewise came up with an almost biblical connotation referring to Pentecost and the Holy Spirit. Landauer's notion of 'Geist', present throughout his writings, implicated creative unity of work, culture and thought, and represented the superordinate principle of each group of interest.[83]

Part of Landauer's theory were so called 'conscious' Jews.[84] They formed a particular group of interest, still in the process of its formation. His essay 'Are These the Ideas of a Heretic?' (1913) put this process down in writing, reshaping the Jewish notion of *tikkun olam* ('repair of the world'), which had an effect on various Jewish traditions reaching from Orthodoxy to Kabbalah,[85] and also influenced Landauer's reasoning on anarchist Socialism.[86] The Jews among those willing to build the stateless future, according to Landauer, could profit from a valuable advantage compared to other pioneers: their preserved, deep-rooted nationality. Regardless of any disruption in the course of history, the Jews, in Landauer's reading, remained united in a league to serve mankind. For him, it was their duty to send out an impulse by changing themselves, side by side with mankind, into society, people, corporation and organism anew. To work among the peoples for redemption meant the actual completion of their Judaism, Landauer underlined. Neither Zionism nor a Jewish state, but the cooperation of pioneer-like Jews and non-Jews, should help to overcome the problems of his age, among them stigmatization and inequality: 'Nation means duty, and my fatherland is the place of my duty'.[87] An age-old longing deep within the Jewish soul, he added, would lead the way for a coming reign of man. Tradition, Landauer asserted, implied nothing else than revolution and the renaissance of mankind. In his conclusion he argued, the Jew could only be redeemed together with humanity: 'To wait for the messiah in exile and diaspora, and to be the messiah of all peoples, is one and the same'.[88]

The perception of a Jewish renewal for the sake of mankind in Landauer's writings shows plainly that secularity falls back on religious categories in a renewed interpretation, combining, in his case, religious-messianic with worldly political notions.[89] Mühsam echoed this 'iteration' in the way he talked about his Jewish belonging as a given fact, providing him with strength for his mission.[90] Because of the existing deep Jewish relationship,[91] and because Jews had maintained their particularity, even 'their race',[92] they could have the effect of sourdough on society, he declared.[93] What is more, Mühsam correlated the anarchist idea of freedom with the religious. Unlike those positivists, who would abuse the revolution as a sheer means to their ends, only those aiming for freedom in their revolution were, to Mühsam, truly religious.[94] In both Landauer's and Mühsam's reasoning, it seems, 'the "religious" and "the secular" are continuously made and remade'.[95] But, if we speak of a transformed though outlasting religious constituting the secular in German-Jewish anarchism, do we not tend to overlook an actual ongoing shrinking of religion in favour of an individualism, which reduces 'the religious' to a functional notion, mostly related to the political and social sphere, serving mainly the self-stylization of modern man? On the other hand, has the religious itself not revealed its heterogeneous, alterable character throughout history? Did the secular not evolve from a religious society?[96] Would it thus be plausible to add a transformed and ever-transforming religious to a likewise non-fixed secular, as Landauer's and Mühsam's cases seem to suggest?

A Conclusion

The impact of the Enlightenment, modernization and pluralization, as well as the nineteenth-century development of Jewish emancipation and acculturation, combined to render the term 'Jewish' an ambiguity. It no longer specified a person's identity according to religious criteria alone. Rather, it underwent a process of secular opening: 'Jewish' in the modern age could also mark individual, national or even ethnic affiliations, either imposed as a classifying and often downgrading category from the outside, or used in an affirmative self, as well as group-attributing manner.[97] The transitional individualizing complexity of the term became evident when Landauer stressed:

> The German and the Jewish in me do not obstruct but enrich each other. Like two brothers, the first born and a Benjamin, who are not loved by their mother the same way but with the same intensity, … I experience this strange and familiar coexistence as precious. There is nothing primary or secondary in this relation. I never felt the need to simplify or negate myself to appear more unified. I accept the complex being, who I am, and I hope to be even more manifold in my personality than I already know I am.[98]

Mühsam echoed: 'I am a Jew and I will stay a Jew as long as I live. … I consider it neither an advantage nor a deficit to be Jewish. It simply belongs to me like my red beard, my body weight or the nature of my interests'.[99]

Among those semantic levels of 'Jewish' in modernity, German-Jewish anarchism represented one variety of a heterogeneous left-wing field, just as it was one option among the many possibilities of (self-)positioning in society between the middle and working class, orthodoxy, neo-orthodoxy, progressive Judaism and the manifold Zionisms. Regarding their anarchisms, Landauer's and Mühsam's recourse to the Jewish and Christian tradition upheld the illusion of a persisting religious in the secular. But in fact, their religious 'iteration' was much more part of the secular than their language, impregnated by religious terms, together with the patterns they draw on and the figures they referred to, might suggest. Being part of a generation in search of a way out of the crisis of acculturation, Landauer and Mühsam adapted an identity-related construed notion of 'the Jewish', which they included in their revolutionary concept of a stateless future. To a certain extent, their anarchisms formed a melting pot uniting their complex individualities as Jews, Germans, writers, poets, politicians and revolutionaries.

Within the plurality the secular had brought about, a rediscovered and reinterpreted Jewish tradition arose as one option among others to create distinction, but against the background of anti-Semitism and further existing discrimination it was certainly not one of choice alone.[100] Still, the religious was redefined by the secular in Landauer's and Mühsam's globally couched concepts, not the reverse. The German-Jewish-anarchist reception of the religious came as a worldly utopian political attitude, and, in Landauer's and Buber's writings, was further infused with a mystical tone.[101] Just like Mühsam and Landauer had been political renegades fighting monarchy as well as Marxism,[102] they reinterpreted the religious, too, as heretics, relying on figures and personalities like Caine, Spinoza[103] and Jesus as Jewish rebels. In contrast, the Jewish body of laws, the synagogue, holidays, Jewish dietary requirements, or the Hebrew language were not major points of reference they would have considered anew. Instead, Jewish elements in their works were further determined by contemporary, secular attributes like history,[104] race, nation and individuality in an often neo-romantic reading. We should therefore be careful to draw a line, however twisted, of reliable historical continuity while observing the religious in nineteenth-century German-Jewish anarchism.

Then again, the major problems with tracing the religious and the secular are caused by the phenomenologically open and controversial concept of the secular.[105] Moreover, its definitional vagueness is further deepened by the lack of an effective definition of religion. The term itself strongly relies on the Christian model, its faith contents, values and denominations.[106] If it is hard to specify the religious and the secular related to a Christian example, it is even harder when the focal point of analysis is a non-Christian one. Without a clear identification of the secular and the religious, it therefore remains a challenge to clarify and substantiate the exact implications of 'the Christian' or 'the Jewish' in modern times. Not withstanding these difficulties, we have to take into consideration that Judaism, unlike most of the Christian denominations, is characterized by 'a strong *worldliness*',[107] and that a 'Jewish heretic who transcends Jewry [still] belongs to a Jewish tradition'.[108] The messianic elements present in Landauer's and Mühsam's libertarian theories might thus indicate the presence of the religious in the secular precisely because, not despite, the original Torah content recurring in social politics.[109] To put it the other way around, the secular appears as shaped by the specific, religiously grounded background of its agents, and proves to be as diverse and adaptable as the religious.[110] In the case of German-Jewish anarchism, both categories constitute two sides of a coin, stamped by a heterogeneous set of influences and social circumstances. Although the references are fractured and transformed, we must take into account the fact that a secularly modified 'religious' – with every awareness of the notion's problematics – is not only present in, but crucial to, Landauer's and Mühsam's anarchism.

Carolin Kosuch graduated from Leipzig University with an MA degree in history and religious studies. She received her PhD in 2014 at the Simon Dubnow Institute for Jewish History and Culture at Leipzig University. Her dissertation dealt with philosopher of language Fritz Mauthner, and the anarchists Gustav Landauer and Erich Mühsam, shedding light on the connection between generational experience and critique of their lifeworld (*Missratene Söhne: Anarchismus und Sprachkritik im Fin de Siècle*, Vandenhoeck & Ruprecht, 2015). In 2014, she joined the German Historical Institute in Rome as a research associate. Her new project aims to explore the cultural history of cremation in a comparative way, reading together nineteenth-century history of philosophy, technology and culture.

Notes

1. G. Landauer, 'Volk und Land: Dreißig sozialistische Thesen', in S. Wolf (ed.), *Gustav Landauer: Antipolitik* (Lich and Hessen: Verlag Edition AV, [1907] 2010), 109–22.
2. Ibid.
3. Ibid., 113f.
4. See H.J. Becker, *Fichtes Idee der Nation und das Judentum: Den vergessenen Generationen der jüdischen Fichte-Rezeption* (Amsterdam: Rodopi, 2000), 305–10; and M. Löwy, 'Romantic Prophets of Utopia: Gustav Landauer and Martin Buber', in P.M. Flohr and A. Mali (eds), *Gustav Landauer: Anarchist and Jew* (Berlin: De Gruyter, 2015), 73.
5. See D. Kerbs and J. Reulecke (eds), *Handbuch der deutschen Reformbewegungen 1880–1933* (Wuppertal: P. Hammer, 1998).
6. See G. Merlio, 'Die Reformbewegung zwischen Progressismus und Konservatismus', in M. Cluet and C. Repussard (eds), *'Lebensreform': Die soziale Dynamik der politischen Ohnmacht* (Tübingen: Francke, 2013), 63–74.
7. See C. Kosuch, *Missratene Söhne: Anarchismus und Sprachkritik im Fin de Siècle* (Göttingen: Vandenhoeck & Ruprecht, 2015), 209–304.
8. Landauer considered anarchism to be the essence of 'true' socialism. He used the terms, if not synonymously, then aligned to each other. See G. Landauer, 'Anarchism–Socialism', in G. Kuhn and R. Day (eds), *Gustav Landauer: Revolution and Other Writings* (Oakland, CA: PM Press, [1895] 2010), 70–74. The spectrum of modern anarchisms in general traces C. Levy, 'Social Histories of Anarchism', *Journal for the Study of Radicalism* 4(2) (2010), 1–44.
9. See D. Turcato, 'Nations without Borders: Anarchists and National Identity', in C. Bantman and B. Altena (eds), *Reassessing the Transnational Turn: Scales of Analysis in Anarchist and Syndicalist Studies* (New York: Routledge, 2015), 25–42.
10. B. Wilson, *Religion in Secular Society: A Sociological Comment* (London: Watts, 1969), 21–108.
11. See J. Most, *Die Gottespest* (New York: Verlag der Freiheit, 1883); M.A. Bakunin, *Gott und der Staat: Ein Wort zum Austritt aus der Landeskirche nebst Anleitung zum Austritt* (Berlin: Grunau, 1901); and F. Brupbacher, *Seelenhygiene für gesunde Heiden* (Zurich: Oprecht, 1943).
12. G. Landauer, 'A Few Words on Anarchism', in G. Kuhn and R. Day (eds), *Gustav Landauer: Revolution and Other Writings* (Oakland, CA: PM Press, [1897] 2010), 80.
13. O. Tschannen, 'The Secularization Paradigm: A Systematization', *Journal for the Scientific Study of Religion* 30 (1991), 395.
14. S. Bruce, *God is Dead: Secularization in the West* (Malden, MA: Blackwell, 2002).
15. S.N. Eisenstadt (ed.), *Multiple Modernities* (New Brunswick, NJ: Transaction, 2002), 1–29.
16. M. Burchardt and M. Wohlrab-Sahr, 'Multiple Secularities: Religion and Modernity in the Global Age', *International Sociology* 28(6) (2013), 605–6.
17. Regarding German-Jewish anarchism, it seems appropriate to substitute 'middle class' with the politicized, connected to the city and to cultural hegemony term 'bourgeois'. The

notion points to the main source of friction leading Landauer and his fellow anarchists to their positions. It will be used not exclusively, but preferably, throughout the chapter to indicate this tense relationship. The multidimensional process of Jewish emancipation is discussed in J. Katz, *Aus dem Ghetto in die bürgerliche Welt: Jüdische Emanzipation 1770-1880* (Frankfurt/Main: Athenaeum, 1988); and A. Gotzmann, *Eigenheit und Einheit: Modernisierungsdiskurse des deutschen Judentums der Emanzipationszeit* (Leiden: Brill, 2002).
18. D. Diner, 'Geschichte der Juden: Paradigma einer europäischen Historie', in G. Stourzh (ed.), *Annäherung an eine europäische Geschichtsschreibung* (Vienna: Verlag der Österreichischen Akademie der Wissenschaften, 2002), 85f.
19. Due to its descriptive and neutral character, the term 'acculturation' is given preference over assimilation in this chapter. The latter carries an often negative connotation of self-denial and complete renouncement of Jewish tradition and culture. Its underlying meaning mirrors the normative power of the (Christian) majority. Acculturation, on the other hand, points to the selectiveness of Jewish adaption to Christian society. It indicates the possibility of a perpetuation of certain values, habits and norms, unaltered or through modification, in the process of emancipation. See also C. Wiese, *Wissenschaft des Judentums und protestantische Theologie im wilhelminischen Deutschland: Ein Schrei ins Leere?* (Tübingen: Mohr Siebeck, 1999), 45.
20. See W.E. Mosse, '"From Schutzjuden to Deutsche Staatsbürger jüdischen Glaubens": The Long and Bumpy Road to Jewish Emancipation in Germany', in P. Birnbaum and I. Katznelson (eds), *Paths of Emancipation: Jews, States, and Citizenship* (Princeton, NJ: Princeton University Press, 1995), 59-93. Both the reduction and persistence of restrictions and Jewish social, professional, economic and cultural participation in the society of the German Empire in general are discussed in P. Pulzer, *Jews and the German State: The Political History of a Minority 1848-1933* (Oxford: Blackwell, 1992), 69-193; and M. Brenner et al., *Deutsch-Jüdische Geschichte in der Neuzeit*, vol. 2, *Emanzipation und Akkulturation 1780-1871* (Munich: Beck, 1996), 287-327.
21. Nineteenth-century Jewish life in Buttenhausen is examined by R. Deigendesch, *Juden in Buttenhausen: Ständige Ausstellung in der Bernheimer'schen Realschule Buttenhausen* (Münsingen: Stadtarchiv, 1994). The Landauer family in Buttenhausen traces C. Knüppel (ed.), 'Siegfried Mühsam: Erinnerungen eines jüdischen Arztes aus Schwaben', in *Allmende 45 – Wir gingen stumm und tränenlos: Jüdische Lebens- und Leidensbilder* (1995), 158-61.
22. See IISG Amsterdam, Landauer Papers, 'Jugendschriften', letter of Gustav Landauer to Ida Wolf, 15 June 1891, inv. no. 100; and IISG Amsterdam, Landauer Papers, diary entry, 25 April 1885, inv. no. 1.
23. See T. van Rahden, 'Von der Eintracht zur Vielfalt: Juden in der Geschichte des deutschen Bürgertums', in A. Gotzmann et al. (eds), *Juden, Bürger, Deutsche: Zur Geschichte von Vielfalt und Differenz 1800-1933* (Tübingen: Mohr Siebeck, 2001), 9-32; and S. Lässig, *Jüdische Wege ins Bürgertum: Kulturelles Kapital und sozialer Aufstieg im 19. Jahrhundert* (Göttingen: Vandenhoeck & Ruprecht, 2004).
24. S. Mühsam, *Geschichte des Namens Mühsam: Nach amtlichen Urkunden und mündlicher Überlieferung. Familien-Chronik*, 2nd edn (Lübeck: Werner & Hörnig, 1912), 12f.; and C. Hamann, *Die Mühsams: Geschichte einer Familie* (Teetz: Hentrich & Hentrich, 2005), 12-42.
25. See F. Leimkugel, *Wege jüdischer Apotheker: Die Geschichte deutscher und österreichisch-ungarischer Pharmazeuten* (Frankfurt/Main: Govi, 1991), 27.

26. P. Guttkuhn (ed.), *Charlotte Landau-Mühsam: Meine Erinnerungen* (Lübeck: Erich Mühsam-Gesellschaft, 2010), 34.
27. See M.A. Kaplan, *Jüdisches Bürgertum: Frau, Familie und Identität im Kaiserreich* (Hamburg: Dölling und Galitz, 1991), 130–66.
28. See H.D. Hellige, 'Generationskonflikt, Selbsthaß und die Entstehung antikapitalistischer Positionen im Judentum: Der Einfluß des Antisemitismus auf das Sozialverhalten jüdischer Kaufmanns- und Unternehmersöhne im Deutschen Kaiserreich und in der k. und k.-Monarchie', *Geschichte und Gesellschaft* 4 (1979), 474–518.
29. See Z. Bauman, *Moderne und Ambivalenz* (Hamburg: Hamburger Edition, 2005), 174–88.
30. See Guttkuhn, *Charlotte Landau-Mühsam*, 26–30.
31. See M. Richarz, *Der Eintritt der Juden in die akademischen Berufe: Jüdische Studenten und Akademiker in Deutschland 1678–1848* (Tübingen: Mohr Siebeck, 1974), 164–217.
32. E. Albanis, *German-Jewish Cultural Identity from 1900 to the Aftermath of the First World War: A Comparative Study of Moritz Goldstein, Julius Bab and Ernst Lissauer* (Tübingen: Niemeyer, 2002), 16.
33. See Lässig, *Jüdische Wege ins Bürgertum*, 669.
34. See M. Zimmermann and N. Berg, 'Berliner Antisemitismusstreit', in D. Diner (ed.), *Enzyklopädie jüdischer Geschichte und Kultur*, Vol. 1 (Stuttgart: Metzler, 2011), 277–82.
35. R. Rürup stated that the Jewish question during the 1880s reverted from an emancipatory to an anti-Semitic one – R. Rürup, 'Emanzipation und Krise: Zur Geschichte der "Judenfrage" in Deutschland vor 1890', in W.E. Mosse (ed.), *Juden im Wilhelminischen Deutschland, 1890–1914* (Tübingen: Mohr Siebeck, 1998), 1.
36. See S. Feiner, *Haskala – Jüdische Aufklärung: Geschichte einer kulturellen Revolution* (Hildesheim: Georg Olms, 2007), 455–64.
37. See, for the following, Kosuch, *Missratene Söhne*, 93–111 and 142–207.
38. For an in-depth analysis of Berlin's associations, see W. Wülfing et al. (eds), *Handbuch literarisch-kultureller Vereine, Gruppen und Bünde 1825–1933* (Stuttgart: Metzler, 1998); and H.M. Bock, 'Die "Literaten- und Studenten-Revolte" der Jungen in der SPD um 1890', *Das Argument* 63 (1971), 22–41.
39. On the conflicts between Landauer and his father, see IISG Amsterdam, Landauer Papers, family correspondence, letter of Gustav Landauer to Grete Landauer-Leuschner, 23 April 1894, inv. no. 71.
40. See R. Kauffeldt and G. Cepl-Kaufmann, *Berlin Friedrichshagen – Literaturhauptstadt der Jahrhundertwende: Der Friedrichshagener Dichterkreis* (Munich: Boer, 1994).
41. See W. Fähnders, *Anarchismus und Literatur: Ein vergessenes Kapitel deutscher Literaturgeschichte zwischen 1890 und 1910* (Stuttgart: Metzler, 1987).
42. G. Landauer, 'Vor 25 Jahren: Zum Regierungsjubiläum Wilhelms II', in S. Wolf (ed.), *Gustav Landauer: Anarchismus* (Lich and Hessen: Verlag Edition AV, [1913] 2009), 90.
43. G. Landauer, 'Majestät Masse', in S. Wolf (ed.), *Gustav Landauer: Anarchismus* (Lich and Hessen: Verlag Edition AV, [1893] 2009), 122–24.
44. See K. Bruns, 'Die neue Gemeinschaft (Berlin-Schlachtensee)', in W. Wülfing et al. (eds), *Handbuch literarisch-kultureller Vereine, Gruppen und Bünde 1825–1933* (Stuttgart: Metzler, 1998), 358–71.
45. E. Mühsam, 'Bohème', in M. Fritzen (ed.), *Sich fügen heißt lügen: Ein Lesebuch* (Göttingen: Steidl, [1904] 2003), 40f.
46. For a useful analysis of the Bohemian world, see E. Kleemann, *Zwischen symbolischer Rebellion und politischer Revolution: Studien zur deutschen Bohème zwischen Kaiserreich*

und Weimarer Republik (Frankfurt/Main: Lang, 1985). Mühsam's anti-bourgeois stance is reflected in E. Mühsam, 'Das Lebensprogramm', in E. Mühsam, *Ausgewählte Werke*, Vol. 1 (Berlin: Volk und Welt, [1900] 1978), 247–52.
47. See IISG Amsterdam, Brupbacher Papers, letter of E. Joël to F. Brupbacher, 14 October 1904, inv. no. 141.
48. See A.G. von Olenhusen, 'Psychoanalyse und Anarchismus: "Die Eroberung des Luftreiches"', in J.W. Goette (ed.), *Anarchismus und Psychoanalyse zu Beginn des 20. Jahrhunderts* (Lübeck: Erich Mühsam-Gesellschaft, 2000), 84–99.
49. See E. Mühsam, 'Leserbrief und Weihelied', *Der arme Teufel* 3 (1904), 5.
50. Landauer, 'Anarchism–Socialism', 71.
51. See L. Hölscher, 'Secularization and Urbanization in the Nineteenth Century: An Interpretative Model', in H. McLeod (ed.), *European Religion in the Age of Great Cities, 1830–1930* (London: Routledge, 1995), 263–88.
52. The long tradition of the secular in Judaism is examined by D. Biale, *Not in the Heavens: The Tradition of Jewish Secular Thought* (Princeton, NJ: Princeton University Press, 2011).
53. The way the church and Christian faith adapted to modern needs and challenges is shown in R. Schlögl, *Alter Glaube und modern Welt: Europäisches Christentum im Umbruch 1750–1850* (Frankfurt/Main: Fischer, 2013).
54. See, e.g., E. Mühsam, *Tagebücher*, vol. 10, 8 and 29 September 1912.
55. Guttkuhn, *Charlotte Landau-Mühsam: Meine Erinnerungen*, 34. The almost religious value of education in nineteenth-century Jewish culture is highlighted in E. Bahr, 'Goethe and the Concept of Bildung in Jewish Emancipation', in K.L. Berghahn and J. Hermand (eds), *Goethe in German-Jewish Culture* (Rochester, NY: Camden House, 2001), 16–30.
56. See S. Mühsam, *Die Killeberger: Nach der Natur aufgenommen von Onkel Siegfried*, 3rd edn (Leipzig: Kaufmann, 1910); and Guttkuhn, *Charlotte Landau-Mühsam*, 22.
57. See, e.g., E. Mühsam, 'Soll dieses Herz denn ewig darben', in E. Mühsam, *Wüste-Krater-Wolken: Die Gedichte Erich Mühsams* (Berlin: Cassirer, 1914), 213.
58. See ibid., 'Golgatha', 211; and ibid., 'Ich weiß von allem Leid', 214. See also G. Landauer, 'Die Kriegsfeier', in R. Kauffeldt and M. Matzigkeit (eds), *Gustav Landauer: Zeit und Geist. Kulturkritische Schriften 1890–1919* (Munich: Boer [1895] 1997), 41f.
59. Mühsam hoped to find like-minded combatants among thieves, beggars and prostitutes. According to him, society anyway had no need for them. Thus, they seemed natural allies willing to overcome the current status, precisely because they were not part of it. See, e.g., Landesarchiv Berlin, APrBr Rep 030, 16384, 1 May 1904.
60. E. Mühsam, 'Kain', in *Kain* 1(1) (1911), 1–4.
61. See IISG Amsterdam, Landauer Papers, manuscripts, inv. no. 36.
62. See E. Mühsam, 'Und Moses blickte ins gelobte Land', in E. Mühsam, *Wüste-Krater-Wolken. Die Gedichte Erich Mühsams* (Berlin: Cassirer, 1914), 207; and G. Landauer, 'Kiew', in R. Kauffeldt and M. Matzigkeit (eds), *Gustav Landauer: Zeit und Geist. Kulturkritische Schriften 1890–1919* (Munich: Boer, [1913] 1997), 227.
63. I borrowed the concept of 'iteration' from S. Benhabib, 'Demokratische Iterationen: Das Lokale, das Nationale, das Globale', in idem (ed.), *Kosmopolitismus und Demokratie: Eine Debatte* (Frankfurt/Main: Campus, 2008), 46.
64. On Stirner's philosophy of radical, anti-autoritarian individualism, see M. Stirner, *Der Einzige und sein Eigentum*, 3rd edn (Leipzig: Wigand, 1901).

65. G. Landauer, 'Through Separation to Community', in G. Kuhn and R. Day (eds), *Gustav Landauer: Revolution and Other Writings* (Oakland, CA: PM Press, [1901] 2010), 94–108.
66. See G. Wehr, *Martin Buber: Leben, Werk, Wirkung* (Zurich: Diogenes, 1991), 15–107.
67. Buber's reading of Hasidism becomes apparent in M. Buber, *Mein Weg zum Chassidismus* (Frankfurt/Main: Rütten & Loening, 1918).
68. See R. Link-Salinger, 'Friends in Utopia: Martin Buber and Gustav Landauer', *Midstream* 24(1) (1978), 67–72; and P. Mendes-Flohr and B. Susser, '"Alte und neue Gemeinschaft": An Unpublished Buber Manuscript', *AJS Review* 1 (1976), 41–56.
69. E. Mühsam, *Namen und Menschen: Unpolitische Erinnerungen* (Berlin: K. Guhl, 1977), 23.
70. G. Landauer, 'Die Legende des Baalschem', in S. Wolf (ed.), *Gustav Landauer: Philosophie und Judentum* (Lich and Hessen: Verlag Edition AV, [1910] 2012), 345.
71. M. Buber, 'Unser Nationalismus', *Der Jude* 2(1) (1917), 1.
72. G. Landauer, 'Notizen zum Aufbau und Gedankengang der Rede Martin Bubers: "Der Geist des Orients und das Judentum"', in S. Wolf (ed.), *Gustav Landauer: Philosophie und Judentum* (Lich and Hessen: Verlag Edition AV, [1915] 2012), 372.
73. See E. Lunn, *Prophet of Community: The Romantic Socialism of Gustav Landauer* (Berkeley: University of California Press, 1973), 176–79.
74. G. Landauer, 'Revolution', in G. Kuhn and R. Day (eds), *Gustav Landauer: Revolution and Other Writings* (Oakland, CA: PM Press, [1907] 2010), 130 and 136; emphasis in the original. Landauer's reading of Christian philosophy is also discussed in J. Willems, *Religiöser Gehalt des Anarchismus und anarchistischer Gehalt der Religion? Die jüdisch-christlich-atheistische Mystik Gustav Landauers zwischen Meister Eckhart und Martin Buber* (Albeck bei Ulm: Verlag Ulmer Manuskripte, 2001), 130–49.
75. G. Landauer, 'What Does the Socialist Bund Want?', in G. Kuhn and R. Day (eds), *Gustav Landauer: Revolution and Other Writings* (Oakland, CA: PM Press, [1908] 2010), 189.
76. Ibid., 190.
77. G. Landauer, 'The Settlement', in G. Kuhn and R. Day (eds), *Gustav Landauer: Revolution and Other Writings* (Oakland, CA: PM Press, [1909] 2010), 197.
78. For the 'Socialist League', see U. Linse, *Organisierter Anarchismus im Deutschen Kaiserreich von 1870* (Berlin: Duncker & Humblot, 1969), 275–301.
79. See M. Fölling-Albers and W. Fölling, *Kibbutz und Kollektiverziehung: Entstehung, Entwicklung, Veränderung* (Opladen: Leske+Budrich, 2000), 33–38; and J. Horrox, *A Living Revolution: Anarchism in the Kibbutz Movement* (Edinburgh: AK Press, 2009), 61.
80. See Linse, *Organisierter Anarchismus*, 293.
81. For Mühsam's participation in the 'Socialist League', see G.W. Jungblut, *Erich Mühsam: Notizen eines politischen Werdegangs*, 2nd edn (Marburg: Schlitz, 1986), 8–38.
82. Landauer, 'Anarchism–Socialism', 70f.
83. Landauer's notion of 'Geist' is traced in Lunn, *Prophet of Community*, 179–81.
84. G. Landauer, 'Sind das Ketzergedanken?', in R. Kauffeldt and M. Matzigkeit (eds), *Gustav Landauer: Zeit und Geist. Kulturkritische Schriften 1890-1919* (Munich: Boer, [1913] 1997), 218.
85. The notion *tikkun olam* is explicated in M.L. Morgan, 'Tikkun olam', in D. Diner (ed.), *Enzyklopädie jüdischer Geschichte und Kultur*, Vol. 5 (Stuttgart: Metzler, 2015), 102f.
86. See M. Löwy, 'Jewish Messianism and Libertarian Utopia in Central Europe (1900–1933)', *New German Critique* 8(20) (1980): Special Issue 2, *Germans and Jews*, 105–15.
87. Landauer, 'Sind das Ketzergedanken?', 221.

88. Ibid., 220.
89. See also P. Breines, 'The Jew as Revolutionary: The Case of Gustav Landauer', *Leo Baeck Institute Yearbook* 12 (1967), 75–84.
90. Mühsam, *Tagebücher*, Vol. 1, 1 October 1910.
91. Ibid., Vol. 10, 14 October 1912.
92. E. Mühsam, 'Die Jagd auf Harden', in G. Emig (ed.), *Erich Mühsam Gesamtausgabe*, Vol. 3 (Berlin: Verlag Europäische Ideen, [1908] 1978), 227.
93. Ibid.
94. E. Mühsam, 'Bismarxismus', *Fanal* 1(5) (1927), 65.
95. T. Asad, *Formations of the Secular: Christianity, Islam, Modernity* (Stanford, CA: Stanford University Press, 2003), 99.
96. Ibid., 42.
97. Diner, 'Geschichte der Juden', 89–93.
98. Landauer, 'Sind das Ketzergedanken?', 221f.
99. E. Mühsam, 'Zur Judenfrage', in J.W. Goette (ed.), *Erich Mühsam und das Judentum* (Lübeck: Erich Mühsam-Gesellschaft, [1920] 2002), 13.
100. See I. Bertz, 'Jüdische Renaissance', in D. Kerbs and J. Reulecke (eds), *Handbuch der deutschen Reformbewegungen 1880–1933* (Wuppertal: P. Hammer, 1998), 551–64.
101. See C.B. Maurer, *Call to Revolution: The Mystical Anarchism of Gustav Landauer* (Detroit, MI: Wayne State University Press, 1971), 48–76.
102. See, e.g., Mühsam, 'Bismarxismus'.
103. See H. Delf, 'In die größte Nähe zu Spinozas Ethik: Zu Gustav Landauers Spinoza-Lektüre', in H. Delf and G. Mattenklott (eds), *Gustav Landauer im Gespräch: Symposium zum 125. Geburtstag* (Tübingen: Niemeyer, 1997), 69–90.
104. The turn to history in modern Jewish thinking is highlighted in Wiese, *Wissenschaft des Judentums*, 59–68.
105. See D. Pollack, *Säkularisierung: Ein moderner Mythos?* (Tübingen: Mohr Siebeck, 2003), 1–20.
106. F. Stolz, *Grundzüge der Religionswissenschaft*, 3rd edn (Göttingen: Vandenhoeck & Ruprecht, 2001), 12.
107. Biale, *Not in the Heavens*, 4.
108. I. Deutscher, *The Non-Jewish Jew and other Essays* (London: Oxford University Press, 1968), 26.
109. For messianism in modern times, see E. Dubbels, *Figuren des Messianischen in Schriften deutsch-jüdischer Intellektueller 1900–1933* (Berlin: De Gruyter, 2011).
110. Burchardt and Wohlrab-Sahr, 'Multiple Secularities', 606.

Bibliography

Albanis, E. *German-Jewish Cultural Identity from 1900 to the Aftermath of the First World War: A Comparative Study of Moritz Goldstein, Julius Bab and Ernst Lissauer*. Tübingen: Niemeyer, 2002.

Asad, T. *Formations of the Secular: Christianity, Islam, Modernity*. Stanford, CA: Stanford University Press, 2003.

Bahr, E. 'Goethe and the Concept of Bildung in Jewish Emancipation', in K.L. Berghahn and J. Hermand (eds), *Goethe in German-Jewish Culture* (Rochester, NY: Camden House, 2001), 16–30.
Bakunin, M.A. *Gott und der Staat: Ein Wort zum Austritt aus der Landeskirche nebst Anleitung zum Austritt*. Berlin: Grunau, 1901.
Bauman, Z. *Moderne und Ambivalenz*. Hamburg: Hamburger Edition, 2005.
Becker, H.J. *Fichtes Idee der Nation und das Judentum: Den vergessenen Generationen der jüdischen Fichte-Rezeption*. Amsterdam: Rodopi, 2000.
Benhabib, S. 'Demokratische Iterationen: Das Lokale, das Nationale, das Globale', in idem (ed.), *Kosmopolitismus und Demokratie: Eine Debatte* (Frankfurt/Main: Campus, 2008), 43–74.
Bertz, I. 'Jüdische Renaissance', in D. Kerbs and J. Reulecke (eds), *Handbuch der deutschen Reformbewegungen 1880–1933* (Wuppertal: P. Hammer, 1998), 551–64.
Biale, D. *Not in the Heavens: The Tradition of Jewish Secular Thought*. Princeton, NJ: Princeton University Press, 2011.
Bock, H.M. 'Die "Literaten- und Studenten-Revolte" der Jungen in der SPD um 1890'. *Das Argument* 63 (1971), 22–41.
Breines, P. 'The Jew as Revolutionary: The Case of Gustav Landauer'. *Leo Baeck Institute Yearbook* 12 (1967), 75–84.
Brenner, M. et al. *Deutsch-Jüdische Geschichte in der Neuzeit: Emanzipation und Akkulturation 1780–1871*. Munich: Beck, 1996.
Bruce, S. *God is Dead: Secularization in the West*. Malden, MA: Blackwell, 2002.
Bruns, K. 'Die neue Gemeinschaft (Berlin-Schlachtensee)', in W. Wülfing et al. (eds), *Handbuch literarisch-kultureller Vereine, Gruppen und Bünde 1825–1933* (Stuttgart: Metzler, 1998), 358–71.
Brupbacher, F. *Seelenhygiene für gesunde Heiden*. Zurich: Oprecht, 1943.
Buber, M. 'Unser Nationalismus'. *Der Jude* 2(1) (1917), 1–3.
———. *Mein Weg zum Chassidismus*. Frankfurt/Main: Rütten & Loening, 1918.
Burchardt, M., and M. Wohlrab-Sahr. 'Multiple Secularities: Religion and Modernity in the Global Age'. *International Sociology* 28(6) (2013), 605–11.
Deigendesch, R. *Juden in Buttenhausen: Ständige Ausstellung in der Bernheimer'schen Realschule Buttenhausen*. Münsingen: Stadtarchiv, 1994.
Delf, H. 'In die größte Nähe zu Spinozas Ethik: Zu Gustav Landauers Spinoza-Lektüre', in H. Delf and G. Mattenklott (eds), *Gustav Landauer im Gespräch: Symposium zum 125. Geburtstag* (Tübingen: Niemeyer, 1997), 69–90.
Deutscher, I. *The Non-Jewish Jew and other Essays*. London: Oxford University Press, 1968.
Diner, D. 'Geschichte der Juden: Paradigma einer europäischen Historie', in G. Stourzh (ed.), *Annäherung an eine europäische Geschichtsschreibung* (Vienna: Verlag der Österreichischen Akademie der Wissenschaften, 2002), 85–103.
Dubbels, E. *Figuren des Messianischen in Schriften deutsch-jüdischer Intellektueller 1900–1933*. Berlin: De Gruyter, 2011.
Eisenstadt, S.N. (ed.). *Multiple Modernities*. New Brunswick, NJ.: Transaction, 2002.
Fähnders, W. *Anarchismus und Literatur: Ein vergessenes Kapitel deutscher Literaturgeschichte zwischen 1890 und 1910*. Stuttgart: Metzler, 1987.
Feiner, S. *Haskala – Jüdische Aufklärung: Geschichte einer kulturellen Revolution*. Hildesheim: Georg Olms, 2007.
Fölling-Albers, M., and W. Fölling. *Kibbutz und Kollektiverziehung: Entstehung, Entwicklung, Veränderung*. Opladen: Leske+Budrich, 2000.

Gotzmann, A. *Eigenheit und Einheit: Modernisierungsdiskurse des deutschen Judentums der Emanzipationszeit*. Leiden: Brill, 2002.

Guttkuhn, P. (ed.). *Charlotte Landau-Mühsam: Meine Erinnerungen*. Lübeck: Erich Mühsam-Gesellschaft, 2010.

Hamann, C. *Die Mühsams: Geschichte einer Familie*. Teetz: Hentrich & Hentrich, 2005.

Hellige, H.D. 'Generationskonflikt, Selbsthaß und die Entstehung antikapitalistischer Positionen im Judentum: Der Einfluß des Antisemitismus auf das Sozialverhalten jüdischer Kaufmanns- und Unternehmersöhne im Deutschen Kaiserreich und in der k. und k.-Monarchie'. *Geschichte und Gesellschaft* 4 (1979), 474–518.

Hölscher, L. 'Secularization and Urbanization in the Nineteenth Century: An Interpretative Model', in H. McLeod (ed.), *European Religion in the Age of Great Cities 1830–1930* (London: Routhledge, 1995), 263–88.

Horrox, J. *A Living Revolution: Anarchism in the Kibbutz Movement*. Edinburgh: AK Press, 2009.

Jungblut, G.W. *Erich Mühsam: Notizen eines politischen Werdegangs*. Marburg: Schlitz, 1986.

Kaplan, M.A. *Jüdisches Bürgertum: Frau, Familie und Identität im Kaiserreich*. Hamburg: Dölling und Galitz, 1991.

Katz, J. *Aus dem Ghetto in die bürgerliche Welt: Jüdische Emanzipation 1770–1880*. Frankfurt/Main: Athenaeum, 1988.

Kauffeldt, R., and G. Cepl-Kaufmann. *Berlin Friedrichshagen – Literaturhauptstadt der Jahrhundertwende: Der Friedrichshagener Dichterkreis*. Munich: Boer, 1994.

Kerbs, D., and J. Reulecke (eds). *Handbuch der deutschen Reformbewegungen 1880–1933*. Wuppertal: P. Hammer, 1998.

Kleemann, E. *Zwischen symbolischer Rebellion und politischer Revolution: Studien zur deutschen Bohème zwischen Kaiserreich und Weimarer Republik*. Frankfurt/Main: Lang, 1985.

Knüppel, C. (ed.). 'Siegfried Mühsam: Erinnerungen eines jüdischen Arztes aus Schwaben'. *Allmende 45 – Wir gingen stumm und tränenlos: Jüdische Lebens- und Leidensbilder* (1995), 152–87.

Kosuch, C. *Missratene Söhne: Anarchismus und Sprachkritik im Fin de Siècle*. Göttingen: Vandenhoeck & Ruprecht, 2015.

Landauer, G. 'Majestät Masse', in S. Wolf (ed.), *Gustav Landauer: Anarchismus* (Lich and Hessen: Verlag Edition AV, [1893] 2009), 122–24.

———. 'Anarchism–Socialism', in G. Kuhn and R. Day (eds), *Gustav Landauer: Revolution and Other Writings* (Oakland, CA: PM Press, [1895] 2010), 70–74.

———. 'Die Kriegsfeier', in R. Kauffeldt and M. Matzigkeit (eds), *Gustav Landauer: Zeit und Geist. Kulturkritische Schriften 1890–1919* (Munich: Boer, [1895] 1997), 35–42.

———. 'A Few Words on Anarchism', in G. Kuhn and R. Day (eds), *Gustav Landauer: Revolution and Other Writings* (Oakland, CA: PM Press, [1897] 2010), 79–83.

———. 'Through Separation to Community', in G. Kuhn and R. Day (eds), *Gustav Landauer: Revolution and Other Writings* (Oakland, CA: PM Press, [1901] 2010), 94–108.

———. 'Revolution', in G. Kuhn and R. Day (eds), *Gustav Landauer: Revolution and Other Writings* (Oakland, CA: PM Press, [1907] 2010), 110–87.

———. 'Volk und Land: Dreißig sozialistische Thesen', in S. Wolf (ed.), *Gustav Landauer: Antipolitik* (Lich and Hessen: Verlag Edition AV, [1907] 2010), 109–22.

———. 'What Does the Socialist Bund Want?', in G. Kuhn and R. Day (eds), *Gustav Landauer: Revolution and Other Writings* (Oakland, CA: PM Press, [1908] 2010), 188–90.

———. 'The Settlement', in G. Kuhn and R. Day (eds), *Gustav Landauer: Revolution and Other Writings* (Oakland, CA: PM Press, [1909] 2010), 196–200.

———. 'Die Legende des Baalschem', in S. Wolf (ed.), *Gustav Landauer: Philosophie und Judentum* (Lich and Hessen: Verlag Edition AV, [1910] 2012), 345–47.

———. 'Kiew', in R. Kauffeldt and M. Matzigkeit (eds), *Gustav Landauer: Zeit und Geist. Kulturkritische Schriften 1890-1919* (Munich: Boer, [1913] 1997), 224–28.

———. 'Sind das Ketzergedanken?', in R. Kauffeldt and M. Matzigkeit (eds), *Gustav Landauer: Zeit und Geist. Kulturkritische Schriften 1890–1919* (Munich: Boer, [1913] 1997), 216–23.

———. 'Vor 25 Jahren: Zum Regierungsjubiläum Wilhelms II', in S. Wolf (ed.), *Gustav Landauer: Anarchismus* (Lich and Hessen: Verlag Edition AV, [1913] 2009), 89–104.

———. 'Notizen zum Aufbau und Gedankengang der Rede Martin Bubers: "Der Geist des Orients und das Judentum"', in S. Wolf (ed.), *Gustav Landauer: Philosophie und Judentum* (Lich and Hessen: Verlag Edition AV, [1915] 2012), 371–74.

Lässig, S. *Jüdische Wege ins Bürgertum: Kulturelles Kapital und sozialer Aufstieg im 19. Jahrhundert*. Göttingen: Vandenhoeck & Ruprecht, 2004.

Leimkugel, F. *Wege jüdischer Apotheker: Die Geschichte deutscher und österreichisch-ungarischer Pharmazeuten*. Frankfurt/Main: Govi, 1991.

Levy, C. 'Social Histories of Anarchism'. *Journal for the Study of Radicalism* 4(2) (2010), 1–44.

Link-Salinger. R. 'Friends in Utopia: Martin Buber and Gustav Landauer'. *Midstream* 24(1) (1978), 67–72.

Linse, U. *Organisierter Anarchismus im Deutschen Kaiserreich von 1870*. Berlin: Duncker & Humblot, 1969.

Löwy, M. 'Jewish Messianism and Libertarian Utopia in Central Europe (1900-1933)'. *New German Critique* 8(20) (1980), Special Issue 2: *Germans and Jews*, 105–15.

———. 'Romantic Prophets of Utopia: Gustav Landauer and Martin Buber', in P.M. Flohr and A. Mali (eds), *Gustav Landauer: Anarchist and Jew* (Berlin: De Gruyter, 2015), 64–81.

Lunn, E. *Prophet of Community: The Romantic Socialism of Gustav Landauer*. Berkeley: University of California Press, 1973.

Maurer, C.B. *Call to Revolution: The Mystical Anarchism of Gustav Landauer*. Detroit, MI: Wayne State University Press, 1971.

Mendes-Flohr, P., and B. Susser. '"Alte und neue Gemeinschaft": An Unpublished Buber Manuscript'. *AJS Review* 1 (1976), 41–56.

Merlio, G. 'Die Reformbewegung zwischen Progressismus und Konservatismus', in M. Cluet and C. Repussard (eds), *'Lebensreform' die soziale Dynamik der politischen Ohnmacht* (Tübingen: Francke, 2013), 63–74.

Morgan, M.L. 'Tikkun olam', in D. Diner (ed.), *Enzyklopädie jüdischer Geschichte und Kultur*, Vol. 5 (Stuttgart: Metzler, 2015), 102–6.

Mosse, W.E. '"From Schutzjuden to Deutsche Staatsbürger jüdischen Glaubens": The Long and Bumpy Road to Jewish Emancipation in Germany', in P. Birnbaum and I. Katznelson (eds), *Paths of Emancipation: Jews, States, and Citizenship* (Princeton, NJ: Princeton University Press, 1995), 59–93.

Most, J. *Die Gottespest*. New York: Verlag der Freiheit, 1883.

Mühsam, E. 'Das Lebensprogramm', in E. Mühsam, *Ausgewählte Werke*, Vol. 1 (Berlin: Volk und Welt, [1900] 1978), 247–52.

———. 'Bohème', in M. Fritzen (ed.), *Sich fügen heißt lügen: Ein Lesebuch* (Göttingen: Steidl, [1904] 2003), 37–41.

———. 'Leserbrief und Weihelied'. *Der arme Teufel* 3 (1904), 5.

———. 'Die Jagd auf Harden', in G. Emig (ed.), *Erich Mühsam Gesamtausgabe* (Berlin: Verlag Europäische Ideen, [1908] 1978), 209–56.

———. 'Kain'. *Kain* 1(1) (1911), 1–4.

———. 'Soll dieses Herz denn ewig darben', in E. Mühsam, *Wüste-Krater-Wolken: Die Gedichte Erich Mühsams* (Berlin: Cassirer, 1914), 213.

———. 'Und Moses blickte ins gelobte Land', in E. Mühsam, *Wüste-Krater-Wolken: Die Gedichte Erich Mühsams* (Berlin: Cassirer, 1914), 207.

———. 'Zur Judenfrage', in J.W. Goette (ed.), *Erich Mühsam und das Judentum* (Lübeck: Erich Mühsam-Gesellschaft, [1920] 2002), 11–15.

———. 'Bismarxismus'. *Fanal* 1(5) (1927), 65–71.

———. *Namen und Menschen: Unpolitische Erinnerungen*. Berlin: K. Guhl, 1977.

———. *Tagebücher* (http://www.muehsam-tagebuch.de/tb/diaries.php), 13 July 2016.

Mühsam, S. *Die Killeberger: Nach der Natur aufgenommen von Onkel Siegfried*. Leipzig: Kaufmann, 1910.

———. *Geschichte des Namens Mühsam: Nach amtlichen Urkunden und mündlicher Überlieferung. Familien-Chronik*. Lübeck: Werner & Hörnig, 1912.

Olenhusen, A.G. von. 'Psychoanalyse und Anarchismus. "Die Eroberung des Luftreiches"', in J.W. Goette (ed.), *Anarchismus und Psychoanalyse zu Beginn des 20. Jahrhunderts* (Lübeck: Erich Mühsam-Gesellschaft, 2000), 84–99.

Pollack, D. *Säkularisierung: Ein moderner Mythos?* Tübingen: Mohr Siebeck, 2003.

Pulzer, P. *Jews and the German State: The Political History of a Minority 1848–1933*. Oxford: Blackwell, 1992.

Rahden, T. van. 'Von der Eintracht zur Vielfalt: Juden in der Geschichte des deutschen Bürgertums', in A. Gotzmann et al. (eds), *Juden, Bürger, Deutsche: Zur Geschichte von Vielfalt und Differenz 1800–1933* (Tübingen: Mohr Siebeck, 2001), 9–32.

Richarz, M. *Der Eintritt der Juden in die akademischen Berufe: Jüdische Studenten und Akademiker in Deutschland 1678–1848*. Tübingen: Mohr Siebeck, 1974.

Rürup, R. 'Emanzipation und Krise: Zur Geschichte der "Judenfrage" in Deutschland vor 1890', in W.E. Mosse (ed.), *Juden im Wilhelminischen Deutschland, 1890–1914* (Tübingen: Mohr Siebeck, 1998), 1–56.

Schlögl, R. *Alter Glaube und moderne Welt: Europäisches Christentum im Umbruch 1750–1850*. Frankfurt/Main: Fischer, 2013.

Stirner, M. *Der Einzige und sein Eigentum*. Leipzig: Wigand, 1901.

Stolz, F. *Grundzüge der Religionswissenschaft*. Göttingen: Vandenhoeck & Ruprecht, 2001.

Tschannen, O. 'The Secularization Paradigm: A Systematization'. *Journal for the Scientific Study of Religion* 30 (1991), 395–415.

Turcato, D. 'Nations without Borders: Anarchists and National Identity', in C. Bantman and B. Altena (eds), *Reassessing the Transnational Turn: Scales of Analysis in Anarchist and Syndicalist Studies* (New York: Routledge, 2015), 25–42.

Wehr, G. *Martin Buber: Leben, Werk, Wirkung*. Zurich: Diogenes, 1991.

Wiese, C. *Wissenschaft des Judentums und protestantische Theologie im wilhelminischen Deutschland: Ein Schrei ins Leere?* Tübingen: Mohr Siebeck, 1999.

Willems, J. *Religiöser Gehalt des Anarchismus und anarchistischer Gehalt der Religion? Die jüdisch-christlich-atheistische Mystik Gustav Landauers zwischen Meister Eckhart und Martin Buber*. Albeck bei Ulm: Ulmer Manuskripte, 2001.

Wilson, B. *Religion in Secular Society: A Sociological Comment*. London: Watts, 1969.

Wülfing, W., et al. (eds). *Handbuch literarisch-kultureller Vereine, Gruppen und Bünde 1825–1933*. Stuttgart and Weimar: Metzler, 1998.

Zimmermann, M., and N. Berg. 'Berliner Antisemitismusstreit', in D. Diner (ed.), *Enzyklopädie jüdischer Geschichte und Kultur*, Vol. 1 (Stuttgart: Metzler, 2010), 277–82.

6
Catholic Women as Global Actors of the Religious and the Secular

Relinde Meiwes

Catholic female congregations developed out of small communities of women with common interests in the German-speaking world and other European societies over the course of the nineteenth century. Here, Catholic women gathered who wanted to combine a communal religious life in imitation of Christ with forms of social or pedagogic engagement. In addition, they swore the traditional monastic vows of poverty, obedience and chastity. The combination of religiosity with works of practical neighbourly love marked the congregations as distinct from traditional female orders, which placed contemplation and the observance of strict moral codes at the centre of their lives. Women such as Clara Fey and Franziska Schervier, who came from Aachen industrialist families, founded female congregations, as did Pauline von Mallinckrodt in Westphalian Paderborn, Aline Bonzel in Olpe, in the Sauerland, and Clara Wolff and her companions in Silesia, at Neisse. In Prusssia alone, the largest German state, whose Catholic minority comprised only a third of the total population, twenty-three female congregations had been founded before the onset of the *Kulturkampf* in the 1870s. Newly founded communities of this kind had to receive official recognition from the local Catholic bishop, and quite a few went even further and sought papal acknowledgement. Those communities successful in this regard were no longer under the jurisdiction of the local bishop, but rather the Pope in Rome, with the consequence that their scope for action did not end with the borders of their diocese or secular state.

The founders of these congregations were often inspired by similar efforts in the Netherlands, Belgium, and above all in France, where the restrictions imposed on Catholic orders and congregations in the course of the French

Revolution were lifted by Napoleon in the years up to 1807. As a consequence, there was a positive boom in female religious life, and a diverse female congregational life developed; this proved influential, and established itself beyond France's borders in confessionally mixed Germany.[1] French members of female orders often opened German establishments in cooperation with their German counterparts, as in Cologne, Trier and Koblenz. Four sisters of the Borromeus Order moved from Nancy in Lorraine to the Prussian capital, Berlin, in 1846. The 'Clemens Sisters' in Münster and the 'Vinzentinerinnen' in Paderborn had already been set up on the French model as independent congregations. But these transnational influences did not flow exclusively from France, but also from Heythuysen in the Netherlands and Aspel in Belgium, from where sisters were also sent to begin work in Prussia.[2]

These impulses also motivated older congregations to develop new activities. The Sisters of Holy Catherine, for example, who had been based in East Prussia from the sixteenth century, began to expand their educational activities in the 1820s, under the leadership of their head, Rosa Schrade, and also took new members into their community. A similar trend can be observed in the medical care provided by the Sisters of Holy Elizabeth in Aachen, who had operated in the city since 1622.[3]

After an establishment phase of varying duration, these female congregations themselves often went on to open dependencies in their immediate localities, with some extending across national borders. These female communities often lived and worked in neighbouring European countries, but soon looked even further afield, to North and South America. Some congregations even dared to establish branches in Asia, and, following in the footsteps of European colonialism and imperialism, sought to extend their networks into Africa. But wherever these female communities were established, they practised a form of communal religious life, and sought to evangelize local populations with their own living example of piety. To that end they worked in education, in the care of the sick and disabled, and in all spheres of social work.[4]

My argument is that the entanglement of the religious with the secular and vice versa – the central topic of this volume – was already in evidence in the founding principles of these female Catholic communities. The members of the female congregations followed a religiously determined life in nunneries and convents, but also worked as teachers, nurses and carers in the world. They governed schools, hospitals and welfare institutions, and were involved in the practice of pastoral care and religious services. For these congregations there could be no division between the religious and the secular, and this unusual way of life excited great interest among Catholics across Europe and beyond in the nineteenth and early twentieth centuries.

These communities were, moreover – and this is my second argument – transnational from their very beginnings. As we have seen, influences from France and the Low Countries proved crucial in establishing such congregations in the German states themselves in the early nineteenth century, and, as of

1870, they spread beyond Europe's shores. Transnationally entangled networks, in other words, were not only constructed by men in the nineteenth century, but also by women.[5] This fact has, until now, barely been recognized in historiography or Catholic Church history, despite its obvious relevance for the classic question concerning the 'feminization of religion' in the nineteenth and twentieth centuries. This venerable debate is certainly to be congratulated for focusing attention on women in a religious context in this period, and for opening up new questions concerning the influence of gender. Most importantly, we have come to realize that women found spaces in churches and religious communities that afforded them opportunities to socialize and gain influence within a secular world and in institutions dominated by men.[6] I am sceptical, however, about whether my topic should be entirely subsumed within the 'feminization' thesis. Indeed, the very search for the secular as well as the religious – as we are doing in this volume – shows that the history of women in this period can be located in wider contexts.[7] I am especially keen to inquire how the sisters of these congregations managed to establish themselves across national borders, and where, geographically, they were most active. Which activities and forms of work were most important for them, and how did they organize their transnational work? Did it diverge markedly from that of comparative male communities?

The self-understanding of these congregations' founders and their successors had the consequence that each individual congregation had unique goals and ways of pursuing them.[8] Due to their position within ecclesiastical law, most of the congregations were under papal jurisdiction, as opposed to that of their local bishop. They could ignore the instructions of their local clerical hierarchy, even if, on the whole, they strove for cooperation and harmony. This independence led to the establishment of a wide range of educational and welfare institutions and establishments, often without precedent in the immediate locality. My argument is that the success of these congregations, both at home and abroad, can, to a large extent, be explained with reference to transnational experiences and exchanges. German congregation leaders had access to knowledge and information, for example, that extended far beyond the Reich's own borders. The sisters operated in a complicated constellation of influences, and it was seldom easy to simply replicate practices, developed in Germany, elsewhere. This might work in a German community in southern Brazil, but not an African village in Cameroon or Togo.

Entanglements of the Religious and the Secular

As late as 1800, there were only a handful of female congregations in the largest German state, Prussia, even in its majority-Catholic regions.[9] The Enlightenment, the French Revolution and the secularization of ecclesiastical lands had led to the situation that venerable orders such as the Dominicans, who followed a contemplative life – one of prayer and religious devotion – increasingly became less attractive. And this trend continued, as it was only those female orders involved in education, such as that of St Ursula, that were embraced by the expansion of female piety in the nineteenth century; and it was only those communities, newly founded and without strict examination requirements, but which still featured a monastic environment combined with worldly activity, that gained more female members. (This focus on worldly activity, had, of course, been integral to individual Catholic female orders since the early sixteenth century.) It is extraordinary to note that this upswing in female congregation membership ocurred at exactly the moment that educational and professional opportunities were increasingly opening up for bourgeois women in nineteenth-century Germany.

From the 1830s and 1840s onwards, countless new communities were established in the German states. This trend continued until national unification in 1871, and the growth was especially pronounced among congregations specializing in the provision of education and medical care. Even in Protestant-dominated Prussia, these communities expanded largely free from state interference. Female congregations, for example, were able to establish a very wide network of Catholic primary schools. In the rural Ermland in the far Prussian north, the 'Catherine Sisters' taught, prior to the *Kulturkampf*, in fourteen schools, controlled the only senior girls' school in the region, in Rössel, and even assumed control of teacher education through the establishment of a teacher training college for women.[10] The sisters instructed not only young women and girls from bourgeois backgrounds, but also those from lower-middle-class and peasant families, opening up for them a path to knowledge and education, in a fashion that was far from commonplace in the later nineteenth century. In Aachen, a centre of early western German industrialization, the congregation of the Sisters of the Poor Child Jesus furnish another example of this tendency. From 1844 onwards, they provided education to children from the local working class, who, until that point, had rarely been able to attend school. Clara Fey, the daughter of an industrialist, along with her female friends, built up a network of primary schools in Aachen in this period, at a time when the secular municipal authorities were showing little interest in the task.

The provision of secular as well as religious knowledge was central to the activities of the female congregations, and this ensured that they afforded their pupils a solid grounding in writing, mathematics and geography, as well as Bible stories, the Catechism and church history. A systematic interlocking of secular and spiritual pedagogies was especially evident in the care of the sick. Their treatment and care were afforded a special importance by the sisters, in addition to attention to their spiritual needs. As in classrooms, those in hospitals featured the religious symbol of the cross, and the sisters prayed with schoolchildren and the sick, and led them through the rituals of the ecclesiastical year. They accompanied the children in their journey into the world of adult Catholics, by preparing them for the sacraments of confession, communion and confirmation. A chapel was rarely missing from the hospitals, with a present priest ensuring that patients could receive the sacraments. The female congregations also placed great importance on ensuring that terminally ill people would receive the last rights, so that they could leave this world free of sin.

This motivation to care for the sick naturally came from religious faith. The founder of the Grey Sisters in Silesia, Clara Wolff, located her activities, and those of the other sisters, squarely within the ambit of her religious convictions, stating that they were 'caring for the wounded members and bodies of the Divine Saviour'.[11] In 1851, the sisters began to practise the door-to-door care of the sick of all social classes, providing them with food, if that was necessary. Stationary care was provided later, mostly in small localities, as in Langenbielau after 1858 and Reichenbach as of 1870. From the 1890s onwards, large hospitals were established in cities such as Breslau, Dresden and Königsberg.[12] This care, whether provided in a hospital or individual homes, was perceived by the sisters as an opportunity to evangelize, by attempting to win over the sick to their faith.[13]

As exemplified by Franziska Schervier, a daughter of the Aachen bourgeoisie, over the course of the nineteenth century more and more young women, including Protestants, came to care for the sick. In industrial centres, in particular, the period witnessed the emergence of medical conditions and problems in such numbers that the traditional option of care within the home was rendered inadequate. Schervier's own order, the 'Poor Sisters', began in 1851 to provide care for the sick – its chief charitable activity in the secular world. In so doing, the sisters provided individuals with practical help in times of traumatic social and economic change, and were thus incorporated into the realms of church and confessional politics. For example, the Aachen Sisters took over the care duties in a Catholic hospital in the city located near its main Protestant hospital, the 'Kaiserswerther Diakonissenkrankenhaus', and were also not afraid to establish a Catholic hospital, the St Francis, in heavily Protestant Bielefeld. The sisters had learned the propaganda value of such acts from the Borromeus Order, which, in 1846, had established the first Catholic social institution in Berlin, by founding the St Hedwig Hospital next to its established Protestant and Jewish equivalents.

The female congregations' focus on combining religious and secular approaches in the provision of care continued, reflecting the development of medical science and of increasingly specialized doctors. Inviting the latter to work in the hospitals was easiest when the congregations owned the buildings themselves. The sisters thereby moved between ecclesiastical and secular spheres, and were also successful in ensuring that their nunneries, hospitals, schools, orphanages and welfare institutions served as advertisements for Catholicism. It was often the case that the female congregations constructed buildings right across the areas in which they and their dependents and employees lived, provided social care and education, and held religious services in chapels and churches. In Simpelveld, just over the Dutch border from Aachen, the Sisters of the Poor Child of Jesus constructed such a tangible bastion of Catholicism during the *Kulturkampf* of the 1870s.[14]

Even in Protestant-dominated cities, such as Bielefeld, Berlin, Königsberg and Hamburg, the female congregations managed to draw attention to themselves not only through their actions, but also their eager building work and clothing. With their congregation-specific attire, members presented an external image that earned respect and recognition, which they indeed needed in order to realize their projects. The congregations were not only reliant on support from the Catholic Church itself, but also state institutions, as they typically took over several tasks in the provision of public welfare, and did not by any means restrict their activities to the ecclesiastical sphere. This particular aspect of congregation activity has long been overlooked by historical research, and underestimated in its importance. For example, the major industrial regions of the German Empire – the Ruhr, Saarland and Silesia – would not have been able to develop without the presence of an extensive network of social and hospital care, or a form of school system. Even in 1900, adequate infrastructure in these key areas was lacking. Municipal authorities, welfare associations and business leaders asked the female congregations to help out, often paying out of their own pocket to facilitate this request, or supporting the orders in other ways. The sisters therefore often acted following an introduction or invitation from a secular authority.[15]

This expansion of communitarian female religious life only embraced traditional orders, such as the Ursulinites, when they were active in education. The Order of St Clare, or the Dominicans, for example, who followed the principles of a 'vita contemplativa' – of prayer and religious exercise – did not benefit from this upswing. The public presence of Catholic nuns, acting out their religious convictions in the world, predictably received criticism from various quarters, especially from liberal politicians, medical professionals and Protestants.[16] These prejudices culminated in the *Kulturkampf* of the 1870s, whose legislation enacted successive restrictions on the activities and freedoms of Catholic religious orders and congregations, afforded by the Prussian constitution of 1850. The Bismarckian legislation of the 1870s indeed explicitly targeted congregations involved in the provision of school education. In March 1872, the ecclesiastical administration of schools was abolished, and a few months later, Catholic orders and congregations were banned from public schools in the Kingdom of Prussia. Ultimately, their presence in higher and professional schools, as well as in the upbringing of small children and orphans, was banned. Only involvement in the care of the sick was spared by these anti-clerical laws. The Prussian state was nevertheless attempting to achieve a complete separation of the secular from the religious. This ensured that members of religious orders were expelled from teaching in public schools, and were only permitted to do so in Catholic primary schools. Those congregations involved in the care of the sick proved less controversial than those in education, as state officials were reliant on their services in this field.[17] These religious orders nevertheless feared that they too would at some point be subjected to similarly restrictive pieces of legislation. For this reason, they often searched, as their peers involved in education did, to establish activities outside of the German Reich.

Kulturkampf and Gender

That men such as the Prussian minister president and German chancellor Otto von Bismarck, the immunologist and Reichstag member Rudolf Virchow, the church lawyer Paul Hinschius and his colleague, the old Catholic Johann Friedrich von Schulte, regarded female religious orders with suspicion, was the result of multiple factors. For one thing, the boom in female religious orders provoked a sense of unease. Men such as Bismarck and Virchow suspected the orders of educating children in a manner that stood in direct contradiction to the culture and character of the Protestant nation state, which they had established in 1871.[18] As celibate women, who had thereby rejected the dominant cultural association of feminity with reproduction, members of female orders rapidly became the targets of anti-Catholic polemic and criticism, along with the male clergy and members of male orders. Celibacy in particular was seen by many liberal polemicists as the antithesis of the normative, bourgeois lifestyles that they themselves championed.[19]

The culture wars of the mid to late nineteenth century can certainly be interpreted as a struggle regarding the position of the Catholic Church in the political realm, especially within majority-Protestant states. New research has, moreover, highlighted that the culture wars of this period can be read not only as classic examples of church–state conflict, rivalry between varying confessions or battles over the cultural identity of new nation states, but also as manifestations of contemporary anxieties concerning questions of gender. Michael Gross's research highlights the profound misogyny of many liberal *Kulturkämpfer*, who, when confronted with public manifestations of female Catholic piety, were appalled by women 'who literally did not know their place'.[20] In this sense, the logic of the *Kulturkampf* was to drive Catholic women out of the public sphere – an explicitly sexist, rather than a narrowly party-political goal. As Gross argues: 'At the center of liberal anti-Catholicism was the sexism typical of the middle class'.[21] Shifts in gender identities and roles in the nineteenth century thereby also profoundly shaped the contours of the *Kulturkampf* itself.

Michael Borruta's work has, in turn, examined liberal conceptions of gender. These assumed the existence of separate spheres – the one public and political, the other religious and private. Both of these spaces were understood by liberals as properly belonging to one gender – it was the place of men to be active in public life and politics, and that of women to attend to religious piety. The 'feminization of religion' was produced by this newly gendered division of labour.[22] A mixing of these spheres, as liberals perceived to be the case in devout, ultra-Montanist Catholic circles, was deemed inappropriate and even dangerous.[23] Within liberal thought, these separate spheres existed in a close relationship with one another, with state and church entering into a form of marriage, according to the Swiss jurist and politician Johann Casper Bluntschli.[24]

Female religious orders violated this liberal conception of spheres and of the secular through their social work, and the construction of schools, nurseries and hospitals. For the nuns themselves, the notion of a separation of spheres between public and private made no sense. This attitude had the potential to cause conflict, as it directly contradicted the notion that religion was a private matter, and did not follow the logic of a 'gendering of church and state'.[25]

The difficulties in neatly separating the appropriate spheres of the secular state and the religious shows that contemporary liberal notions of a clear division represented an ideal type rarely found in reality. The borders between the secular and the religious were continually contested and disrespected, as the example of the Catholic female congregations clearly underlines. But, as Manuel Borutta has argued, these women campaigned for the privileges of their church, and not for the civic rights of women. Nevertheless, in so doing, they inadvertently expanded the spheres of social activity available to women. Female congregations – and this was later seized upon by Catholic missionaries outside Europe – took up fields of work that were deemed especially appropriate for their gender, such as the upbringing of children, elementary education and the care of the sick. Finally, hospital care developed over the course of the nineteenth century into a female domain. In the few hospitals in existence in the early nineteenth century, one could find salaried employees of both genders, but, over the decades, men were increasingly replaced by nuns and female members of Protestant welfare organizations, such as the *Diakonie*.[26]

Women Initiate Transnational Activities

Those female orders that had experienced major increases in their memberships in previous decades were suddenly confronted by the *Kulturkampf* in the 1870s, and with the decision of whether or not to relocate their personnel and expertise elsewhere. From the 1840s onwards, most female orders had developed their regulations and patterns of work, refined their statutes and constitutions, and received recognition from the institutional church. Moreover, they possessed the appropriate qualifications and permissions to be active in the upbringing of small infants and orphans. It rapidly became clear that the religious orders possessed horizons that stretched far beyond the borders of newly formed nation states, and that many individual members possessed contacts within the international Catholic Church, above all via the transnational networks of religious orders. This was a key point of difference between German Catholicism and Protestantism in the late nineteenth century – with the latter organized as individual state churches of the Reich's constituent *Länder* and kingdoms. Possessed of transnational Catholic networks stretching beyond the German state's borders, nuns and sisters were more than capable of evading the anti-Catholic policies of the Bismarckian government in the *Kulturkampf* era.

A vigorous exchange of people, spiritual ideas, rules and regulations across state boundaries had, of course, been a defining characteristic of Catholic Europe from the medieval period onwards. One of the earliest of the newly formed female religious orders in Germany indeed began to form branches abroad, even prior to the formation of the German Empire in 1871. The first, 'Poor Sisters of Holy Francis' from Aachen, arrived in the United States as early as 1858, where they established a hospital for sick German and Irish immigrants in Cincinnati, before proceeding to do so in Kansas and New York, among other cities. Nuns from this order could hold onto and rely on these establishments during the *Kulturkampf*, even as the Bismarckian government closed down its institutions for the education of children, in flagrant disregard for the order's provision of medical care for the Prussian and German armed forces during the wars of unification between 1864 and 1871.[27]

The *Kulturkampf* indeed served, for practical reasons, to accelerate the tendency for female religious orders to establish foreign branches. Their members searched for alternative means to develop their model and visions of work and piety beyond Germany's borders. Economic considerations played a role here, too. As sisters joining an order had the right to lifelong provision and care, members had to contribute, via their work, to ensuring that this was affordable. Nuns who were not active in education, or the provision of social care, due to anti-clerical legislation were indeed difficult to support. The nuns in this unfortunate position sought alternative forms of employment beyond Germany's borders, and established a range of transnational communities. Typically, they drew on existing contacts, or sought to establish new ones. When one closely examines the activities of these orders and communities, several patterns of behaviour become clear.

Into Neighbouring Countries

Religious congregations located close to the Reich's borders typically established a branch or institution in the neighbouring state. This allowed them to respond flexibly to political developments in Germany itself. Nuns in the Rhineland logically looked westwards to Belgium, France and the Netherlands. The Sisters of the Poor Child Jesus from Aachen established a new Mother House in the Netherlands. This institution in turn financed the order in the Reich itself, as of 1878 – it had previously supported itself through its educational activities, which were now banned in the Kingdom of Prussia. The Sisters of Divine Providence, traditionally located in Münster and also involved in education, relocated in 1876 to Blerick, just over the Dutch border.

Some orders moved further away. Silesian congregations such as the Grey Sisters moved to the Habsburg Monarchy, before proceeding to Sweden and Norway. Orders involved in the care of the sick were not subjected to such bans as their peers involved in education, but were restricted in their recruitment of new members.[28] A relocation abroad was therefore not only attractive to many congregations as a means of escaping the bans on educational activities recently passed in Germany, but also because there was a genuine demand for their services in neighbouring countries. Due to the mass migrations set in motion by industrialization, the confessional map of Europe was changing fast. For example, industrial workers brought their Catholic faith to overwhelmingly Protestant societies, such as England and Wales, which demanded that the local Catholic Church construct a form of religious and pastoral care for these new arrivals from Ireland, Poland and Lithuania, in addition to nurseries, schools and hospitals. Female religious congregations often rode to the rescue of overwhelmed local clergymen in such regions.[29]

The Sisters of the Poor Child Jesus took up educational roles in England from 1872 onwards. On Saturday 16 January 1876, the first sisters met in Southam, to the north of Oxford, and found what they deemed to be outrageous circumstances. As one noted: 'In this small town, which barely had any prosperous inhabitants in 1780, only a handful of Catholics lived, scattered among members of other confessions, partly in marriages with Protestants, and alienated from all forms of regular pastoral care'.[30] Here, in rural Warwickshire, unfamiliar tasks awaited the sisters, who had previously been accustomed to working in overwhelmingly Catholic Aachen. The congregation's own history states: 'The sisters nevertheless set to work bravely, filled their rooms with orphaned children of all ages from England, Ireland and Scotland, and brought local Catholic children to the school they had just opened in the town'.[31] The Poor Service Girls of Jesus Christ from Westerwald began to work in London in 1876.[32] From 1895 onwards, the Sisters of St Catherine from East Prussia attended to the pastoral needs of Polish and Lithuanian migrants in the industrial region around Liverpool.[33] Female German religious orders nevertheless represented a minority in comparison to their peers from France and Belgium, who had also been forced to leave their countries for political reasons.[34] In terms of pull factors, there was even a demand for the services provided by female Catholic orders in the Tsarist Empire and Scandinavia.[35]

Into North and South America

Following in the footsteps of the emigrants themselves, many nuns and members of female congregations moved to areas further afield, such as North and South America. The founder of the Congregation of the Poor School Sisters of our Dear Lady, Karolina Gerhardinger, travelled to North America with five sisters as early as 1847 in order to establish a network of establishments in Baltimore and beyond. It was only later that the community expanded on the European continent itself – to Württemberg and Prussia, into the Habsburg Monarchy and Great Britain. During the *Kulturkampf*, those congregations involved in education saw their houses closed in Prussia, Hessen and Baden.[36] Even in Bavaria restrictions were introduced, and the establishment of new institutions was not approved, even if those already in existence were left alone. Ultimately, however, as Sister Maria Liobgid Ziegler notes in a monograph on the congregation's history, the Bavarian government decided to 'spare' the 'religious sentiments' of its population.[37] The attempt of the liberal government to drive the clergy and religious orders out of schools thereby failed.[38] Nevertheless, the Poor School Sisters sought new fields of activity abroad. They achieved this goal in Great Britain, the Habsburg Monarchy and the United States, where, by 1908, over five thousand sisters were working in 252 branches of the order, in contrast to 3,443 nuns in 260 European institutions.[39] The female orders were moreover present in South as well as North America.

The first German nuns – Franciscans – arrived in Brazil in 1872 from Nonnenwerth in the Rhineland. Over two decades later, the Sisters of Divine Providence from Münster and the Sisters of St Catherine from East Prussia joined them. The three orders chose to locate themselves in southern Brazil, as it was there that most German migrants had established themselves in the country from the 1820s onwards. The Sisters of Holy Catherine, for example, could practise their educational work fully in this new location, as well as their duties of social work and care for the sick. In so doing, they served to construct a form of Catholic community or milieu in southern Brazil. Moreover, in this South American context, the sisters added the evangelization of local populations to their list of activities.[40]

The Sisters of Christian Love found new opportunities in Chile to accomplish their spiritual and pastoral goals. They originally followed the movements of German migrants to the country, before later embracing the conversion and evangelization of local populations as a central task. Initially twelve sisters arrived in the city of Ancud in September 1874, where the order's first Chilean house was established, with attached girls' school, orphanage and hospital. In the port city of Puerto Montt, the nuns opened the Casa San José, a boarding school, in addition to an orphanage and a training college for craftworks and domestic science, and the Colegio de la Immaculada Concepción – a school for the city. In the cities of Valdivia, Osorno, Puerto Varas and Puerto Octay, similar institutions were established by the congregation. Its members did not, however, confine themselves to Chile. In Montevideo, Uruguay's capital, the sisters founded the Colegio de la Immaculada Concepción in 1884, a school centre that ran from nursery through to senior girls' school. Further establishments of this kind followed, and in 1905, the Sisters of Christian Love moved to Argentina, where in Buenos Aires the Colegio Mallinckrodt was opened.[41] The sisters based in the Americas were in permanent contact with the order's leadership in Europe, which had been forced by the *Kulturkampf* to relocate its headquarters to the more welcoming environment of Belgium.

Evangelization in Africa and Asia

For female Catholic congregations, the German Reich's colonial expansionism, embraced from the 1880s onwards, opened up new fields of evangelization and pastoral work in Africa and Asia. At the international 'Togo Conference' held in Berlin in 1884/85, it was not only economic and trade policies that were discussed, but also matters pertaining to religion, and particularly, those organizations that would be permitted to travel to Africa in the name of Christian Mission, and the secular powers who would exercise jurisdiction over them. At this conference, the powers guaranteed African populations religious freedom, and all religions present on the continent the right to construct buildings for the purpose of religious practice.[42] By contrast, developments on the ground in Africa rapidly revealed that Catholic and Protestant missionaries displayed little respect for the religious traditions and practices of African populations. In marked contrast to the *Kulturkampf* of the 1870s and 1880s, in these colonial contexts outside Europe – in Africa and Asia – the skill sets of the female orders were actively sought out by the German state, to support its imperialist objectives.

The Catholic Church also saw advantages in the use of female religious orders in these African and Asian contexts, and in contrast to the early modern era, many sisters worked in missionary activity over the course of the nineteenth century. Michael Sievernich estimates that, in addition to around forty Catholic female congregations, which were founded explicitly for the purpose of missionizing, around three hundred female congregations were directly or indirectly involved in this evangelization activity.[43] As in Europe, in the missionary field, the competencies of the sisters in health care and education were much in demand. Moreover, contemporary missionaries followed concepts of evangelization, which placed a great premium on the roles played by European women among local populations. Male missionaries often entrusted nuns and sisters with the task of winning local women over to the Catholic faith, and of instructing them how to live a Christian family life.

Congregations, such as that of the Servants of the Holy Spirit, founded in the Netherlands in 1889 to avoid the *Kulturkampf*'s legislative restrictions, embraced these tasks in the newly acquired German colony of Togo. This order had been founded at the behest of the Dutch-German priest and missionary Arnold Janssen, who did so in 1875, that it might follow and support his own example and work. The Servants of the Holy Spirit thereby became part of a wider movement of Catholic women, which remains extensively unresearched. However, Katharina Stornig demonstrates, in an informative study, that nuns took over an extensive part of missionary work in the colonies themselves, and that they had particular understandings of the evangelization work undertaken by their church. Stornig also underlines the gendered impact that the missionary activities of the sisters had on local women. The former expected the latter to transform their ways of life radically, including their relationships with their bodies as well as their roles as wives and mothers. With this multiplicity of perspectives, she impressively demonstrates that European nuns and sisters embraced a wide variety of roles, as representatives of German Catholicism as well as the German state. In so doing, they transported the European model of a Christian community and a colonial state to Africa.[44]

Worldwide Mission

Female French congregations also served as a model for their German equivalents when it came to their international orientation and organization. Large female orders, such as that established by Vincent St Paul and Luise de Marillac in 1634, had a long tradition of global organization and missionary work stretching back to the early modern period.⁴⁵ For example, this order had established itself in Poland as early as 1652. By the nineteenth century, such female orders were active in Spain, Portugal, the Habsburg Monarchy, Germany and Great Britain, among other locations. In the 1870s, more female orders took up work in Latin America, for example, in Peru, Chile and Ecuador, as well as in the Ottoman Empire at Constantinople, and in Palestine at Jerusalem, Nazareth and other locations. Female orders were already working in China and Persia, and it is hardly surprising that others were to be found in the Belgian Congo.⁴⁶ A similar story can be told regarding the Women of the Good Shepherd, a congregation founded in Angers, France, in 1829. Between 1838 and 1868, its members were active worldwide, working in Rome as of 1838, London as of 1839, and from 1842 onwards in Louisville, Kentucky. The order established branches in Canada in 1844, Egypt in 1846, and Australia in 1863, in addition to other outposts in Asia and South America.⁴⁷

According to the studies of the Jesuit and historian Alfons Väth, fifteen female congregations with mother houses in Germany sent nuns to the mission field, to the Indian subcontinent, Palestine, Syria, Egypt, Japan, South Africa, East Africa, Zanzibar, the Belgian Congo, Korea, Brazil, China, the Dutch East Indies, New Guinea, Paraguay, British Honduras,⁴⁸ the Philippines and the United States.⁴⁹ Many female congregations found a new theatre of operations in this context, as their skill sets were especially in demand on the ground. This trend was also eased by the fact that the Catholic Church was able to draw on its centuries of organizational experience in these territories, and construct its pastoral structures in the mission field.⁵⁰ A central part of this project was the construction of a system of Catholic schools, in contrast to the Protestant-dominated system constructed by the German state in its colonies. Nuns overwhelmingly served as teachers in these institutions. Drawing on the studies of José Casanova, Frank Adloff has highlighted in his research on the United States that these schools 'made a significant contribution to the identification of the laity with Catholicism, and the construction of an American Catholic subculture'.⁵¹

Nuns from Germany, Ireland, Poland and France also played a role here, and contributed to the construction of transnational Catholic structures outside their own countries. A significant number of German sisters had indeed already worked in the Reich itself with people who had migrated to the German states or later empire. The sisters' flexibility, and their commitment to their Catholic faith and not the nation state, allowed them to appeal to wide constituencies. Nevertheless, Catholic communities in the United States increasingly changed over the course of the nineteenth century, initially distancing themselves from their 'polyglot and cosmopolitan' origins, and increasingly reflecting a greater level of ethnic homogeneity, before (from the 1880s onwards) returning to a multi-ethnic composition, possessed of an 'organizational substructure, which was primarily created by women and members of female congregations'.[52] This organization embraced education, health care, and a range of other charitable and welfare activities. This infrastructure was available to the whole population of a given locality.

In short, the construction of international Catholic networks in the nineteenth century was undertaken not only by men, but also women, who were able to do so with, but also without, the support of the institutional church.

The Establishment of Local and Transnational Networks of Experience and Knowledge

The *Kulturkampf* paradoxically accelerated the further development of female Catholic congregations. Due to the restrictive conditions present in the German Empire itself, they were compelled to seek fields of engagement beyond its borders. Through their activities abroad, many orders were indeed able to stabilize their positions in Germany itself. The leaderships of individual congregations could expand their horizons, and realizing that their services and skills were in demand elsewhere. Many communities in the German Empire were able to send novices and trained nuns to establishments in other countries. These nuns, who moved within the transnational networks of Roman Catholicism, served as transmitters of knowledge and information concerning religious and secular themes, which in turn influenced the Catholicism of their home country.

Such transfers are clearly illustrated by the example of the Sisters of Christian Love. The order's founder, Pauline von Mallinckrodt, (1817–1881), had already travelled extensively in the 1830s and 1840s to study welfare institutions, schools and monasteries in Berlin and Munich, but also in Liége, Brussels, Prague, Strasbourg, Vienna and Paris.[53] Drawing on what she had learned during these visits, she in turn established a community in Paderborn in 1849 that was dedicated to the education of the blind and young girls. Shortly before her death in 1881, Pauline von Mallinckrodt embarked on a journey to the Americas, departing from Bordeaux in October 1879, from which she returned to Paderborn on 28 December 1880.[54] Scarcely anyone else from provincial Westphalia could have undertaken such a journey in this period. These new establishments were so successful that, as early as 1907, there were more sisters of the order working outside Europe than within it. In Europe, the congregation possessed 501 nuns in twenty-three establishments, whereas in the United States alone the numbers were 737 and fifty-seven respectively, and in Chile, 351 and twenty-seven.[55]

The extent to which international experiences shaped orders' practices in Germany itself is revealed by the activities of the Sisters of our Dear Lady from

Coesfeld in the Münster region. In the summer of 1874, four of its sisters travelled to the United States, and, three years later, the order's entire leadership relocated itself to Cleveland, Ohio. Under the leadership of M. Chrysostoma Heck, over the following years an extensive network of primary schools and higher girls' schools were established in the region. The order's leadership returned to Germany in 1888, and concentrated its activities on the construction of senior schools for girls, as, even as late as 1887, following the end of the *Kulturkampf*, it was still illegal for nuns to teach in Prussian state schools.[56] The history of the Sisters of St Catherine is similarly transnational in character. They gathered their initial experiences in the administration of a large hospital in São Paulo, rather than in Germany. It was drawing on these experiences gained in Brazil that the order later began to open hospitals in the German Empire itself.[57]

These dynamic and transnational developments were naturally underpinned not only by the political context of church–state conflict in Bismarckian Germany, but also the wishes of the female congregations themselves to spread their own zeal abroad. By the 1870s at the latest, these female German Catholics had become part of an international movement of religious women, who were active on all continents. Reflecting the traditions of divine orders, their activities were also inspired by the desire to mission and evangelize. Transnational movements and exchanges across state borders shaped the communal religious life of these women, and it was rare that a community remained closely bound to a single locality.

The spheres in which the sisters and nuns were able to act in the later nineteenth century were indeed great, as the papacy had not yet acquired the power of later years, and was itself surprised by the boom of new female orders in Europe. Parallel to the rise of nation states, such as the formation of the German Empire in 1871, the papacy sought to renew itself, construct a genuinely global church, and encourage the cooperation of Catholics belonging to differing nationalities. At the same time, it must be remembered that Catholic missionaries often carried the regional and national peculiarities of their own religious backgrounds with them into the mission fields outside Europe.

The boom of Catholic religious orders in the nineteenth century reflected the fact that the church provided spaces and opportunities to women that were simply not available in the secular realm. The transnational activities of female religious orders, moreover, underlines that they were more than capable of harnessing the age of industrialization and migration to expand their spheres of social activity. Without integration in these religious networks, the women in question would never have had the opportunity to take on qualified, professional work in foreign countries.

This in turn highlights that, in the Bismarckian and Wilhelmine eras, German Catholics drew upon their experiences gleaned internationally in the provision of welfare and education when they ultimately returned to the Reich itself. The practice of social work and debates about the 'social question' in Imperial Germany were indeed profoundly shaped by religious understandings of social conditions in industrial regions. Rebekka Habermas's research has shown that even the atheist Friedrich Engels was not immune from this tendency.[58] It is therefore all the more surprising that the religious dimensions of social debates in Imperial Germany have been neglected within historiography, as have the roles played by women as actors in this field.[59] The important contribution made by Catholic and Protestant missionary activities (including the roles of women within them) to the exchange of knowledge about life in Germany and Europe – and the flow of information to the imperial metropole itself concerning conditions in Africa, Asia and elsewhere – has long been neglected.[60] Further research will be necessary to properly evaluate the consequences of the transnational organizational structures employed by Catholic female congregations in this period, and their roles in missionary activities.

One interesting field of inquiry concerns the forms of network established by the women to facilitate their transnational labours. The development of operations on an international scale typically involved an adaptation of organizational systems, resulting in the emergence of new provinces and chapters, which were incorporated within the individual order's hierarchy, but at the same time permitted to respond to local conditions. The *Generaloberin*, or head of a congregation, was nominally in charge – but on the ground, local officials could undertake their own initiatives according to the congregation's statutes. Nevertheless, the real balance of power within individual congregations did not always reflect these fixed rules. Much evidence indeed implies that a regional leader in Chile or Brazil possessed a considerable amount of independence from a mother house in Europe, given the distances, and slow speeds of communication, involved.[61]

On the whole, congregations did not incorporate nuns recruited abroad into their leadership structures. As a consequence, it took a very long time before the new extra-European establishments of these orders acquired status as provinces with a fully developed leadership of their own, and locally recruited sisters. Governing boards were dominated by nuns from Germany. It was only following the reforms initiated by the Second Vatican Council (1962–65) that this practice began to change, and sisters from a wider range of societies were able to enter into managerial and leadership roles. It nevertheless remained very much the exception rather than the rule that a sister from abroad would be elected to the overall leadership of an order.[62] Recent research underlines just how long it took for female Catholic organizations in Africa to gain independence from the European leaderships of their congregation.[63]

Among the Servants of the Holy Spirit, for example, new forms of identification ultimately emerged within the order itself. As early as 1960, its head demanded that the congregation 'no longer strive to achieve the dissolution of national and cultural differences', but rather to 'propagate the fundamental recognition of difference, but without this being seen in hierarchical terms, or according to hierarchical principles'. In so doing, she departed from the order's traditional 'ideal of homogeneity', embracing all its members.[64]

Today, it is not only African women who benefit from the transnational entanglements, which were first established by European nuns from the late nineteenth century onwards (even if these networks were not established with the aim of achieving an equal treatment of native populations). As Stornig notes: 'Spiritual and religious women found room for action here, which permitted them a degree of autonomy virtually unknown in other areas of society'.[65]

The history of female Catholic orders in the nineteenth and early twentieth centuries demonstrates overwhelmingly that 'modernity' does not represent the simple departure from religion, but rather emerges out of the interactions between the religious and the secular. Catholic women founded and became members of life communities due to their religious convictions, and, simultaneously, practised a *vita activa* in response to the economic and social conditions of their age. The countless new congregations established in this period saw their place as being both in a convent and the world outside: they lived in convents, but worked in the public realm.

The sisters of female congregations were pioneers – they learned how to stand up for their faith, and defend their church, in the public sphere. Due to their position within ecclesiastical law and their recognition from the wider Catholic community, the orders had the opportunity to help to shape the development of emerging church structures, and the confessional identities of lay communities. These opportunities could be used in very different ways and were not equally open to all. For example, the Steyler Missionaries in Togo did not permit Africans to become sisters like themselves. The virgin status was supposed to be a preserve of 'white' women, whereas African women were intended to expand the Catholic community through the upbringing of many Christian children.[66] This may surprise, as female orders themselves typically intended to recruit new members from the societies in which they were working. Whereas in Great Britain or Lithuania, it was self-evident that local Catholic women could be welcomed into a congregation, this matter was seen very differently in colonial Africa, or indeed South America.

Most female orders did little to document and record the histories of their transnational activities. As Kristine Ashton Gunnell has recently noted: 'Taught to blend into the background, the sisters could easily fade away into the historical abyss'.[67] If we are to locate their stories adequately within the historiography of the German Empire, much micro-historical research will be required, particularly focusing on the documentary records of individual congregations. Reading sources against the grain will also be necessary to see beyond the veneer of hierarchical relations seemingly existing between leaderships based in Germany, and their members operating abroad.

Research in this area could reveal that religion – as feared by liberal *Kulturkämpfer* – was not only operating in the private sphere, but that nuns and sisters were using their Catholicism as a platform for social action in the public realm. In short, Catholic women in this context were emerging as global players as well as global prayers! They emerged as the transmitters of 'German virtues' and religious agendas, and were some of the first institutional representatives of Germany outside the European continent. If the nineteenth century did indeed witness a 'triumphal rebirth and spread of "religion" in the sense we employ the term today', this would scarcely have been possible in the Catholic world without the efforts and work of women in religious orders and communities.[68]

Relinde Meiwes has worked as a researcher at the University of Bielefeld and at the University of Siegen. She received her PhD from the University of Bielefeld with a study on female congregations in nineteenth-century Germany: *'Arbeiterinnen des Herrn': Katholische Frauenkongregationen im 19. Jahrhundert* (Campus, 2000). She has published two books on the Katharinenschwestern: *Von Ostpreußen in die Welt: Die Geschichte der ermländischen Katharinenschwestern (1772–1914)* (Schöningh, 2011); and *Klosterleben in bewegten Zeiten: Die Geschichte der ermländischen Katharinenschwestern (1914–1962)* (Schöningh, 2016). She currently is preparing a book on Franciscan nuns in the nineteenth and twentieth centuries.

Notes

1. C. Langlois, *Le catholicisme au féminin: Les congrégations françaises à supérieure générale au XIXe siècle* (Paris: Le Cerf, 1988), 112–23, 207. The writer Clemens Brentano travelled once to France, to study this trend in person, presenting his findings to a German audience in 1831. See C. Brentano, *Die barmherzigen Schwestern in Bezug auf Armen- und Krankenpflege* (Koblenz: Hölscher, 1831).
2. R. Meiwes, *'Arbeiterinnen des Herrn': Katholische Frauenkongregationen im 19. Jahrhundert* (Frankfurt/Main: Campus, 2000), 82.
3. For the significance of foreign congregations, see Meiwes, *'Arbeiterinnen des Herrn'*, 89–97; and R. Meiwes, *Von Ostpreußen in die Welt: Die Geschichte der ermländischen Katharinenschwestern, 1772–1914* (Paderborn: Schöningh, 2011), 58f., 69–90.
4. An overview of this development in Western Europe is provided by J. De Maeyer, S. Leplae and J. Schmiedl (eds), *Religious Institutes in Western Europe in the nineteenth and twentieth Centuries: Historiography, Research and Legal Position* (Leuven: Leuven University Press, 2004). Coverage of a larger chronology is offered in J.A.K. McNamara, *Sisters in Arms: Catholic Nuns through Two Millennia* (Cambridge, MA: Harvard University Press, 1996). For France, see Langlois, *Le catholicisme au féminin*; for Belgium, A. Tihon, 'Les religieuses en Belgique du XVIIIe au XXe siècle: Approche statistique', *Belgisch Tijdschrift voor nieuwste geschiedenis/Revue Belge d'Histoire contemporaine* 7 (1976), 1–54; for Germany, Meiwes, *'Arbeiterinnen des Herrn'*; for England and Wales, B. Walsh, *Roman Catholic Nuns in England and Wales, 1800–1937* (Dublin: Irish Academic Press, 2002). Various studies have emerged within the context of Catholic Church history, but increasingly 'secular' historiography has developed an interest in the phenomenon. An exception is, however, provided by comparative studies across wider geographies, which extend beyond the boundaries of individual states.
5. See S. Conrad and J. Osterhammel (eds), *Das Kaiserreich transnational: Deutschland in der Welt 1871–1914* (Göttingen: Vandenhoeck & Ruprecht, 2004).

6. See the pioneering study of B. Welter, 'The Feminization of American Religion, 1800–1860', in M.S. Hartmann and L. Banner (eds), *Clio's Consciousness Raised: New Perspectives on the History of Women* (New York: Octagon Books, 1976), 137–57. See also the German version, B. Welter, '"Frauenwille ist Gottes Wille": Die Feminisierung der Religion in Amerika, 1800–1860', in C. Honegger and B. Heintz (eds), *Listen der Ohnmacht* (Frankfurt/Main: Europäische Verlagsanstalt, 1981), 326–55, in whose pages many important debates concerning the feminization of religion were developed. Also, H. McLeod, 'Weibliche Frömmigkeit – männlicher Unglaube? Religion und Kirche im bürgerlichen 19. Jahrhundert', in U. Frevert (ed.), *Bürgerinnen und Bürger: Geschlechterverhältnisse im 19. Jahrhundert* (Göttingen: Vandenhoeck & Ruprecht, 1988), 134–56; R. Habermas, 'Weibliche Religiosität – oder: Von der Fragilität bürgerlicher Identitäten', in K. Tenfelde and H.U. Wehler (eds), *Wege zur Geschichte des Bürgertums* (Göttingen: Vandenhoeck & Ruprecht, 1994), 125–48; P. Pasture, J. Art and T. Buermann (eds), *Gender and Christianity in Modern Europe: Beyond the Feminization Thesis* (Leuven: Leuven University Press, 2012), as well as the recently published edited volume of M. Sohn-Kronthaler (ed.), *Feminisierung oder (Re-)Maskulinisierung der Religion im 19. und 20. Jahrhundert: Forschungsbeiträge aus Christentum, Judentum und Islam* (Vienna: Böhlau, 2016); and O. Blaschke, 'Religion ist weiblich. Religion ist männlich: Geschlechterumwandlungen des Religiösen in historischer Perspektive', in K. Sammet, F. Benthaus-Apel and Christel Gärtner (eds), *Religion und Geschlechterordnungen* (Wiesbaden: Springer VS, 2017), 77–97. See also the important research of K. Stornig, *Sisters Crossing Boundaries: German Missionary Nuns in Colonial Togo and New Guinea, 1897–1960* (Göttingen: Vandenhoeck & Ruprecht, 2013), which, using a German order, places transnational entanglements at the heart of its analysis.
7. The Dutch historian Marjet Derks suggested in 2012 that the term should be avoided altogether, as it does not help to understand 'the ambiguities of gender [or] the complex symbolic meanings of womanhood and manhood within religion' – see M. Derks, 'Female Soldiers and the Battle for Gold: Gender Ambiguities and a Dutch Catholic Conversation Movement, 1921–1942', in P. Pasture, J. Art and T. Buermann (eds), *Gender and Christianity in Modern Europe: Beyond the Feminization Thesis* (Leuven: Leuven University Press, 2012), 188f. Catholic Church history has also developed reservations concerning the concept. Gisela Muschiol deems it a 'catgeory of analysis, and, in accordance with Derks, 'dispensible'. G. Muschiol, 'Dienste, Ämter und das Geschlecht: Anfragen an die Feminisierungsthese aus katholischer Perspektive', in M. Sohn-Kronthaler (ed.), *Feminisierung oder (Re-)Maskulinisierung der Religion im 19. und 20. Jahrhundert: Forschungsbeiträge aus Christentum, Judentum und Islam* (Vienna: Böhlau, 2016), 49. For Bernhard Schneider it remains a 'useful hypothesis', albeit one in urgent need of nuance and correction. Further research will be required to further improve and expand our understandings of the relationships between gender and religion; see B. Schneider, 'Feminisierung und (Re-)Maskulinisierung der Religion im 19. Jahrhundert: Tendenzen der Forschung aus der Perspektive des deutschen Katholizismus', in M. Sohn-Kronthaler (ed.), *Feminisierung oder (Re-)Maskulinisierung der Religion im 19. und 20. Jahrhundert: Forschungsbeiträge aus Christentum, Judentum und Islam* (Vienna: Böhlau, 2016), 11–41, 24–27, 35.
8. Information regarding all Catholic orders and congregations can be found in this 10 volume work: *Dizionario degli Istituti de Perfezione (DIP)*, G. Pelliccia and G. la Rocca (eds). For the content of this Lexicon, see K.S. Frank, 'Das "Dizionario degli Istituti di

Perfezione" (DIP)', *Beiträge zur Neueren Ordens- und Frömmigkeitsgeschichte (BnOFG)* 3 (2005), 4–16.
9. A rare exception is provided by 'Die Schwestern von der hl. Katharina'; Meiwes, *Von Ostpreußen in die Welt*.
10. Ibid., 107–12.
11. J. Mertens, *Geschichte der Kongregation der Schwestern von der heiligen Elisabeth, 1842–1992*, 2 vols (Reinbeck, 1998; not available in bookshops), Vol. 1, 21.
12. Mertens, *Geschichte der Kongregation*, Vol. 2, 422, 426; Mertens, *Geschichte der Kongregation*, Vol. 1, 363.
13. Mertens, *Geschichte der Kongregation*, Vol. 1, 359.
14. Meiwes, 'Arbeiterinnen des Herrn', 204f.
15. Rebekka Habermas noted in the Introduction that there are only a few studies that properly unpackage and analyse the secular, rather than using it as a self-evident category.
16. Meiwes, 'Arbeiterinnen des Herrn', 288–93; and M. Borutta, *Antikatholizismus: Deutschland und Italien im Zeitalter der europäischen Kulturkämpfe* (Göttingen: Vandenhoeck & Ruprecht, 2010).
17. Meiwes, 'Arbeiterinnen des Herrn', 293–301.
18. The 'Orientalization of Catholicism', as Manuel Borutta terms it, ensured that Catholic nuns were deemed innapropriate to teach in Prussian schools (Borutta, *Antikatholizimus*, 150).
19. Ibid., 216.
20. M.B. Gross, 'Kulturkampf and Geschlechterkampf: Anti-Catholicism, Catholic Women, and the Public', in F. Biess, M. Roseman and H. Schissler (eds), *Conflict, Catastrophe and Continuity: Essays on Modern German History* (New York: Berghahn Books, 2007), 39.
21. Ibid.
22. Borutta, *Antikatholizimus*, 281; idem, 'Kulturkampf als Geschlechterkampf? Geschlecht als Grenze der Säkularisierung im 19. Jahrhundert', in B. Stollberg-Rilinger (ed.), *'Als Mann und Frau schuf er sie': Religion und Geschlecht* (Würzburg: Ergon-Verlag, 2014), 109–37.
23. Borutta, *Antikatholizimus*, 274.
24. Ibid., 276f.
25. Ibid., 274. Borutta extensively studies the attitudes of Heinrich von Sybel and Johann Casper Bluntschi.
26. Meiwes, 'Arbeiterinnen des Herrn', 157–60.
27. J. Jeiler, *Die gottselige Mutter Franziska Schervier, Stifterin der Genossenschaft der Armenschwestern vom hl. Franziskus* (Freiburg i.B.: Herdersche Verlagsbuchhandlung, 1897), 238f., 527, 573.
28. Mertens, *Geschichte der Kongregation*, Vol. 1, 109–11, 115.
29. Walsh, *Roman Catholic Nuns in England and Wales*.
30. O. Pfülf, *M. Clara Fey vom armen Kinde Jesus* (Freiburg i.B.: Herdersche Verlagsbuchhandlung, 1907), 427.
31. Ibid., 428.
32. Walsh, *Roman Catholic Nuns in England and Wales*, 167.
33. Meiwes, *Von Ostpreußen in die Welt*, 171–74.
34. Walsh, *Roman Catholic Nuns in England and Wales*.
35. Y.M. Werner (ed.), *Nuns and Sisters in the Nordic Countries after the Reformation: A Female Counter-Culture in Modern Society* (Uppsala: SIM, 2004); Meiwes, *Von Ostpreußen in die Welt*, 148–54; and R. Meiwes, 'Im Schatten des Kulturkampfes: Katholische Schwestern

in Skandinavien. Beitrag zum Themenschwerpunkt "Europäische Geschichte – Geschlechtergeschichte"', in *Themenportal Europäische Geschichte* (2012). Retrieved 28 January 2014 from http://www.europa.clio-online.de/2012/Article=543.
36. H.K. Wendlandt, *Die weiblichen Orden und Kongregationen der katholischen Kirche und ihre Wirksamkeit in Preußen 1818–1918* (Paderborn: Schöningh, 1924), 260f.; and M.L. Ziegler, *Die Armen Schulschwestern von Unserer Lieben Frau: Ein Beitrag zur bayerischen Bildungsgeschichte* (Munich: Filser, 1935).
37. Ziegler, *Arme Schulschwestern*, 87.
38. Borutta, *Antikatholizismus*, 304–7.
39. Wendlandt, *Die weiblichen Orden*, 262.
40. Meiwes, *Von Ostpreußen in die Welt*, 174–98.
41. Die Schwestern der christlichen Liebe, *Genossenschaft der Schwestern der christlichen Liebe. Töchter der allerseligsten Jungfrau Maria von der Unbefleckten Empfängnis* (Paderborn: Bonifacius-Druckerei, 1930), 89–105.
42. M. Sievernich, *Die christliche Mission: Geschichte und Gegenwart* (Darmstadt: Wissenschaftliche Buchgesellschaft, 2009), 93.
43. Sievernich, *Die christliche Mission*, 97. In the early 1920s, 12,700 priests, and double this number of nuns, were active in missionary activity. References to these 24,000 women in historical works are rare.
44. Stornig, *Sisters Crossing Boundaries*; and idem, '"… denn die ganze Sorge der Schwestern war darauf gerichtet, die Lage des weiblichen Geschlechts zu verbessern": Geschlecht, Religion und Differenz in der Missionspraxis deutscher Ordensfrauen im kolonialen Togo (1896–1918)', in R. Habermas and R. Hölzl (eds), *Mission global: Eine Verflechtungsgeschichte seit dem 19. Jahrhundert* (Cologne: Böhlau, 2014), 111–34.
45. Many of these communities ultimately became independent organizations.
46. M. Heimbucher, *Die Orden und Kongregationen der katholischen Kirche* (Paderborn: Schöningh [1933] 1987), Vol. 2, 461–68.
47. Ibid., 477–79.
48. Ibid., 46.
49. In the United States, missionary work typically consisted of evangelizing Native Americans and African Americans. A. Väth, *Die Frauenorden in den Missionen: Eine Untersuchung über die Beteiligung der katholischen Ordensschwestern am Weltapostolat der Kirche vom 16. Jahrhundert bis zur Gegenwart* (Aachen: Xaverius, 1920), 46.
50. Väth, *Die Frauenorden in den Missionen*, 112f.
51. F. Adloff, *Im Dienste der Armen: Katholische Kirche und amerikanischen Sozialpolitik im 20. Jahrhundert* (Frankfurt/Main: Campus, 2003), 114.
52. Ibid., 117.
53. P. von Mallinckrodt, *Kurzer Lebensabriss unserer theuern Würdigen Mutter und Stifterin Pauline von Mallinckrodt bis zu ihrer ersten Gelübdeablegung von ihr selbst verfaßt* (Paderborn: Bonifatius Druckerei, 1889), 22f., 38–58.
54. Die Schwestern der christlichen Liebe, *Genossenschaft der Schwestern der christlichen Liebe*, 3638.
55. Wendlandt, *Die weiblichen Orden*, 113f.
56. M.R. Böckmann and M.B. Morthorst, *Geschichte der Kongregation der Schwestern Unserer Lieben Frau von Coesfeld, Deutschland*, 5 vols (Coesfeld, 1993–1997; not available in book shops).
57. Meiwes, *Von Ostpreußen in die Welt*, 188f.

58. R. Habermas, 'Piety, Power, and Powerlessness: Religion and Religious Groups in Germany, 1870–1945', in H.W. Smith (ed.), *The Oxford Handbook of Modern German History* (Oxford University Press, 2011), 461f.
59. Ibid., 462.
60. Ibid., 462; R. Habermas, 'Mission im 19. Jahrhundert: Globale Netze des Religiösen', *Historische Zeitschrift* 287 (2008), 647–52.
61. It would be fascinating here to examine the social backgrounds of the orders' leaderships.
62. The Sisters of St Catherine began to establish an international leadership committee in the aftermath of the Second World War, but it was only in 1995 that a Brazilian sister was elected to the order's overall leadership. The African sisters from Togo, Benin and Cameroon remain to this day under the jurisdiction of the Mother House in Italy, and do not form independent provinces of the order. See R. Meiwes, *Klosterleben in bewegten Zeiten: Die Geschichte der ermländischen Katharinenschwestern, 1914–1962* (Paderborn: Schöningh, 2016).
63. See the work of G. Hüwelmeier, 'Ordensfrauen unterwegs: Transnationalismus, Gender und Religion', *Historische Anthropologie* 13 (2005), 91–110; K. Langewiesche, 'Aus Töchtern werden Schwestern: Afrikanische katholische Ordensfrauen in kolonialen und postkolonialen Zeiten', in R. Habermas and R. Hölzl (eds), *Mission global: Eine Verflechtungsgeschichte seit dem 19. Jahrhundert* (Cologne: Böhlau, 2014), 297–326; and K. Stornig, 'Kosmopolitische Praktiken? Katholische Frauenkongregationen im 20. Jahrhundert', in B. Gißibl and I. Löhr (eds), *Bessere Welten: Kosmopolitismus in den Geschichtswissenschaften* (Frankfurt/Main: Campus, 2017), 135–65.
64. Stornig, 'Kosmopolitische Praktiken?', 136, 159.
65. Ibid., 325.
66. Stornig, 'Geschlecht, Religion und Differenz', 131–34.
67. K.A. Gunnell, 'Archival Research and the Daughters of Charity', *Newsletter of the UCLA Center for the Study of Women* (Winter 2014), 19.
68. C.A. Bayly, *Die Geburt der modernen Welt: Eine Globalgeschichte, 1780–1914* (Frankfurt/Main: Campus, 2008), 400.

Bibliography

Adloff, F. *Im Dienst der Armen: Katholische Kirche und amerikanischen Sozialpolitik im 20. Jahrhundert*. Frankfurt/Main: Campus, 2003.

Bayly, C.A. *Die Geburt der modernen Welt: Eine Globalgeschichte, 1780–1914*. Frankfurt/Main: Campus, 2008.

Blaschke, O. 'Religion ist weiblich. Religion ist männlich: Geschlechterumwandlungen des Religiösen in historischer Perspektive', in K. Sammet, F. Benthaus-Apel and Christel Gärtner (eds), *Religion und Geschlechterordnungen* (Wiesbaden: Springer VS, 2017), 77–97.

Böckmann, M.R., and M.B. Morthorst. *Geschichte der Kongregation der Schwestern Unserer Lieben Frau von Coesfeld, Deutschland*, 5 vols. Coesfeld, 1993–1997; not available in bookshops.

Borutta, M. *Antikatholizismus: Deutschland und Italien im Zeitalter der europäischen Kulturkämpfe*. Göttingen: Vandenhoeck & Ruprecht, 2010.

———. 'Kulturkampf als Geschlechterkampf? Geschlecht als Grenze der Säkularisierung im 19. Jahrhundert', in B. Stollberg-Rilinger (ed.), *'Als Mann und Frau schuf er sie': Religion und Geschlecht* (Würzburg: Ergon-Verlag, 2014), 109–37.

Brentano, C. *Die barmherzigen Schwestern in Bezug auf Armen- und Krankenpflege*. Koblenz: Hölscher, 1831.

Conrad, S., and J. Osterhammel (eds). *Das Kaiserreich transnational: Deutschland in der Welt 1871–1914*. Göttingen: Vandenhoeck & Ruprecht, 2004.

De Maeyer, J., S. Leplae and J. Schmiedl (eds). *Religious Institutes in Western Europe in the nineteenth and twentieth Centuries: Historiography, Research and Legal Position*. Leuven: Leuven University Press, 2004.

Derks, M. 'Female Soldiers and the Battle for Gold: Gender Ambiguities and a Dutch Catholic Conversation Movement, 1921–1942', in P. Pasture, J. Art and T. Buermann (eds), *Gender and Christianity in Modern Europe: Beyond the Feminization Thesis* (Leuven: Leuven University Press, 2012), 173–90.

Die Schwestern der christlichen Liebe. *Genossenschaft der Schwestern der christlichen Liebe. Töchter der allerseligsten Jungfrau Maria von der Unbefleckten Empfängnis*. Paderborn: Bonifacius-Druckerei, 1930.

Frank, K.S. 'Das "Dizionario degli Istituti di Perfezione" (DIP)'. *Beiträge zur Neueren Ordens- und Frömmigkeitsgeschichte (BnOFG)* 3 (2005), 4–16.

Gunnell, K.A. 'Archival Research and the Daughters of Charity'. *Newsletter of the UCLA Center for the Study of Women* (Winter 2014), 16–23.

Gross, M. 'Kulturkampf and Geschlechterkampf: Anti-Catholicism, Catholic Women, and the Public', in F. Biess, M. Roseman and H. Schissler (eds), *Conflict, Catastrophe and Continuity: Essays on Modern German History* (New York: Berghahn Books, 2007), 27–43.

Habermas, R. 'Weibliche Religiosität – oder: Von der Fragilität bürgerliche Identitäten', in K. Tenfelde and H.U. Wehler (eds), *Wege zur Geschichte des Bürgertums* (Göttingen: Vandenhoeck & Ruprecht, 1994), 125–48.

———. 'Mission im 19. Jahrhundert: Globale Netze des Religiösen'. *Historische Zeitschrift* 287 (2008), 629–79.

———. 'Piety, Power, and Powerlessness: Religion and Religious Groups in Germany, 1870–1945', in H.W. Smith (ed.), *The Oxford Handbook of Modern German History* (Oxford University Press, 2011), 453–80.

Heimbucher, M. *Die Orden und Kongregationen der katholischen Kirche*. Paderborn: Schöningh, (1933) 1987.

Hüwelmeier, G. 'Ordensfrauen unterwegs: Transnationalismus, Gender und Religion'. *Historische Anthropologie* 13 (2005), 91–110.

Jeiler, J. *Die gottselige Mutter Franziska Schervier, Stifterin der Genossenschaft der Armenschwestern vom hl. Franziskus*. Freiburg i.B.: Herdersche Verlagsbuchhandlung, 1897.

Langewiesche, K. 'Aus Töchtern werden Schwestern: Afrikanische katholische Ordensfrauen in kolonialen und postkolonialen Zeiten', in R. Habermas and R. Hölzl (eds), *Mission global: Eine Verflechtungsgeschichte seit dem 19. Jahrhundert* (Cologne: Böhlau, 2014), 297–326.

Langlois, C. *Le catholicisme au féminin: Les congrégations françaises à supérieure générale au XIXe siècle*. Paris: Le Cerf, 1984.

Mallinckrodt, P. von. *Kurzer Lebensabriss unserer theuern Würdigen Mutter und Stifterin Pauline von Mallinckrodt bis zu ihrer ersten Ge*lübdeablegung von ihr selbst verfaßt. Paderborn: Bonifatius Druckerei, 1889.

McLeod, H. 'Weibliche Frömmigkeit – männlicher Unglaube? Religion und Kirche im bürgerlichen 19. Jahrhundert', in U. Frevert (ed.), *Bürgerinnen und Bürger:*

Geschlechterverhältnisse im 19. Jahrhundert (Göttingen: Vandenhoeck & Ruprecht, 1988), 134–56.

McNamara, J.A.K. *Sisters in Arms: Catholic Nuns through Two Millennia*. Cambridge, MA: Harvard University Press, 1996.

Meiwes, R. *'Arbeiterinnen des Herrn': Katholische Frauenkongregationen im 19. Jahrhundert* Frankfurt/Main: Campus, 2000.

———. *Von Ostpreußen in die Welt: Die Geschichte der ermländischen Katharinenschwestern, 1772–1914*. Paderborn: Schöningh, 2011.

———. 'Im Schatten des Kulturkampfes: Katholische Schwestern in Skandinavien. Beitrag zum Themenschwerpunkt "Europäische Geschichte – Geschlechtergeschichte"'. *Themenportal Europäische Geschichte*, 2012. Retrieved 28 January 2014 from http://www.europa.clio-online.de/2012/Article=543.

———. *Klosterleben in bewegten Zeiten: Die Geschichte der ermländischen Katharinenschwestern, 1914–1962*. Paderborn: Schöningh, 2016.

Mertens, J. *Geschichte der Kongregation der Schwestern von der heiligen Elisabeth, 1842–1992*. Reinbeck, 1998 (not available in bookshops).

Muschiol, G. 'Dienste, Ämter und das Geschlecht: Anfragen an die Feminisierungsthese aus katholischer Perspektive', in M. Sohn-Kronthaler (ed.), *Feminisierung oder (Re)Maskulinisierung der Religion im 19. und 20. Jahrhundert: Forschungsbeiträge aus Christentum, Judentum und Islam* (Vienna: Böhlau, 2016), 42–51.

Pasture, P., J. Art and T. Buermann (eds). *Gender and Christianity in Modern Europe: Beyond the Feminization Thesis*. Leuven: Leuven University Press, 2012.

Pfülf, O. *M. Clara Fey vom armen Kinde Jesus*. Freiburg i.B.: Herdersche Verlagsbuchhandlung, 1907.

Schneider, B. 'Feminisierung und (Re-)Maskulinisierung der Religion im 19. Jahrhundert. Tendenzen der Forschung aus der Perspektive des deutschen Katholizismus', in M. Sohn-Kronthaler (ed.), *Feminisierung oder (Re-)Maskulinisierung der Religion im 19. und 20. Jahrhundert: Forschungsbeiträge aus Christentum, Judentum und Islam* (Vienna: Böhlau, 2016), 11–41.

Sievernich, M. *Die christliche Mission: Geschichte und Gegenwart*. Darmstadt: Wissenschaftliche Buchgesellschaft, 2009.

Sohn-Kronthaler, M. (ed.). *Feminisierung oder (Re-)Maskulinisierung der Religion im 19. und 20. Jahrhundert: Forschungsbeiträge aus Christentum, Judentum und Islam*. Vienna: Böhlau, 2016.

Stornig, K. *Sisters Crossing Boundaries: German Missionary Nuns in Colonial Togo and New Guinea, 1897–1960*. Göttingen: Vandenhoeck & Ruprecht, 2013.

———. '"… denn die ganze Sorge der Schwestern war darauf gerichtet, die Lage des weiblichen Geschlechts zu verbessern": Geschlecht, Religion und Differenz in der Missionspraxis deutscher Ordensfrauen im kolonialen Togo (1896–1918)', in R. Habermas and R. Hölzl (eds), *Mission global: Eine Verflechtungsgeschichte seit dem 19. Jahrhundert* (Cologne: Böhlau, 2014), 111–34.

———. 'Kosmopolitische Praktiken? Katholische Frauenkongregationen im 20. Jahrhundert', in B. Gißibl and I. Löhr (eds), *Bessere Welten: Kosmopolitismus in den Geschichtswissenschaften* (Frankfurt/Main: Campus, 2017), 135–65.

Tihon, A. 'Les religieuses en Belgique du XVIIIe au XXe siècle: Approche statistique'. *Belgisch Tijdschrift voor nieuwste geschiedenis/Revue Belge d'Histoire contemporaine* 7 (1976), 1–54.

Väth, A. *Die Frauenorden in den Missionen: Eine Untersuchung über die Beteiligung der katholischen Ordensschwestern am Weltapostolat der Kirche vom 16. Jahrhundert bis zur Gegenwart.* Aachen: Xavernius, 1920.

Walsh, B. *Roman Catholic Nuns in England and Wales, 1800–1937.* Dublin: Irish Academic Press, 2002.

Welter, B. 'The Feminization of American Religion, 1800–1860', in M.S. Hartmann and L. Banner (eds), *Clio's Consciousness Raised: New Perspectives on the History of Women* (New York: Octagon Books, 1976), 137–57.

———. '"Frauenwille ist Gottes Wille". Die Feminisierung der Religion in Amerika, 1800–1860', in C. Honegger and B. Heintz (eds), *Listen der Ohnmacht* (Frankfurt/Main: Europäische Verlagsanstalt, 1981), 326–55.

Wendlandt, H.K. *Die weiblichen Orden und Kongregationen der katholischen Kirche und ihre Wirksamkeit in Preußen 1818–1918.* Paderborn: Schöningh, 1924.

Werner, Y.M. (ed.). *Nuns and Sisters in the Nordic Countries after the Reformation: A Female Counter-Culture in Modern Society.* Uppsala: SIM, 2004.

Ziegler, M.L. *Die Armen Schulschwestern von Unserer Lieben Frau: Ein Beitrag zur bayerischen Bildungsgeschichte.* Munich: Filser, 1935.

7
Negotiating the Fundamentals?
German Missions and the Experience of the Contact Zone, 1850–1918

Richard Hölzl and Karolin Wetjen

Famously, Edward Said in his seminal essay *Orientalism* set out to demonstrate that British and French – to a lesser extent German and Italian – artists, writers and scholars created a hegemonic image of 'the Orient' in close relation to imperial political power, and that 'European culture gained in strength and identity by setting itself off against the Orient as a sort of surrogate and even underground self'.[1] Said also held that modern orientalism was to some extent formed by a secularization of earlier ideas of religious difference of the *mundus christianus* from the 'heathen rest'.[2] Orientalism in the sense of Said has long been regarded as an ideological foundation of European colonialism, and most historians of German colonialism have stuck to this secularized framework of Said's interpretation.[3] German imperialism and colonial discourse was an exercise either in ruthless power politics, in liberal Western secular civilizing mission, or a merely accidental outpouring of male adventurism. If missionaries are mentioned, they figure as one more subgroup within the horde of self-proclaimed civilizers who entered colonial space and discourse with the primarily secular civilizing mission as a common master narrative.[4]

We argue, however, that the missionary understanding of culture and civilization warrants a closer scrutiny by historians. In two ways, in particular, missionaries occupied a central role for European colonialism: (1) in practice, they dominated the fields of education, health care and cultural policy in the colonies; and (2) they operated powerful communication networks, which together with popular and academic media outlets constituted the field of imperial communication.⁵ Both aspects make missionaries key brokers of cultural contact and agents of cultural translation. Missionaries, in a very particular way, constituted relays between colony and metropole, as well as between the secular and the religious. They negotiated the experience of contact and metropolitan discourse about the colonies within both a secular and a religious framework. In the process, they blurred and reshaped the boundaries of these frameworks.

Missions hardly ever made clear distinctions between a religious and a secular colonial sphere, between cultural work (or civilizing mission) and evangelism. Missionary experience in the contact zone fleshed out their contribution to the debate on the character and aims of colonialism in the colonial metropole. Missions fought to add a very particular position to the master narrative of the civilizing mission, emphasizing that 'civilization' was essentially Christian and that supremacy rested not on secular, materialist or liberal concepts, but on Christian values, morals and faithfulness. This will be demonstrated in the first part of this chapter.

At the same time missions were in a liminal position in Europe itself, and their interpretation of a Christian civilizing mission was a contested one. Liberal intellectuals, who set the tone in the political debate in Imperial Germany, were far from denying the role of Christian values and clerical institutions in producing Western supremacy – but only at a sort of early stage. Max Weber, for instance, saw the Catholic Church (its ascetic traditions), and to a certain extent the Protestant churches, as early stepping stones long superseded by bourgeois capitalism's rational organization of society.⁶ From this angle, religion and religiosity did exist as a subordinate and privatized field distinct from the secular spheres of politics, economy and the social at large. Both the historical context of the European culture wars – in which Catholicism, but also conservative neo-confessional Protestants had been subjected to a quasi-orientalist brushing over– and the experience of the contact zone have led to a redrawing of the boundaries of the religious and the secular among religious intellectuals and activists.⁷ This was at least a century-long process, beginning early in the nineteenth-century, when theologians and romantic philosophers fought the ideas of the *lumières* and the French Revolution 'on their own territory', developing alternative narratives to enlightened ideas of progress and civilization.⁸ Given the pivotal but also liminal position of missions, we ask how they negotiated and rearranged the boundaries of the religious and the secular in colonial discourse, in theology and in practical mission work.

The reorganization of the boundaries of the religious and the secular played out in the much narrower academic field of (mission) theology in a different way than in colonial politics, as will be demonstrated in the second part of this chapter. The focus on theology allows us to argue that negotiating the boundaries of the religious and the secular was a multilevel process with sometimes contradictory trajectories. While missionaries in the political field fiercely argued for a religious understanding of colonialism, they frantically tried to distinguish the religious and the secular in mission theology and practice. Missionary encounters set religious and cultural boundaries in motion, and this was acknowledged and questioned among theologians, missionaries and other religious actors at the time. They discussed how much change to the fundamentals of Christianity could be tolerated in the process of expansion and conversion. This was in essence a debate about the boundaries of the religious and the secular. While the secular (or the cultural) seemed open to negotiation and adaption, religious fundamentals would not be compromised as a matter of principle. European religious actors discussed this question under the impression that they held the key to defining what was fundamentally religious and what was merely a cultural by-product that could be sacrificed in a process of 'accommodation'. The practice of negotiating the fundamentals – in particular baptism, and the theological debates ensuing from it – lead directly into the centre of the missionary principle, namely religious and cultural conversion. In the second part of this chapter, we look at how this negotiating of fundamentals was narrated in mission theology.

This story is not one confined to metropolitan discourse, but one of entanglement and of cultural encounter. As missionaries realized, very few things remained 'sacred' in the contact zone; the fundamentals and sacraments were subject to strife, cultural translation, and compromise. Most of the intellectual and theological work went into the question of how traditions, customs and cultural rituals could be distinguished from pastoral questions (marriage, socialization, reference to ancestors, healing, etc.) and dogmatic rules, where the theological fundament of faith stood against allegedly heathen, superstitious, heretic, or simply devilish incursions and practice.

In the third part of this chapter we will provide cases of how German Protestant and Catholic missionaries in East Africa negotiated religious fundamentals during the German colonial period. In a comparative perspective we look at the sacrament of baptism in Protestant and Catholic missions, which lay at the heart of any Christian mission's work. But it was also – as we intend to demonstrate – a key site of negotiating the religious and the secular. The case studies cover the north-east and the south of the German colony East Africa. These mission fields were characterized by a high level of competition among Christian confessions, African religions, and Islam.[9] The competitive layout was an important factor, as it opened a range of possibilities for potential converts. It gave mission work a sense of urgency that influenced mission practices. All this points us at the agency of the people targeted by missionary theory and practice. They certainly had a share in negotiating conversion and thereby Christianity in the mission field. We argue here and in the following paragraphs that missionary practice in the contact zone, mission theology, and metropolitan colonial discourse are to be treated as interrelated fields of study.[10] Conversion was a spiritual and a political affair in the colonies, and it shaped the way missionaries engaged in both the theological and the political debates. The simple necessity to negotiate with potential and actual converts about what was held to be fundamentally Christian led to a shift in the boundaries of the religious and the secular.

Politicizing Mission: Missionary Interventions in the Colonial Discourse

Imperial rule was a process of continuous and sometimes discontinuous feedback loops that are hard to pin down to a linear narrative of cause and effect. To develop our argument, we begin by asking how Christian mission was articulated in the political arena of the colonial metropole and how missionaries negotiated the boundaries of the religious and the secular with respect to the colonial civilizing mission. The role of missions in the colonies, and in particular the role of Catholic missions, was hotly debated within the German Empire. The anti-Catholic bias of liberals and Protestant conservatives alike and the 'culture war' provided the background for Catholic missions to address the questions about the means and ends of German colonialism.[11] Missionaries navigated the narrow straits of the colonial discourse by pointing out their crucial role with respect to the civilizing mission of the German Empire. They underlined their 'cultural work' and the results achieved and to be achieved in educating, healing and pacifying the populations in the German colonies. At the same time, they argued that, since European civilization was rooted in Christianity, any colonial civilizing mission would also have to be based on Christianity.

The early years of German colonialism had been characterized by the parallel establishment of formal colonies and of German-based Catholic mission societies – this had been negotiated by Bismarck and Pope Leo XIII, and was also institutionalized by the Berlin Conference of 1884, which among other things agreed on the 'freedom of religion' (i.e. freedom for Christian missions to enter the colonies). The 1900s were characterized by an increasingly heated debate on the means and ends of colonialism, its cost and benefits, and the repercussions of the colonies on Germany's 'national character', or the reasons for the colonial wars in the German colonies of Southwest Africa and East Africa (see the so-called 'Hottentotten' elections in 1907; the miscegenation debate in the Reichstag in 1912). Missionaries and in particular Catholics were called upon to justify their role in the colonies, and also questioned colonial administration in its efficacy, the legitimacy of its means, and the ethical conduct of its personnel. The years after 1900 also saw a number of colonial scandals involving missionaries as whistle-blowers denouncing sexual deviance and exploitation, as well as excessive violence.[12]

Under the impression of these public political clashes, Catholic missions sought to present a more united and cooperative position on colonial rule and administration, on education and coerced labour. Father Amandus Acker CSSp (1847–1923),[13] head of the German branch of the French Holy Ghost Fathers and also head of the Conference of Superiors that assembled Catholic mission leaders and coordinated political interventions of missions, published a summary on the missionaries' cultural work in the German colonies in 1909. Acker put his emphasis on the obligation of a colonial power 'to address the important question of how to treat and to educate the natives adequately'.[14] If colonialism failed to bring 'higher culture', 'ethical principles' and 'modern technology', it would amount to 'nothing more than exploitation'.[15] The colonized were 'human beings in relation to their creator', a fact that made introducing 'Christian civilization' in the colonies paramount, as part of the missions quest to lead the allegedly sinful heathen back to God and to a life combining a strong will, ethical values, and the holy sacraments of the Catholic Church. All this would automatically work to the benefit of the colonizing nation.[16] Acker presented a bleak picture of African life, including violent oppression by slave raiders, cruel indigenous subordination, ethical deviance (humans sacrificed in cults, polygamy, abuse of women, warfare and violence), but emphasized the ability of Africans to basic though tyrannical social formation and the rudiments of religion. These religious and social structures had, according to Acker, allowed the 'blacks' to sustain themselves and to procreate. Were colonialism to simply destroy these structures without replacement – by putting exploitation, mere technical education, and political subordination before a Christian civilizing mission – the consequences would 'wipe the natives from the face of the earth'. 'Even fetishism' was to be preferred to 'the literary scepticism, materialism, naturalism of the rising nations', because 'religion is the cement, without which any house will fall'.[17] Commerce and colonial administration were passing on 'appearances' without 'instilling conscience, responsibility and ... Christian civilization and true progress among the colonized'. Missionaries were the ones who approached the colonized at grass-roots level, in day-to-day encounters, and gave a living 'model of the European'.[18] Only 'Christian religion' would in the long run 'penetrate the soul', 'sentence the secret and hidden vices and oblige to inner virtues'.[19] In another political piece, Acker argued that the colonial state was merely to provide the material infrastructure, while mission would facilitate changes in hearts, minds and souls.[20]

Much of this presentation of African lives and religion reminds of nineteenth-century theological racism.[21] Acker's account of colonialism is a ranting critique of liberal and modern values. And although Protestants are not mentioned directly, his insistence on the sound ethical fundament of Catholicism, the holy sacraments and the church marks the difference. Acker's views on the nature of colonialism and the penetration of the soul of the colonized exhibit to the point Catholic (Jesuit) ideas of the clerical guidance of the lay soul, so brilliantly interpreted by Michel Foucault as the nucleus of modern discipline.[22] In the end, Catholic missions claimed a key role in the process of colonization, not only to the betterment of the colonized, but also by advocating the cause of the 'native' and thereby maintaining the perfunctory civil and humanitarian character of the colonial enterprise.[23] Acker denounced the decadence of the colonized, but also warned against the destructive force of liberal, materialist colonialism and the superficial effect of a merely secular civilizing mission. His claim was epitomized in the syntactic unity of 'true, i.e. Christian, civilization', as a combination of ethical values, orthodox faith and Catholic Church ritual.[24]

But then, Acker was a veteran of the European culture wars and the early days of Catholic mission in East Africa. He had gone to Zanzibar in 1875, where he had worked as a missionary until 1893. Arriving in Germany, he began to re-erect the German province of the Holy Ghost Fathers that had been closed down during the culture war.[25] His focus lay on Central Africa and the colonial debate on the exploitation of resources, plantation economy and African labour.

The Benedictine archabbot Norbert Weber OSB (1870–1956) belonged to a younger generation who had neither lived through the culture wars nor the early years of ruinous mission efforts in East and Central Africa.[26] In his writings on colonial policy and mission strategy he employed a wider, really global lens that stretched from the direct colonialism in Africa to East Asia and the question of Germany's ability to compete with Britain, France and the United States on the field of 'soft power', to attract the emerging Asian nations to Germany's culture and to render them receptive to economic and political efforts.[27] The two main mission fields of Weber's Benedictine congregation at the time lay in the German colony of East Africa and in Korea.

Much like Amandus Acker, Weber interpreted the European civilizing mission as a Christian project, and missions as its key actors, 'the life-giving ingredient of progress'.[28] For him, British and American initiatives in health, education and development were Protestant mission activities that intended both cultural and religious conversion. In Weber's opinion, Germany, with her high level of technological and scientific development and her allegedly strong ethical values, was to take on the 'burden' of elevating the world's people by passing on 'European culture'.[29]

Weber's argument connected Christian mission, German cultural power and commercial expansion closely – much closer indeed than Acker had done, who still juxtaposed the worldly and the divine as antagonistic principles, the latter checking and balancing the former. While Weber saw a cultural conflict with Buddhism and Confucianism, his main argument rested not on theology, ritual or the church, but on the higher education work of missions. He underlined that British and American global success had depended more on hard power than on cultural attraction – for example, the English language: 'From Port Said or Aden … to the ministries in Korea and Japan, the English language enhances England's esteem, and upon this esteem cultural influence and economic success depend … The language alone, spread by schools and universities, is overpowering propaganda … and missions are always marching in the vanguard'.[30] Weber's appeal was aimed at Germany's industrial elite, urging them to fund missions on a grand scale, much as American and English entrepreneurs did. He actively conflated the worldly and the divine to a degree that must have been difficult to digest within Catholic mission circles, and, indeed, it was criticized in his own organization at the time.[31] Nevertheless, he provided a sharp analysis of international politics to a national audience that in its reasoning largely adhered to categories of military strength, *Geo-* and *Realpolitik*.[32]

Germany's African colonies featured second in Weber's programme. Similar to Acker, he emphasized the ethical value of missions in the field. Religious conversion, however, is hardly mentioned, and mission work is presented as an appeal to the mind rather than the soul of the colonized population: 'The force of the mind – which drives the physical resistance [of the colonized] – will in the long run only be overpowered by the powers of the mind [of the colonizer]. If there is a peaceful way to secure the possession of the colonies, then it is the holy awareness of gratitude to the bearer of culture and of the civil duties, both instilled by religion'.[33]

Protestants in Germany had not been in the focus of the culture wars during the nation building of the Bismarck era to the same extent as their Catholic counterparts. Nonetheless, the Protestant mission movement on the whole took a careful stance towards Germany's colonialism.[34] One year after the Berlin Congo Conference of 1884, Protestant German mission leaders held an extraordinary conference in Bremen in order to discuss their position towards the German colonial project and the weight of secular, civilizing activities in contrast to spreading the gospel.[35] Well aware that the German public counted them among imperial actors, they needed to define a position that was in accordance with their conservative and pietistic worldview and took the changed political situation into account. After heated debates concerning questions like 'What do we need to do, so that German colonial politics will not harm but support mission?', resolutions were passed defining the Protestant position: German missions should pursue their mission work in other colonies, just as non-German mission societies continued their work in German colonies. Only if there were areas in German colonies where no Protestant mission was working should German mission societies become active.[36] Because of the international character of mission work, neither mission nor politics should interfere in the affairs of the other.[37] Although German missionaries could never neglect being German, they could not work as agents of the colonial power but should instead focus on the needs of the indigenous people. Hence, their civilizing and educational work should be considered as only a 'side effect'.[38] The older and more conservative representatives of protestant mission organizations asserted their critical position, and rejected, for example, Friedrich Fabri's plans for a mission that primarily worked for colonial aims.

Although their position did not change profoundly during the German Empire, a pragmatic approach was taken over the years. In 1890, when the German mission leaders met in Halle to discuss their position towards colonial affairs again, no other than Gustav Warneck, the leading missiologist, invited the governmental representative in order to enhance the relationship with the colonial administration.[39] Warneck published several articles and books on the relationship of colonialism, civilization and mission. As early as 1879 he analysed the 'mutual relationship between modern mission and culture', referring directly to the culture wars that he saw in straight connection with this question.[40] Culture, he argued, consisted of material, intellectual and ethical aspects. Mission fostered all of them, especially ethical aspects, which were undeniably a consequence of religiosity or rather Christianity: 'Culture most effectively prospered under the rule of Christianity'.[41] By this, he defined culture as a part, or rather as an outcome, of Christianity and claimed appreciation of missions' work in the colonial field.

In later years, Warneck geared those general arguments on civilization and civilizing mission towards colonialism. Again, he did not deny the civilizing mission (*Kulturaufgabe*) that was fulfilled by missions, but subordinated it to the religious aim. Cultural work in all its ethical, intellectual and material aspects was done only for the need of indigenous people, but not for colonial power.[42] In this, Warneck and the other Protestants did not much differ from the Catholic position that also interpreted civilization and culture as an outcome of Christianity.

Although the civilizing mission with its focus on health, education and work ethics was in this argumentation only a side aspect, it legitimized a mission's claims for appreciation. Carl Paul, pastor in Lorenzkirch and later director of Leipzig mission, like many others pointed to the importance of the missionaries' work for scientific enterprises; mission stations were 'cultural oases'[43] because of the missionaries' medical work and the different schools for general education and professional training. Thereby, the mission reconciled 'the subjected with their new mistress Germania'.[44] In reward, Paul claimed, the German colonial administration should be Christianized. Colonial officials, for example, were supposed to live in a Christian and moral way, the missionaries' decisions, especially that indigenous people were primarily to be taught in their mother tongue, were to be respected, and above all the rights of indigenous people should not be infringed on.[45]

Carl Mirbt, professor of church history and missiology in Göttingen, followed a similar path in his piece 'Mission and Colonial Politics', published 1910. Mirbt analysed different domains in which mission and colonial politics were deeply intertwined. The education of the indigenous people served the two main goals of colonial politics – the economic exploitation and the cultural enhancement – and constituted the relationship between politics and mission.[46] Although they might differ about goals and methods of their work,[47] both provided key services for each other. If they worked together – which was deeply wished for – it had to be clear that they were different entities, following their own approach and goals.[48] Therefore mutual understanding and respect was necessary,[49] especially because the aspects that were regarded as most important by colonial authorities – for example, the education for work – might only be a method for missionaries to inspire moral energy and stimulate working through character building.[50]

The majority of the older Protestant mission movement took, as these examples show, a critical stance on colonialism and fiercely questioned its secular, or 'merely' cultural and materialist fashion. They did not wish to give up the international character of mission, and nor did they regard themselves as agents of colonialism. On the contrary, they adhered to their religious task as they underlined that they worked as advocates for the indigenous communities, and demanded for a Christian colonial government and law. Nevertheless, they did not hesitate to benefit from colonial enthusiasm in order to finance their work. Colonial congresses and expositions were seen as possibilities to broaden the missionary movement that was frowned upon in liberal and bourgeois circles. Together with other mission societies, the Leipzig missionary society, for example, organized the first colonial mission days in Dresden in 1911. Such an event was considered a good opportunity 'to draw public attention to mission' and gain new supporters.[51] In his opening speech of the first colonial mission days, Prof. D. Ludwig Ihmels, member of the mission board, argued in a similar way to Warneck and Mirbt, but expressed in the same breath his wish that colonial and mission supporters converge, because they 'were under obligation to both the colonies and the gospel'.[52] As the older mission societies took this pragmatic approach towards colonialism, there were, of course, other Protestant societies that clearly underlined their national obligation, propagating a direct collaboration. This is especially true for the German Mission for East Africa (Berlin III), founded 1886. The society, which was deeply connected to Carl Peters, argued for a national and colonial approach to mission work rather than emphasizing religious or humanitarian goals ranking culture higher than religion. The well-established societies, as well as their leading figure Gustav Warneck, openly discountenanced this.[53]

As this comparison underlines, missions of both denominations, Catholics and Protestants, often took a tactical approach to colonial politics and policies. While subscribing to colonial ideologies (European cultural supremacy, civilizing mission, and economic exploitation to a certain degree), they remained wary of the (colonial) state's hegemony in areas where the secular and the religious overlapped, such as education, health care, and church discipline. In their political statements, both denominations demanded that the colonial state embrace the Christian character of European civilization, and castigated an alleged modern materialism present in the colonial movement. In a way, the colonial state and colonial civilizing programmes were seen as synonymous to the secular sphere as such by missionary activists in the metropole. Against this perception, these activists envisioned an explicitly Christian colonial state whose primary aim was building Christian civilizations, and not 'merely' civilizations in a secular sense.

Theologizing Mission: Debates on the Essence of Conversion

To this day, comparative denominational approaches in mission history are rare, but nonetheless called for. The religious divide that characterized the German cultural and political landscape during the long nineteenth-century, and shaped the respective theologies, extended to the colonies. This added considerable complexity to the negotiation of Christian fundamentals, since European missionaries not only looked to their constituencies in the mission fields and home countries, but also to their competitors. This was the case especially in a colony like German East Africa. The colony came under the jurisdiction of the Berlin Treaty of 1884, which granted unrestricted access to missions. Members of several denominations did Christian mission work in East Africa, where Islam spread as well.

After the early endeavour of the Tranquebar mission during the eighteenth century, German Protestant mission came, with the exception of the Moravians, to a halt until about the 1850s. By then, the missionary endeavour had become popular once more in German pietistic and neo-confessionalist conservative circles. As a consequence, new mission societies emerged.[54] Those societies did not stand directly under ecclesiastical control but worked as free associations. Two decades later, questions as to how far an accommodation of faith could be tolerated, how key terms and concepts of Christianity should be translated, and how missionary methods should be applied, were heatedly debated in practice and theory among the leaders of these societies. The debate engendered theological and theoretical publications on mission, propagating its importance in the theological discipline and often demanding a special subdiscipline, missiology.[55] Important questions of mission practice and theology were debated at university level, in mission literature, and at conferences all over Germany.[56]

Although Protestant mission societies differed in their theological orientation, common ground was sought regarding a basic understanding of conversion, of the character of baptisms in the mission field, and of the essential requirements for candidates to receive this sacrament. These standards show what was seen as the essence of Christianity in the mission field. Much like in the Catholic case, as will be demonstrated, the debate about the fundamentals was at the same time a debate about the boundaries of the religious and the secular. The latter was treated as a cultural addendum that could positively underpin Christianity, but was also negotiable to a certain extent. Moving the boundaries between the secular and the religious was a clandestine way of making fundamentals the object of negotiating.

Again, it was one of the continental mission conferences that laid the ground for a Protestant position. When Protestant mission leaders and theologians met 1893 in Bremen they fervently discussed to whom, when and on the basis of which beliefs and knowledge baptism could be granted. Franz Michael Zahn's input paper and the ensuing discussion illustrate how the importance of baptism and the standards of Christianity were consolidated, while spaces for negotiation and adaption were opened simultaneously. The Bremen mission inspector's report was based on two main assumptions. First, Zahn stated that a heathen who after sermon declared his willingness to become a Christian should be baptized. Secondly, God, as founder of baptism, wanted those baptized who knowingly wished to be guided by Jesus Christ to come out of sinful life into the community of the triune God and into the community of brothers. Nevertheless, he also remarked, 'one should not forget that the candidate of baptism could only be a beginner'.[57]

In the contemporary understanding, conversion was mainly defined by the intention of willingly and knowingly leaving sinful life and heathendom, and becoming a Christian.[58] Everyone was – in theory – to be granted baptism just because of his longing in accordance with the then presumed Apostles' practice. The restrictions 'willingly' and 'knowingly' indeed were intended to ensure that baptism was not granted 'too early'. Missionaries were given the official power to decide who was baptized and, thereby, to safeguard their outstanding position in missionary communities.

Problems arose when missionaries and in the aftermath mission leaders had to deal with local rites and customs that seemed improper for Christians. Abandoning polygamy was declared essential, while other rituals and lifestyles should be carefully examined whether they were truly incompatible with Christianity or merely a secular 'folk custom'.[59] If the latter, they might be declared *adiaphora* – issues that, affecting the conversion neither positively nor negatively, should stand outside ecclesiastical influence. Hence, this doctrine allowed shifts of the boundaries between the religious and the secular without questioning a theologically based and comprehensive interpretation of Christianity itself.

To make sure that baptism was not granted too early, all aspects of Christianity were to be taught during a preparation period, the catechumenate, which also aimed at testing the candidates' willingness and preparedness for baptism. To evangelize meant, as Zahn stated, to teach the history of salvation. Bible stories were seen as the key to soteriology.[60] In addition, the Lutheran catechism, along with the most common prayers and hymns, was also seen as essential Christian knowledge. In the end, missionaries in the field decided whether a candidate knew enough to be baptized. Nevertheless, a focus was laid on inner conversion and piety, and that is why it was frequently pointed out that belief and consistent action were more important than knowledge learnt by heart.

Mission theologians oscillated between theological fundamentalism adhering to their pious self-conception and the need not to preclude baptisms in the mission field. As a consequence, the latter's quality became a point of contention. Focusing on the question of whether baptism implied the permission to attend the Lord's Supper, contemporaries' (lack of) appreciation of so-called 'heathen Christians' becomes obvious.[61]

Zahn stated in his report on baptism in 1893 that baptized adults were in general to be admitted to the sacrament, although there might be reasons why the day of baptism and the day of first communion were not identical. Zahn justified this by the emotional quality of baptism. Most of the participants of the conference agreed on the principle that baptized adults should be allowed to attend the sacrament. However, most of them also affirmed that, as practical experiences had allegedly shown, baptized 'heathen Christians' were not mature enough to attend the Lord's Supper due to their 'unsteady character'.[62] Von Schwartz, director of Leipzig mission, additionally referred to the fact that even in the Apostle's case there had been three years between baptism and the Lord's Supper.[63] At the same time, he underlined the dogmatic weight of the sacrament in Lutheran thought. The fact that the question of maturity was discussed at all, points to the fact that, for one, mission theologians never considered newly baptized Christians as equals; secondly, it underlines that, despite of all these efforts and preconditions, European mission leaders were not sure whether those 'heathen Christians' had truly converted.

Most of the discussants, however, were at the same time mission inspectors or directors. Their positions on baptism and related issues were highly influenced by the urgency of the mission project and confessional conflicts with Catholicism – Catholic missions were always accused of baptizing too early and without thorough tuition – and sometimes even more importantly with other Protestant theological positions which did not regard Christianity as absolute.[64] Because they refused to see Christianity subjected to historical development, like for example Ernst Troeltsch did, it was crucial for these mission theologians to preserve the purity of the Christian message. They ascertained their own piety and orthodoxy while at the same time opening – due to the necessities in the mission field – a space for negotiation and accommodation in their discussions, especially in cases of ritual practices defined as secular. This underlines the impact of the missionaries' boundary work in the mission fields, even in the Protestant case, where mission societies were strictly organized hierarchically, and steered by mission directors and boards in Europe.

Catholic missiology was established in the German-speaking countries comparatively late. Joseph Schmidlin, a key figure in the movement, who in 1910 occupied the first Catholic chair for missiology in Münster, followed Warneck's example closely, but accentuated the dogmatic differences of the confessions.[65] Schmidlin's definition of the aims of mission work is an example of this. Not only would Catholic mission be aiming at individual conversion and local community building, but it would also focus on extending the Roman Catholic Church and its hierarchy to non-Christian areas.[66] Concerning the central questions of conversion, baptism and the catechumenate, missiological knowledge was closely tied to the early church history and the church fathers, but also to the canonical texts issued by the Congregatio Propaganda Fide, the governing body of missions at the Holy See, and the prescriptions of mission superiors. Charles de Lavigerie's (Bishop of Algiers and founder of the White

Fathers) instructions laid out in letters and memoires, for instance, were particularly influential for Catholic missions in Africa. Lavigerie intended to renew the practice of intensive and extended teaching – prescribing at least four years of preparation and several stages of development (*postulantes, catechumenii, electi*) towards baptism – after the alleged example of early Christianity.[67] Jean Joseph Hirth (White Fathers), bishop to the Central African Vicariate Nyanza, elaborated on Lavigerie's provisions and issued a detailed regulation on the catechumenate and baptism, which set standards for other missions in Central and East Africa.[68]

As Schmidlin observed in 1923, the *Propaganda Fide*'s regulations on the catechumenate were 'rather sparse' and left the details to the Apostolic Vicars in the mission fields.[69] As will be demonstrated below, Catholic missions in Africa practised various versions of the catechumenate and with time sought to ensure regional coherence in the respective conferences of bishops. The Catholic hierarchy granted ample jurisdiction to the local missions, which were headed by bishops or apostolic vicars responsible only to the Holy See. Relevant decisions on church and parish matters were made not by the mission societies in the home countries, but in the mission field, and they varied from vicariate to vicariate.[70] After 1900, conferences of bishops – for example, in the German colonies of Cameroon (1906) and German East Africa (1912) – agreed on a framework and criteria for the catechumenate.[71] One may speculate that the tightening of regulations was inspired by the spirit of discipline characteristic for the colonial environment of these particular missions, and also by Protestant debates on the relative laxness of Catholic proselytizing.[72]

Debates among missiologists and mission leaders focused on the length of the preparatory period, on the theological depth and precision of the teachings, and on the general character of the process, with positions varying from a period of probation including cultural, church and family matters to merely teaching a somehow adapted catechism.

When most of the German missionaries were forced to return home during and after the First World War, the Conference of Mission Superiors seized the opportunity to gather experience and find common approaches to cultural and pastoral questions in the various mission fields. More than a hundred missionaries from seventeen mission organizations assembled in Düsseldorf in October 1919 for a workshop.[73] They discussed matters that touched the critical intersections of practical mission work and theology, such as the 'mission sermon', 'catechism and ethical education', 'the vernacular in church and school', 'admission to baptism', 'superstition', the 'tendency to reify faith before and after baptism', 'marriage among non-Christian peoples', 'chastity in the tropics', 'health care', 'preserving indigenous customs' and 'ethnography, sociology and phonetics'. This event may well be regarded as an attempt to summarize the experiences German Catholic missionaries had collected over the preceding decades in the mission fields all over the globe on the difficulties of the practice of evangelization, pastoral work and cultural adaption. One of the more controversial issues discussed was the question of when a candidate should be eligible for baptism, since it led right into the missionary dilemma of preserving the fundamentals while adapting to the expectations of converts. In his input paper, Franziskus Hennemann PSM (Priests of St Mary of Tinchebray), apostolic vicar of Cameroon, sketched the problem as to when a candidate was sufficiently prepared to receive baptism, and as to which ethical and moral standards would be prerequisite.[74] Quite typically the background for the debate was the anxiety that converts would relapse, water down or corrupt the message, and discredit the Christian civilizing mission, while an overly prohibitive attitude would foreclose conversions in the first place.[75] Hennemann emphasized the particular 'burden' of African missions whose supposed task was not only to change religious convictions, but alter lifestyles and moral standards, and to supervise not only the catechumenate but closely 'monitor' the new parishes with the help of teachers, catechists and Catholic elders.[76] While he discussed different ways and durations of the catechumenate, it was the historical example he gave to illustrate the problem that proved contentious. Hennemann referred back to the year 1879 when the White Father Siméon Lourdel denied baptism to King Mtesa of Buganda, who would not refrain from polygamy. While Lourdel had presented his decision as a matter of dogmatic principle, Cardinal Lavigerie, the head of the mission congregation, later criticized this. He contemplated the missed opportunity and presented Mtesa's polygamy as a problem to be overcome by time and pastoral work:

> I do lament that Father Lourdel did not make the King a catechumen, when he asked to be baptized! How big a misapprehension to think that a man like Mtesa would do without his flock of women and the other heathen prerogatives of an African potentate! I always thought it would have been of much better service to the mission if we had let him promise to make efforts with respect to the Christian ethic and to gradually refrain from his heathen ways and opinions, and to promise in turn holy baptism at a later date, and surely in the hour of death.[77]

While Hennemann preferred Lourdel's clear-cut views to Lavigerie's pastoral compromise, others were not so sure. Robert Streit OMI (Oblates of Mary Immaculate) asked whether 'heathens had sufficient understanding and means to work for their salvation' in the first place? This would have to be determined on the spot by experienced missionaries, who would 'know best, if and how the heathen conceived of God, of sin, and of repentance'.[78] And Meinulf Küsters OSB (Missionary Benedictines of St Ottilien) even put forward that the 'Old Testament allowed polygamy; therefore it was part of natural law'.[79] While the discussants would not embrace polygamy as legitimate practice without consequence for baptism, it was clear that the catechumenate provided missions with some leeway to manoeuvre the boundaries of the cultural, the pastoral and the dogmatic in a practical way.

Another hotly debated issue was the aims and the theological finesse of the catechumenate. Were missionaries to explain and define what a 'sacrament' was, or were they to teach by way of narrative, allegory and imagery? While some advocated a pragmatic approach, underlining practical translations into the social realities of the catechumen, even preferring the use of pictures and illustrations instead of catechetical texts and definitions, others held that theological soundness was paramount in the face of Protestant competition.[80]

Quite similar to Protestant missiology, Catholic mission theology acknowledged the dilemma of preserving 'sound' dogmatic positions in the face of practical challenges in the mission fields and expectations of potential converts. In contrast to Protestant missions, however, theoretical debates in the colonial metropole had to bow to the jurisdiction of the bishops in the field and the *Propaganda Fide* in Rome, whose rulings left ample space for the bishops' jurisdiction. Accordingly, Catholic missiology rather tried to elaborate on missionary methods than finding normative solutions to pastoral and dogmatic problems. Both Catholic and Protestant mission protagonists had in common that they separated the spheres of the religious and the secular inasmuch as they tried to define what was essential to Christianity, and where spaces for negotiation lay. Moreover, neither Catholic nor Protestant theologians questioned that the power of defining what made up the religious fundamentals of Christianity lay first and foremost with European experts, and least of all with new Christians in other parts of the world. Catholic and Protestant mission experts in the metropole performed most of the boundary work by ascertaining this power of defining the fundamentals, and a self-understanding of being keepers of the uncompromised message in the face of cultural change. In the field, sacrament and theological fundamentals also were paramount, albeit as a point of everyday negotiation. This will be discussed in the following section.

Doing Mission: Baptism and Conversion in the Contact Zone

In 1893, missionaries of the Leipzig mission society had settled in the north of the German colony East Africa in the Kilimanjaro region, which was inhabited by an ethnic group known by Europeans and Swahili traders as Chagga.[81] By 1913, ten years after the foundation of the first Lutheran mission station on Mount Kilimanjaro, fourteen stations had been established. More than four thousand new Lutheran Christians had been baptized by the German missionaries.[82]

Looking at the mission fields explains why metropolitan experts were struggling to delineate the fundamentals and the boundaries of the religious and the secular. In the day-to-day encounters with possible and actual converts, missionaries in the field developed their own standards of baptism even though they constantly referred to missiological debates and findings in the metropole. Because of the importance of baptism and conversion, these issues are well suited to illustrate the boundary work of missionaries in the field.

The missionaries saw achieving conversion as their main goal. Baptisms were announced in letters to the Mission Board[83] who shared these latest reports of success with a wider Lutheran public.[84] To avoid disappointment not only for themselves and the whole missionary public, but also for already existing parishioners, missionaries generally held high expectations for their candidates. Therefore, the sacrament stood at the end of a process in which future Christians were not only taught the main contents of Christian belief but were also closely monitored in order to find out whether their way of life was in accordance with what missionaries regarded as Christian principles. In this, they directly referred to the missiologists' debate. For example, they developed a catalogue of essentials of Christianity that was quite similar to and probably influenced by Zahn's ideas. The catalogue included mainly Bible stories of the New Testament focusing on the work and death of Jesus Christ, and some Lutheran prayers and hymns alongside the main aspects of the Lutheran catechism.[85] Thereby, Leipzig missionaries defined the religious or rather the Christian in a Lutheran way, projecting the European confessional divide right into the colony.

Already baptized Chagga who worked as catechists or teachers were not allowed to baptize under any circumstances. Indeed, until the 1930s Chagga Christians were not allowed to become pastors. Even though the process of becoming a Christian and the ritual itself was largely dominated by male European missionaries, conversion and baptism still became objects of constant negotiation in the mission field. This was especially true for those cases in which the boundaries between the secular and the religious were challenged by local rites and customs. When the missionaries learnt that the Chagga practised circumcision and polygamy,[86] the question of whether these practices were compatible with baptism arose. Even though both practices were regarded as sinful, unethical and, as a consequence, incompatible with Christianity in the metropole, this was not so clear in the mission field.

As Leipzig missionaries in the first years mainly taught young men in mission schools, the question of whether circumcision was a reason for not being granted baptism had to be answered, even before the first baptism was performed. The Chagga practised circumcision of girls and boys, but only the latter was heatedly debated in the missionaries' circle. Boys were circumcised in groups, and at the same time initiated in adult life.[87] At first, Leipzig missionaries did not regard circumcision as a problem as their pupils had not told them about any ritual practices in connection with circumcision that were regarded as incompatible with Christianity.[88] Missionary Raum, one of the eldest missionaries in Moshi, practised circumcision even on the mission station.[89] A few years after the missionaries' arrival, they had gained more information on the issue. Missionary Ovir, for example, wrote a detailed report to the mission director, remarking that 'circumcision was not merely a civilian custom but a heathen ritual'.[90] Missionary Müller, founder of the first mission station, held that in Chagga culture circumcision was, in theory, not demanded by spirits;

in practice, however, circumcision was deeply connected with sacrifices, dances and 'uncontrollable immoralities'.[91] Despite these evaluations, circumcision never became a reason to deny baptism. On the contrary, the essence of circumcision – not the practice – was declared a secular 'cultural rite' (*Volkssitte*) that did not clash with the promise to renounce the 'devil's service' and 'sinful life' that the candidates of baptism had to give in order to be accepted.[92] This declaration was, firstly, underlined by the assumption that circumcision as practised in the Kilimanjaro region could never be compared with the Jewish and Christian symbol of the purification of the heart. This meaning should therefore never be mentioned.[93] Secondly, this decision was – although often questioned by missionaries having other experiences – seen as legitimate for practical reasons: missionaries feared baptizing 'unworthy' candidates less than the risk of candidates turning away from Christianity if they were not allowed to be circumcised. Thirdly, the decision with all its implications was not only the missionaries': the mission director and the society's board had decided to treat the circumcision of boys in Chagga culture as an *adiaphoron*.

In the case of polygamy, the dilemma was similar. Monogamous, lifelong marriage was seen as a central feature of Christianity. Nevertheless, the question of whether it was legitimate to baptize 'polygamists' or not was at least debated in the Lutheran Chagga mission. In 1903, Missionary Althaus, who chaired the mission council, provided regulations for the catechumenate, in which he treated the matter. On the one hand, he took for granted that polygamists would somehow be included in the catechumenate but not baptized, as he regarded polygamy as a 'basic trait of heathendom'. On the other hand, his position had become ambivalent. He stated that the candidate of baptism might be drawn into 'moral conflict' as he had to abandon wives and children. Therefore, he regarded baptism for polygamists as possible, even though, he qualified, 'polygamists would not have the qualification for parish council'.[94] Actually, the mission director agreed with Althaus that polygamy was not an official reason for denying baptism, because the candidate was morally obliged to his wives and children, and marriage constituted a moral bond.[95] Missionaries, on the other hand, could not be forced into baptizing polygamists, and in the end all of them, it seems, refused to do so.[96] Altogether, the missionaries were not able to come to a principle agreement on the matter, but deferred the issue again and again. As they had agreed not to baptize until a definite decision had been taken, polygamists were not baptized but were welcome to attend services and school lessons.[97] This was especially true for chiefs, who in general had numerous wives. Baptism of polygamists, in practice, became the decision of the individual missionary – it was neither allowed nor forbidden. But if a polygamist had been baptized, the ritual would have been performed secretly because: 'Catholics and other mission societies would point a finger at us if a missionary was known to baptize a polygamist'.[98]

These examples show how even strict boundaries were probed and sound dogmas softened when challenged in the mission field. Practical experiences and expectations of the Chagga led to modifications and adjustments that were afterwards justified by moral considerations, by anthropological learning and by theological argumentation. If adaptions were not popular in Germany, they were conducted secretly. But – and this was part of the strict organization of Protestant mission societies – the mission board was kept informed on the decisions in the mission field.[99] Because of their theological outlook, emphasizing the authority of the Bible and Lutheran principles, the mission board was sometimes even more liberal than the missionaries in the field.

Despite missionaries' efforts to control, Chagga highly influenced mission strategy, the preaching of the gospel and as a consequence the missions' understanding of what was fundamental to Christian faith and what was to be regarded as secular tradition. Motivations for becoming a Christian in the mission field ranged from material, economic or social advantages to spiritual longing.[100] An important factor for Chagga to maintain a close relationship with the missionaries was the possibility to learn European cultural techniques such as writing and reading, which became more and more useful in colonial economy and administration. For that reason, Leipzig missionaries had to alter their mission strategy and increasingly focused on schooling.[101] In fact, schooling soon became their main missionary method as they established a variety of different school forms. In 1906, Kiswahili, the most commonly used language in the colony, became a subject in higher classes, and in 1912 even a language of instruction in the seminary for teachers and catechists. By this, supposedly secular contents were integrated into the religious sphere, making the boundary work even more complex.

As the Leipzig mission was wary of converts and so-called 'heathen Christians' administering sacraments, the work of Chagga interpreters and catechists was vitally important for missionaries' success. In order to follow Luther's example to preach the gospel in local languages, the missionaries had to learn Chagga dialects before even starting their missionary efforts.[102] Language brokers and interpreters played a crucial part in translating the message and transferring Chagga dialects into a written language. In addition, advanced learners were used as teachings assistants. In 1913, 152 assistants (*Gehilfen*) worked as catechists and teachers, teaching mainly Bible stories and language skills.[103] The missionaries were not able to monitor the teachings of those assistants, although they tried very hard in order to secure their definitions of Christianity. For example, assistants and teachers were kept under strict surveillance regarding their moral conduct and their adherence to Christian belief. Nevertheless, these teachers and catechists became the first who strove for an independent church, challenging the boundary work the missionaries had carried out before.

The second case of this section focuses on the Missionary Benedictines of St Ottilien. Established in 1884, the Benedictines arrived in East Africa in 1887 and were assigned the Apostolic Vicariate of South Zanzibar. After failing on the mainland coast near Dar es Salaam, they established themselves in an area that extends over Tanzania's southern highlands and southern coastal zone from the mid-1890s. The mission field was reduced to today's Njombe, Ruvuma, Mtwara and Lindi regions after 1919. By 1915 the mission had twenty-four stations, with a European staff of 97 male and female missionaries and 657 African teacher-catechists (lay missionaries) addressing a Catholic population of just over eighteen thousand.[104]

The number and quality of converts was the single most important marker of success in any mission.[105] The first baptism of a mission station, for instance, was celebrated and remembered as a kind of symbolic initiation.[106] Nevertheless, baptism was also a prime object of negotiation in the process of conversion. As a consequence, baptism in the Catholic missions in the southern part of today's Tanzania, much as elsewhere in the world, followed not one but a variety of courses depending on the changing historical contexts and immediate circumstances. Generally speaking, however, one may distinguish 'extraordinary' or 'emergency' from 'ordinary' baptisms. The former would be administered ad hoc, with a minimum of ritual by priests, African lay missionaries and female missionaries to willing – and in some cases unwilling or unwitting – converts in lethal danger or in the hour of death. However, missionaries were also prepared to fast-track procedures for sultans, chiefs and other dignitaries.[107] Ordinary baptisms followed a period of preparation, probation and examination – the catechumenate – which would take several years and was performed by priests, and it involved the full range of Roman Catholic ritual with certain features added for the African context (e.g. candidates would receive medals showing the Virgin Mary, which were to be worn as a sign of their applicant status). Ordained European priests, sister and brothers, and also African lay missionaries, saw baptism as the litmus test to their missionary ability. Looking back at more than three decades as a Catholic mission teacher-catechist, Pauli Holola recalled his earliest mission post at the court of Chabruma Tawete, a notorious Ngoni king/*nkosi*. Pauli Holola's involvement in baptisms was a focal point in his recollections. In the six years before his mission at Chabruma's was put to an abrupt end by the outbreak of the Maji Maji war in 1905, Holola had not only taught seventy pupils, but baptized forty-seven children and eleven adults. He had hardly been more than fifteen years of age when he arrived at Chabruma's court, and had converted only a few years earlier.[108] African catechists routinely functioned in lieu of priests in times of crisis, at the early stages of a new mission area – catechists being the ones who spearheaded into a territory and prepared the ground, and if their place was too far out of the way to be seen to regularly by an ordained priest. Similarly, female European missionary staff performed baptisms routinely in emergency cases. Since the Catholic Sisters often worked in the health sector, in hospitals, dispensaries, and leprosy settlements, emergency baptisms were frequent. Baptizing one's first 'heathen' became almost a formal initiation ritual for the newly arrived, and an opportunity for the sisters to appropriate missionary functions and practices.[109]

The number of such extraordinary and emergency baptisms increased during the hunger crisis in the aftermath of the Maji Maji war. The most prominent examples were the forty-eight Ngoni leaders hanged by German troops at Songea in February 1906, thirty-one of whom received baptism by a Benedictine father before being murdered.[110] As a consequence, Bishop Thomas Spreiter sought clarification of the procedure in a pastoral letter explicitly directed to priests, sisters and brothers, as well as African catechists. He laid out the minimum provisions given by church law, and the rulings of the Congregatio Propaganda Fide: adult converts had to believe in (1) God as the retributor of good and evil, (2) salvation through God, (3) Christ's incarnation, and (4) the Holy Trinity. While the first point marked the difference to Lutheran ideas on divine grace, the Holy Church as a marker of distinction was strangely absent in the list. Children should be baptized without causing offence, in particular to their parents. The bishop warned his missionaries against violating parental or 'tribal' feelings, and suggested secrecy, so as not to give competitors the opportunity to blame baptism for the death of a child. Should a child survive a possibly lethal illness, the mission had to ensure a Christian upbringing by all means. Spreiter, however, exhorted his missionaries to act *ad personam* and not simply attempt mass baptisms in times of hunger and high infant mortality.[111] In the face of about two hundred emergency baptisms in the Benedictine mission field in 1909 alone, Spreiter renewed his appeal in 1910, explicitly encouraging medical missionary staff to 'heal the wounded souls' without turning hospitals and dispensaries into 'some kind of factory for conversions'.[112]

The gradual intensification in the regulation of extraordinary baptisms was complemented by the development of the catechumenate as a period of instruction and probation for prospective juvenile and adult converts. The catechumenate was hardly a fixed and universal institution in the early twentieth century, but was put together as missions settled and grew. The Catholic missions in East Africa reached an agreement in 1912 on the minimum length of the catechumenate – two years for schoolchildren, three years for adults.[113] While the White Fathers in Central Africa adhered to their four-year catechumenate and demanded three successful examinations of their prospective converts, the Benedictines considered three years and one examination sufficient preparation.[114]

Having discussed how missionaries used emergency baptisms and the catechumenate as instruments to negotiate the boundaries of the secular and the spiritual by explicitly avoiding the dogmatic question of whether converts had knowingly and truly subscribed to the fundamentals of Catholic faith, a change of perspective is called for. How had the African counterparts of mission, prospective converts, and political and spiritual leaders perceived the missions' efforts? The first Christians of the 1890s were mainly former slaves bailed out by the mission. These – mostly young – converts lived at the mission stations, were taught the catechism and provided cheap physical labour for the maintenance and expansion of the mission.[115] In many cases these Christians remained apart from the surrounding population, were even considered 'slaves of the wafranza' ('the French', as Catholic missionaries were termed in Kiswahili at the time).¹¹⁶ Only gradually did missions also gather sizeable groups of pupils from among the villagers living in the vicinity of the stations, most of whom were also enlisted for the catechumenate. Early on in the process of Christianization, African leaders in the Benedictine mission field will have realized that missions not merely offered a new form of education, but aimed at spiritual-cum-cultural conversion. The motivations of those leaders who invited and supported missionary settlement, as well as the backgrounds of those parents who sent children to mission schools and allowed baptism, are largely unknown. Ngoni leaders, such as King Mputa Gama of Njelu or King Chabruma Tawete of Mshope – both of whom were later engaged in the Maji Maji war against German colonialism – seem to have valued educational skills without giving way to spiritual or cultural conversion attempts. They, however, did not stop those among the Ngoni who were willing to receive baptism; that receiving baptism was seen as a holistic (spiritual-cultural) conversion in the way missionaries aspired is unlikely. When Father Francis Leuthner, head of the Peramiho mission station, destroyed the ancestral shrine at Mputa's residence in 1903, thereby challenging the authority and spiritual leadership of the *nkosi* (king), the flow of pupils all but dried up. Chabruma and Mputa among others turned against the mission during the Maji Maji war in 1905/6, destroyed the stations and had Fr. Francis, killed.¹¹⁷

The Ngoni case demonstrates that conversion epitomized in baptism was a process that thrived when the related cultural translation was vague, unspecific, and open for interpretation, when the boundaries of the religious and the secular were actively negotiable rather than dogmatically fixed. On the other hand, the conversion process was halted when moral and spiritual anxiety regarding the faithfulness of candidates got the better of European missionaries. This may be demonstrated by a second specific cultural and spiritual conflict, at the Ndanda mission in the south-east of the colony. It came to a virtual standstill after the Benedictines learnt the details of the initiation procedures of the surrounding Mwera, Makua, Yao and Makonde people in 1908 – *unyago*. The fathers judged these rituals as being deeply immoral violations of the sixth commandment and afflicted by the workings of Satan. Rather than acknowledging the holistic social and cultural character of initiation, the fathers focused on the aspects of male circumcision and female genital modification and cutting, as well as sex education for youths and young adults which was regarded not only as immoral, but as sinful and as an entry point for the work of the devil. As a consequence of violent suppression, many non-Christians kept their distance from the mission, and Christian converts resorted to secrecy to reconcile fundamental principles of their sociocultural environment and the religious community they had recently joined. For the mission, the consequences were dire, since the flock of willing converts all but dried up until the late 1930s, when suppressive policies were called off and a form of Christian *unyago* became possible under the guidance of venerable African mission activists.¹¹⁸

Ancestral cults, initiation rites, traditional forms of healing ('witch doctors'), and (extra-) marital relations deviating from Catholic orthodoxy's understanding of marriage at the turn of the twentieth century – trial marriage, polygamy, separation, bridewealth, various contraceptive forms of sexual intercourse, contraceptive procedures – were major points of conflict. While missionaries feared and complained about the immorality of converts who adhered to or relapsed into allegedly heathen practices, or led supposedly defunct marriages, these problems were to be solved by pastoral care or oblivion, by penitence, by threatening loss of material support and jobs, or by exclusion from the Eucharist. Designating a problem to the cultural or the pastoral sphere rather than the dogmatic, meant that boundaries of the religious and the secular could be manoeuvred and African Christianity could evolve without, however, being underpinned by changes to the dogma.

Polygamy, however, marked a very serious barrier for conversion and a real stumbling block for missions, inasmuch as it prevented affluent and powerful leaders from entering the Church. Non-Christian marriages, even of polygamous character, were accepted as an expression of natural law. Church law, however, provided a clause for the mission context, the Pauline Privilege, which allowed marriage vows to be annulled if a partner was willing to convert to Catholicism. In practice, long-married polygamous believers would be referred to baptism 'at the eleventh hour'.[119]

For the Benedictine mission in Southern Tanzania, African teacher-catechists stood in the centre of attention and anxiety. These activists performed extraordinary baptisms, executed the teaching of the candidates and were regarded as model converts, the lapsing of whom was dreaded by mission superiors. They held the key to success with respect to the mission's prime goal. Looking briefly at the 'language of conversion', the catechists' role as cultural and spiritual brokers becomes transparent. The Benedictine mission field extended over a large territory, with dozens of ethnic groups and an equal number of languages. Although the colonial government and the colonial office in Berlin tried to push German in education programmes, it never became relevant in practice. Kiswahili was established as the language of administration in government and church. The vast majority of East Africans – with the exception of the coastal area – spoke local and regional languages. Even Kiswahili-speaking Europeans, therefore, largely relied on interpreters. Teaching materials and catechisms used in preparation for baptism were written in Kiswahili in most cases, translated from European models in collaboration with African mission teachers.[120] The actual instruction, therefore, depended on the language skills, on the didactic zeal, and on the cultural literacy of the African catechists in charge who translated the Kiswahili catechism into the spoken language of the respective schooling area. According to a reporting missionary in 1912, the teacher Cassian of Manda-Ngawi, a village on the eastern shore of Lake Nyasa/Malawi, for instance, gave regular religious lessons to 166 adults (126 of them women). His self-assured teaching style was the key to success: 'First, religious education.

Teacher Cassian teaches the catechism very nicely. He addresses the question even to the older students. Most give apt answers, even though the sacrament lessons are not really easy. ... The understanding of the truths is induced by the practical explanations, which Cassian knows how to provide'.[121] Much as in the Protestant case, teachers were liminal figures – key to the success of a mission, but a constant threat to the defining powers European missionaries. The framing of teachers' agency in European missionary media is telling in this respect. Far from being represented as self-reliant missionary actors, they were objectified as instances of missionary success. A great many of them were criticized, even denigrated for a supposed lack of stability in faith and lifestyle in the mission's internal correspondence. In 1911 the Bishop decided to intensify the training of catechists, and issued stricter regulations, for example about their marital status.[122]

If there was a corresponding emotion among European missionaries to the 'anxiety' of the colonizer described by Ranajit Guha,[123] it was connected to baptism and the process of conversion it stood for. Comparing the two missions' baptizing practices highlights contradictory trends in both cases. On the one hand, the urge to baptize – fuelled by the expectations of the mission supporters in Europe and the aspirations of African and European mission personnel – afforded adaption to the cultural-cum-spiritual environment of the mission field. On the other hand, European missionaries' anxiety to avoid relapsing of converts and compromising religious *and* civil norms would often arrest adaption and cross-cultural negotiation of conversion. The failure to endorse circumcision by the Lutheran Chagga mission, and the moral panic of the Benedictines encountering the initiation process of the Mwera, the Makua and the Makonde, are cases in point. The confessional divide, transferred to the mission fields, also produced contradictory effects. For one, the competition seems to have provided leverage to potential African converts and leaders, and underpinned the role of African missionary actors. In the Benedictine case, many African lay missionaries regularly conducted baptisms in emergency cases. Nevertheless, the respective missions shied away from public endorsement of African norms, cultural traditions, and African Christian initiatives, for fear of being castigated about the watering down of Christian civilizing mission just as theological doctrine. However, the institute of the catechumenate, in combination with baptism 'at the eleventh hour', emergency baptisms, and the secret acquiescence and referral to the cultural or pastoral sphere of practices that were publicly denounced, provided the common ground for a certain degree of leeway for the negotiation of fundamentals.

Hopes and anxieties of missionaries were fuelled by theological and political debate, just as much as the encounter in the mission field. Missions were heard in the metropolitan colonial discourse, because they were able to establish themselves as the voice of practical experience in 'civilizing' the colonized populations, by providing an ample number of concrete cases from the colonies and by setting themselves off from other colonial actors. African agency in the 'ifs, whens and hows' of baptism – be it by potential and actual converts or by teachers and catechists – was, however, narrated as assisting, as passive, and sometimes negatively as a lack of moral stability and theological training. This form of boundary work complemented the metropolitan discourse on the preservation of the fundamentals, and fed back into the delineation of the divide of the religious and the cultural.

Conclusion

This chapter has taken a comparative multilevel approach to analysing the boundaries of the religious and the secular in Imperial Germany. The boundary work of Catholic and Protestant missions during Germany's colonial period was twofold. For one, both missions actively reworked the boundaries of the religious and the secular by demanding a civilizing effort of colonialism that was based on Christian faith, perhaps best captured in the historico-political term 'Christian civilization'. Secondly, this chapter has employed the lens of entangled history by looking closely at missions' boundary work in the mission field. The two case studies of Catholic and Protestant missions in the German colony East Africa, which focused on the key missionary practice of baptism, have underlined the ambiguity of missionary activity in the colonies. Mission practice was confronted with conflicting expectations from home constituencies and possible converts. Missionaries had to comply with theological standards often set in the metropole and were influenced by their own personal cultural backgrounds and inhibitions. This was a common experience for both denominations, even though pastoral and ecclesiastical jurisdiction in the Catholic case lay with the mission leaders in the field, who had the powers of bishops and were subordinated directly to the Holy See, while Protestant missions were supervised by their home missionary boards.

In addition, much like in the metropolitan discourse on 'Christian civilization', the common ground was tinged by the deep theological and cultural rift of (neo-)confessionalism. The contradictory and diverging expectations as well as the political and theological formations resulted in deep-rooted ambiguities in missionary practice. Conversion, epitomized in baptism, was redefined partly as a civilizing practice. Catholic and Protestant missions were eager to ensure that conversion to Christianity was also seen as a change of lifestyle. In practice, however, conversion remained negotiable. Emergency baptisms, loose affiliations of catechumen, baptisms 'at the eleventh hour', and secret condoning of 'heathen' rituals were instruments for keeping up appearances and securing the success of mission work. The catechumenate in particular became an ambiguous practice – in the theoretical reading, a period of formation and change; in the practical, an instrument to negotiate the meaning of conversion. The ambiguity had two effects; on the one hand, Eurocentric and imperial definitions of conversion prevented the public acknowledgement that Christianity was slowly becoming African, and that African actors – first and foremost African catechists – were incremental to this process. Whether in metropolitan discourse or in practical mission work, non-Europeans were subjected to cultural othering on a massive scale, and a 'Christian civilizing mission' in the period of German colonialism never treated African Christians as equals, but as 'heathen Christians'; nor did it intend the full-scale emancipation of non-European individuals, societies or churches. On the other hand, ambiguity, denominational competition, and the quest for converts provided the inroads for non-European missionary actors and concepts. Baptisms turned out to be key cultural and religious turning points for individuals and for the colonial endeavour as a whole, inasmuch as it represented the success or failure of the civilizing mission.

As this study has shown, a considerable amount of cultural translation was necessary to turn the complexities of cultural and religious conversion in the everyday encounter into self-assured well-crafted contributions to metropolitan discourses. A symmetrical approach integrating the political, theological and practical layers of mission highlights a stark contrast: missionaries presented a confident and self-assured position in the debate about the means and ends of colonialism, namely the claim that European supremacy rested first and foremost on a common Christian civilizing mission; equally confident, they claimed authority over the definition of the theological fundamentals of Christian faith. Strangely disconnected from this message are the anxieties, the self-consciousness, and the ambiguities relating to the highly volatile and improvised (spiritual and cultural) conversion procedures in the mission field. The continuous feedback loops that entangled and irritated colonial metropole and periphery produced both the powerful missionary interventions in the colonial discourse that claimed legitimacy by citing experience in the practice of a 'Christian civilizing mission', and the profound anxieties as well as the theological uncertainties, which ensued from the continuous negotiation of fundamentals.

What do the findings laid out here add to our understanding of German colonialism in a more general way? First of all, understanding colonialism means paying attention to a share of different religious actors – many of them conservative Protestants and Catholics – and to the ways those actors negotiated colonial and metropolitan relations. They put forward alternative interpretations of the means and ends of colonialism as well as the key trajectories of the history of modern civilization. We realize that the civilizing mission and European cultural supremacy – key concepts of modern imperialism – were much more embattled and a lot less secular than is currently acknowledged in historical research. We do not pretend that missionary actors achieved a complete change of the colonial discourse; but they established a platform for alternative positions highlighting idealist aims beyond material and exploitative strategies of contemporary liberalism – a platform that did not exist before due to the lines of conflict during the culture war, which effectively rendered these religious voices outsiders to the political discourse of the Kaiserreich. As key actors in the colonial field who epitomized the partly Christian character of colonialism, missionaries introduced once again the religious to a seemingly secular political arena, redefining the boundaries of the religious and the secular.

Richard Hölzl is a lecturer and researcher at the University of Göttingen, Germany. Previously, he held positions at Erfurt University, Kassel University and The New School in New York. His research interests include the history of forests, of environmentalism, and of colonialism and Christian missions. He has authored a book on scientific forestry in Germany (*Umkämpfte Wälder*, Campus, 2010), and co-edited collections on the global history of missions (*Mission Global*, Böhlau, 2013) and European forestry (*Managing Northern Europe's Forests*, Berghahn Books, 2018). Currently, he is preparing a book on the history of Catholic missions in Germany and East Africa, 1830s to 1940s.

Karolin Wetjen studied history, Latin, and education at Göttingen University, where she also worked as a lecturer and researcher. Since 2013, she has been working on her PhD thesis 'Mission and Modernity: Christianity Making and Negotiations of Religion at the End of the Nineteenth Century', under the supervision of Prof. Dr Rebekka Habermas. Karolin Wetjen co-edited (with Linda Ratschiller) a volume on new approaches in mission history (*Verflochtene Mission: Perspektiven auf eine neue Missionsgeschichte*, Böhlau, 2018). Her research interests include the history of cultural entanglements with regards to religion, knowledge, power and gender.

Notes

1. E. Said, *Orientalism* (New York: Vintage Books, 1979), 3.
2. On the German impact on orientalism, see R. Loimeier, 'Edward Said und der deutschsprachige Orientalismus. Eine kritische Würdigung', *Stichproben: Wiener Zeitschrift für kritische Afrikastudien* 1(2) (2001); S. Friedrichsmeyer et al. (eds), *The Imperialist Imagination, German Colonialism and Its Legacy* (Ann Arbor: University of Michigan Press, 1998); S.L. Marchand, *German Orientalism in the Age of Empire: Religion, Race, and Scholarship* (Washington, DC: Cambridge University Press, 2009).
3. Said, *Orientalism*, 120–21. See, however, on missionary inputs to cultural othering, V.Y. Mudimbe, *Invention of Africa: Gnosis, Philosophy, and the Order of Knowledge* (Bloomington: Indiana University Press, 1988).
4. To name but a view works on the general character of German colonialism: J. Osterhammel, *Europe, the 'West', and the Civilizing Mission* (London: German Historical Institute, 2006); S. Zantop, *Colonial Fantasies: Conquest, Family, and Nation in Precolonial Germany, 1770–1870* (Durham, NC: Duke University Press, 1997); B. Kundrus (ed.), *Phantasiereiche: Zur Kulturgeschichte des deutschen Kolonialismus* (Frankfurt/Main: Campus, 2003); B. Kundrus, *Moderne Imperialisten: Das Kaiserreich im Spiegel seiner Kolonien* (Cologne: Böhlau, 2003); S. Conrad and J. Osterhammel

(eds), *Das Kaiserreich transnational: Deutschland in der Welt 1871–1914* (Göttingen: Vandenhoeck & Ruprecht, 2004); G. Steinmetz, *The Devil's Handwriting: Precoloniality and the German Colonial State in Quingdao, Samoa, and Southwest Africa* (Chicago: University of Chicago Press, 2007); U. Lindner, *Koloniale Begegnungen: Deutschland und Großbritannien als Imperialmächte in Afrika 1880–1914* (Frankfurt/Main: Campus, 2011).

5. R. Hölzl, 'Imperiale Kommunikationsarbeit: Zur medialen Rahmung von Mission im 19. und 20. Jahrhundert', *Medien und Zeit: Kommunikation in Vergangenheit und Gegenwart* 31(2) (2016).

6. M. Borutta, 'Genealogie der Säkularisierungstheorie: Zur Historisierung einer großen Erzählung der Moderne', *Geschichte und Gesellschaft* 36 (2010); R. Hölzl, 'Aus der Zeit gefallen? Katholische Mission zwischen Modernitätsanspruch und Zivilisierungskritik', in C. Bultmann, J. Rüpke and S. Schmolinisky (eds), *Religionen in Nachbarschaft: Pluralismus als Markenzeichen europäischer Religionsgeschichte* (Münster: Aschendorff, 2012).

7. See on the European culture wars: M. Borutta, *Antikatholizismus Deutschland und Italien im Zeitalter der europäischen Kulturkämpfe* (Göttingen: Vandenhoeck & Ruprecht, 2011); M.B. Gross, *The War against Catholicism Liberalism and the Anti-Catholic Imagination in Nineteenth-Century Germany* (Ann Arbor: University of Michigan Press, 2005); C. Clark, *Culture Wars: Secular–Catholic Conflict in Nineteenth-Century Europe* (Cambridge: Cambridge University Press, 2004).

8. B. Plongeron, 'Affirmation et transformation d'une "civilization chrétienne" à la fin du XVIIIe siècle', in J.-R. Derre et al. (eds), *Civilisation chrétienne: approche historique d'une idéologie XVIIIe-XXe siècle* (Paris: Beauchesne, 1975), 10; see also, all in ibid., J. Gadille, 'Le concept de civilisation chretienne dans la pensée romantique', and X. de Montclos, 'Lavigerie, le christianisme et la civilization', and J. Prévotat, 'Remarques sur la notion de civilisation catholiques dans la Revue "L'action française" (juillet 1899 – mars 1908)'; also, S. Weichlein, 'Mission und Ultramontanismus im frühen 19. Jahrhundert', in G. Fleckenstein and J. Schmiedl (eds), *Ultramontanismus: Tendenzen der Forschung* (Paderborn: Bonifatius, 2005). In a different vein, debates about the differences of West European civilization and German culture had ensued by the end of the Kaiserreich – see, J. Fisch, 'Zivilisation, Kultur', in O. Brunner, W. Conze and R. Koselleck (eds), *Geschichtliche Grundbegriffe: Historisches Lexikon zur politisch-sozialen Sprache in Deutschland* (Stuttgart: Klett-Cotta, 1992), Vol. 7.

9. See, e.g., F. Becker, *Becoming Muslim in Mainland Tanzania, 1890–2000* (Oxford: Oxford University Press, 2008); and T.O. Ranger and I.N. Kimambo (eds), *The Historical Study of African Religion* (Berkeley: University of California Press, 1972).

10. A.L. Stoler and F. Cooper, 'Between Metropole and Colony: Rethinking a Research Agenda', in idem (eds), *Tensions of Empire: Colonial Culture in a Bourgeois World* (Berkeley: University of California Press, 2001).

11. Hölzl, 'Aus der Zeit gefallen?', 143–64.

12. See R. Habermas, *Skandal in Togo: Ein Kapitel deutscher Kolonialherrschaft* (Frankfurt/Main: Campus, 2016); see also the quite different political setting of the Rechenberg scandal, when an allegedly mission- and native-friendly governor had to step down over a homosexual scandal. See H.I. Schmidt, 'Colonial Intimacy: The Rechenberg Scandal and Homosexuality in German East Africa', *Journal of the History of Sexuality* 17(1) (2008).

13. L. Dohmen CSSp, 'Acker, Amandus', in *Neue Deutsche Biographie*, Vol. 1 (1953). Retrieved 29 June 2017 from https://www.deutsche-biographie.de/sfz117.html#ndbcontent.
14. A. Acker, 'Die Aufgabe der katholischen Mission in den Kolonien', *Jahrbuch über die deutschen Kolonien* 2 (1909), 119. All translations in this chapter are by Richard Hölzl and Karolin Wetjen.
15. Ibid., 124.
16. Ibid., 119, see also 124. H. Heines MSC, 'Erziehung eines Naturvolkes durch das Mutterland', in *Verhandlungen des deutschen Kolonialkongresses zu Berlin am 5., 6. und 7. Oktober 1905* (Berlin: Reimer, 1906), 452, discusses Germany's challenges as a 'Christian cultural power'.
17. Acker, 'Die Aufgabe', 133.
18. Ibid., 129.
19. Ibid., 130.
20. See A. Acker CSSp, 'Die Erziehung des Negers zur Arbeit', *Jahrbuch über die deutschen Kolonien* 1 (1908), 124. See more detailed and nuanced F. Schwager SVD, 'Die Bedeutung der Arbeitserziehung für die Hebung der primitiven Rassen', *Zeitschrift für Missionswissenschaft* 4 (1914). Schwager argued against biological racism and coerced labour, but in favour of educational efforts to achieve social differentiation and class societies.
21. R. Hölzl, 'Rassismus, Ethnogenese und Kultur: "Afrikaner" im Blickwinkel der deutschen katholischen Mission im 19. und frühen 20. Jahrhundert', *WerkstattGeschichte* 60 (2012).
22. M. Foucault, *Religion and Culture*, ed. by J.R. Carette (Manchester: Manchester University Press, 1999); idem, *Security, Territory, Population: Lectures at the Collège de France 1977–78* (Houndmills/Basingstoke: Palgrave Macmillan 2007), here: 15 February 1978.
23. See F. Schwager SVD, 'Katholische Missionstätigkeit und nationale Propaganda', *Zeitschrift für Missionswissenschaft* 6 (1916), 126.
24. The distinction of 'true' and 'false/superficial' civilization was characteristic for missionary interventions in the colonial discourse. See also Heines, 'Erziehung', 450.
25. F.W. Bautz, 'Acker, Amandus', in *Biographisch-Bibliographisches Kirchenlexikon*, 2nd edn, Vol. 1 (Hamm: Bautz, 1990), col. 19.
26. Also, the missionary Benedictines had underlined the German character of the mission from its foundation in 1884, indeed, had received the direct assistance of Bismarck and the State Department in retrieving the East African mission field from the Vatican. See C. Schäfer OSB, *Stella Maris: Größe und Grenzen des ersten Erzabtes von St. Ottilien P. Norbert Weber OSB 1870–1956* (St Ottilien: Eos, 2005).
27. N. Weber OSB, 'Am Scheideweg: Nationalpolitische Bedeutung der Mission', *Das Hochland* 8(2) (1910).
28. Ibid., 16.
29. Ibid., 11.
30. Ibid., 19.
31. Schäfer, *Stella Maris*, 104.
32. See N. Weber OSB, 'Der Krieg und die Mission', *Zeitschrift für Missionswissenschaft* 5 (1915), 1.

33. Weber, 'Am Scheideweg', 23. See also N. Weber OSB, 'Ziele und Wege der Eingeborenen Erziehung', in *Verhandlungen des deutschen Kolonialkongresses, zu Berlin am 5., 6. und 7. Oktober 1905* (Berlin: Reimer, 1906).
34. Still, there were marked exceptions, like the Rhenish mission inspector Friedrich Fabri, who had strongly advocated a German colonial empire since 1859. See K.J. Bade, *Friedrich Fabri und der Imperialismus in der Bismarckzeit: Revolution, Depression, Expansion* (Freiburg i.B.: Atlantis, 1975).
35. M. Hamilton, *Mission im kolonialen Umfeld* (Göttingen: Universitätsverlag, 2009), 56. Nine German Protestant missionary societies had sent their deputies: Basel, Barmen, Berlin I and II, Brekklum, Bremen, Herrnhut, Hermannsburg and Leipzig. Additionally, some other important partakers of the missionary movement attended the conference, which was chaired by Friedrich Fabri. Fabri was the former director of the Rheinische Missionsgesellschaft, and well known for his colonial enthusiasm. See G. Warneck, 'Eine bedeutsame Missionskonferenz', *Allgemeine Missionszeitschrift* 12 (1885), 544–45.
36. Ibid., 553–54.
37. Ibid., 557.
38. Ibid., 557–58.
39. For this he was criticized by several colleagues, especially by Bremen missionary inspector Zahn, who was also a member of the committee that had been working as a negotiation partner for the colonial administration since 1885. See W. Ustorf, *Die Missionsmethode Franz Michael Zahns und der Aufbau kirchlicher Strukturen in Westafrika. Eine missionsgeschichtliche Untersuchung* (Erlangen: Verlag der Evangelisch-Lutherischen Mission, 1989), 64–65; Hamilton, *Mission im kolonialen Umfeld*, 61; Warneck, 'Eine bedeutsame Missionskonferenz', 563.
40. G. Warneck, *Die gegenseitigen Beziehungen zwischen der modernen Mission und Cultur: Auch eine Culturkampfstudie* (Gütersloh: Bertelsmann, 1879).
41. Ibid., 9.
42. G. Warneck, *Evangelische Missionslehre. Ein missionstheoretischer Versuch. Dritte Abteilung: Der Betrieb der Sendung. Erste Hälfte* (Gotha: Perthes, 1897), 180.
43. C. Paul, 'Die Leistungen der Mission für die Kolonien und ihre Gegenforderungen an die Kolonialpolitik', *Evangelisch-lutherisches Missionsblatt* 57 (1902), 498.
44. Ibid., 500.
45. Ibid., 519–20. See also K. von Schwartz, *Mission und Kolonisation in ihrem gegenseitigem Verhältnis* (Leipzig: Verlag der Evangelisch-Lutherischen Mission, 1908), 19–27. Von Schwartz pointed to the fact that the colonial regiment needed the mission to teach the indigenous people the moral value of work. In response, the colonial authorities had to respect the rights of the Christianized people. Nevertheless, von Schwartz as well as other leading Protestants never questioned the legitimacy of colonialism itself. See, e.g., C. Mirbt, *Mission und Kolonialpolitik in den deutschen Schutzgebieten* (Tübingen: Mohr, 1910), 235.
46. Mirbt, *Mission*, 229–37, 237.
47. Ibid., 239.
48. Ibid., 251.
49. Ibid., 253.
50. Ibid., 251–54.
51. Kolonialmissionstage. Letter from mission director to Herrnhuter mission society, 4 Dec. 1910, ALMW II.32.277.

52. L. Ihmels, *Wir sind Schuldner beides unsern Kolonien und dem Evangelium: Predigt über Röm. 1, 14.15 zur Eröffnung der Kolonialmissionstage in Dresden am 25. Juni 1911* (Leipzig: Verlag der Evang.-luth. Mission, 1911).
53. See J. Bückendorf, *'Schwarz-weiß-rot über Ostafrika!' Deutsche Kolonialpläne und afrikanische Realität* (Münster: Lit, 1997), 320.
54. See T. Altena, *'Ein Häuflein Christen Mitten in der Heidenwelt des dunklen Erdteils': Zum Selbst- und Fremdverständnis protestantischer Missionare im kolonialen Afrika 1884–1918* (Münster: Waxmann, 2003), 19.
55. For a short overview of the pioneers of the discipline, see H.-J. Findeis, 'Missionswissenschaft', in K. Müller and T. Sundermeier (eds), *Lexikon Missionstheologischer Grundbegriffe* (Berlin: Reimer, 1987). Apart from Gustav Warneck, Karl Graul is often named as father of the discipline. He defined the discipline in his inauguration speech in Erlangen but died soon afterwards. K. Graul, *Über Stellung und Bedeutung der christlichen Missionen im Ganzen der Universitätswissenschaften* (Erlangen: Deichert, 1864).
56. See T. Yates, 'Mission Conferences', in J. Bonk (ed.), *Encyclopedia of Missions and Missionaries* (New York: Routledge, 2007).
57. *Protokoll über die Verhandlungen der neunten Kontinentalen Missionskonferenz zu Bremen am 9., 10. und 12. Mai 1893* (Gütersloh: Bertelsmann, 1893), 22–23, theses 3 and 10. Similarly, Warneck, *Der Betrieb der Sendung. Erste Hälfte*, 214.
58. See Warneck, *Der Betrieb der Sendung. Erste Hälfte*, 209.
59. See J. Triebel, 'Polygamie als Taufhindernis: 100 Jahre Auseinandersetzung dargestellt am Beispiel Südwest-Tanzanias', in J. Ngeiyama and J. Triebel (eds), *Gemeinsam auf eigenen Wegen. Ev.-Luth. Kirche Tanzanias nach hundert Jahren* (Erlangen: Verlag der Evangelisch-Lutherischen Mission, 1994); J. Warneck, 'Evangelisieren oder Christianisieren', *Allgemeine Missionszeitschrift* 40 (1913), 435.
60. See *Protokoll*, 67.
61. See ibid., 23 and 79–80. The positions of different missionary societies were also reported in M. Nathuslus, 'Die Konfirmationspraxis in der Mission', *Allgemeine Missionszeitschrift* 29 (1902).
62. *Verhandlungen der neunten Kontinentalen Missionskonferenz zu Bremen am 25., 26. und 28. Mai 1897* (Berlin: Martin Warneck, 1897), 7. On the conference Warneck held this opinion, but a few years later he changed his view and pleaded for a direct admission. See also G. Warneck, *Evangelische Missionslehre. Ein missionstheoretischer Versuch. Dritte Abteilung: Der Betrieb der Sendung. 3. Teil: Das Missionsziel* (Gotha: Perthes, 1903), 186.
63. See *Protokoll*, 30–31.
64. See, for an overview, U. Berner, 'Religionsgeschichte und Mission: Zur Kontroverse zwischen Ernst Troeltsch und Gustav Warneck', in V. Drehsen and W. Sparn (eds), *Vom Weltbildwandel zur Weltanschauungsanalyse: Krisenwahrnehmung und Krisenbewältigung um 1900* (Berlin: Akademie, 1996).
65. See, for a brief summary, Sievernich, *Die christliche Mission*, 143–45.
66. J. Schmidlin, *Einführung in die Missionswissenschaft* (Münster: Aschendorff, 1917), 15.
67. T. Ohm OSB, *Das Katechumenat in den Katholischen Missionen* (Münster: Aschendorffsche Verlagsbuchhandlung, 1959), 14.
68. See J. Schmidlin, 'Katechumenat', in *Lexikon für Theologie und Kirche*, Vol. 5 (Freiburg: Herder, 1933).

69. J. Schmidlin, *Katholische Missionslehre im Grundriss* (Münster: Aschendorff, 1919), 393–99. Some rulings, however, were unambiguous, e.g. the prohibition of polygamy. See J. Mausbach, 'Das sechste Gebot in der Missionsseelsorge', *Zeitschrift für Missionswissenschaft* 4 (1914), 195–96.
70. See the detailed provisions of the Vicariate Nyanza by Jean Joseph Hirth, as cited in Schmidlin, *Katholische Missionslehre*, 394–96.
71. Ibid., 394.
72. Spontaneous mass conversions were practised during the early Middle Ages and in the sixteenth and seventeenth centuries. See Schmidlin, 'Katechumenat'.
73. F. Schwager SVD (ed.), *Der Düsseldorfer Missionskursus für Missionare und Ordenspriester 7.–14. Oktober 1919: Vorträge, Aussprachen und Beschlüsse des Missionskursus* (Aachen: Xaverius, 1920).
74. F. Hennemann PSM, 'Anforderungen und Kriterien für die Zulassung zur Taufe', in ibid.
75. See R.M. Fontaine SDS, 'Wie ist der Kampf gegen den Aberglauben und die Neigung zur Materialisierung der Religion vor und nach der Taufe zu führen?', in ibid.; M. Küsters OSB, 'Der Aberglaube im Heidentum', in ibid.
76. Hennemann PSM, 'Anforderungen', 16–17.
77. 'Instructions de Son Eminence Le Card: Lavigerie à ses Missionaires', 313, as cited in Hennemann PSM, 'Anforderungen', 20.
78. 'Discussion on "Hennemann PSM, Anforderungen"', in Schwager, *Düsseldorfer Missionskursus*, 22–23.
79. Ibid., 23.
80. 'Discussion on "O. Schwab, Wie wird die Katechese ihrer Aufgabe als Pflanzschule lebendiger Religiosität und sittlichen Strebens gerecht?"', in Schwager, *Düsseldorfer Missionskursus*, 32–35.
81. For the name 'Chagga', see M.V. Bender, 'Being "Chagga": Natural Resources, Political Activism, and Identity on Kilimanjaro', *The Journal of African History* 54 (2013).
82. See N.-P. Moritzen, *Werkzeug Gottes in der Welt: Leipziger Mission 1836 – 1936 – 1986* (Erlangen: Verlag der Evangelisch-Lutherischen Mission, 1986), 35.
83. The *Missionskollegium* was the management commitee of Leipzig missionary society. For missionary societies as institutions, see H. Tyrell, 'Weltgesellschaft, Weltmission und religiöse Organisation', in A. Bogner, B. Holtwick and H. Tyrell (eds), *Weltmission und religiöse Organisationen* (Würzburg: Ergon, 2004).
84. Successfully performed baptisms were described at length in the *Evangelisches Missionsblatt*, the journal of the Leipzig missionary society. Additionally, statistics underlining the success of the mission were published annually.
85. G. Althaus, *Chagga Mission. Protokolle der Chaggakonferenzen IV. Protokoll der 18. Konferenz, Dezember 1903. Beilage Nr. 7: Katechumenatsordnung der Dschagga-Mission*, ALMW II.32.95.
86. The missionaries undertook anthropological studies of the Chagga in order to adjust their preaching to the local situation. See A. Nehring, 'Missionsstrategie und Forschungsdrang: Anmerkungen zu Mission und Wissenschaft in Südindien im 19. Jahrhundert', in H. Liebau, A. Nehring and B. Klosterberg (eds), *Mission und Forschung: Translokale Wissensproduktion zwischen Indien und Europa im 18. und 19. Jahrhundert* (Halle: Harrassowitz, 2010), 23. D. Livingstone, 'Scientific Inquiry and the Missionary Enterprise', in R. Finnegan (ed.), *Participating in the Knowledge Society: Researchers Beyond the University Wall* (Basingstoke: Palgrave Macmillan, 2005).

87. The Chagga initiation is described in S.F. Moore, 'The Secret of Man: A Fiction of Chagga Initation and its Relation to the Logic of Chagga Symbolism', *Journal of the International African Institute* 46(4) (1976); P. Hasu, *Desire and Death: History through Ritual Practice in Kilimanjaro* (Saarijärvi: Finnish Anthropological Society, 1999), 65–84 and 176–89; K. Wetjen, 'Der Körper des Täuflings: Konstruktionen von Körper und die Beschneidungsdebatte der Leipziger Missionsgesellschaft 1890–1914', in S. Weichlein and L. Ratschiller (eds), *Der schwarze Körper als Missionsgebiet: Mission, Ethnologie, Theologie in Afrika und Europa, 1880–1960* (Cologne: Böhlau, 2016).
88. Stationstagebuch Mamba I, 17 March 1896, ALMW II.32.129.
89. 'Die 18. Konferenz der Wadschagga-Missionare', *Evangelisch-lutherisches Missionsblatt* 59 (1904), 145.
90. Die Beschneidung bei den Wamadschame, ALMW II.32.71.
91. Letter from Emil Müller to the mission director, 16.6.1896, ALMW II.32.71. Dances were generally forbidden on mission stations for this reason. See R. Eves, 'Colonialism, Corporeality and Character: Methodist Missions and the Refashioning of Bodies in the Pacific', *History and Anthropology* 10(1) (1996).
92. Protokoll der Generalversammlung 1897. Thesen des Direktors zur Beschneidung, ALMW II.2.2.
93. As a matter of fact, New Year, the feast of the circumcision of Jesus Christ, was never celebrated as a religious festival in the Chagga mission. Chagga Mission. Protokolle der Chaggakonferenzen II. Protokoll der 14. Konferenz, Januar 1902. Beilage Nr. 4: Wann dürfen Christen zum hl. Abendmahl gehen, ALMW II.32.92, 6.
94. G. Althaus, Chagga Mission. Protokolle der Chaggakonferenzen IV. Protokoll der 18. Konferenz, Dezember 1903. Beilage Nr. 7: Katechumenatsordnung der Dschagga-Mission, ALMW II.32.95, 12.
95. This decision was taken at the Dresdener mission committee. The mission director was present when the missionaries discussed this matter at their conference in East Africa. Protokolle der Chaggakonferenzen IV. Protokoll der 18. Konferenz, Dezember 1903, ALMW II.32.95, 199–200.
96. Chagga Mission. Protokolle der Chaggakonferenzen IV. Protokoll der 18. Konferenz, Dezember 1903, ALMW II.32.95, 199–200.
97. In fact, the matter was completely removed from the order of the catechumenate, and became therefore an individual decision of the missionary in charge. See Ordnungen für Kirchen, Gemeinden, Missionare und Gehilfen, ALMW II.32.61.
98. Chagga Mission. Protokolle der Chaggakonferenzen IV. Protokoll der 18. Konferenz, Dezember 1903, ALMW II.32.95, 209.
99. T. Altena, '"Brüder" und "Väter im Herrn": Notizen zum inneren Machtgefüge protestantischer deutschsprachiger Missionsgesellschaften 1884–1918', in U. van der Heyden and H. Stoecker (eds), *Mission und Macht im Wandel politischer Orientierungen: Europäische Missionsgesellschaften in politischen Spannungsfeldern in Afrika und Asien zwischen 1800 und 1945* (Stuttgart: Steiner, 2005).
100. Moritzen, *Werkzeug*, 35.
101. See J. Eggert, *Missionsschule und sozialer Wandel in Ostafrika: Der Beitrag der evangelischen Missionsgesellschaften zur Entwicklung des Schulwesens in Tanganyika 1891–1939* (Bielefeld: Bertelsmann, 1970), 175.
102. Several 'dialects' were spoken at the Kilimanjaro mission. The missionaries tried to homogenize at least some of them into a language called KiChagga. This plan failed.
103. See Moritzen, *Werkzeug*, 35.

104. See Statistik der Benediktiner-Mission in Ostafrika 1897 bis Ende 1920, ArchOtt Z. 1. 30.
105. It also was the bench mark for the respect and support missions received from the home branches of their organization and from the public. See Bishop Spreiter, Concluding Report on the Visitation of the Apostolic Vicariate South Zanzibar, 25 March 1911, 7, ArchOtt Z. 1. 01.
106. See for instance the chronicle of the Kigonsera mission (17 May 1902). ArchOtt Z. 2.1. 30.
107. See, for instance, *Missionsblätter: Illustrierte Zeitschrift für das katholische Volk* 1 (1897), col. 254. Father Anton Ruedel reports the baptizing of Chief Rasso of Nanyungu, and his wife Regina; in *Missionsblätter* 8 (1903), 34, Father Francis Leuthner reports the baptizing of Chief Heinrich Mchota.
108. See, on Pauli Holola and mission teachers in general, R. Hölzl, 'Educating Missions: Catholic Teachers and Catechists in Southern Tanganyika, 1890–1940', *Itinerario: International Journal on the History of European Expansion and Global Interaction* 40(3) (2016).
109. See R. Hölzl, 'Lepra als *entangled disease*: Leidende afrikanische Körper in Medien und Praxis der katholischen Mission in Ostafrika, 1911–1945', in S. Weichlein and L. Ratschiller (eds), *Der schwarze Körper als Missionsgebiet: Mission, Ethnologie, Theologie in Afrika und Europa, 1880–1960* (Cologne: Böhlau, 2016).
110. L. Doerr, *Peramiho 1898–1998: In the Service of the Missionary Church*, Vol. I (Ndanda-Peramiho: Benedictine Publications, 1998), 48–49.
111. Spreiter, Pastoral Letter, Dec. 12, 1906, ArchOtt Z. 1. 01.
112. Spreiter, Pastoral Letter, Jan 15, 1910, ArchOtt Z. 1. 01.
113. Beschlüsse der ersten Konferenz der ostafrikanischen Bischöfe im Juli 1912, 9, ArchOtt Z. 1. 31.
114. See Bishop Spreiter, 'Concluding Report'.
115. See Doerr, *Peramiho 1898–1998*, 15.
116. See *Missionsblätter* 4 (1900), 75; and L. Doerr, 'Afrikaner und Missionar', in F. Renner (ed.), *Der fünfarmige Leuchter: Beiträge zum Werden und Wirken der Benediktinerkonkgregation von Sankt Ottilien. Vol. II: Klöster und Missionsfelder der Kongregation von St. Ottilien* (St Ottilien: Eos, 1971), 208.
117. See the detailed account in E. Ebner OSB, *The History of the Wangoni*, Reprint (Peramiho-Ndanda: Benedictine Publications, 2009), 131–33; Doerr, 'Afrikaner und Missionar', 215.
118. See Hölzl, 'Arrested Circulation: Catholic Missionaries, Anthropological Knowledge and the Politics of Cultural Difference in Imperial Germany, 1880–1914', in H. Fischer-Tiné and C. Whyte (eds), *Empires on the Verge of a Nervous Breakdown: Crisis, Anxiety and Panic in the Age of Imperialism, c. 1860–1960* (Basingstoke: Palgrave Macmillan, 2017).
119. See Bishop Spreiter, 'Concluding Report'.
120. A report to the colonial administration in 1939 reveals that 10 of 62 Benedictine Fathers of Peramiho Abbey, all of whom spoke Kiswahili, knew other local/regional languages (Kingoni, Kibena, Kimatengo, Kikisi). See Letter of Abbot Gallus Steiger, 10 May 1939. The Benedictines produced a Kiswahili catechism ('*Maurus-Katechismus*') in 1902 in collaboration with teacher-catechists based on a European model – in the Benedictine case, the catechism of Augsburg Diocese; in addition, a short biblical history (*Usimulio pungufu*, 1902) was produced. A journal, including regular addenda of catechetical instruction was started in 1910 ('*Rafiki yangu*'). See S. Hertlein, 'Die

Entwicklung katechetischer Literatur in der ostafrikanischen Benediktinermission 1888–1968', in F. Renner (ed.), *Der fünfarmige Leuchter: Beiträge zum Werden und Wirken der Benediktinerkonkgregation von Sankt Ottilien. Vol II: Klöster und Missionsfelder der Kongregation von St. Ottilien* (St Ottilien: Eos, 1971), 245–47. The Archive of St Ottilia Abbey (ArchOtt 'Lehrmittel Suaheli 1/2') contains a Kihehe-catechism (by Fr. Severin Hofbauer, 1903); a translation of the Kiswahili-catechism into Kibena (approx. 1930); and catechisms in Kisongwe and Kikulwe (both undated).

121. *Missionsblätter* 17 (1912/13), 48.
122. See Bishop Spreiter, 'Concluding Report'; and Hölzl, 'Educating Missions'.
123. R. Guha, 'Not at Home in Empire', *Critical Inquiry* 23(3) (1997).

Bibliography

Acker, A., CSSp. 'Die Erziehung des Negers zur Arbeit'. *Jahrbuch über die deutschen Kolonien* 1 (1908), 117–24.

———. 'Die Aufgabe der katholischen Mission in den Kolonien'. *Jahrbuch über die deutschen Kolonien* 2 (1909), 119–34.

Altena, T. *'Ein Häuflein Christen mitten in der Heidenwelt des dunklen Erdteils': Zum Selbst- und Fremdverständnis protestantischer Missionare im kolonialen Afrika 1884–1918*. Münster: Waxmann, 2003.

———. '"Brüder" und "Väter im Herrn": Notizen zum inneren Machtgefüge protestantischer deutschsprachiger Missionsgesellschaften 1884–1918', in U. van der Heyden and H. Stoecker (eds), *Mission und Macht im Wandel politischer Orientierungen: Europäische Missionsgesellschaften in politischen Spannungsfeldern in Afrika und Asien zwischen 1800 und 1945* (Stuttgart: Steiner, 2005), 51–70.

Bade, K.J. *Friedrich Fabri und der Imperialismus in der Bismarckzeit: Revolution, Depression, Expansion*. Freiburg i.B.: Atlantis, 1975.

Bautz, F.W. 'Acker, Amandus', in *Biographisch-Bibliographisches Kirchenlexikon*, Vol. 1 (Hamm: Bautz, 1990), 19.

Becker, F. *Becoming Muslim in Mainland Tanzania, 1890–2000*. Oxford: Oxford University Press, 2008.

Bender, M.V. 'Being "Chagga": Natural Resources, Political Activism, and Identity on Kilimanjaro'. *The Journal of African History* 54 (2013), 199–220.

Berner, U. 'Religionsgeschichte und Mission: Zur Kontroverse zwischen Ernst Troeltsch und Gustav Warneck', in V. Drehsen and W. Sparn (eds), *Vom Weltbildwandel zur Weltanschauungsanalyse: Krisenwahrnehmung und Krisenbewältigung um 1900* (Berlin: Akademie, 1996), 103–16.

Borutta, M. 'Genealogie der Säkularisierungstheorie: Zur Historisierung einer großen Erzählung der Moderne'. *Geschichte und Gesellschaft* 36 (2010), 347–76.

———. *Antikatholizismus Deutschland und Italien im Zeitalter der europäischen Kulturkämpfe*. Göttingen: Vandenhoeck & Ruprecht, 2011.

Bückendorf, J. *'Schwarz-weiß-rot über Ostafrika!' Deutsche Kolonialpläne und afrikanische Realität*. Münster: Lit, 1997.

Clark, C. *Culture Wars: Secular–Catholic Conflict in Nineteenth-Century Europe*. Cambridge: Cambridge University Press, 2004.

Conrad, S., and J. Osterhammel (eds). *Das Kaiserreich transnational: Deutschland in der Welt 1871–1914*. Göttingen: Vandenhoeck & Ruprecht, 2004.
De Montclos, J.X. 'Lavigerie, le christianisme et la civilization', in J.-R. Derre et al. (eds), *Civilisation chrétienne: approche historique d'une idéologie XVIIIe-XXe siècle* (Paris: Beauchesne, 1975), 309–48.
'Die 18. Konferenz der Wadschagg-Missionare'. *Evangelisch-lutherisches Missionsblatt* 59 (1904), 141–45.
Doerr, L., OSB. 'Afrikaner und Missionar', in F. Renner (ed.), *Der fünfarmige Leuchter: Beiträge zum Werden und Wirken der Benediktinerkonkgregation von Sankt Ottilien. Vol. II: Klöster und Missionsfelder der Kongregation von St. Ottilien* (St Ottilien: Eos, 1971), 200–20.
———. *Peramiho 1898–1998: In the Service of the Missionary Church*. Ndanda-Peramiho: Benedictine Publications, 1998.
Dohmen, L., CSSp. 'Acker, Amandus', in *Neue Deutsche Biographie*, Vol. 1 (1953), 34–35. Retrieved 28 June 2017 from https://www.deutsche-biographie.de/sfz117.html#ndbcontent.
Ebner, E., OSB. *The History of the Wangoni*. Reprint. Peramiho-Ndanda: Benedictine Publications, 2009.
Eggert, J. *Missionsschule und sozialer Wandel in Ostafrika: Der Beitrag der evangelischen Missionsgesellschaften zur Entwicklung des Schulwesens in Tanganyika 1891–1939*. Bielefeld: Bertelsmann, 1970.
Eves, R. 'Colonialism, Corporeality and Character: Methodist Missions and the Refashioning of Bodies in the Pacific'. *History and Anthropology* 10(1) (1996), 86–138.
Findeis, H.-J. 'Missionswissenschaft', in K. Müller and T. Sundermeier (eds), *Lexikon Missionstheologischer Grundbegriffe* (Berlin: Reimer, 1987), 323–27.
Fisch, J. 'Zivilisation, Kultur', in O. Brunner, W. Conze and R. Koselleck (eds), *Geschichtliche Grundbegriffe: Historisches Lexikon zur politisch-sozialen Sprache in Deutschland*, Vol. 7 (Stuttgart: Klett-Cotta, 1992), 679–774.
Fontaine, R.M., SDS. 'Wie ist der Kampf gegen den Aberglauben und die Neigung zur Materialisierung der Religion vor und nach der Taufe zu führen?', in F. Schwager SVD (ed.), *Der Düsseldorfer Missionskursus für Missionare und Ordenspriester 7.–14. Oktober 1919: Vorträge, Aussprachen und Beschlüsse des Missionskursus* (Aachen: Xaverius, 1920), 98–103.
Foucault, M. *Religion and Culture*, ed. by J.R. Carette. Manchester: Manchester University Press, 1999.
———. *Security, Territory, Population: Lectures at the Collège de France 1977–78*. Houndmills/Basingstoke: Palgrave Macmillan, 2007.
Friedrichsmeyer, S., et al. (eds). *The Imperialist Imagination: German Colonialism and Its Legacy*. Ann Arbor: University of Michigan Press, 1998.
Gadille, J. 'Le concept de civilisation chretienne dans la pensée romantique', in J.-R. Derre et al. (eds), *Civilisation chrétienne: approche historique d'une idéologie XVIIIe-XXe siècle* (Paris: Beauchesne, 1975), 183–209.
Graul, K. *Über Stellung und Bedeutung der christlichen Missionen im Ganzen der Universitätswissenschaften*. Erlangen: Deichert, 1864.
Gross, M.B. *The War against Catholicism: Liberalism and the Anti-Catholic Imagination in Nineteenth-Century Germany*. Ann Arbor: University of Michigan Press, 2005.
Guha, R. 'Not at Home in Empire'. *Critical Inquiry* 23(3) (1997), 482–93.

Habermas, R. *Skandal in Togo: Ein Kapitel deutscher Kolonialherrschaft*. Frankfurt/Main: Campus, 2016.

Hamilton, M. *Mission im kolonialen Umfeld*. Göttingen: Universitätsverlag, 2009.

Hasu, P. *Desire and Death: History through Ritual Practice in Kilimanjaro*. Saarijärvi: Finnish Anthropological Society, 1999.

Heines, H., MSC. 'Erziehung eines Naturvolkes durch das Mutterland', in *Verhandlungen des deutschen Kolonialkongresses zu Berlin am 5., 6. und 7. Oktober 1905* (Berlin: Reimer, 1906), 442–60.

Hennemann, F., PSM. 'Anforderungen und Kriterien für die Zulassung zur Taufe', in F. Schwager SVD (ed.), *Der Düsseldorfer Missionskursus für Missionare und Ordenspriester 7.–14. Oktober 1919: Vorträge, Aussprachen und Beschlüsse des Missionskursus* (Aachen: Xaverius, 1920), 13–23.

Hertlein, S., OSB. 'Die Entwicklung katechetischer Literatur in der ostafrikanischen Benediktinermission 1888–1968', in F. Renner (ed.), *Der fünfarmige Leuchter: Beiträge zum Werden und Wirken der Benediktinerkonkgregation von Sankt Ottilien. Vol II: Klöster und Missionsfelder der Kongregation von St. Ottilien* (St Ottilien: Eos, 1971), 245–47.

Hoch, M. *Die Taufbewerber in der indischen Mission, ihre Beweggründe und ihre Verhandlung*. Basel: Verlag der Missionsbuchhandlung, 1901.

Hölzl, R. 'Aus der Zeit gefallen? Katholische Mission zwischen Modernitätsanspruch und Zivilisationskritik', in C. Bultmann (ed.), *Religionen in Nachbarschaft: Pluralismus als Markenzeichen der Europäischen Religionsgeschichte* (Münster: Aschendorff, 2012), 143–64.

———. 'Rassismus, Ethnogenese und Kultur: "Afrikaner" im Blickwinkel der deutschen katholischen Mission im 19. und frühen 20. Jahrhundert'. *WerkstattGeschichte* 60 (2012), 7–34.

———. 'Educating Missions: Catholic Teachers and Catechists in Southern Tanganyika, 1890–1940'. *Itinerario: International Journal on the History of European Expansion and Global Interaction* 40(3) (2016), 405–28.

———. 'Lepra als *entangled disease*: Leidende afrikanische Körper in Medien und Praxis der katholischen Mission in Ostafrika, 1911–1945', in S. Weichlein and L. Ratschiller (eds), *Der schwarze Körper als Missionsgebiet: Mission, Ethnologie, Theologie in Afrika und Europa, 1880–1960* (Cologne: Böhlau, 2016), 95–121.

———. 'Imperiale Kommunikationsarbeit: Zur medialen Rahmung von Mission im 19. und 20. Jahrhundert'. *Medien und Zeit: Kommunikation in Vergangenheit und Gegenwart* 31(2) (2016).

———. 'Arrested Circulation: Catholic Missionaries, Anthropological Knowledge and the Politics of Cultural Difference in Imperial Germany, 1880–1914', in H. Fischer-Tiné and C. Whyte (eds), *Empires on the Verge of a Nervous Breakdown: Crisis, Anxiety and Panic in the Age of Imperialism, c. 1860–1960* (Basingstoke: Palgrave Macmillan, 2016), 307–344.

Ihmels, L. *Wir sind Schuldner beides unsern Kolonien und dem Evangelium: Predigt über Röm. 1, 14.15 zur Eröffnung der Kolonialmissionstage in Dresden am 25. Juni 1911*. Leipzig: Verlag der Evang.-luth. Mission, 1911.

Kasdorf, H. *Gustav Warnecks missiologisches Erbe: Eine biographisch-historische Untersuchung*. Giessen: Brunnen, 1990.

Kundrus, B. (ed.). *Phantasiereiche: Zur Kulturgeschichte des deutschen Kolonialismus*. Frankfurt/Main: Campus, 2003.

———. *Moderne Imperialisten: Das Kaiserreich im Spiegel seiner Kolonien*. Cologne: Böhlau, 2003.
Küsters, M., OSB. 'Der Aberglaube im Heidentum', in F. Schwager SVD (ed.), *Der Düsseldorfer Missionskursus für Missionare und Ordenspriester 7.–14. Oktober 1919: Vorträge, Aussprachen und Beschlüsse des Missionskursus* (Aachen: Xaverius, 1920), 98–103.
Lindner, U. *Koloniale Begegnungen: Deutschland und Großbritannien als Imperialmächte in Afrika 1880–1914*. Frankfurt/Main: Campus, 2011.
Livingstone, D. 'Scientific Inquiry and the Missionary Enterprise', in R. Finnegan (ed.), *Participating in the Knowledge Society: Researchers beyond the University Wall* (Basingstoke: Palgrave Macmillan, 2005), 50–64.
Loimeier, R. 'Edward Said und der deutschsprachige Orientalismus: Eine kritische Würdigung'. *Stichproben: Wiener Zeitschrift für kritische Afrikastudien* 1(2) (2001), 63–84.
Marchand, S.L. *German Orientalism in the Age of Empire: Religion, Race, and Scholarship*. Washington, DC: Cambridge University Press, 2009.
Mausbach, J. 'Das sechste Gebot in der Missionsseelsorge'. *Zeitschrift für Missionswissenschaft* 4 (1914), 189–98.
Mirbt, C. *Mission und Kolonialpolitik in den deutschen Schutzgebieten*. Tübingen: Mohr, 1910.
Missionsblätter: Zeitschrift für das katholische Volk, New Series 1 (1897 ff.).
Moore, S.F. 'The Secret of Man: A Fiction of Chagga Initiation and its Relation to the Logic of Chagga Symbolism'. *Journal of the International African Institute* 46(4) (1976), 357–70.
Moritzen, N.-P. *Werkzeug Gottes in der Welt: Leipziger Mission 1836 – 1936 – 1986*. Erlangen: Verlag der Evangelisch-Lutherischen Mission, 1986.
Mudimbe, V.Y. *Invention of Africa: Gnosis, Philosophy, and the Order of Knowledge*. Bloomington: Indiana University Press, 1988.
Nathusius, M. 'Die Konfirmationspraxis in der Mission'. *Allgemeine Missionszeitschrift* 29 (1902), 422–433, 476–85.
Nehring, A. 'Missionsstrategie und Forschungsdrang: Anmerkungen zu Mission und Wissenschaft in Südiniden im 19. Jahrhundert', in H. Liebau, A. Nehring and B. Klosterberg (eds), *Mission und Forschung: Translokale Wissensproduktion zwischen Indien und Europa im 18. und 19. Jahrhundert* (Halle: Harrassowitz, 2010), 21–32.
Ohm OSB, T. *Das Katechumenat in den Katholischen Missionen*. Münster: Aschendorffsche Verlagsbuchhandlung, 1959.
Osterhammel, J. *Europe, the 'West', and the Civilizing Mission*. London: German Historical Institute, 2006.
Paul, C. 'Die Leistungen der Mission für die Kolonien und ihre Gegenforderungen an die Kolonialpolitik'. *Evangelisch-lutherisches Missionsblatt* 57 (1902), 495–500, 519–21.
Plongeron, B. 'Affirmation et transformation d'une "civilization chrétienne" à la fin du XVIIIe siècle', in J.-R. Derre et al. (eds), *Civilisation chrétienne: approche historique d'une idéologie XVIIIe-XXe siècle* (Paris: Beauchesne, 1975), 9–21.
Prévotat, J. 'Remarques sur la notion de civilisation catholiques dans la Revue "L'action francaise" (juillet 1899–mars 1908)', in J.-R. Derre et al. (eds), *Civilisation chrétienne: approche historique d'une idéologie XVIIIe-XXe siècle* (Paris: Beauchesne, 1975), 349–65.
Protokoll über die Verhandlungen der neunten Kontinentalen Missionskonferenz zu Bremen am 9., 10. und 12. Mai 1893. Gütersloh: Bertelsmann, 1893.

Ranger, T.O., and I.N. Kimambo (eds). *The Historical Study of African Religion*. Berkeley: University of California Press, 1972.

Said, E. *Orientalism*. New York: Vintage Books, 1979.

Schäfer, C., OSB. *Stella Maris: Größe und Grenzen des ersten Erzabtes von St. Ottilien P. Norbert Weber OSB 1870–1956*. St Ottilien: Eos, 2005.

Schmidlin, J. *Einführung in die Missionswissenschaft*. Münster: Aschendorff, 1917.

———. *Katholische Missionslehre im Grundriss*. Münster: Aschendorff, 1919.

———. 'Katechumenat', in *Lexikon für Theologie und Kirche*, Vol. 5 (Freiburg: Herder, 1933), col. 884–88.

Schmidt, H.I. 'Colonial Intimacy: The Rechenberg Scandal and Homosexuality in German East Africa'. *Journal of the History of Sexuality* 17(1) (2008), 25–59.

Schwab, O. 'Wie wird die Katechese ihrer Aufgabe als Pflanzschule lebendiger Religiosität und sittlichen Strebens gerecht?', in F. Schwager (ed.), *Der Düsseldorfer Missionskursus für Missionare und Ordenspriester 7.–14. Oktober 1919: Vorträge, Aussprachen und Beschlüsse des Missionskursus* (Aachen: Xaverius, 1920), 24–35.

Schwager, F., SVD. 'Die Bedeutung der Arbeitserziehung für die Hebung der primitiven Rassen'. *Zeitschrift für Missionswissenschaft* 4 (1914), 278–98.

———. 'Katholische Missionstätigkeit und nationale Propaganda'. *Zeitschrift für Missionswissenschaft* 6 (1916), 109–34.

———. (ed.). *Der Düsseldorfer Missionskursus für Missionare und Ordenspriester 7.–14. Oktober 1919: Vorträge, Aussprachen und Beschlüsse des Missionskursus*. Aachen: Xaverius, 1920.

Schwartz, K. von. *Mission und Kolonisation in ihrem gegenseitigem Verhältnis*. Leipzig: Verlag der Evangelisch-Lutherischen Mission, 1908.

Sievernich, M., SJ. *Die christliche Mission: Geschichte und Gegenwart*. Darmstadt: Wissenschaftliche Buchgesellschaft, 2009.

Steinmetz, G. *The Devil's Handwriting: Precoloniality and the German Colonial State in Quingdao, Samoa, and Southwest Africa*. Chicago: University of Chicago Press, 2007.

Stoler, A.L., and F. Cooper. 'Between Metropole and Colony: Rethinking a Research Agenda', in idem (eds), *Tensions of Empire Colonial Culture in a Bourgeois World* (Berkeley: University of California Press, 2001), 1–56.

Triebel, J. 'Polygamie als Taufhindernis: 100 Jahre Auseinandersetzung dargestellt am Beispiel Südwest-Tanzanias', in J. Ngeiyama and J. Triebel (eds), *Gemeinsam auf eigenen Wegen: Ev.-Luth. Kirche Tanzanias nach hundert Jahren* (Erlangen: Verlag der Evangelisch-Lutherischen Mission, 1994), 307–23.

Tyrell, H. 'Weltgesellschaft, Weltmission und religiöse Organisation', in A. Bogner, B. Holtwick and H. Tyrell (eds), *Weltmission und religiöse Organisationen* (Würzburg: Ergon, 2004), 255–72.

Ustorf, W. *Die Missionsmethode Franz Michael Zahns und der Aufbau kirchlicher Strukturen in Westafrika: Eine missionsgeschichtliche Untersuchung*. Erlangen: Verlag der Evangelisch-Lutherischen Mission, 1989.

Verhandlungen der neunten Kontinentalen Missionskonferenz zu Bremen am 25., 26. und 28. Mai 1897. Berlin: Martin Warneck, 1897.

Warneck, G. *Die gegenseitigen Beziehungen zwischen der modernen Mission und Cultur: Auch eine Culturkampfstudie*. Gütersloh: Bertelsmann, 1879.

———. 'Eine Bedeutsame Missionskonferenz'. *Allgemeine Missionszeitschrift* 12 (1885), 545–63.

———. *Zur Abwehr und Verständigung. Offener Brief an Herrn Major von Wißmann, Kaiserlicher Reichskommissar. Ein Wort der Erwiderung auf seine Urteile über die Missionen beider christlichen Konfessionen*. Gütersloh: Bertelsmann, 1890.

———. *Evangelische Missionslehre. Ein missionstheoretischer Versuch. Dritte Abteilung: Der Betrieb der Sendung. Erste Hälfte*. Gotha: Perthes, 1897.

———. *Evangelische Missionslehre. Ein missionstheoretischer Versuch. Dritte Abteilung: Der Betrieb der Sendung. Zweite Hälfte: Die Missionsmittel*. Gotha: Perthes, 1900.

———. *Die Christliche Mission und die überseeische Politik: Vortrag auf der Missionskonferenz der Provinz Sachsen am 12. Februar 1901 zu Halle*. Berlin: Martin Warneck, 1901.

———. *Evangelische Missionslehre. Ein missionstheoretischer Versuch. Dritte Abteilung: Der Betrieb der Sendung. 3. Teil: Das Missionsziel*. Gotha: Perthes, 1903.

Warneck, J. 'Evangelisieren oder Christianisieren'. *Allgemeine Missionszeitschrift* 40 (1913), 433–47.

Weber, N., OSB. 'Ziele und Wege der Eingeborenen Erziehung', in *Verhandlungen des deutschen Kolonialkongresses zu Berlin am 5., 6. und 7. Oktober 1905* (Berlin: Reimer, 1906), 673–83.

———. 'Am Scheideweg: Nationalpolitische Bedeutung der Mission'. *Das Hochland* 8(2) (1910), 10–27.

———. 'Der Krieg und die Mission'. *Zeitschrift für Missionswissenschaft* 5 (1915), 1–9.

Weichlein, S. 'Mission und Ultramontanismus im frühen 19. Jahrhundert', in G. Fleckenstein and J. Schmiedl (eds), *Ultramontanismus: Tendenzen der Forschung* (Paderborn: Bonifatius, 2005), 93–109.

Wetjen, K. 'Der Körper des Täuflings: Konstruktionen von Körper und die Beschneidungsdebatte der Leipziger Missionsgesellschaft 1890–1914', in S. Weichlein and L. Ratschiller (eds), *Der schwarze Körper als Missionsgebiet: Mission, Ethnologie, Theologie in Afrika und Europa, 1880–1960* (Cologne: Böhlau, 2016), 73–94.

Yates, T. 'Mission Conferences', in J. Bonk (ed.), *Encyclopedia of Missions and Missionaries* (New York: Routledge, 2007), 256–59.

Zantop, S. *Colonial Fantasies: Conquest, Family, and Nation in Precolonial Germany, 1770–1870*. Durham, NC: Duke University Press, 1997.

Index

Aachen, 179
acculturation, 150, 152–53, 158
Acker, Amandus, 199, 201
Anarchism, 16, 147–159
   Jewish anarchists, 15
Anthropology, 2, 5, 199, 122, 208
   evolutionary, 43
Anti-Catholicism/anti-Catholic, 38, 109, 118–19, 121, 123, 127, 133n18, 177–78, 199
Anti-Semitism, 150–51, 158
Argentina, 181
Asad, Talal, 2, 5–7, 17, 44–45, 119, 131, 134n26
Association of Independent Socialists, 151
Atheism, 4, 9, 108

Bakunin, Mikhail Alexandrovich, 148
Baptism, 198, 205, 210, 214–15, 217
Bavaria, 180
belief system, 10–11, 17, 33, 43, 105
Belgium, 179
Benedictins, 209, 213, 216
Benzinger, Immanuel, 71, 79
Berlin, 151, 175
Berlin (Congo) Conference/Berlin Treaty, 182, 199, 205
Bernstein, Eduard, 105
Bible, 57, 59, 123, 174, 206, 213
   Old Testament, 59–67
   New Testament, 60, 65, 76, 156
Bildungsreligion, 107
Bismarck, Otto von, 128, 176–77, 199
Bluntschli, Johann Casper, 177
Bonzel, Aline, 171
Borutta, Manuel, 38, 177–78
Bourdieu, Pierre, 102
Brazil, 187

Brussels, 184
Buber, Martin, 149, 155–56
Buber, Salomon, 155
Buddhism, 42–43, 108, 123, 201
Brahmanism, 42

Caine, 154, 159
Cameroon, 208
Catechumenate, 207, 209–10, 214, 219
Catholicism, 3, 37–38, 43, 105. See also theology.
Catholic Church, 124, 127, 172, 176, 178, 183, 197, 207
Chagga, 210
Chile, 181, 184
Christianity, 40, 42, 57, 62–66, 123
circumcision, 211, 216,
civilization, 6, 10, 56, 73, 122, 196, 204, 220
   Christian civilization, 200, 204, 209, 218–19
civil religion. See under religion
class, 8, 67, 109, 115, 121, 125, 127– 28, 131, 150, 174
colonies/colonialism, 14–16, 122, 182, 196, 219–220
colony – metropole, 197
confession/Konfession, 103, 106
confessionalism (Konfessionalismus), 106, 117, 205
confessionalist primary schools, 107, 174
Confucianism, 108, 123, 201
congregations, female, 15, 171–177, 184, 186, 187
Congo, 183
contact zone, 15, 197, 210
conversion, 198, 202, 206, 210, 214
Cornill, Carl Heinrich, 65

Coulanges, Numa Denis Fustel de, 34–36, 39, 43
Cultural Protestantism (Kulturprotestantismus). See under Protestantism
Culture wars (Kulturkampf), 4, 8, 14, 37, 107, 109, 121, 123, 126, 171, 176–78, 184, 197, 203, 220

Dalman, Gustav, 71–71,79
Deutsches Evangelisches Institut für Altertumswissenschaft des Heiligen Landes (DEIAHL), 58, 68, 70, 72
Deutsche Morgenländische Gesellschaft (DMG), 69
Deutsche Orient-Gesellschaft (DOG), 71
Deutscher Palästina-Verein (DPV), 58, 70–72
Durkheim, Emile, 4, 6, 13, 34–36, 39, 43–44

East Africa (German), 16, 198, 208, 210, 219
Eckhart von Hochheim (Meister Eckhart), 154
education, 176, 218
Eisenstadt, Shmuel, 148
Emerson, Ralph Waldo, 148
emotionality, 129–130, 218
England, 8, 102, 108
Enlightenment, 36, 106, 125, 151, 155, 158, 173
Engels, Friedrich, 105, 186
Evangelization, 181–82

femininity, 38, 120
feminization of religion, 3, 121, 173, 177
Fetishism, 8, 10, 40, 200
Fey, Clara, 171, 174
Fichte, Johann Gottlieb, 148
France, 9, 21n31, 34–36, 39, 106, 108, 171, 180
freedom of thought, 107, 124, 157
Freethinker associations/freethinker clubs, 10, 14, 116, 118, 130

gender, 3, 120–21, 128, 131, 173, 177–78
Gerhardinger, Karolina, 180
German Mission for East Africa, 195–230
Globalization/global, 7–11, 57, 196
Goethe, Johann Wolfgang von, 109, 125, 154

Gogarten, Friedrich, 104
Gross, Otto, 152
Guthe, Hermann, 61, 67–69, 71, 73

Häckel, Ernst, 105, 116–18
Halle, 201
Harden, Maximilian, 147
Harnack, Adolf, 65
Hart, Heinrich, 154
Heck, M. Chrysostoma, 185
Hegel, Georg Wilhelm Friedrich, 10, 42, 116
Hennemann, Franziskus, 209
Herder, Johann Gottfried, 148
Hinduism, 8, 42–43
Historiography, 10, 23n52, 76–77
    conceptual history, 101–103
Holyoake, George J., 102, 108
Holy Ghost Fathers, 199, 201

Ihmels, D. Ludwig, 204
Innere Mission. See under Mission
Islam, 123, 126, 198.
Israel, 56–79

Janssen, Arnold, 182
Jesuits, 37, 108, 121, 127, 128, 130, 200
Jews, 60, 64, 67, 75, 149–159
Judaism, 40, 43, 57, 60–65, 75–76, 153, 155

Kant, Immanuel, 39–42, 109
Kautsky, Karl, 105
King Chabrum Tawete, 216
King Mputa Gama, 216
König, Eduard, 60
Kropotkin, Pyotr Alexeyevich, 148, 155
Küsters, Meinulf, 209

Lachmann, Hedwig, 152, 155
Laïcité, 9, 104, 109
Landauer, Gustav, 15, 147–159
Landauer, Hermann, 149
language, 101, 103, 201, 213, 217
Lavigerie, Charles de, 207–219
Lebensreform, 148
Leipzig missionary society, 204, 210, 213
liberal, 38, 104, 106
liberty of the individual, 148
Lithuania, 180
Lourdel, Siméon, 209
Lübbe, Hermann, 4, 116

Lutheranism, 42, 56

magic, 42
Mallinckrodt, Pauline von, 171, 184
Maistre, Joseph de, 35–36
Marillac, Luise de, 183
Marx, Karl, 105, 116
Marxism, 159
masculinity, 120, 122, 125, 130
masculinization of the secular, 212
Masuzawa, Tomoko, 8, 122
Matthes, Joachim, 44–45
May, Karl, 125
Mauthner, Fritz, 154
middle class values (Bürgerlichkeit), 127
Mirbt, Carl, 203
Mission, 122, 183, 197, 207, 212
   Innere, 115, 127, 130
   civilizing mission, 196, 199, 201, 218
   societies, 212
   missiology, 203, 205, 210
missionaries, 8, 15, 126
   Catholic missionaries, 185, 199–202, 208
   Protestant missionaries, 202
modernity/Modernization Theory, 3, 6, 45, 124, 149, 187
Mtesa of Buganda (king), 209
Mühsam, Erich, 15, 149–59

nation, 5, 59, 147, 150, 157, 178, 185
Netherlands, 179, 182
Nietzsche, Friedrich, 109, 151, 154

Orientalism, 76, 196
Orthodoxy, 129, 207, 217

Palestine, 56–79, 183
Palestine Exploration Fund (PEF), 68, 69, 72
Pappenheim, Pinkus Seligman, 150
Paul, Carl, 203
Pietists, 108
Poland, 180
polygamy, 200, 205, 208, 217
Pope Leo XIII, 199
Pope Pius IX, 105, 107
postcolonial (studies), 2, 10, 75, 122
Protestantism, 3, 13, 107–108. See also Theology
   Cultural Protestantism, 38, 41, 70, 123, 129–30

Liberal Protestantism, 14
Proudhon, Pierre-Joseph, 148, 151
Prussia, 179–180

race, 73, 77, 120, 128, 131, 159
Reformation, 44–45, 67, 70
religion, 7, 44, 50n71, 108. See under World Religion
   and nationbuilding, 9
   and globalization, 9
   civil religion, 17, 39, 44, 109
   natural religion, 10
religion-making, 119
religious revival, 7, 17, 33
religious studies, 2, 12
religious women, 121, 187
Rome, 37, 171, 183

Scandinavia, 180
Schervier, Franziska, 171, 175
Schleiermacher, Friedrich, 41, 109
Schmidlin, Joseph, 207–208
school, 104, 107, 172
Schopenhauer, Arthur, 41–43, 109, 151
Schulte, Johann Friedrich von, 177
secular, 4, 102, 116–131
secularisation, 4, 9, 39, 44, 102
secularism, 6, 104
secularity, 38, 105
   multiple secularities, 6, 148, 153
silencing, 58, 78–79
Simmel, Georg, 36, 41, 126
Smend, Rudolf, 59
Socialdemocrats, 20n21, 104, 105, 107
sociology, 2, 5, 7, 34, 208
Sociology of religion, 4, 12, 17, 36, 40
spiritual, 103, 116, 127, 147, 149, 174, 213
Stade, Bernhard, 60, 65
Stirner, Max, 151, 154
Stroumsa, G.G., 33–34
St Paul, Vincent, 183
superstition / superstitious, 6, 9, 40, 67, 125, 198, 208

Thomsen, Peter, 67–68, 73
Tolstoy, Lev Nikolayevich, 148
theology, 5, 56–57, 70
   Catholic theology, 37, 210
   Mission theology, 197, 208, 210
   Protestant theology, 42, 104, 205
Togo, 182
transnational, 2, 45, 66, 148–49, 172

entanglements, 7–9, 179, 187
  networks, 15, 178, 184
Treitschke, Heinrich von, 5, 116
Troeltsch, Ernst, 36, 38, 116, 207

United States, 181, 184
Uruguay, 181

Virchow, Rudolf, 115–16, 124, 177

Warneck, Gustav, 202–204, 207
Weber, Max, 3–6, 9, 13, 34–45, 115, 124, 126, 197

Weber, Norbert, 201
Weir, Tedd H., 57, 116–17, 132n6
Welter, Barbara, 3
Windthorst, Ludwig, 105
Wolff, Clara, 171, 175
World Religion, 8, 10, 38, 122–23.

Zahn, Franz Michael, 205–207, 211
Zanzibar, 201, 213
Ziegler, Maria Liobgid, 180
Zionism, 157–58

www.ingramcontent.com/pod-product-compliance
Lightning Source LLC
Chambersburg PA
CBHW072049110526
44590CB00018B/3097